EMBERS OF EMPIRE

AUSTRIAN AND HABSBURG STUDIES
General Editor: Howard Louthan, Center for Austrian Studies, University of Minnesota

Before 1918, Austria and the Habsburg lands constituted an expansive multinational and multiethnic empire, the second largest state in Europe and a key site for cultural and intellectual developments across the continent. At the turn of the twentieth century, the region gave birth to modern psychology, philosophy, economics, and music, and since then has played an important mediating role between Western and Eastern Europe, today participating as a critical member of the European Union. The volumes in this series address specific themes and questions around the history, culture, politics, social, and economic experience of Austria, the Habsburg Empire, and its successor states in Central and Eastern Europe.

Recent volumes:

Volume 22
Embers of Empire: Continuity and Rupture in the Habsburg Successor States after 1918
Edited by Paul Miller and Claire Morelon

Volume 21
The Art of Resistance: Cultural Protest against the Austrian Far Right in the Early Twenty-First Century
Allyson Fiddler

Volume 20
The Monumental Nation: Magyar Nationalism and Symbolic Politics in Fin-de-siècle Hungary
Bálint Varga

Volume 19
Tropics of Vienna: Colonial Utopias of the Habsburg Empire
Ulrich E. Bach

Volume 18
Sacrifice and Rebirth: The Legacy of the Last Habsburg War
Edited by Mark Cornwall and John Paul Newman

Volume 17
Understanding Multiculturalism: The Habsburg Central European Experience
Edited by Johannes Feichtinger and Gary B. Cohen

Volume 16
The Viennese Café and Fin-de-siècle Culture
Edited by Charlotte Ashby, Tag Gronberg, and Simon Shaw-Miller

Volume 15
Territorial Revisionism and the Allies of Germany in the Second World War: Goals, Expectations, Practices
Edited by Marina Cattaruzza, Stefan Dyroff, and Dieter Langewiesche

Volume 14
Journeys into Madness: Mapping Mental Illness in the Austro-Hungarian Empire
Edited by Gemma Blackshaw and Sabine Wieber

Volume 13
Sexual Knowledge: Feeling, Fact and Social Reform in Vienna, 1900–1934
Britta McEwen

For a full volume listing, please see the series page on our website: http://berghahnbooks.com/series/austrian-habsburg-studies.

EMBERS OF EMPIRE

Continuity and Rupture in the Habsburg Successor States after 1918

Edited by Paul Miller and Claire Morelon

First published in 2019 by
Berghahn Books
www.berghahnbooks.com

© 2019, 2021 Paul Miller and Claire Morelon
First paperback edition published in 2021

All rights reserved. Except for the quotation of short passages
for the purposes of criticism and review, no part of this book
may be reproduced in any form or by any means, electronic or
mechanical, including photocopying, recording, or any information
storage and retrieval system now known or to be invented,
without written permission of the publisher.

Library of Congress Cataloging-in-Publication Data
Names: Miller, Paul B., 1964- editor. | Morelon, Claire, 1984- editor.
Title: Embers of Empire: Continuity and Rupture in the Habsburg Successor States after 1918 / edited by Paul Miller and Claire Morelon.
Description: New York: Berghahn Books, 2019. | Series: Austrian and Habsburg Studies; Volume 22 | Includes bibliographical references and index.
Identifiers: LCCN 2018040252 (print) | LCCN 2018047121 (ebook) | ISBN 9781789200232 (ebook) | ISBN 9781789200225 (hardback: alk. paper)
Subjects: LCSH: Europe, Eastern--History--1918-1945. | Europe, Eastern--Politics and government--1918-1945. | Europe, Central--History. | Europe, Central--Politics and government. | Habsburg, House of.
Classification: LCC DJK49 (ebook) | LCC DJK49 .E44 2019 (print) | DDC 943.0009/041--dc23
LC record available at https://lccn.loc.gov/2018040252

British Library Cataloguing in Publication Data
A catalogue record for this book is available from the British Library

ISBN 978-1-78920-022-5 hardback
ISBN 978-1-80073-212-4 paperback
ISBN 978-1-78920-023-2 ebook

Contents

List of Illustrations — vii
Acknowledgments — ix

Introduction — 1
Claire Morelon

Part I. Permanence and Revolution: National Politics in the Transition to the Successor States

Chapter 1. Negotiating Post-Imperial Transitions: Local Societies and Nationalizing States in East Central Europe — 15
Gábor Egry

Chapter 2. State Legitimacy and Continuity between the Habsburg Empire and Czechoslovakia: The 1918 Transition in Prague — 43
Claire Morelon

Chapter 3. Strangers among Friends: Leon Biliński between Imperial Austria and New Poland — 64
Iryna Vushko

Chapter 4. Ideology on Display: Continuity and Rupture at Exhibitions in Austria-Hungary and Czechoslovakia, 1873–1928 — 90
Marta Filipová

Part II. The Habsburg Army's Final Battles

Chapter 5. Reflections on the Legacy of the Imperial and Royal Army in the Successor States — 117
Richard Bassett

Chapter 6.	Imperial into National Officers: K. (u.) k. Officers of Romanian Nationality before and after the Great War *Irina Marin*	136
Chapter 7.	Shades of Empire: Austro-Hungarian Officers, Frankists, and the Afterlives of Austria-Hungary in Croatia, 1918–1929 *John Paul Newman*	157

Part III. Church, Dynasty, Aristocracy: The Postwar Fate of Imperial Pillars

Chapter 8.	"All the German Princes Driven Out!" The Catholic Church in Vienna and the First Austrian Republic *Michael Carter-Sinclair*	177
Chapter 9.	Wealthy Landowners or Weak Remnants of the Imperial Past? Central European Nobles during and after the First World War *Konstantinos Raptis*	203
Chapter 10.	Sinner, Saint—or Cipher? The Austrian Republic and the Death of Emperor Karl I *Christopher Brennan*	229

Part IV. History, Memory, Mentalité: Processing The Empire's Passing

Chapter 11.	"What Did They Die For?" War Remembrance in Austria in the Transition from Empire to Nation State *Christoph Mick*	261
Chapter 12.	"The First Victim of the First World War": Franz Ferdinand in Austrian Memory *Paul Miller*	284
	Afterword *Pieter M. Judson*	318

Index	327

ILLUSTRATIONS

Figure 4.1. The Palace of Industries, Prague, 1891. Postcard. Author's collection.   94

Figure 4.2. The German-Bohemian exhibition, Reichenberg/Liberec, 1906. Postcard. Author's collection.   97

Figure 4.3. The Exhibition of Contemporary Culture in Czechoslovakia, Brno, 1928 (statue of President Masaryk in the center). Postcard. Author's collection.   107

Figure 9.1. Prugg Palace (Bruck an der Leitha), rear side, 12 September 2008. Author's photo.   210

Figure 9.2. Harrach Palace in Vienna's First District (Freyung 3), June 2006. Photo courtesy of Gryffindor, Wikimedia Commons.   213

Figure 9.3. Hradek Palace (bei Nechanic), front view, 30 April 2008. Author's photo.   215

Figure 10.1. Karl on his deathbed in Madeira, 1922. Author's collection.   232

Figure 10.2. Memorial Bust of Emperor Karl I of Austria (Blessed Karl) in Vienna's Imperial (Capuchin) Crypt. Dedicated in a memorial mass on Karl's name day, 4 November 1931. Author's photo.   236

Figure 11.1. War memorial in Vienna's Central Cemetery (*Zentralfriedhof*). Photo courtesy of Dr. Christopher Brennan.   264

Figure 11.2. The outer castle gate (*Äußeres Burgtor*) on Vienna's Heroes' Square (*Heldenplatz*). Photo courtesy of Tofko, Wikimedia Commons.   267

Figure 11.3. Heroes' Memorial (*Heldendenkmal*) inside the castle gate. Photo courtesy of Paul Miller.   271

Figure 12.1. Artstetten crypt with tombs of Franz Ferdinand and Sophie von Hohenberg. Author's photo.   285

Figure 12.2. Vienna *Weltmuseum* exhibition: "Franz is here!" 2014. Photo courtesy of Dr. David Schriffl.   301

Figure 12.3. 1986 Memorial Plaque in Vienna's Imperial Crypt. Author's photo.   305

Acknowledgments

This book traces its roots to a scholarly gathering held at the University of Birmingham (UK) in June 2012, under the generous auspices of the European Research Institute. Back then, we editors hardly knew each other—Paul having recently arrived to Birmingham as a Marie Curie Fellow, and Claire in the midst of writing her thesis while living in London. But in the process of planning a conference and then preparing a book, we have come a long way both in terms of professional collaboration and personal friendship, and thus our first thanks inevitably goes to each other for the mutual support, encouragement, prodding, patience, and diligence that allowed us to reach our goal of a published volume. Neither of us could have imagined the amount of time, effort, and sheer stamina such a project would take, and neither could have seen it through without the other at his/her side.

The same goes for our authors, four of whom (not including the editors) have waited for six years to see their work in print. We are grateful to Richard Bassett, Marta Filipová, Christoph Mick, and John Paul Newman for sticking it out with us from the beginning, and for allowing their superb scholarship to become part of this collection. The editors additionally owe special thanks and recognition to Alan Sked who not only gave a characteristically engrossing paper in 2012 (on the historian Heinrich Ritter von Srbik and "the survival of the Austrian idea after 1918"), but was also an enthusiastic and steadfast supporter of this book project from the get-go.

Many other friends, colleagues, and family members kept this project going through their personal generosity and sheer enthusiasm for its theme of continuity and rupture with the Habsburg Empire across the World War I divide. Of particular note is a conference in London on World War I in Central and Eastern Europe, organized by Jonathan Kwan in September 2014. Professor Kwan not only graciously allowed us to use his conference as a forum to advertise our book, but we also recruited five of the volume's chapters there. We thank them for joining the project. We also extend our appreciation to the volume's last but certainly not least contributor to come onboard in order to write the conclusion, Pieter Judson.

Finally, we would like to thank the two anonymous peer reviewers for Berghahn Books, and above all the publisher itself for improving the overall quality of the manuscript and seeing it through to print in such an outstanding and professional manner. In this respect, Gary Cohen, Chris Chappell, Amanda Horn, Soyolmaa Lkhagvadorj, and Lizzie Martinez all played key roles, from helping us to understand the submission process to fine-tuning the final product. Of course, any errors or imperfections that may remain in the work are the editors' sole responsibility.

—Paul and Claire

Introduction

Claire Morelon

In the Austrian writer Joseph Roth's short story *The Bust of the Emperor* (1935), a fictional Count Morstin returns home to Galicia after the First World War, only to question the very meaning of home itself after the disappearance of Austria-Hungary:

> Seeing as this village . . . now belongs to Poland and not Austria: can it still be said to be my home? What is home, anyway? Are not the particular uniforms of the customs men and the gendarmes that we were used to seeing in our childhood, are they not just as much home as the pines and firs, the swamp and the meadow, the cloud and the stream.[1]

The void left by the collapse of the Habsburg Monarchy produced a rich literature, with Roth as one of its prime exemplars. Yet while Morstin lamented the loss of old uniforms, the reality in Central Europe's new nation-states was that many officials remained in place after 1918. In Roth's Galicia, for example, old Austrians willingly integrated into the interwar Polish State Police.[2] The dislocations emphasized by authors bereft of *Heimat* (homeland) often obscured more latent continuities in everyday life. Maintaining general law and order had been a priority for many of the new states. In Czechoslovakia, the first general law published on 28 October 1918 stated that all the current laws were to remain in effect, "as if there had been no revolution at all," in the words of one of the coup organizers, Alois Rašín.[3]

When the Austro-Hungarian Empire disintegrated at the end of World War I, it was far more than a political phenomenon—it directly affected the lives of millions of ordinary people across the whole of East Central Europe. Despite the nationalist agitations understood by some contemporaries and, until recently, most scholars as foreshadowing the Empire's collapse, the regime not only lasted longer than expected, but as the British military historian B. H. Liddell Hart pointed out, "the loosely knit conglomeration of races withstood the shock and strain of war for four years in a way that surprised and dismayed her opponents."[4] How Austria-Hungary did so, and what this can tell us about the effectiveness of the Monarchy's institutions and our assumptions about their viability, is crucial to understanding the complex history of East Central Europe during the disruptive transformation from Empire to nation-states.[5]

The historian Pieter Judson has argued recently that nation and empire were not binary opposites in the context of the Habsburg Monarchy, and that the regime's collapse in 1918 was due to the state's transformation under the pressures of war conditions rather than any internal nationalist tensions.[6] Numerous studies of national movements in the late Habsburg era have revealed them to be more variegated and less imperially antagonistic than previously assumed. Instead of targeting the regime itself, these movements sought to mobilize their own nationalistically indifferent populations.[7] National activists (be they German, Czech, or Slovene) had to fight against the ambivalence of people without clearly defined national allegiances.[8] In this respect, they sometimes competed with each other to "demonstrate their loyalty to the Habsburg dynasty."[9] In parallel, scholars have reevaluated the role of loyalty in Habsburg political culture, arguing that the focus on national mobilization has impeded our appreciation of the forces for imperial loyalty, some of which sprung from the national movements themselves.[10] Such questions have shifted late Habsburg historiography away from searching for weaknesses to explain the Monarchy's fall toward understanding the regime's longevity and the elements that sustained it. Once we consider the relative successes of the Empire's institutions even in its final years, the obvious ensuing question becomes: Did these structures and the *habitus* linked to them last even beyond the collapse of the *ancien régime* in 1918? This issue is the central theme of this collection.

As long as scholars generally viewed the Habsburg Monarchy as a surviving anachronism, the continuities with its successor states were downplayed or ignored altogether.[11] Of course, to varying degrees, these states sought to break free from their Habsburg legacies and present a modern new image.[12] Yet in addition to the aforementioned research on prewar nationalisms,[13] recent local studies on both sides of the 1918 divide have highlighted the permanence of some political, social, and even cultural elements alongside the obvious ruptures engendered by the transition.[14] Furthermore, several historians have pointed to the similarities between the Habsburg monarchy and the successor states (as mini-Empires). It thus makes sense to interrogate the manifestations of the Habsburg regime's post-1918 legacies in East Central Europe.¹⁵

National historiographies, especially in Czechoslovakia and Yugoslavia, have traditionally been so focused on the break with the past that the novelty of the postwar states has largely occluded scholars from seeing relevant instances of imperial continuity. This was reflected in the language used to describe the monarchy's demise: "disintegration" or even "catastrophe" for Austria and Hungary; "liberation" and "beginning" in the Czech and Slovak cases.¹⁶ While the continuity issue for Germany's transformation from Empire to Republic has been well examined, virtually nothing comparable has been done for post-Habsburg East Central Europe despite its crucial place in the interwar jockeying for power.¹⁷ As long as the predominant lens for viewing the region was that of national groups, its only stable feature was the nations themselves: states varied, but the nations remained the same.

When historians did consider elements of continuity with the Habsburg Empire, it was usually in the context of the new Austrian Republic (or, less often, Hungary) rather than states like Czechoslovakia or Yugoslavia.¹⁸ This imbalance gave the false impression that only the two defeated states, Austria and Hungary, had to come to terms with the Habsburg past, while the newly created nation-states were unencumbered by their imperial legacies. A broader regional comparison is thus necessary to reveal the imprint of the Empire in all its former provinces.

That comparison, moreover, needs to go beyond the main fields through which the postwar survival of the Habsburg Empire has been envisaged: literature and intellectual history, with their singular focus on the nostalgic vision created by the monarchy's disappearance. The "Habsburg myth," identified by Claudio Magris, has long been central to scholarship on the persistence of post-1918 Austria-Hungary, sometimes blurring the line between analyzing the myth and actually sustaining it.¹⁹ These studies tend to concentrate on prominent writers and other intellectuals who influenced public discourse on the monarchy.²⁰ More recent work that convincingly deconstructs the myth still largely focuses on intellectual circles and the idea that the monarchy's most lasting legacy was its nostalgic image.²¹

Yet other, more concrete forms of institutional, economic, political, and cultural continuity also deserve examination. Social scientists have pointed to the weight of historical legacies to explain the present in East Central Europe, but historians have not always followed suit (and even less so for the interwar period). Debates around the post-communist transition in the social sciences were long dominated by the notion of path dependency, which posits that institutional legacies shaped the transformation period.²² Recent reflections on 1989 have also tended to downplay the paradigm of complete transformation and analyze how various political actors used the past in the transition of the early 1990s.²³ More recently, a new project on "ghost borders" led by historians and geographers tackles regional continuities in the *longue durée* and highlights the permanence of old imperial divisions in political or infrastructural terms through the present day. For example, Dietmar Müller examines how legal cultures and expectations toward the institutions in interwar Romania show the impact of former borders on individual decisions and strategies.[24] New studies in economic history already indicate a permanence of structures and local elites after 1918 that could be extended to other fields.[25]

The present work also builds on the new trends in the historiography of World War I, which expand our conception of the war and increasingly question the relevance of the 1918 divide. Recent studies have shifted the focus from Western Europe toward those transformations taking place in the Middle East and Eastern Europe, thus transferring the conflict's center of gravity both in terms of chronology (with a focus on the postwar period) and experience (civilians and population movements, for example).[26] As both regions were affected by the war in similar ways, it would be interesting to expand on comparisons between empires that have been so fruitful for studies of these regions in the nineteenth century.[27] For example, thinking in terms of continuities can help us to compare both the new mandates system and their nationalizing policies with that of the successor states.[28] Scholars of the Ottoman Empire have already demonstrated the value of an approach that questions the narrative of rupture after 1918.[29] Our aim is to adopt such an approach in the case of the Habsburg Empire.

The present collection consists of twelve chapters on the issue of continuity and rupture with the Austro-Hungarian Empire after World War I. Together, these studies extend the ongoing scholarly debate over the efficacy and long-term viability of Habsburg political culture well into the twentieth century. By exploring the continuance of people, institutions, and ideas, we can better understand the Empire's legacy in the successor states' political, military, and intellectual cultures. These chapters track remnants of the imperial world through institutional hysteresis and other continuities that characterized the interwar years beyond elegiac nostalgia. They also offer a variety of approaches to tracing adaptations to the new order and the persistence of old habits and *mentalités* of, for example, a specific group, individual, or locality.

Part I examines the transition in local contexts across the region. The chapters in this section explore the experiences of permanence and revolution through the lens of a city (Morelon), two regions (Egry), an individual (Vushko), and institutionalized events (Filipová). Their common premise is that in order to approach this chronological turning point, it is essential to go from the high-level diplomatic discussions down to the grassroots level. Local studies offer insights into institutional continuity that belie discourses of rupture. The transition from the Habsburg monarchy to the new national states has long been viewed through the prism of the new states' teleological narratives, whereby 1918 is presented as the culmination of national liberation. Yet this has obscured the period's complex reality, which was marked by demobilization, revolutionary and counter-revolutionary movements, and an economic crisis.[30] The first two chapters, by Gábor Egry and Claire Morelon, grapple with these issues through case studies of Slovakia, Transylvania, and Prague, where realities on the ground sometimes diverged from the plans imagined by the new state leaders. Both studies show how local societies responded to the postwar transformations and adapted them for their own goals in negotiation with the central authorities. By comparing the Romanian and Czechoslovak cases, Egry shows that, in this period of uncertainty, definitions of national interest not only varied across regions and localities, but were often at odds with decisions taken in the new capital cities. He highlights the role played in the transition by remaining local officials, and the continuity of middle-class cultural practices in areas with strong regional identities.

Morelon's study of Prague explores the different interpretations of regime change within the Czechoslovak capital. In particular, she uncovers the sense of disappointment generated by the perception of continuity between the pre- and postwar governments. Iryna Vushko's chapter complements Egry and Morelon by focusing on an individual rather than local trajectory—that of the statesman Leon Biliński, who was shaped by the political culture of the Empire yet came to play a key role in the new Polish state. Through her study of Biliński, Vushko examines the fate of imperial networks in postwar Poland and shows how the continuity between the two regimes was also apparent in personal biographies. The last chapter in this section, by Marta Filipová, shows how regional and state-sponsored exhibitions before and after 1918 adopted similar political and cultural strategies in constructing national identities. Exhibitions served as vectors of state ideology for both the monarchy and the new Czechoslovak republic; although presented as very different, they had numerous official and ideological commonalities. This first part complicates our understanding of national politics in postwar states by highlighting the persistence of imperial dimensions in their political and cultural fabrics.

Parts II and III focus on the postwar predicament of institutions traditionally considered as mainstays of the Habsburg monarchy—the army, dynasty, church, and nobility. Studies of the Austro-Hungarian common army have, at least since István Deák's pathbreaking work, insisted on its key role for social cohesion and the development of a supranational Habsburg identity.[31] Given its even more prominent position during the world war, the army is the subject of several chapters in this book. Richard Bassett explores its general experience during the war, and then offers vivid reflections on the army's legacies in the successor states. Irina Marin and John Paul Newman chart the personal trajectories of Habsburg officers from Austria-Hungary to postwar Romania and Yugoslavia, respectively, emphasizing the links between the two eras for many prominent figures. Newman additionally shows how the "culture of defeat" of former Austro-Hungarian officers nurtured the fascist Croatian Ustashe movement, while Marin traces the capacity of Romanian officers to adapt to the new regime back to the compatibility of their national and imperial loyalties.

The army was not the only "centripetal force"—to use the sociologist Oscar Jászi's famous phrase—holding the monarchy together, and the book's next section thus turns to the fate of other pillars of the former Empire: the Catholic Church, the dynasty, and the nobility. Michael Carter-Sinclair's chapter explores the Church's reaction to the demise of a regime with which it had long been closely aligned, as well as its attitudes toward the new Austrian Republic. This chapter challenges existing narratives of the Church's quick reconciliation to the Republic, showing that the upper ecclesiastical hierarchy never fully came to terms with the destruction of the old regime of orders. Although not named by Jászi, the nobility also saw its *raison d'être* as deeply linked to the Habsburg dynasty. The fate of these noble families after the war, which is the subject of Konstantinos Raptis's chapter, illustrates their efforts to maintain social status despite the establishment of republics in both Austria and Czechoslovakia. The most prominent members of these families were able to preserve their prewar lifestyles to a surprising degree, while poorer nobles were more directly affected by the social changes of the interwar years. Christopher Brennan's chapter centers on the reactions in Austria to Emperor Karl's death in 1922. The attitudes revealed by this intrusion of the old order into the new are, Brennan argues, indicative of the Austrian population's more general relationship to its recent imperial past.

The last section of this book deals with the memory of the Empire after its passing and its role in different legitimization strategies. Christoph Mick assesses attempts to give meaning to the world war in interwar Austria through public remembrance of the dead soldiers. His analysis of war monuments highlights the use of memory to legitimize the new political order. Shifting the focus away from Franz Joseph, Empress Elisabeth, and other well-studied figures of the Habsburg legacy, Paul Miller's chapter on Franz Ferdinand reveals the ambivalence about the imperial past that characterized postwar Austrian society. Miller shows how, even in the present day, the Archduke's memory has engaged little with his activity as heir to the throne, but rather focused on his assassination and the world war.

Collectively, these chapters show how the Habsburg Empire continued to shape the region it had long ruled. This continuity, moreover, was not so much manifested in a nostalgic desire to return to the past, but rather in concrete aspects of society and political culture. Indeed, the (often literary) nostalgic discourse on the Habsburg Empire, which stresses feelings of loss and confines debate to subjective assessments of the monarchy, has obscured its actual, if often more mundane legacy in the successor states. Yet nostalgic intellectuals were not the only ones who kept the Empire as a frame of reference: parts of the former military, social, and political elite continued to play key roles in public life throughout the interwar period, and not just in Austria and Hungary. Despite the forceful discourse of rupture, these biographical connections to the past were well marked in all the successor states and had an important impact on their development. These chapters thus also help us to rethink the chronologies of the turbulent twentieth century in East Central Europe, where dramatic regime changes have long hid important continuities on the individual, local, and even state levels.

Notes

1. Joseph Roth, "The Bust of the Emperor," in *Collected Shorter Fiction of Joseph Roth*, transl. Michael Hofmann (London: Granta Books, 2002), 244.
2. Andrzej Misiuk, "Police and Policing under the Second Polish Republic, 1918–39," in *Policing Interwar Europe: Continuity, Change, and Crisis, 1918–1940*, ed. Gerald Blaney (Basingstoke: Palgrave, 2007), 162.
3. Quoted in Ladislav Rašín, *Paměti Dra Aloise Rašína* (Praha: Nákladem vlastním, 1929), 216. Cited in: Gary Cohen, "Nationalist Politics and the Dynamics of State and Civil Society in the Habsburg Monarchy, 1867–1914," *Central European History* 40 (2007): 278.
4. Captain B. H. Liddell Hart, *The Real War: 1914–1918* (Boston: Little, Brown and Company, 1930), 39.
5. For a recent reappraisal of the Habsburg monarchy, see Pieter Judson, *The Habsburg Empire: A New History* (Cambridge, MA: Harvard University Press, 2016). For earlier studies against the still commonplace narratives of decline, see Alan Sked, *The Decline and Fall of the Habsburg Empire, 1815–1918* (London: Longman, 1989); Gary Cohen, "Neither Absolutism nor Anarchy: New Narratives on Society and Government in Late Habsburg Austria," *Austrian History Yearbook* 29 (1998) part 1: 37–61.
6. Pieter Judson, "'Where Our Commonality Is Necessary . . .': Rethinking the End of the Habsburg Monarchy," *Austrian History Yearbook* 48 (2017): 1–21.
7. See *Austrian History Yearbook* 43 (April 2012) on "Sites of Indifference to Nationhood"; Pieter Judson, *Guardians of the Nation: Activists on the Language Frontiers in Imperial Austria* (Cambridge, MA: Harvard University Press, 2006); Pieter Judson and Marsha Rozenblit, eds., *Constructing Nationalities in East Central Europe* (New York: Berghahn Books, 2005).
8. Tara Zahra, "Imagined Noncommunities: National Indifference as a Category of Analysis," *Slavic Review* 69 (2010): 93–119.
9. Tara Zahra, *Kidnapped Souls: National Indifference and the Battle for Children in the Bohemian Lands, 1900–1948* (Ithaca: Cornell University Press, 2008), 12.
10. Laurence Cole and Daniel Unowsky, eds., *The Limits of Loyalty: Imperial Symbolism, Popular Allegiances, and State Patriotism in the Late Habsburg Monarchy* (New York: Berghahn Books, 2007).
11. See, for example, Oscar Jászi, *The Dissolution of the Habsburg Monarchy* (Chicago: University Press of Chicago, 1929), 7.
12. The most extreme example of this self-presentation is Czechoslovakia, while Hungary, for example, had a more ambivalent relationship to the Habsburg past. On the Czechoslovak

interwar myth, see Andrea Orzoff, *Battle for the Castle: The Myth of Czechoslovakia in Europe, 1914–1948* (New York: Oxford University Press, 2009).

13. On this so-called "quiet revolution" in Habsburg historiography, see Pieter M. Judson's review of Cole/Unowsky, "The Limits of Loyalty," in *Central European History* 42 (2009): 152–54; and Jonathan Kwan, "Nationalism and All That: Reassessing the Habsburg Monarchy and Its Legacy," *European History Quarterly* 41, no. 1 (2011): 88–108. Before this "revolution," there were, of course, important arguments in favor of the Monarchy's resilience. In particular, see Joachim Remak, "The Healthy Invalid: How Doomed the Habsburg Empire?" *The Journal of Modern History* 41, no. 2 (June 1969): 127–43.

14. See Peter Švorc and Harald Heppner, eds., *Veľká doba v malom priestore. Zlomové zmeny v mestách stredoeurópskeh priestoru a ich dôsledky (1918–1929)/Große Zeit im kleinen Raum. Umbrüche in den Städten des mitteleuropäischen Raumes 1918–1929* (Prešov/Graz: Universum, 2012). On Trieste, see Marco Bresciani, "Lost in Transition? The Habsburg Legacy, State- and Nation-Building, and the New Fascist Order in the Upper Adriatic," in *Ignoring the Nation's Call: National Indifference and the History of Nationalism in Modern Europe*, ed. Maarten Van Ginderachter and Jon Fox (London: Routledge, forthcoming).

15. Judson, *The Habsburg Empire*, 442–52. On Czechoslovakia's ambitions for overseas colonies, see Sarah Lemmen, "The 'Return to Europe': Intellectual Debates on the Global Place of Czechoslovakia in the Interwar Period," *European Review of History/Revue européenne d'histoire* 23, no. 4 (2016): 610–22.

16. Gernot Heiss et al., "Habsburg's Difficult Legacy: Comparing and Relating Austrian, Czech, Magyar, and Slovak National Historical Master Narratives," in *The Contested Nation: Ethnicity, Class, Religion and Gender in National Histories*, ed. Stefan Berger and Chris Lorenz (London: Palgrave, 2008), 374.

17. For example, Conan Fischer, "Continuity and Change in Post-Wilhelmine Germany: From the 1918 Revolution to the Ruhr Crisis," in *Wilhelminism and Its Legacies: German Modernities, Imperialism and the Meanings of Reform, 1890–1930*, ed. Geoff Eley and James Retallack (New York: Berghahn Books, 2003), 185–201. For a detailed study of the Prussian administration, see Marie-Bénédicte Vincent, *Serviteurs de l'Etat: les élites administratives en Prusse de 1871 à 1933* (Paris: Belin, 2006). For estimates in the Czechoslovak case, see Ivan Šedivý, "K otázce kontinuity nositelů státní moci: jmenování vedoucích úředníků v kompetenci ministerstva vnitra v letech 1918–1921," in *Moc, vliv a autorita v procesu vzniku a utváření meziválečné ČSR (1918–1921)*, ed. Jan Hájek, Dagmar Hájková et al. (Prague: Masarykův ústav, 2008), 184–97.

18. On the Austrian Republic, see several essays in Günter Bischof, Fritz Plasser, Peter Berger, eds., *From Empire to Republic: Post-World War I Austria* (New Orleans: University of New Orleans Press, 2010); Douglas P. Campbell, "The Shadow of the Habsburgs: Memory and National Identity in Austrian Politics and Education, 1918–1955" (PhD diss., University of Maryland, 2006).

19. Claudio Magris, *Der habsburgische Mythos in der modernen österreichischen Literatur* (Salzburg: O. Müller, 1966).

20. Ritchie Robertson, Edward Timms, eds., *The Habsburg Legacy: National Identity in Historical Perspective* (Edinburgh: Edinburgh University Press, 1994). On the role of the Habsburg myth in Austrian political discourse, see: Laurence Cole, "Der Habsburger-Mythos," in *Memoria Austriae I: Menschen Mythen Zeiten*, ed. Emil Brix,

Ernst Bruckmüller, and Hannes Stekl (Wien: Verlag für Geschichte und Politik, 2004), 473–504.
21. For example, Gergely Romsics's study of the political elite's memoirs: *Myth and Remembrance: The Dissolution of the Habsburg Empire in the Memoir Literature of the Austro-Hungarian Political Elite* (New York: Columbia University Press, 2006); Adam Kożuchowski, *The Afterlife of Austria-Hungary: The Image of the Habsburg Monarchy in Interwar Europe* (Pittsburgh: Pittsburgh University Press, 2013).
22. For an overview of the debate on path dependency in post-socialist contexts, see Jürgen Beyer and Jan Wielgohs, "On the Limits of Path Dependency Approaches for Explaining Postsocialist Institution Building: In Critical Response to David Stark," *East European Politics and Societies* 15, no. 2 (2001): 356–88.
23. Adéla Gjuričová et al., *Rozděleni minulostí: vytváření politických identit v České republice po roce 1989* (Praha: Knihovna Václava Havla, 2011).
24. Béatrice von Hirschhausen, Hannes Grandits, Claudia Kraft et al. *Phantomgrenzen: Räume und Akteure in der Zeit neu denken* (Göttingen: Wallstein Verlag, 2015), 57–83.
25. See Máté Rigó's work on the survival of business elites in Transylvania: "The Long First World War and the Survival of Business Elites in East-Central Europe: Transylvania's Industrial Boom and the Enrichment of Economic Elites," *European Review of History/Revue européenne d'histoire* 24, no. 2 (2017): 250–72. See also Nikolaus Wolf, "1918 als Zäsur? Die wirtschaftliche Entwicklung und Periodisierung der neueren Geschichte Ostmitteleuropas," *Comparativ* 20, no. 1/2 (2010): 30–52.
26. See Robert Gerwarth, *The Vanquished: Why the First World War Failed to End* (London: Allen Lane, 2016); Julia Eichenberg and John Paul Newman, "Aftershocks: Violence in Dissolving Empires after the First World War," *Contemporary European History* 19, no. 3 (August 2010): 183–94. For studies on the war's impact in former Habsburg lands, see Mark Cornwall, John-Paul Newman, eds., *Sacrifice and Rebirth: The Legacy of the Last Habsburg War* (New York: Berghahn Books, 2016).
27. Jörn Leonhard and Ulrike von Hirschhausen, eds., *Comparing Empires: Encounters and Transfers in the Long Nineteenth Century* (Göttingen: Vandenhoeck & Ruprecht, 2011); For a more precise example linked to some of the chapters in this volume, see Tim Buchen and Malte Rolf, eds. *Eliten im Vielvölkerreich: Imperiale Biographien in Russland und Österreich-Ungarn (1850–1918)* (Göttingen: De Gruyter, 2015).
28. See Benjamin Thomas White, *The Emergence of Minorities in the Middle East: The Politics of Community in French Mandate Syria* (Edinburgh: Edinburgh University Press, 2011).
29. Michael Meeker, *A Nation of Empire: The Ottoman Legacy of Turkish Modernity* (Berkeley: University of California Press, 2002); Sener Akturk, "Persistence of the Islamic Millet as an Ottoman Legacy: Mono-religious and Anti-ethnic Definition of Turkish Nationhood," *Middle Eastern Studies* 45, no. 6 (2009): 893–909.
30. Robert Gerwarth and John Horne, eds., *War in Peace: Paramilitary Violence in Europe After the Great War* (Oxford: Oxford University Press, 2012).
31. István Deák, *Beyond Nationalism: A Social and Political History of the Habsburg Officer Corps, 1848–1918*, (New York: Oxford University Press, 1990); Laurence Cole, *Military Culture and Popular Patriotism in Late Imperial Austria* (New York: Oxford University Press, 2014).

Bibliography

Akturk, Sener. "Persistence of the Islamic Millet as an Ottoman Legacy: Mono-religious and Anti-ethnic Definition of Turkish Nationhood." *Middle Eastern Studies* 45, no. 6 (2009): 893–909.

Bischof, Günter, Fritz Plasser, Peter Berger, eds. *From Empire to Republic: Post-World War I Austria*. New Orleans: University of New Orleans Press, 2010.

Buchen, Tim, and Malte Rolf, eds. *Eliten im Vielvölkerreich: Imperiale Biographien in Russland und Österreich-Ungarn (1850–1918)*. Göttingen: De Gruyter, 2015.

Campbell, Douglas P. "The Shadow of the Habsburgs: Memory and National Identity in Austrian Politics and Education, 1918–1955." PhD diss., University of Maryland, 2006.

Cohen, Gary. "Nationalist Politics and the Dynamics of State and Civil Society in the Habsburg Monarchy, 1867–1914." *Central European History* 40 (2007): 241–78.

———. "Neither Absolutism nor Anarchy: New Narratives on Society and Government in Late Habsburg Austria." *Austrian History Yearbook* 29 (1998) part 1: 37–61.

Cole, Laurence. "Der Habsburger-Mythos," In *Memoria Austriae I: Menschen Mythen Zeiten*, edited by Emil Brix, Ernst Bruckmüller, and Hannes Stekl, 473–504. Wien: Verlag für Geschichte und Politik, 2004.

———. *Military Culture and Popular Patriotism in Late Imperial Austria*. New York: Oxford University Press, 2014.

Cole, Laurence, and Daniel Unowsky, eds. *The Limits of Loyalty: Imperial Symbolism, Popular Allegiances, and State Patriotism in the Late Habsburg Monarchy*. New York: Berghahn Books, 2007.

Cornwall, Mark, and John-Paul Newman, eds. *Sacrifice and Rebirth: The Legacy of the Last Habsburg War*. New York: Berghahn Books, 2016.

Deák, István. *Beyond Nationalism: A Social and Political History of the Habsburg Officer Corps, 1848–1918*. New York: Oxford University Press, 1990.

Fischer, Conan. "Continuity and Change in Post-Wilhelmine Germany: From the 1918 Revolution to the Ruhr Crisis." In *Wilhelminism and Its Legacies: German Modernities, Imperialism and the Meanings of Reform, 1890–1930*, edited by Geoff Eley, James Retallack, 185–201. New York: Berghahn Books, 2003.

Gerwarth, Robert. *The Vanquished: Why the First World War Failed to End*. London: Allen Lane, 2016.

Gerwarth, Robert, and John Horne, eds. *War in Peace: Paramilitary Violence in Europe After the Great War*. Oxford: Oxford University Press, 2012.

Gjuričová, Adéla, Michal Kopeček, Petr Roubal, Jiří Suk, and Tomáš Zahradníček. *Rozděleni minulostí: vytváření politických identit v České republice po roce 1989*. Praha: Knihovna Václava Havla, 2011.

Jászi, Oscar. *The Dissolution of the Habsburg Monarchy*. Chicago: University of Chicago Press, 1929.

Judson, Pieter. *Guardians of the Nation: Activists on the Language Frontiers in Imperial Austria*. Cambridge, MA: Harvard University Press, 2006.

———. *The Habsburg Empire: A New History*. Cambridge, MA: Harvard University Press, 2016.

———. "'Where Our Commonality Is Necessary . . .': Rethinking the End of the Habsburg Monarchy." *Austrian History Yearbook* 48 (2017): 1–21.

Judson, Pieter, and Marsha Rozenblit, eds. *Constructing Nationalities in East Central Europe*. New York: Berghahn Books, 2005.
King, Jeremy. *Budweisers into Czechs and Germans: A Local History of Bohemian Politics, 1848–1948*. Princeton: Princeton University Press, 2002.
Kożuchowski, Adam. *The Afterlife of Austria-Hungary: The Image of the Habsburg Monarchy in Interwar Europe*. Pittsburgh: Pittsburgh University Press, 2013.
Kwan, Jonathan. "Nationalism and All That: Reassessing the Habsburg Monarchy and Its Legacy." *European History Quarterly* 41, no. 1 (2011): 88–108.
Lemmen, Sarah. "The 'Return to Europe': Intellectual Debates on the Global Place of Czechoslovakia in the Interwar Period." *European Review of History/Revue européenne d'histoire* 23, no. 4 (2016): 610–22.
Leonhard, Jörn, and Ulrike von Hirschhausen, eds. *Comparing Empires: Encounters and Transfers in the Long Nineteenth Century*. Göttingen: Vandenhoeck & Ruprecht, 2011.
Magris, Claudio. *Der habsburgische Mythos in der modernen österreichischen Literatur*. Salzburg: O. Müller, 1966.
Meeker, Michael. *A Nation of Empire: The Ottoman Legacy of Turkish Modernity*. Berkeley: University of California Press, 2002.
Misiuk, Andrzej. "Police and Policing under the Second Polish Republic, 1918–39." In *Policing Interwar Europe: Continuity, Change, and Crisis, 1918–1940*, edited by Gerald Blaney, 159–71. Basingstoke: Palgrave, 2007.
Orzoff, Andrea. *Battle for the Castle: The Myth of Czechoslovakia in Europe, 1914–1948*. New York: Oxford University Press, 2009.
Remak, Joachim. "The Healthy Invalid: How Doomed the Habsburg Empire?" *The Journal of Modern History* 41, no. 2 (June 1969): 127–43.
Rigó, Máté. "The Long First World War and the Survival of Business Elites in East-Central Europe: Transylvania's Industrial Boom and the Enrichment of Economic Elites." *European Review of History/Revue européenne d'histoire* 24, no. 2 (2017): 250–72.
Robertson, Ritchie, and Edward Timms, eds. *The Habsburg Legacy: National Identity in Historical Perspective*. Edinburgh: Edinburgh University Press, 1994.
Romsics, Gergely. *Myth and Remembrance: The Dissolution of the Habsburg Empire in the Memoir Literature of the Austro-Hungarian Political Elite*. New York: Columbia University Press, 2006.
Šedivý, Ivan. "K otázce kontinuity nositelů státní moci: jmenování vedoucích úředníků v kompetenci ministerstva vnitra v letech 1918–1921." In *Moc, vliv a autorita v procesu vzniku a utváření meziválečné ČSR (1918–1921)*, edited by Jan Hájek, Dagmar Hájková et al., 184–97. Prague: Masarykův ústav, 2008.
Sked, Alan. *The Decline and Fall of the Habsburg Empire, 1815–1918*. London: Longman, 1989.
Švorc, Peter, and Harald Heppner, eds. *Veľká doba v malom priestore. Zlomové zmeny v mestách stredoeurópskeh priestoru a ich dôsledky (1918–1929)/Große Zeit im kleinen Raum. Umbrüche in den Städten des mitteleuropäischen Raumes 1918–1929*. Prešov/Graz: Universum, 2012.
Vincent, Marie-Bénédicte. *Serviteurs de l'Etat: les élites administratives en Prusse de 1871 à 1933*. Paris: Belin, 2006.
von Hirschhausen, Béatrice, Hannes Grandits, Claudia Kraft, Dietmar Müller, and Thomas Serrier. *Phantomgrenzen: Räume und Akteure in der Zeit neu denken*. Göttingen: Wallstein Verlag, 2015.

White, Benjamin Thomas. *The Emergence of Minorities in the Middle East: The Politics of Community in French Mandate Syria*. Edinburgh: Edinburgh University Press, 2011.
Wolf, Nikolaus. "1918 als Zäsur? Die wirtschaftliche Entwicklung und Periodisierung der neueren Geschichte Ostmitteleuropas." *Comparativ* 20, no. 1/2 (2010): 30–52.
Zahra, Tara. "Imagined Noncommunities: National Indifference as a Category of Analysis." *Slavic Review* 69 (2010): 93–119.
———. *Kidnapped Souls: National Indifference and the Battle for Children in the Bohemian Lands, 1900–1948*. Ithaca: Cornell University Press, 2008.

Part I

PERMANENCE AND REVOLUTION: NATIONAL POLITICS IN THE TRANSITION TO THE SUCCESSOR STATES

Chapter 1

NEGOTIATING POST-IMPERIAL TRANSITIONS
Local Societies and Nationalizing States in East Central Europe

Gábor Egry

Scholars typically attribute the demise of empires in the wake of World War I to their struggle with emerging nation-states.[1] Yet making the nation into the primary subject of analysis often obscures crucial differences within the new political entities. Of course, this is not to overlook the important scholarship that tackles local and regional issues either directly or as part of a larger narrative. This includes studies of transitional events in Upper Silesia; a collection of local stories from Austria-Hungary; new work on postwar violence throughout East-Central Europe; and even more targeted studies of such ethnic groups as the Mazurians and the Budweisers.[2] All these works depict important episodes in the broader history of the crystallization of sometimes rather heterogeneous nations around their new nation-states.[3]

However, what are generally lacking in the historiographical literature are comprehensive comparative studies of local level transitions. We know surprisingly little, for example, about how the various revolutions assumed administrative and political power in individual localities; to what extent the old elite was replaced; and whether there was a period of revolutionary or counter-revolutionary cooperation across ethnic boundaries (and if so, how long it lasted). Similarly under-researched topics include the installation of local governments in the new nation-states; the nature and extent of local measures; personnel changes in local institutions; and the reconfiguration of politics, social roles, and public practices.

Not even the top-down nationalizing efforts have been thoroughly surveyed at the local level. Indeed, most studies simply assume—on the basis of randomly selected examples and the not necessarily unbiased reports collected by state officials—that central orders and regulations were implemented "seamlessly."[4]

This chapter operates from the opposite assumption—that is, once the Habsburg Empire and its political institutions had collapsed, local elites and ordinary citizens, although their role in state affairs had grown markedly in the preceding decades,[5] were confronted with daunting tasks that previously had been left to the state, and for which they had little, if any, experience.[6] Regardless of whether local leaders had been revolutionaries, they were forced to govern during this transitional period in unfamiliar roles and, largely, without effective support from central organs. Additionally, in the struggle to determine the territorial extent of the successor states, those people living in areas occupied and claimed by the new sovereigns had to face the emerging state and its homogenizing visions on their own. This led to the creation of what may be considered a new state space at the local level—one which directly affected the outcome of the state-building process itself, not least of all due to the limited capacity and efficiency of the new states but also, as we will see, the perseverance of local structures and institutions.[7]

In this chapter, I address these issues through the state-building processes in regions that had belonged to Hungary and came under Czechoslovak and Romanian rule in 1919—Slovakia (or Upper Hungary, as it was called in the dualist era) and Transylvania, respectively. These were diverse, multiethnic areas with predominantly Hungarian and German urban populations despite an overall higher proportion of Slovaks and Romanians. While the majority of inhabitants spoke the language of their new rulers, the border zones contained Hungarian-speaking majorities, even in the countryside. And some areas further from the new frontiers (the Saxon settlements in Southern Transylvania, the Banat, the Szeklerland, Maramureș, and the Spiš) were characterized by a strong Hungarian and German presence, often constituting the regional majority.

Nor was diversity limited to language or nationality. Some of these areas were industrial zones (most notably the mining towns in the Banat or Jiu Valley) with large working-class populations. Others were home to sizable groups of religious minorities, such as Jews and Greek Catholics in Northern Transylvania and Carpatho-Ukraine. These regions had distinct social, cultural, and administrative traditions as well.[8] How they would confront state-building efforts based on different and even foreign practices remained to be seen.

In order to highlight the important ways in which a local perspective can change our understanding of state formation, this chapter begins by discussing the different faces—social, national, and democratic—of the revolutions in 1918. It then examines the process of establishing a political administration, with an emphasis on the peculiar linguistic and symbolic features of the new local regimes and landscapes. The last part assesses how the different regions expressed themselves politically and socially in this early state-building period.

The Three Faces of One Revolution

The revolutions that took place in Eastern Europe between 1917 and 1919 strove to reconfigure politics, economics, and society such that more people would be enfranchised and national development would go hand-in-hand with greater economic equality. Of course, revolutionary elites were typically more interested in preserving their prerogatives than in acceding to the demands of ordinary people, who often made their own, local revolutions. But the leaders of the new nation-states promised to solve their problems together.

Hungary was a prominent case with respect both to the national and social aspects of revolutionary state-building. When the Hungarian National Council, the interim legislative body of the country, declared independence from Austria-Hungary, it not only extended political rights through universal suffrage, but also created integrating institutions like workers' and soldiers' councils; promised minority rights and proper representation for nationalities; and offered to alleviate social ills by redistributing wealth (mainly through agrarian reform and the introduction of extensive social benefits). But these efforts confronted the similar goals of the Slovak, Czech, and Romanian National Councils, which sought to implement change on their own terms and in their own, respective national frameworks. From this perspective, then, national initiatives were crucial in the early phases of nation–state-building in that they prevented cross-ethnic cooperation at the highest government levels.

Rather than simply accepting historical Hungary's existence and reform efforts, the Czech, Slovak, and Romanian National Councils envisioned their own independent nation-states. Thus, the national/political aspect of state-building overshadowed the social/economic one already by late October 1918. Unsurprisingly, differing political visions were the main sources for rivalry between revolutionary bodies, often disrupting interethnic cooperation among administrative elites. An oft-cited example is the negotiations between Oszkár Jászi, the Hungarian Minister for National Minorities, and representatives of the Romanian National Council at Arad. The stakes of these negotiations in late November 1918 were no less than the territorial consolidation of Hungary, as the Romanian National Council was demanding the immediate takeover of twenty-three counties with Romanian populations (thereby extending its rule to the Eastern zone of the Great Plain and the whole of the Banat). Despite the wide-ranging concessions offered by Jászi, who proposed establishing a system of national cantons with broad autonomy, the Romanian politicians insisted upon having full sovereignty over all Romanian inhabited territories.[9]

A similar scenario played out in Upper Hungary. On 6 December 1918, Milan Hodža, a former member of the Hungarian Parliament and a representative of the Slovak National Council, came to terms with the Hungarian government over a demarcation line that left most of the contested territories with predominantly Hungarian populations under Hungarian control. However, he was soon denounced by the Czechoslovak government, which had been working with delegates to the Paris Peace Conference in order to establish a new border that put the disputed zone in its hands. As it happens, this border runs very close to the present one.

At the local level, by contrast, cross-ethnic cooperation was more common, thus making it harder to distinguish the political and social aspects of the revolution. Moreover, local revolutions were often truly local in that they did not simply replicate what happened in the centers of national power. Instead, their main drivers were the social discontent of their respective populations, as well as the violence engendered by returning soldiers. Unsurprisingly, then, local leaders were often less concerned with national, state-building issues than material problems at home, which likewise meant that their construction of enemies did not straightforwardly fall along ethnic lines.

Transylvania, a new province of Romania that was approximately 30 percent ethnic Hungarian and 10 percent German, is a case in point. There, the local revolution and violence targeted everything associated with the old order. Not only did returning soldiers loot rampantly, but the local population took advantage of the breakdown in authority, which in any case was more often concerned with disarming the returning veterans than pursuing the local bands.[10] People in multiethnic regions often attacked state authorities regardless of their ethnicity, and looting was by no means confined to Hungarian property. The Romanian National party politician Ilie Lăzar learned this first-hand when, as a *Honvéd* (Hungarian military) officer, he travelled to Máramarossziget (Sighetu Marmației) in order to establish Romanian rule in the county. Instead, he was robbed clean by a band of returning Romanian soldiers who had come to "rescue" the Orthodox priest with whom Lăzar was lodging, and who were not deterred by the fact that the "Hungarian" officer also happened to be an ethnic Romanian.[11]

Faced with such violence, state authorities often had to rely on National Councils to regain control. A circular from the Hungarian Interior Ministry admitted as much in December 1918: "During those unforgettable days, when the people's will broke centuries of forced servitude, the National Councils provided an invaluable service for the true cause of liberty. . . . Hungary's liberated people owe their eternal gratitude to them."[12] The Councils had the capacity to run local administrations, organize armed national guards, and distribute provisions as part of their larger effort to reorganize society along national lines. But to what extent were local Councils the true embodiment of grassroots demands for a national order? At least three aspects of their activities indicate that the situation was more complex than the Councils typically presented it.

First, many of these National Councils were organized following external initiatives, often by the delegates of county or even regional Councils.[13] In these cases, the delegates brought with them a blueprint for action, describing whom to mobilize and how to legitimize the takeover. The scripted nature of these events in many localities suggests that the vision of a spontaneous revolution generating new institutions along national lines found much less support at the local level than it did among urban intellectuals and political elites. Moreover, the sequence of events was surprisingly similar in such disparate regions as the Barcaság (Burzenland, Țară Bârsei) around Brassó (Kronstadt, Brașov); the Nagy-Küküllő (Târnava Mare) river zone; and Szászrégen (Sächisch Reen, Reghin), especially north and south. First, the Councils were established in the major regional cities (Brassó, Nagyszeben [Hermannstadt, Sibiu], and Szászrégen), all of which declared some form of national autonomy. A few days or weeks later, after securing the cooperation of county administrators, they sent representatives to villages in which the National Council had less presence. These representatives sought out influential local figures, instructed them on how to set up their own councils, and participated in the festivities for newly elected officials tasked with "initiating" the council. Control over the local councils could be quite strict as well. A memorandum adopted by the inaugural session of the Maroslaka (Huduc, today Maiorești) Romanian National Council, for example, contained a verbatim paragraph on the rejection of false compromises from a memo issued by the Reghin National Council.[14]

Second, most of the National Councils prioritized material issues over national ones. Some were eager to reopen old conflicts over property rights irrespective of their opponents' nationality. The Romanian communities in the Görgény Valley (Ghurghiul) offer a telling example. In the village of Görgényhodák (Hodac), the first session of the Romanian National Council adopted a resolution demanding that the Great Council (*sfatul cel mare*), which would discuss the rightful demands of oppressed nations, include the village's claim to the surrounding forests they had lost in 1848.[15] In the nearby village of Görgényorsova (Orșova), the National Council met on 1 December 1918, the same day as the Great Assembly of Alba Iulia, which declared the union of Transylvania with Romania. The participants decided to increase defense of the community forests and to send delegates to neighboring villages to warn them not to enter without permission.[16] The deliberate timing of the Görgényorsova "Great National Assembly" illustrates the extent to which locals went to manipulate national politics for their material aims—in this case drawing upon the legitimacy conferred by events in Alba Iulia.

Finally, despite numerous references to "the nation" in histories of this transformational period, there is evidence to suggest that, at least during the initial phase of the revolution, the concept of Romanian nationhood was less clear-cut than contemporaries claimed and historians and politicians have largely accepted since.[17] Indeed, Romanian exertions in favor of self-determination appear ambiguous if we examine some National Councils' declarations in the immediate aftermath of the regime change. On 10 November 1918 in Erdőidecs (Idicel Pădure), for example, the Council referred to Romanian self-determination from Hungary and Transylvania, without mentioning union with the Old Kingdom of Romania. Yet more astoundingly, on 8 November 1918, the National Council from Görgénynádas (Nădașa Română) announced and greeted the formation of the Hungarian National Council in Budapest, as well as the nomination of Mihály Károlyi as Prime Minister. It then declared its adherence to the program of the Budapest Hungarian National Council. Another passage from this declaration asserted that the Romanians had gained their right for self-government "in this country" (i.e., Hungary), which would be realized through the Romanian National Council in Arad.[18] This Council thus viewed its legitimacy as derived from the Hungarian national revolution rather than the Romanian one.

These organizational and ideological aspects of the local National Councils can also be found on the territory of present-day Slovakia, where the revolution unfolded in similar ways at the local level in terms of the collapse of administrations, the influence of National Councils, and the predominance of material issues over national ones.[19] In the case of Nyitra (Nitra)—the seat of a Catholic bishopric—the National Council was initially formed by representatives of the Social Democrats, the Christian Socialists, and the Hungarian opposition parties. They were soon joined by ethnic Slovaks from the ranks of the Catholic clergy (like Jozef Tiso) and the Christian Socialist association, though many, including Tiso, initially referred to themselves as Hungarians. With the advent of political events in Prague and Budapest, however, more ethnically narrow National Councils were formed.[20]

In the Slovakian capital Pozsony (Pressburg, Bratislava), studied by Pieter van Duin, organized labor also became a factor in the local administration, in sharp contrast to its minimal role in mainly agrarian Transylvania.[21] The Social Democrats in particular—including Germans, Hungarians, and Slovaks—dominated the transitional period in Pozsony, acting as a stabilizing force through their exceptional organization and connections to Budapest and, to a lesser extent, Vienna. Although not necessarily indifferent to nationality, the Social Democrats' admirable ethnic tolerance lasted through the mid-1920s, when the new Czechoslovak state began undermining their position with nationalizing policies that favored Czechs and Slovaks even among the ranks of organized labor. These policies eventually led to the dissolution of the Hungarian-German Social Democratic Party. Romanian regions with similar social fabrics, such as mining districts and industrial Temesvár (Temeschwar, Timișoara), underwent comparable transitions: initially, organized workers and their parties fended off nationalizing efforts, only to be pushed aside by the state administrations appointed by the military authorities in early January 1919.[22]

These relatively exceptional cases of industrial areas raise the broader question of interethnic cooperation. The very purpose of National Councils was to dissociate national communities, despite the fact that local, everyday social and political life was well-entwined nationally. For this reason, local-level cooperation among National Councils tended to be the norm. Common bodies were established to oversee food and firewood provisions, collect local taxes and fees, and to distribute the confiscated property. Different national guards coordinated security measures and patrols.[23] And at least in one case, in Nagymoha (Grănări, Mukendorf), the Hungarian National Council refused to begin operations until its Romanian counterpart was established and they could run the locality together.[24]

In county seats, most National Councils initially operated in an ethnically mixed manner.[25] Jozef Tiso was not the only politician who came to prominence as the leader of a nation-state (i.e., the Slovak Republic formed under the tutelage of Nazi Germany), but started his political career in a National Council that sustained peaceful, interethnic cooperation.[26] The Romanian National Council in Deva was headed by the future Romanian Prime Minister Petru Groza, who, despite the intransigent position of the general Romanian National Council concerning sovereignty over eastern Hungary and Transylvania, waited until early December 1918 to order the removal of ethnic Romanians from the local Hungarian National Council.[27]

In addition to these individual cases, the overall composition of the National Councils had a lasting political impact in the interwar period. The first few weeks featured (partial) elite replacement in which centrally appointed officials often departed, while representatives from the hitherto dominant Hungarian political parties were sidelined (especially István Tisza's Party of National Labor). Those acceding to power through the National Councils either represented the parliamentary opposition or parties that still lacked institutional influence, such as the Social Democrats and Bourgeois Radicals. These parties formed a new ruling class even when the representatives of the traditional opposition, such as the Catholic People's Party in Upper Hungary, already had a strong presence in local communities. The National Councils thus served as nodes in a newly emerging social network, enabling hitherto peripheral groups and personalities to access power at the local, regional, and, often, national levels.[28]

Groza, who maintained ties with the Hungarian elite throughout his life, is a good example of this. Although many of his contacts stemmed from his privileged high school years in Szászváros (Broos, Orăștie), Groza nurtured these relationships to the extent that he even participated in a class reunion in Budapest during his tenure as President of (socialist) Romania in the 1950s. But in the 1920s,

Groza was a regional leader of General Alexandru Averescu's People's Party, in which capacity he served as an interlocutor between the Hungarian minority party and Averescu, with whom the Hungarians concluded an agreement on electoral and political cooperation in 1923.[29] Jozef Tiso also profited from his membership in the Nitra (Nyitra) National Council through his contact with fellow member Jenő Lelley, who went on to become chairman of the Christian Socialist Party in Slovakia. This supposedly transethnic organization was on Budapest's payroll and often toyed with Hungarian revisionism. Nevertheless, after Lelley was ousted as party chairman in 1925, he founded another party (the Christian Socialist Party of Western Slovakia) with a pro-Czechoslovak platform, an apparent volte-face only until one considers the personal connections Lelley established during the revolutionary period, and the overtures made around 1925 toward reconciling the Slovak People's Party and the Czechoslovak government. The party, which Tiso also helped to found, eventually entered the government and became part of the ruling coalition from 1927 to 1929.

The revolutionary period was short and transitory. Overlooking it, however, would be to lose sight of the extent to which state rule had collapsed. During these first few weeks, the "national interest" and the common weal of the nation were defined differently in different places (at least at the local level), and they often deviated from the ideals and interests advocated by the central National Councils.[30] It was only the presence of the conquering states' representatives that ended this practice, which could not have happened without first eliminating the Councils themselves.

Administering the Bitter Pills

Extending state power to the newly acquired regions was complicated by the fact that the new states were often a patchwork of legal systems and administrative cultures. Greater Romania inherited provinces from Cisleithania, Russia, and Hungary, while Czechoslovakia tried to combine Hungarian, Austrian, and provincial legal systems. The transition to a new, unified legal framework supervised by a new administration was thus bound to be a protracted one. Indeed, some important pieces of legislation were never entirely replaced.[31]

The idiosyncrasies of provincial legal traditions required first-hand knowledge, which made employing transferred or newly recruited personnel more problematic. The takeover of the administration and public services typically lasted for months, while new administrative laws were not passed until the mid-1920s. Moreover, despite similarities in the takeover processes, the outcomes in Czechoslovakia and Romania differed significantly in terms of minority participation in the administration and the continuity of pre-1918 personnel.

Initially, the goal was similar in both countries: secure an oath of loyalty from officials in the existing institutions, if necessary by threat of dismissal. The responses, however, differed considerably. In the territories under Czechoslovak rule, officials only pledged their loyalty after receiving permission to do so from Budapest, whereas in Transylvania, they were instructed by Budapest authorities to reject the oath.[32] Many officials actually fled to Budapest, causing serious political and social problems, though a large number of public servants remained at their posts.[33] Ultimately, the fate of those who stayed was not decided by the formal oath, but rather by the human resources available to the new states.

In Transylvania, taking the oath did not necessarily determine whether one kept one's job. As a general rule, high-ranking officials who refused the oath did so as a political gesture, while those serving in less important and publicly exposed positions could more easily take it without fear of repercussions should Hungarian rule be restored or they decide to emigrate.[34] But even those who rejected the oath were not automatically removed from service. While the new rulers certainly preferred qualified Romanian applicants, in places like Târnaveni (Dicsőszentmárton), the new prefect was forced to work with an administrative team that had declared its loyalty to the Romanian National Council despite not speaking Romanian.[35] Even when the administration was totally replaced, as in the county of Solnoc-Dăbâca (Szolnok-Doboka), appointments for low-level positions were not necessarily ethnically biased simply due to the shortage of suitable Romanian applicants.[36] Consequently, the ratio of minority public servants roughly corresponded with the proportion of minorities in Transylvania's population well into the mid-1930s. In many counties, there was much continuity between pre-1918 and post-1918 personnel. For example, in Caraş-Severin (Krassó-Szörény), more than 60 percent of the minority village notaries in 1934 started their careers before 1919. In Trei Scaune (Háromszék) county, two-thirds of village notaries in 1921 held a similar post before 1919, and more than half of those were in the same position before the world war. Among officials of the central county organs, only one-third belonged to this more experienced group, but 59 percent of the newly hired officials were Hungarians.[37]

Administrative institutions were not the only ones faced with a shortage of qualified employees—some public services were simply too essential to function with inexperienced staff. Postal workers thus kept their jobs in Romania regardless of ethnicity and despite nationally motivated attacks.[38] This emphasis on expertise is perhaps best exemplified by the management of postal services by ethnic Hungarians in some remote, predominantly Romanian areas through the first years of the Antonescu era (1940–44).[39] Successful outcomes often superseded ethnic prejudices to such an extent that local authorities would assign politically charged tasks to minority officials. For example, the chief magistrate of the Oradea county court assigned a Hungarian examining magistrate to investigate the murder of two Romanian intellectuals by Hungarian troops in Beiuş

(Belényes) in April 1919. Fearing a biased investigation, the opposition attacked the government in parliament for this specific assignment. Yet the court upheld it on the grounds that this dutiful Hungarian magistrate was the only one who had ample time for such a case.[40] Defending state authority against perceived threats or even illegalities sometimes required the removal of self-appointed Romanian officials. In the county of Cluj (Kolozs), some Hungarian village notaries who had been expelled during the revolution and replaced by local Romanian notables (like a Greek Catholic priest), were later reinstated by the new Romanian administration.[41]

The process unfolded differently in Czechoslovakia, where Hungarian officials retained their posts until enough qualified Czech and Slovak bureaucrats could take over the administration and public services. As a result, layoffs took place gradually depending upon local circumstances and external political events. In Bratislava (Pressburg, Pozsony), for example, the administration was restaffed so cautiously that, in the early 1920s, most local officials still came from the pre-1918 period.[42] Eventually, however, the administration was filled with a new generation of Czech and Slovak officials and the ratio of Hungarian public servants halved between 1921 and 1930, while mainly pre-1918 public servants of Slovak nationality were retained.[43] But these so-called *magyaróns* (pro-Hungarians) had to demonstrate their new national loyalty by adhering to Slovak (or Czechoslovak) customs and social practices, thereby abandoning their earlier means of displaying middle-class status.[44]

Hungarian postal and railway workers faced a harsher fate in Czechoslovakia than in Romania when they refused to take the loyalty oath and/or engaged in strike activity. The latter was quite common due to the strength of organized labor and Social Democracy in these territories of the emerging Czechoslovak Republic. After the creation of the Hungarian Soviet Republic in March 1919, moreover, unionized minority workers became increasingly suspect as supporters of a Bolshevik Revolution. This suspicion accelerated their removal from service.[45]

Local power relations played out differently in Romania and Czechoslovakia. Czechoslovak laws entitled communities to effective self-government based upon proportional representation in local political bodies like city councils and county assemblies (and, after 1927, regional assemblies as well). In localities where minority parties had sufficient support, they could meaningfully influence decisions concerning schools, cultural and social institutions, and even street names.[46] In Romania, by contrast, such elected local bodies served only between 1926 and 1933 (and not without interruptions), and decisions about these issues were made by a centrally appointed commission composed of politicians close to the government. In this way, minority elites in these localities lacked a means for formal influence on local issues, though they often managed to have a voice through personal and professional connections or political pacts between parties.⁴⁷ Romanian political forces competing for power often sought support from minorities by forging such informal compromises. For example, in major Saxon towns, the mayors were still Saxons until the 1930s. And in most Szekler cities, local Hungarian political groups, sometimes in rivalry with each other, gained official positions by the mid-1920s. Every Romanian party had its own Hungarian members and candidates in the most important localities.⁴⁸ It was thus not only the absence of democratic elections that made such informal political settlements easier in Romania, but also the fact that minorities had a strong presence at the mid and low levels of county administration, creating an environment that directly fostered cooperation between politicians.⁴⁹

Yet another example of the continuity of state institutions and the survival of social practices is the voluntary firefighter associations in Transylvania. Such organizations were nonexistent in the Old Kingdom of Romania, where firefighters were subordinated to the military. In Transylvanian cities like Caransebeș (Karansebesch, Karánsebes) and Brașov, by contrast, these associations flourished, assembling public officials and the middle- and lower middle-classes regardless of nationality. Their working language was either Hungarian or German, and it often remained so despite frequent attacks on the associations during the interwar period. When the Romanian General Staff banned them in the province for their alleged irredentism (the circular order claimed that these associations had only been recently founded by Hungarian irredentists), county and local administrators protested and the mayor of Caransebeș sent an emotional, eight-page letter to his superiors denying the presence of irredentist Hungarians and the use of Hungarian language, and defending the firefighter associations as wellsprings of patriotism and altruism:

> We solemnly reject the accusations; those brave people do not deserve the label of irredentist Hungarians.... The Romanians were never excluded from the ranks of the firefighters, [and] even now 10 out of 25 are Romanians, all of them having served 20–30 years. By no means was the association founded by well-known Hungarian irredentists. Nor could it serve Hungarian propaganda and the preservation of the Hungarian spirit, as the firefighters started to work fifty years ago, when not a single Hungarian word was heard in the city. The Germans who founded the association developed it in cooperation with Romanians.... The prefect certainly knows that every loyal son of the country ought to have a place among the voluntary firefighters, irrespective of his mother tongue.⁵⁰

The mayor's argument reveals more than just indignation over the negligence of local traditions—it shows how the nationalizing rhetoric from below was used to fend off nationalizing policies from above. The mayor was probably telling an "official" truth, though police reports confirm that Hungarians belonged to the associations and that their language was one of the firefighters' working languages.⁵¹

Lands of Promise

Historians have analyzed a broad range of symbolic nationalizing efforts in terms of how they transformed cities or forced traditional public practices into the private sphere following regime change. Rituals and festive days from the dualist era that came to be regarded as expressions of Hungarian nationality, for example, were replaced by new festivities and personality cults. Likewise, monuments were destroyed, removed, or relocated; and Hungarian national days were celebrated in private or semi-public spheres such as churches.[52] Yet these efforts to undermine national symbols and practices often had the opposite effect—renewing national consciousness even among social groups that had been indifferent toward Hungarian rituals. Thus, for example, on 20 August 1920, social democratically inclined Hungarian workers in Brașov, who formerly had refrained from demonstrations of religious adherence, attended the feast of Saint Stephen and effusively sang the Hungarian national anthem with the Roman Catholic congregation.[53]

Moreover, the new cults and rituals often possessed their own attractions irrespective of national identity. In Czechoslovakia, large segments of the Hungarian and German populations took part in the Masaryk cult, sometimes to the extent of venerating the president as a benevolent figure whose gestures toward minorities promised to resolve their problems.[54] Local activist (i.e., pro-Czechoslovak) parties were often able to capitalize on Masaryk's personality cult when competing with minority Hungarian parties.[55] After all, this quasi-religious loyalty to the Czechoslovak president had direct links to the dualist era in that it constructed Masaryk as the heir to the venerable Habsburg Emperor Franz Joseph. Similarly, in Romania, allegiance to the ruler (the king of Hungary) was easily transferred to the king of Romania, even by his minority subjects. Numerous royal petitions from mainly lower class Hungarians reached the royal court just as they had in dualist Hungary. Betti Juhász from Petroșani (Petrozsény), for example, asked the king for a dowry, while the Cluj (Kolozsvár) locksmith István Kun just asked for permission to baptize his son after His Majesty's Christian name. In the case of these petitions, socioeconomic status was more decisive than nationality or local context.[56]

Social networks often transcended ethno-national boundaries when it came to resisting central nationalizing initiatives. The importance of these networks is well illustrated by local national markers like street names, statuary, and middle-class cultural activities. Street names in particular constituted crucial indicators of ethnic ownership and a symbolic means of occupation. Hungarian cities had been increasingly nationalized through street renaming before 1914, and the new regimes continued the practice.[57] However, the different patterns of street renaming throughout Romania and Czechoslovakia suggest that these nationalizing initiatives could easily be sidetracked.

This was widely visible in Czechoslovak towns and cities, where effective local self-government enabled the representatives of minority Hungarian and/ or German communities to determine geographic names and nomenclature (if not in Hungarian or German, then often bilingually). As long as a specified percentage of registered minorities lived in any one locality, it was minimally required to have bilingual street signs. With enough votes in the local council, the minority elite could even choose the street names provided they did not explicitly challenge Czechoslovak symbolism.[58] The exceptions were larger, more important cities in which political exigencies and central initiatives prevailed over minority rights. Bratislava was the most flagrant example, as not only was the city rechristened with its largely invented Slovak name, but the official renaming was held just before the 15 March Remembrance Day for the 1848 Hungarian Revolution. Throughout the interwar years, such symbolic conquests gradually erased Hungarian national figures from the city's map, eventually even eliminating the neutral ones.[59]

Similarly, in the Transylvanian capital Cluj, the new prefect provocatively issued his first decree on renaming twenty streets on 15 March 1919. A year later, not one Hungarian street name had been left untouched. These changes were more abrupt and arbitrary than in Czechoslovakia, since local self-government was not practiced in the region until the late 1920s. Interestingly, however, the new nomenclature was neither original nor did it represent a major municipal reinvention. On the contrary, it was the mirror image of a symbolic map in which Hungarian historical figures were replaced by their closest Romanian counterparts from the same period: Romanian military units for Hungarian military units (Dorobanților for Honvéd); heroes of anti-Ottoman wars for anti-Ottoman warriors (Ștefan cel Mare for János Hunyadi); famous writers for famous writers (Ion Heliade Rădulescu for Imre Madách); and revolutionaries for revolutionaries from roughly the same era (Avram Iancu for Sándor Petőfi).[60]

The limited Romanian presence in pre-1918 Cluj (according to the 1910 census, just 12 percent of the population was ethnic Romanian) made it difficult to impose a preexisting, though unofficial Romanian symbolic geography on its streets, as occurred, for example, in the Romanian city of Făgăraș (Fogaras, Fogarasch). Apart from the main roads and squares, it was unclear which areas had the most political and/or cultural relevance for the Romanian community. Consequently, it was hard to determine the most appropriate street names, in which case the new rulers simply adopted what they had inherited. Cluj's obvious political importance, for example, did not permit a more partial renaming as occurred in Oradea (Nagyvárad), where fewer street names were changed and the whole process proceeded rather unsystematically. Indeed, in Oradea several street names considered Hungarian (Ferenc Deák, Kálvin, Saint Ladislaus) continued to be used officially.[61]

Another important variable in renaming patterns was adherence to or deviation from a generalized national pantheon. The former was advocated (or even instructed) from Bucharest and is well illustrated by the city of Lugoj (Lugos, Lugosch), the seat of a Greek-Catholic diocese. The latter, which usually implied recourse to more regional symbols, was evident in Făgăraș and Caransebeș. While all three cities were home to a significant Romanian middle-class, the situation in Lugoj suggests that the presence of competing non-Romanian elites (Serbs, in this case) could adversely affect the behavior of local Romanians. Moreover, when the French had controlled Lugoj in the summer of 1919, they restored the Hungarian administration. Thus, local Romanians faced with such political uncertainty were more likely to adhere to Bucharest's nationalizing expectations than they were in other parts of the Banat.[62]

Statues and other monuments/memorials underwent a parallel fate to street names, especially in regional capitals where the new rulers acted promptly to reconfigure symbolic space. Again, in Czechoslovakia, there were usually still opportunities for minorities to celebrate anti-Habsburg revolutionary traditions in line with the Republic's progressive, anti-Habsburg founding myth. In this way, statues of Hungarian heroes like Petőfi (the poet-hero of 1848) were sometimes tolerated. In 1923, the centenary of his birth was even commemorated in Bratislava.[63] Nevertheless, nationalizing pressures were stronger for monuments than they were for street names, often despite local efforts to preserve elements of the pre-1918 symbolic space. The destruction of the Maria Theresia statue in central Bratislava during the night of 26 October 1921, for example, was a premeditated political act parallel to the city government's resolve to erect a monument to Milan Rastislav Štefánik, the Slovak pilot-hero who died mysteriously in a plane crash in 1919.[64] The new governments also took advantage of their growing differences with previously acculturated or magyarized nationalities to weaken Hungarians by making symbolic concessions to non-Magyar organizations. Even the German-speaking and pro-Hungarian Zipsers from Slovakia established a symbolic topography in 1919, which, they boasted to Budapest, preserved the Hungarian character of the region through the revival of local traditions and the commemoration of local figures and events.[65]

In Romania, conditions on the ground also determined the authorities' attitudes toward statuary. In Oradea, at least six prewar public memorials survived until 1934.[66] In several smaller cities, authorities tolerated statues of Hungarian national figures with local connections, and even some heroes' memorials for the First World War. One of these war memorials depicted a Turul bird, the mythic forefather of Hungarians and a controversial national symbol.[67] More intriguing yet was a professional survey and preservation project of existing statues/memorials undertaken by the new Romanian authorities in the Banat. Although it only lasted until the mid-1920s, it signified a more relaxed official attitude toward these monuments in a region where traditionally strong dynastic loyalty had already produced protests against the removal of Franz Joseph's statue from Caransebeș (1919).[68] This emotional attachment to Habsburg symbols—viewed even by Romanians as an important component of local identity—exemplifies the commonalities of social life across ethnic boundaries. As with the aforementioned voluntary firefighters' associations, specific institutions or practices that were common to Transylvanian Romanians, Germans, and Hungarians could well have been alien to Old Kingdom Romanians.

For middle-class Transylvanians, cultural practices met with particular disapproval from authorities due largely to their alleged non-Romanian character. Gypsy music, suspicious coffeehouse gatherings, and Habsburg military songs could be censured as much as speaking Hungarian in public or, certainly, singing the Hungarian national anthem. Two incidents from around 1930 glaringly illustrate this attachment to old customs. In Brașov, the military band of an elite mountain unit of the Romanian army played the Hungarian song "32-es baka vagyok én" ("I'm a Private from the 32nd Regiment") to the widespread applause of a multiethnic (German, Hungarian, and Romanian) audience. And in Târgu Secuiesc (Kézdivásárhely), the Romanian director of the state lyceum slapped the leader of a gypsy band when he refused to play the Hungarian national anthem. Public officials treated both incidents as signs of Hungarian irredentism. Yet local Romanians used them to express something that was otherwise hard to integrate into the official concept of Romanian national identity.[69] Furthermore, these shared cultural practices reinforced networks and patronage systems that transcended ethnic boundaries and were beneficial in the informal world of local Transylvanian politics.

Some of these practices were also prevalent in Slovakia, but rarely as part of the cultural repertoire of ethnically mixed, socially homogeneous groups. If one exempts the demand for gypsy music (particularly from middle-class Hungarians), then most multicultural social interactions were either isolated acts of defiance from Slovak politicians (a remnant of their socialization in prewar Hungary) or a hidden practice with an ethnic and moral stigma attached.[70] Ferdinand (Ferdiš) Juriga, a Catholic priest and Slovak People's Party politician who served in a village near Budapest for many years before the war, often made gypsy bands play the Hungarian national anthem.[71] Despite such public demonstrations of otherness, the main social group preserving important elements of its dualist era socialization, the so-called *magyaróns*, were depicted by contemporary social researchers as being afraid to display their "Hungarian" cultural practices. Although they still listened to Budapest radio, read Hungarian books and newspapers, and sang Hungarian songs in Bratislava pubs while drinking the *heuriger* (seasonal wine), *magyaróns* often feared the repercussions—including conflict with Slovak nationalists, fights with students, or, in the worst case, removal from office—if they did so too visibly.[72]

Paradoxically, public displays of "Hungarian-ness" were more frequently used to distance oneself from the current Hungarian regime. An alternative, lower middle- and working-class cultural scene developed, often with state assistance and the participation of avant-garde progressivist figures (sometimes from Hungary proper, like Lajos Kassák). This culture was tightly bound to a republican and pro-Czechoslovak Hungarian political current that was extremely critical of Admiral Horthy's Hungary. It thus constituted an alternative national culture from the dominant cultural expressions in mainstream minority Hungarian organizations, and was barely tolerated in Horthy-era Hungary.[73]

In Slovakia, the most striking feature of prewar cultural traditions was thus not their survival, but the gaping hole their absence could leave in the community. This is probably why so many Hungarians misinterpreted their experiences abroad, especially the enthusiastic receptions they often received. When Géza Lakatos, the Hungarian military attaché in Prague and future Prime Minister of Hungary, accompanied President Masaryk to a military exercise in Central Slovakia, he recalled his kingly treatment by waiters, drivers, and hotel boys, who competed to oblige him.[74] Lakatos saw this as an indication of their sincere desire to be reunited with Hungary. However, it may also have suggested nostalgia for the lavish feasts and drinking bouts, not to mention the generous tips that a Hungarian uniform inspired. Meanwhile, Slovaks perceived Czechs as the bearers of a less noble culture, which sidelined such pleasurable pastimes.[75] This interpretation is supported by many contemporary accounts attesting to the lower social distinction of Czechoslovak officers when compared to *k.u.k.* or *Honvéd* officers.[76] For instance, the Czechs often flouted parts of the unwritten, pre-1918 code of conduct by refusing to duel when they were insulted.[77]

On the other hand, some minority Hungarian observers in the 1930s contrasted the democratic, petit bourgeois habits and values of the Czech middle class with the "feudal" Hungarian world of the Habsburg past. The transformation of popular culture and social practices corroborated this. While in Romania, gypsy bands remained popular and played Hungarian music during the interwar years, in Czechoslovakia, this traditional music was gradually replaced by jazz.[78] Alongside the restaurants and coffeehouses where the Hungarian middle-classes often met, new canteens now served food in large quantities and counter service replaced table service, propelling the disappearance of "*Stammtisch*" (regulars' table) culture and entertainment.[79] New social hierarchies and a strong lower-class institutionalized culture emerged—especially in contrast with Romania's oligarchic political structure and predominantly rural population—and did more to transform urban spaces than did forced nationalization.

Ghosts from a Recent Past?

Some of the phenomena outlined above point to non-national allegiances and identifications at the regional level. For instance, institutions unfamiliar to the new rulers and social practices that varied between Romanians and Transylvanians (or Czech[oslovak]s and Slovaks) were often part of a broader pattern of sociocultural specificities that distinguished the center from the province. A discourse that reflected this distinctiveness thus emerged not only in the case of Slovak or Transylvanian Romanian identities (politically represented by strong regionalist parties as they were), but also around more local affinities.[80] The best examples are the small, short-lived republics that emerged during the revolutions. Often regarded by scholars as mere subterfuges to avert incorporation into the new states while still seemingly severing ties with Hungary, they had solid foundations among the local population, most notably in the Banat, in Eastern Slovakia, and in Kalotaszeg (Țară Călaței), near Cluj (Kolozsvár). In these regions of Greater Romania, social affiliations and economic imperatives trumped national ones such that organized labor (Banat) and a rural cooperative movement (Kalotaszeg) produced experiments in self-rule. These movements were not completely devoid of national content and many, in fact, were undertaken by Hungarian and German officials. But they all displayed a distinctly regional attachment—a Kalotaszeg identity as opposed to the Hungarian-ness promoted by prewar Budapest—evident in the political discourse of these localized socioeconomic movements.[81]

In Eastern Slovakia, patterns of regional consciousness promoted by the Hungarian elite before 1918, had aimed to preserve a distinct form of patriotic Slavic attachment to the idea of Hungary, rather than promoting complete assimilation. The changes wrought by World War I gave new impetus to these efforts, and Slovaks were yet more positively portrayed in the Hungarian public sphere.[82] The Eastern Slovak National Council, led by Viktor Dvorčak (Dvorcsák Győző), embodied this political current in its defiance of the Slovak National Council in Turčiansky Svätý Martin (Túrócszentmárton). Although Dvorčak and his companions emigrated (and as émigrés, they collaborated with the Hungarian government and its agents), a group of Slovak intellectuals from the area worked with the local middle classes to preserve this identity after 1919.[83]

The two most striking examples of local identification were in the Transylvanian regions west of the Țară Moților (Motzenland, Mócvidék) and in the small District of Chioar (Kővár-vidék). Both had long traditions of separate administration, distinct local societies, and, in the case of the former, lay partially outside the principality of Transylvania before it merged with Hungary in 1867. The Țară Moților region, moreover, was comprised mainly of small mining towns where local businesses had not yet been taken over by large companies. The town of Beiuș and its surroundings had thus served as a kind of "ethnic contact zone" in which cross-ethnic middle-class practices played an important role in daily life.[84] The District of Chioar was populated by Hungarians and Greek Catholic Romanians with noble status or special liberties that elevated them above serfs in the pre-1848 feudal system. Marketplaces rather than modern urban facilities served as its administrative and economic centers. Visitors often described the regions as non-Romanian and its inhabitants as alien or people of degenerate "Romanian-ness". The locals, in turn, sometimes violently attacked these "intruders" with the help of the local Romanian police or gendarmerie, who slandered the newcomers in Hungarian.[85]

These distinctions explain the reaction of local elites to plans to redraw administrative boundaries in 1919. Although their original administrative units had been abolished almost fifty years earlier, representatives of both regions asked for their reinstatement when the Ruling Council sought proposals for a new administrative territorial system in order to provide better access to public services. Despite using the well-known nationalist arguments to defend their claims (insisting that the redistricting would favor Romanians and disadvantage Hungarians), what they really wanted was to return to a past in which their social and legal status, and the specific rights and privileges associated with it, defined them more than their nationality did.

Conclusion

My aim in this chapter has been to outline aspects of the transition from Austria-Hungary to Czechoslovakia and Romania that shed light on continuities and discontinuities in the establishment of nation-states. As we have seen, most of these elements—the role of civic associations, middle-class culture, administrative personnel and their practices, and regionalist politics—were rooted in the local societies of the contested territories, such that it was hardly possible to integrate them into the homogenizing, unitary framework of the nationalizing successor states. Indeed, the national governments left little room for compromise in their unitary and national visions for Czechoslovakia and Romania. Yet a combination of limited resources, executive constraints, and above all the persistence of local political and social structures often produced exceptions that challenged or even violated the nationalizing regulations.

The above examples are, of course, far from exhaustive, and thus cannot adequately answer such broad questions as how, why, and to what extent these compromises emerged and persisted. But the sheer variety of social practices, institutions, and other local factors points to the potential for further comprehensive research into the clearly crucial role played by local societies in the transition from empire to nation-state. Moreover, such local-level comparative research sheds light not only on the differences and similarities between state-building outcomes, but also on how varying conditions developed within the successor states.

Finally, by discerning patterns of transition in terms of the functioning of different local societies, we gain insight into how nationalizing, postwar successor states were established and managed in the interwar period. Although it is hard to believe that any of the phenomena mentioned above could have derailed the fast-moving train of nationalization, the findings of this study show that, for a significant period, local elites, newly emerged social groups, and their oft-reorganized institutions were strong enough to achieve concessions and compromises. This paints quite a different picture of interwar Czechoslovakia and Romania from that of national government-centered studies: a patchwork of local transitions as opposed to a top-down implementation of state-building measures.

Gábor Egry is director of the Institute of Political History in Budapest. His research focuses on nationalism, ethnicity, and the politics of identity in modern East-Central Europe. His last book, *Etnicitás, identitás, politika: Magyar kisebbségek nacionalizmus és regionalizmus között Csehszlovákiában és Romániában* (Budapest: Napvilág, 2015), was shortlisted for the Felczak-Wereszycki Prize of the Polish Historical Association. Egry has received several prestigious academic fellowships, and is currently the PI for the ERC Consolidator project: "Negotiating Post-imperial Transitions: From Remobilization to Nation-state Consolidation. A comparative study of local and regional transitions in post-Habsburg East and Central Europe."

Notes

1. Jeremy King, "The Nationalization of East Central Europe: Ethnicism, Ethnicity and Beyond," in *Staging the Past: The Politics of Commemoration in Habsburg Central Europe, 1848 to the Present*, ed. Nancy M. Wingfield and Maria Bucur (West Lafayette: Purdue University Press, 2001), 121–23; Gary B. Cohen, "Nationalist Politics and the Dynamics of State and Civil Society in the Habsburg Monarchy, 1867–1914," *Central European History* 40 (2007): 241–78.
2. See T. Hunt Tooley, *National Identity in Weimar Germany: Upper Silesia and the Eastern Border, 1918–1922* (Lincoln: University of Nebraska Press, 1997); Peter Švorc and Harald Heppner, eds., *Veľká doba v malom priestore: Zlomové zmeny v mestách stredoeurópskeh priestoru a ich dôsledky (1918–1929)/Große Zeit im kleinen Raum. Umbrüche in den Städten des mitteleuropäischen Raumes 1918–1929* (Prešov–Graz: Universum, 2012); James E. Bjork, *Neither German nor Pole: Catholicism and National Indifference in a Central European Borderland* (Ann Arbor: The University of Michigan Press, 2008); Robert Gerwarth and John Horne, eds., *War in Peace: Paramilitary Violence in Europe after the Great War* (New York: Oxford University Press, 2012); John Paul Newman, "Post-imperial and Postwar

Violence in the South Slav Lands, 1917–1923," *Contemporary European History* 19, no. 3 (2010): 249–65; Julia Eichenberg, "The Dark Side of Independence: Paramilitary Violence in Ireland and Poland after the First World War," *Contemporary European History* 19, no. 3 (2010): 231–48; Richard Blanke, *Polish Speaking Germans? Language and National Identity among the Masurians since 1871* (Cologne: Böhlau Verlag, 2001); and Jeremy King, *Budweisers into Czechs and Germans: A Local History of Bohemian Politics, 1848–1948* (Princeton: Princeton University Press, 2002).
3. Irina Livezeanu, *Cultural Politics in Greater Romania: Regionalism, Nation-Building and Ethnic Struggle 1918–1930* (Ithaca: Cornell University Press, 1995); Mariana Hausleitner, *Die Rumänisierung der Bukowina: Durchsetzung des nationalstaatlichen Anspruchs Grossrumäniens 1918–1944* (München: Oldenbourg, 2001).
4. See, for example, Gheorghe Iancu, *The Ruling Council. The Integration of Transylvania in Romania 1918–1919* (Cluj-Napoca: Center for Transylvanian Studies, 1995); Gheorghe Iancu, *Justiție românească în Transilvania (1919)* (Cluj-Napoca: Editura Ecumenica Press, 2006); Marián Hronský, *Boj o Slovensko a Trianon 1918–1920* (Bratislava: Národné literárne centrum—Dom slovenskej literatúry, 1998). Somewhat paradoxically, the thesis of a swift takeover and nationalization of the administration is also reflected in the Hungarian historiography, as it seemed and still seems suitable to highlight the injustice suffered by Hungarians in the successor states. See Nándor Bárdi, Csilla Fedinec, and László Szarka, eds., *Minority Hungarian Communities in the Twentieth Century* (Boulder, CO: Social Sciences Monographs, 2011), esp. 52–69, 164–77, 192–218.
5. See Cohen, "Nationalist Politics."
6. Recent research suggests that a shift in roles between state and society occurred much earlier, mainly due to the limited capacity of the state to manage the war effort and to cope with the new social tasks and challenges. See, for example, Joshua A. Sanborn, *Imperial Apocalypse: The Great War and the Destruction of the Russian Empire* (Oxford: Oxford University Press, 2014).
7. Manu Goswami, *Producing India: From Colonial Economy to National Space* (Chicago: University of Chicago Press, 2004).
8. Cohen, "Nationalist Politics." See also Béatrice von Hirschhausen, Hannes Grandits, Claudia Kraft, Dietmar Müller, and Thomas Serrier, eds., *Phantomgrenzen: Räume und Akteure in der Zeit neuzudenken* (Göttingen: Wallstein Verlag, 2015).
9. See Peter Haslinger, *Arad, November 1918: Oszkár Jászi und die Rumänen in Ungarn bis 1918* (Wien: Böhlau, 1993).
10. The reports of the lord lieutenant (county chief administrator) of Maros-Torda (Mureș-Turda) county tell this story in much detail. See Arhivele Naționale Secția Județeană Mureș (Mureș County Section of the Romanian National Archives, ANSJM) Colecție Manuscrise, inventar 75, dosar 256, 111, 120f (folio).
11. Ilie Lăzar, *Amințiri* (București: Editura Fundația Academia civică, 2000), 55–58.
12. Arhivele Naționale Istorice Centrale Bucharest, (Central Historical Archives. ANIC), Consiliul Dirigent Anul 1918, dosar 67/1918, 289f.
13. ANIC, Consiliul Dirigent Anul 1918, dosar 55/1918; ANSJM, Colecție Manuscrise, inventar 75, dosar 256, 15–17, 20f.
14. ANSJM, Colecție Manuscrise, inventar 75, dosar 255. 20f. See also the case of Hodac (4–9f), Turcheș (ANIC), Consiliul Dirigent, Anul 1918, dosar 20/1918, 1–2f.
15. ANSJM, Colecție Manuscrise, inventar 75, dosar 256, 38–39f. The expression "sfatul cel mare" is not entirely clear, and could even refer to the upcoming peace conference.

16. Ibid., 89–90f.
17. See, for example, Ion Popescu-Puțuri, Augustin Deac, eds., *Unirea Transilvaniei cu România. 1 Decembrie 1918* (București: ISISP, 1972), 595–96.
18. ANSJM, Colecție Manuscrise, inventar 75, dosar 255, 22–23, 28f.
19. See Tibor Hajdu, *The Hungarian Soviet Republic* (Budapest: Akadémiai, 1968); Politikatörténeti és Szakszervezeti Levéltár, Budapest (Archives of the Trade Unions and for Political History, PIL), 658 fond, 6/87. ő.e.
20. The list of members was compiled by James M. Ward, who kindly disclosed this material to me. See also Ján Mrva, *Paberky k dejinám štátneho prevratu v Nitre* (Nitra: Miestneho Odboru Matice Slovenskej, 1933); James M. Ward, *Priest, Politician, Collaborator: Jozef Tiso and the Making of Fascist Slovakia* (Ithaca: Cornell University Press, 2013), 39–63.
21. Pieter C. van Duin, *Central European Crossroads: Social Democracy and National Revolution in Bratislava (Pressburg) 1867–1921* (New York: Berghahn Books, 2009).
22. PIL, 658 fond, 5/56. ő.e.
23. Gábor Egry, "Közvetlen demokrácia, nemzeti forradalom: Hatalomváltás, átmenet és a helyi nemzeti tanácsok Erdélyben, 1918–1919," *Múltunk* 55, no. 3 (2010): 92–108.
24. ANIC, Consiliul Dirigent Anul 1918, dosar 45/1918, 14, 17f.
25. Ibid., dosar 55/1918, Minutes of meeting 19 December 1918.
26. Balázs Kiss, "Államfordulat Nyitrán 1918–1923," *Kisebbségkutatás* 18, no. 2 (2008): 161–66; Béla Angyal, *Érdekvédelem és önszerveződés: Fejezetek a csehszlovákiai magyar pártpolitika történetéből* (Somorja, Dunaszerdahely: Lilium Aurum, 2002), 17; Ward, *Priest, Politician, Collaborator*, 39–63; Thomas A. Lorman, "The Christian Social Roots of Jozef Tiso's Radicalism," in *In the Shadow of Hitler: Personalities of the Right in Central and Eastern Europe*, ed. Rebecca Haynes and Martin Rady (London: I. B. Tauris, 2011), 245–60.
27. ANIC, Consiliul Dirigent Anul 1918, dosar 30/1918, 4–5f.
28. Immediately after the National Council was formed in Sighetul Marmației (Máramarosziget), a sizeable portion of its members delegated by the Independence Party (one of the traditional opposition parties) seceded, forming a new local branch of the Bourgeois Radical Party and declaring their allegiance to Minister Oszkár Jászi. Its significance was that the Bourgeois Radicals were an extra-parliamentary fringe opposition organization before 1918, treated by the political mainstream as dangerous and delusional without significant following in "backward" zones such as Sighetul Marmației. See György Litván, *A Twentieth Century Prophet: Oszkár Jászi 1875–1957* (Budapest: CEU Press, 2006).
29. The so-called Pact of Ciucea. See Nándor Bárdi, *Otthon és haza: Tanulmányok a romániai magyarság történetéből* (Csíkszereda: Pro Print, 2013), 114–27.
30. See, for example, the short existence of an Eastern Slovak National Council in contrast to the Martin one, in László Szarka, "A szlovák autonómia alternatívája 1918 őszén," in *". . . ahol a határ elválaszt" Trianon és következményei a Kárpát-medencében*, ed. Cecília Pásztor (Balassagyarmat-Várpalota: Nógrád Megyei Levéltár, 2002), 176–80.
31. For example, the Austrian Civic Code of 1852 was never abolished and remained the basis of private legal relations in Transylvania, even though by the 1930s it was the last region in Europe where this piece of legislation was still in effect. See Magyar Nemzeti Levéltár, Országos Levéltára, Budapest (Hungarian National Archives, MNLOL), P 1077, vol. 5, 421–45; M. M. Vallasek, "Az 1918. évi egyesülést követő jogegyesítés kérdése Romániában," *Magyar Kisebbség* 15, no. 1–2 (2004): 584–85.

32. Angyal, *Érdekvédelem és önszerveződés*, 17–19.
33. István Mócsy, *The Effects of World War I. The Uprooted: Hungarian Refugees and Their Impact on Hungary's Domestic Politics, 1918–1921* (Boulder, CO: Social Science Monographs, 1983). Mócsy cites on pp. 13 and 54 the official figures for the number of refugees between 1918 and 1924 from the Országos Menekültügyi Hivatal (National Office of Refugees). This set of data gave an overall figure of almost 107,000 persons from Czechoslovakia and 197,000 from Romania. However, these detailed statistics should be questioned, as the number of public officials allegedly fleeing from Eastern Hungary and Transylvania (2843 state officials, 1406 county officials) is higher than the number of Hungarians in the same professional category who actually lived there (2728 out of 2949 state officials, 1252 out of 1464 county officials) according to the official prewar statistic: *A Magyar Szent Korona országainak 1910. évi népszámlálása*. Vol. IV. *Magyar Statisztikai Közlemények* 56 (Budapest: Magyar Királyi Központi Statisztikai Hivatal, 1915), 722.
34. See the case of Máramaros (Maramureș) and Zilah (Zălău), in Ioan Scurtu and Liviu Boar, eds., *Minoritățile naționale din România 1918–1925* (București: Arhivele Statului Din Romania, 1995), 267–68, 487–88.
35. ANIC, Consiliul Dirigent Administrația Județeană și Comunală, dosar 79/1919, 111–114f.
36. See the appointments from 17 July 1919 onward in County Caraș-Severin, Arhivele Naționale Secția Județeană Timiș, Timișoara (Timiș County Section of the Romanian National Archives, ANSJTM), fond 223, Prefectură Judeșului Severin, dosar 38/1919, 162–69f.
37. ANSJTM, fond 223, Pref. Jud. Severin dosar 34/1934, 140–46f.; ANIC, Ministerul de Interne, inventar 754, dosar 27/1937, 18f; ANSJCV, fond 9, vols. 10, 48, 49. I am grateful to Botond Nagy for sharing this data from his own research.
38. Gábor Egry, "Navigating the Straits: Changing Borders, Changing Rules and Practices of Ethnicity and Loyalty in Romania after 1918," *Hungarian Historical Review* 2, no. 3 (2013): 466–68.
39. For example, in Abrud (Abrudbánya). ANSJCJ, fond 209, inventar 399, dosar 31/II, 243f., dosar 463, 2f., dosar 29. 1f.
40. ANIC, Ministerul Justiției Direcția Judiciară, Moldvași Țară Românească, dosar 78/1920, 21–23f.
41. ANIC, Consiliul Dirigent Direcția Administrația Generală, dosar 19/1919, 6–8f.
42. Van Duin, *Central European Crossroads*, 341–94; Tamás Gusztáv Filep, "Kormánypárton vagy ellenzében? A pozsonyi magyar polgár és az 1925-ös választások," in *A humanista voksa. Írások a csehszlovákiai magyar kisebbség történetének köréből 1918–1945*, ed. Tamás Gusztáv Filep (Pozsony: Kalligram, 2007), 32, note #12.
43. László Pukkai, *Mátyusföld 1. A Galántai járás társadalmi és gazdasági változásai 1945–2000* (Somorja–Dunaszerdahely: Fórum Kisebbségkutató Intézet—Lilium Aurum Könyvkiadó, 2002).
44. Sándor Vájlok, "Szlovákok és magyarok," in *Magyarok Csehszlovákiában*, ed. Borsody István (Budapest: Az Ország Útja, 1938), 191–94.
45. Attila Simon, *Egy rövid esztendő krónikája: A szlovákiai magyarok 1938-ban* (Somorja: Fórum, 2010), 30–31.
46. Elena Mannová, "'Sie wollen keine Loyalität lernen!': Identitätsdiskurse und lokale Lebenswelten in der Südslowakei 1918–1938," in *Staat, Loyalität und Minderheiten im*

Ostmittel- und Südosteuropa 1918–1941, ed. Joachim von Puttkamer and Peter Haslinger (München: Oldenbourg, 2007), 58.
47. Bárdi, *Otthon és haza*, 106–67.
48. See, for example, ANSJBV, fond 2, inventar 342, Prefectură Județului Brașov, Serviciul Administrativ, dosar 19/1926, 3–4f; ANIC, Direcția Generală a Poliției (General Police Directorate, DGP), dosar 19/1919, 104f.
49. Andrei Florin Sora, *Servir l'État roumain: Le corps préfectoral, 1866–1944* (Bucharest: Editura Universității din București, 2011), 130–52; Andrei Florin Sora, "Être fonctionnaire 'minoritaire' en Roumanie. Idéologie de la nation et pratiques d'État (1918–1940)," in *New Europe College "Ștefan Odobleja" Program Yearbook 2009–2010*, ed. Irina Vainovski-Mihai (Bucharest: New Europe College, 2011), 212–14.
50. ANSJTM Prefectură Județului Severin, dosar 24/1924, 190–91f.
51. Ibid., 172–91f., dosar 40/1932, 1f., dosar 41/1934, 1f., and Legiunea Jandarmilor Severin, dosar 2/1932, 22f.; Arhivele Naționale Secția Județeană Brașov (Brașov County Section of the Romanian National Archives, ANSJBV), Prefectură Județului Brașov Serviciul Administrativ, dosar 551/1940, 125–26f.
52. Ľubomír Lipták, "Transformations politiques des monuments ou monuments des changements politiques," in *Miroirs brisés: Récits régionaux et imaginaires croisés sur le territoire slovaque*, ed. Étienne Boisserie and Clara Royer (Paris: Inst. d'Études Slaves, 2011), 53–82; Miroslav Michela, "'A Home Should Be Home to All Its Sons': Cultural Representations of Saint Stephen in Slovakia During the Interwar Period," in *Overcoming the Old Borders: Beyond the Paradigm of Slovak National History*, ed. Adam Hudek (Bratislava: Institute of History, Slovak Academy of Sciences, 2013), 97–110; Zuzana Motajová, "'Apuskánk' születésnapjai: A személyi kultusz a két világháború közötti Csehszlovákiában," *Sic itur ad astra* 20, no. 3–4 (2006): 303–16; Mannová, "Sie wollen keine," 59; Maria Bucur, *Heroes and Victims: Remembering War in Twentieth Century Romania* (Bloomington: Indiana University Press, 2008).
53. ANIC DGP dosar 4/1920, 157f.
54. Elena Mannová, "'... de most már jó szlovák' A nemzeti identitás variációi két délszlovákiai kisváros egyesületi életében, 1918–1938," *Regio* 11, no. 4 (2000): 98.
55. Attila Agócs, "Hulita Vilmos a füleki gyár változó életlehetőségekhez alkalmazkodni tudó igazgatója," *Neograd: A Nógrád Megyei Múzeumok Évkönyve* 32 (2008): 16.
56. ANIC, Președinția Consiliului de Miniștri, dosar 12/1934, 31–35f.; ANIC, DGP, dosar 18/1934, 167f.
57. Peter Stachel, "Stadtpläne als politische Zeichensysteme: Symbolische Einschreibungen in den öffentlichen Raum," in *Die Besetzung des öffentlichen Raumes: Politische Plätze, Denkmäler und Straßennamen in europäischen Vergleich*, ed. Rudolf Jaworski, Peter Stachel (Berlin: Frank & Timme, 2007), 13–60; Lipták, "Transformations politiques."
58. Mannová, "Sie wollen keine," 58. In practice, it meant the use of a progressivist, revolutionary, and localized nomenclature, and the abandonment of the typical political street names of dualist and interwar Hungary.
59. Elena Mannová, "Von Maria Theresia zum Schönen Náci. Kollektive Gedächtnisse und Denkmalkultur in Bratislava," in *Die Besetzung des öffentlichen Raumes: Politische Plätze, Denkmäler und Straßennamen in europäischen Vergleich*, ed. Rudolf Jaworski, Peter Stachel (Berlin: Frank & Timme, 2007), 203–16; Júlia Lovisek, "Pozsony utcaneveinek politikai indíttatású névváltoztatásai az első Csehszlovák Köztársaság megalakulása után," *Fórum*

Társadalomtudományi Szemle 9, no. 2 (2007): 127–36; Peter Bugge, "The Naming of a Slovak City: The Czechoslovak Renaming of Pressburg/Pozsony/Prešporok in 1918–19," *Austrian History Yearbook* 35 (2004): 205–27.
60. ANIC, Consiliul Dirigent Secția Administrația Județeană și Comunală, dosar 66/1920, 44f, 221–27f. There was likely even deliberate mockery in one case, when the street previously named after the fiction writer Mór Jókai, who often drew upon historical subject matter, was renamed for Nicolae Iorga.
61. ANIC, Consiliul Dirigent Secția Administrația Județeană și Comunală, dosar 46/1920, 130–35f.
62. Egry, "Navigating the Straits," 462–64.
63. Lipták, "Transformations politiques."
64. Ibid.; Tamás Gusztáv Filep, *Főhatalomváltás Pozsonyban 1918–1920* (Pozsony: Kalligram, 2010), 131, 137.
65. MNLOL, Ministry of Foreign Affairs, K64, 27.csomó, 7. tétel, 74–88f. 258/res/1928.
66. ANIC, DGP, dosar 56/1921, 311f.
67. Ibid.
68. ANIC, DGP, dosar 8/1919, 240. Veterans of the border regiments and their descendants highly valued the statue. Its unveiling had already caused a political demonstration in favor of the Emperor and against Hungarian politics. See Alexandru Vaida Voevod's report to Franz Ferdinand from December 1908, in Keith Hitchins, ed., *The Nationality Problem in Austria-Hungary: The Reports of Alexandru Vaida to Archduke Franz Ferdinand's Chancellery* (Leiden: Brill, 1974), 45.
69. ANIC, DGP, dosar 56/1921 200f; ANSJMS Directia Regională Ministerului de Afacerilor Interne Mures Autonomă Maghiară, inventar 1235, dosar 2899, 23f.
70. MNLOL, Department for Minority and Nationality Issues, K28, 168. csomó, 300. tétel, ME1926–P–125, 5–8f.
71. MNLOL, Department for Minority and Nationality Issues, K28, 168. csomó 300. tétel, 1934–P–15314.
72. Vájlok, "Szlovákok és magyarok," 191–94; Mannová, "Sie wollen keine," 63–64.
73. Balázs Ablonczy, "A csehszlovák minta: A masaryki demokrácia és szimpatizánsai a két világháború közti Magyarországon," in *Nyombiztosítás: Letűnt magyarok: Kisebbség- és művelődéstörténeti tanulmányok*, ed. Balázs Ablonczy (Pozsony: Kalligram, 2011), 177–98; Attila Simon, *Az elfeledett aktivisták: Kormánypárti politika az első Csehszlovák Köztársaságban* (Somorja: Fórum Intézet, 2013).
74. MNLOL, K64, 37. csomó, 7. tétel, 245/pol–1930, 587/re/1930.
75. Ablonczy, "A csehszlovák minta," 177–78.
76. Wenzel Ruzicka, *Nordböhmisches Tagebuch: Chronik einer sudetendeutschen Familie 1926–1946* (Bad Reichenhall: E. Thöres, 1995), 15–16.
77. MNLOL, K28, 17. csomó, 59. tétel, 1929–P–332.
78. Mannová, ". . . de most már jó szlovák ő," 98.
79. József Liszka, "A szlovákiai magyarok populáris kultúrája a 20. században (Korszakok és az impériumválásokból eredő hatások)," *Fórum Társadalomtudományi Szemle* 2, no. 3 (2000): 67–80.
80. Ward, *Priest, Politician, Collaborator*; Florian Kührer-Wielach, *Siebenbürgen ohne Siebenbürger? Staatliche Integration und neue Identifikationsangebote zwischen Regionalismus und nationalem Einheitsdogma im Diskurs der Siebenbürger Rumänen 1919–1933* (München: Oldenbourg, 2014); Livezeanu, *Cultural Politics*.

81. Zsolt K. Lengyel, *Auf der Suche nach dem Kompromiß: Ursprünge und Gestalten des frühen Transsilvanismus* (München: Verlag Ungarisches Institut, 1993), 1–67.
82. László Vörös, "Premeny obrázu Slovákov v maďarskej regionálnej tlači v odobí rokov 1914–1918," *Historický časopis* 54, no. 3 (2006): 419–53.
83. Szarka, "A szlovák autonómia"; Balázs Ablonczy, "A magyar revíziós politika szlovák ágensei a két világháború között," in *Nyombiztosítás. Letűnt magyarok. Kisebbség- és művelődéstörténeti tanulmányok*, ed. Balázs Ablonczy (Pozsony: Kalligram, 2011), 69–87.
84. Robert Nemes, "Obstacles to Nationalization on the Hungarian-Romanian Language Frontier," *Austrian History Yearbook* 43 (2012): 28–44.
85. A youth from Craiova fared poorly when he arrived at this border zone in order to make a career. He failed to establish himself in the county seat Carei (Nagykároly), and when he moved to Sieni (Szinérváralja), in the center of the District of Chioar, he faced violent abuse from the locals and gendarmes. In a petition to Queen Maria, the youth described the locals as degenerated, magyarized Romanians. See ANIC, Ministerul Justiţiei Ministerul Justiţiei Direcţia Judiciară, inventar 1116, dosar 103/1923, 6–7f. On national degeneration, see Nicolae Iorga, *Neamul Românesc în Ardeal şi Ţară Românească*, vol. 2 (Bucureşti: Saeculum I. O., 1906), 591–642.

Bibliography

Ablonczy, Balázs. "A csehszlovák minta: A masaryki demokrácia és szimpatizánsai a két világháború közti Magyarországon." In *Nyombiztosítás: Letűnt magyarok: Kisebbség- és művelődéstörténeti tanulmányok*, edited by Balázs Ablonczy, 177–98. Pozsony: Kalligram, 2011.
———. "A magyar revíziós politika szlovák ágensei a két világháború között." In *Nyombiztosítás: Letűnt magyarok: Kisebbség- és művelődéstörténeti tanulmányok*, edited by Balázs Ablonczy, 69–87. Pozsony: Kalligram, 2011.
Angyal, Béla. *Érdekvédelem és önszerveződés: Fejezetek a csehszlovákiai magyar pártpolitika történetéből*. Somorja, Dunaszerdahely: Lilium Aurum, 2002.
Bárdi, Nándor. *Otthon és haza: Tanulmányok a romániai magyarság történetéből*. Csíkszereda: Pro Print, 2013.
Bárdi, Nándor, Csilla Fedinec, and László Szarka, eds. *Minority Hungarian Communities in the Twentieth Century*. Boulder, CO: Social Sciences Monographs, 2011.
Bjork, James E. *Neither German nor Pole: Catholicism and National Indifference in a Central European Borderland*. Ann Arbor: The University of Michigan Press, 2008.
Blanke, Richard. *Polish Speaking Germans? Language and National Identity among the Masurians since 1871*. Cologne: Böhlau Verlag, 2001.
Bucur, Maria. *Heroes and Victims: Remembering War in Twentieth Century Romania*. Bloomington: Indiana University Press, 2008.
Bugge, Peter. "The Naming of a Slovak City: The Czechoslovak Renaming of Pressburg/Pozsony/Prešporok in 1918–19." *Austrian History Yearbook* 35 (2004): 205–27.
Cohen, Gary B. "Nationalist Politics and the Dynamics of State and Civil Society in the Habsburg Monarchy, 1867–1914." *Central European History* 40 (2007): 241–78.
Eichenberg, Julia. "The Dark Side of Independence: Paramilitary Violence in Ireland and Poland after the First World War." *Contemporary European History* 19, no. 3 (2010): 231–48.

Egry, Gábor. "Közvetlen demokrácia, nemzeti forradalom: Hatalomváltás, átmenet és a helyi nemzeti tanácsok Erdélyben, 1918–1919." *Múltunk* 55, no. 3 (2010): 92–108.

———. "Navigating the Straits: Changing Borders, Changing Rules and Practices of Ethnicity and Loyalty in Romania after 1918." *Hungarian Historical Review* 2, no. 3 (2013): 449–76.

Filep, Tamás Gusztáv. *Főhatalomváltás Pozsonyban 1918–1920*. Pozsony: Kalligram, 2010.

———. "Kormánypárton vagy ellenzékben? A pozsonyi magyar polgár és az 1925-ös választások." In *A humanista voksa: Írások a csehszlovákiai magyar kisebbség történetének köréből 1918–1945*, edited by Tamás Gusztáv Filep, 26–55. Pozsony: Kalligram 2007.

Gerwarth, Robert, and John Horne, eds. *War in Peace: Paramilitary Violence in Europe after the Great War*. New York: Oxford University Press, 2012.

Goswami, Manu. *Producing India: From Colonial Economy to National Space*. Chicago: University of Chicago Press, 2004.

Hajdu, Tibor. *The Hungarian Soviet Republic*. Budapest: Akadémiai, 1968.

Haslinger, Peter. *Arad, November 1918: Oszkár Jászi und die Rumänen in Ungarn bis 1918*. Wien: Böhlau, 1993.

Hausleitner, Mariana. *Die Rumänisierung der Bukowina: Durchsetzung des nationalstaatlichen Anspruchs Grossrumäniens 1918–1944*. München: Oldenbourg, 2001.

Hitchins, Keith, ed. *The Nationality Problem in Austria-Hungary: The Reports of Alexandru Vaida to Archduke Franz Ferdinand's Chancellery*. Leiden: Brill, 1974.

Hronský, Marián. *Boj o Slovensko a Trianon 1918–1920*. Bratislava: Národné literárne centrum—Dom slovenskej literatúry, 1998.

Iancu, Gheorghe. *Justiție românească în Transilvania (1919)*. Cluj-Napoca: Editura Ecumenica Press, 2006.

———. *The Ruling Council: The Integration of Transylvania in Romania 1918–1919*. Cluj-Napoca: Center for Transylvanian Studies, 1995.

Iorga, Nicolae. *Neamul Românesc în Ardeal și Țară Românească*, vol. 2. București: Saeculum I. O., 1906.

King, Jeremy. *Budweisers into Czechs and Germans: A Local History of Bohemian Politics, 1848–1948*. Princeton: Princeton University Press, 2002.

———. "The Nationalization of East Central Europe: Ethnicism, Ethnicity and Beyond." In *Staging the Past: The Politics of Commemoration in Habsburg Central Europe, 1848 to the Present*, edited by Nancy M. Wingfield and Maria Bucur, 121–23. West Lafayette: Purdue University Press, 2001.

Kiss, Balázs. "Államfordulat Nyitrán 1918–1923." *Kisebbségkutatás* 18, no. 2 (2008): 161–66.

Kührer-Wielach, Florian. *Siebenbürgen ohne Siebenbürger? Staatliche Integration und neue Identifikationsangebote zwischen Regionalismus und nationalem Einheitsdogma im Diskurs der Siebenbürger Rumänen 1919–1933*. München: Oldenbourg, 2014.

Lăzar, Ilie. *Amintiri*. București: Editura Fundația Academia civică, 2000.

Lengyel, Zsolt K. *Auf der Suche nach dem Kompromiß: Ursprünge und Gestalten des frühen Transsilvanismus*. München: Verlag Ungarisches Institut, 1993.

Lipták, Ľubomír. "Transformations politiques des monuments ou monuments des changements politiques." In *Miroirs brisés: Récits régionaux et imaginaires croisés sur le territoire slovaque*, edited by Étienne Boisserie and Clara Royer, 53–82. Paris: Inst. d'Études Slaves, 2011.

Litván, György. *A Twentieth Century Prophet: Oszkár Jászi 1875–1957*. Budapest: CEU Press, 2006.

Livezeanu, Irina. *Cultural Politics in Greater Romania: Regionalism, Nation-Building and Ethnic Struggle 1918–1930*. Ithaca: Cornell University Press, 1995.

Lorman, Thomas A. "The Christian Social Roots of Jozef Tiso's Radicalism." In *In the Shadow of Hitler: Personalities of the Right in Central and Eastern Europe*, edited by Rebecca Haynes and Martin Rady, 245–60. London: I. B. Tauris, 2011.

Mannová, Elena. "'Sie wollen keine Loyalität lernen!': Identitätsdiskurse und lokale Lebenswelten in der Südslowakei 1918–1938." In *Staat, Loyalität und Minderheiten im Ostmittel- und Südosteuropa 1918–1941*, edited by Joachim von Puttkamer and Peter Haslinger, 45–67. München: Oldenbourg, 2007.

———. "Von Maria Theresia zum Schönen Náci. Kollektive Gedächtnisse und Denkmalkultur in Bratislava." In *Die Besetzung des öffentlichen Raumes: Politische Plätze, Denkmäler und Straßennamen in europäischen Vergleich*, ed. Rudolf Jaworski and Peter Stachel, 203–16. Berlin: Frank & Timme, 2007.

Michela, Miroslav. "'A Home Should Be Home to All Its Sons': Cultural Representations of Saint Stephen in Slovakia During the Interwar Period." In *Overcoming the Old Borders: Beyond the Paradigm of Slovak National History*, edited by Adam Hudek, 97–110. Bratislava: Institute of History, Slovak Academy of Sciences, 2013.

Mócsy, István M. *The Effects of World War I. The Uprooted: Hungarian Refugees and Their Impact on Hungary's Domestic Politics, 1918–1921*. Boulder, CO: Social Science Monographs, 1983.

Mrva, Ján. *Paberky k dejinám štátneho prevratu v Nitre*. Nitra: Miestneho Odboru Matice Slovenskej, 1933.

Newman, John Paul. "Post-imperial and Postwar Violence in the South Slav Lands, 1917–1923." *Contemporary European History* 19, no. 3 (2010): 249–65.

Popescu-Puțuri, Ion, and Augustin Deac, eds. *Unirea Transilvaniei cu România. 1 Decembrie 1918*. București: ISISP, 1972.

Pukkai, László. *Mátyusföld 1. A Galántai járás társadalmi és gazdasági változásai 1945–2000*. Somorja–Dunaszerdahely: Fórum Kisebbségkutató Intézet—Lilium Aurum Könyvkiadó, 2002.

Ruzicka, Wenzel. *Nordböhmisches Tagebuch: Chronik einer sudetendeutschen Familie 1926–1946*. Bad Reichenhall: E. Thöres, 1995.

Sanborn, Joshua A. *Imperial Apocalypse: The Great War and the Destruction of the Russian Empire*. Oxford: Oxford University Press, 2014.

Scurtu, Ioan, and Liviu Boar, eds. *Minoritățile naționale din România 1918–1925*. București: Arhivele Statului Din Romania, 1995.

Simon, Attila. *Az elfeledett aktivisták: Kormánypárti politika az első Csehszlovák Köztársaságban*. Somorja: Fórum Intézet, 2013.

———. *Egy rövid esztendő krónikája: A szlovákiai magyarok 1938-ban*. Somorja: Fórum Intézet, 2010.

Sora, Andrei Florin. "Être fonctionnaire 'minoritaire' en Roumanie. Idéologie de la nation et pratiques d'État (1918–1940)." In *New Europe College "Ştefan Odobleja" Program Yearbook 2009–2010*, ed. Irina Vainovski-Mihai. Bucharest: New Europe College, 2011.

———. *Servir l'État roumain: Le corps préfectoral, 1866–1944*. Bucharest: Editura Universității din București, 2011.

Stachel, Peter. "Stadtpläne als politische Zeichensysteme: Symbolische Einschreibungen in den öffentlichen Raum." In *Die Besetzung des öffentlichen Raumes: Politische Plätze,*

Denkmäler und Straßennamen in europäischen Vergleich, ed. Rudolf Jaworski and Peter Stachel, 13–60. Berlin: Frank & Timme, 2007.

Švorc, Peter, and Harald Heppner, eds. *Veľká doba v malom priestore: Zlomové zmeny v mestách stredoeurópskeh priestoru a ich dôsledky (1918–1929)/Große Zeit im kleinen Raum: Umbrüche in den Städten des mitteleuropäischen Raumes 1918–1929.* Prešov–Graz: Universum, 2012.

Szarka, László. "A szlovák autonómia alternatívája 1918 őszén." In *". . . ahol a határ elválaszt" Trianon és következményei a Kárpát-medencében*, edited by Cecília Pásztor. Balassagyarmat-Várpalota: Nógrád Megyei Levéltár, 2002.

Tooley, T. Hunt. *National Identity in Weimar Germany: Upper Silesia and the Eastern Border, 1918–1922.* Lincoln: University of Nebraska Press, 1997.

Vájlok, Sándor. "Szlovákok és magyarok." In *Magyarok Csehszlovákiában*, edited by Borsody István, 191–94. Budapest: Az Ország Útja, 1938.

van Duin, Pieter C. *Central European Crossroads: Social Democracy and National Revolution in Bratislava (Pressburg) 1867–1921.* New York: Berghahn Books, 2009.

von Hirschhausen, Béatrice, Hannes Grandits, Claudia Kraft, Dietmar Müller, and Thomas Serrier, eds. *Phantomgrenzen: Räume und Akteure in der Zeit neuzudenken.* Göttingen: Wallstein Verlag, 2015.

Ward, James M. *Priest, Politician, Collaborator: Jozef Tiso and the Making of Fascist Slovakia.* Ithaca: Cornell University Press, 2013.

Chapter 2

STATE LEGITIMACY AND CONTINUITY BETWEEN THE HABSBURG EMPIRE AND CZECHOSLOVAKIA
The 1918 Transition in Prague

Claire Morelon

For Prague's inhabitants, the liberation promised by the declaration of independence and the establishment of the Czechoslovak Republic in 1918 did not necessarily represent a clean break with the past. A cabaret play in 1919 featured the following discussion between a worker and a typist, symptomatic of the atmosphere at the time in the city: "You know, sir, we had somehow imagined it differently, the whole thing. People always said republic, liberty, peace, independent state and everything—and what do you have now?" To which the typist retorted: "Yes, yes, same old Austria, worse regulations, war in Slovakia and Poland, a couple of ministers and penury with poverty."[1]

The declaration of independence on 28 October 1918 in Prague, when the Czechoslovak National Committee took over official institutions, is generally considered to mark the end of the war in the Bohemian lands and the birth of the new national democratic state, Czechoslovakia. In the streets of Prague, people marched and spontaneously removed Austrian eagles and other symbols of the monarchy in the first days after the upheaval. The new government emphasized the break with the old regime and rapidly introduced new symbols to fill the vacuum. Yet, looking at the events in the city around the time of the regime change, this turning point does not appear to have coincided with a fundamental change, as social conflicts continued to be commonplace until at least the end of 1920. Beyond the politicians' discourse about a clean break with the past, what were the actual continuities with the Habsburg Empire after Czechoslovak independence?

This chapter examines these continuities as they were experienced and construed by various actors and groups in the new capital city. In so doing, it also explores how the term "revolution" itself was understood by different constituencies.[2] For the new Czechoslovak authorities, the revolution was the process of transformation set forth on 28 October. Revolution could also refer to a more imprecise yearning for greater social justice and a change that was yet to come after the 28th of October. As various sections of the population denounced continuities with the Habsburg Empire, the official revolution of 1918 was sometimes perceived as too limited. The example of Prague sheds light on the 1918 transformation in Central Europe: it emerges as a more complex turning point in twentieth-century Europe than the traditional interpretation of it as either an aftershock of the Bolshevik revolution or a new wave of national self-determination.

By late 1918, the Austro-Hungarian Empire, and particularly its Austrian half, had undergone a progressive "exhaustion" of its entire economy.[3] This process played an important role in the regime's final demise. Austrian cities were especially affected by the lack of food, making their populations desperate for peace. The disintegration of the Austro-Hungarian army had been rapidly accelerating since the summer of 1918, and hungry soldiers were making their way home.[4] These problems could not be resolved as quickly as many hoped in Prague, and the new regime was confronted with many challenges to its legitimacy.

Studies of revolutions and political transitions in general often place continuities at the forefront. In his famous nineteenth-century work on the French Revolution, Alexis de Tocqueville already questioned assumptions about the changes introduced by the revolutionaries in order to shed light on the modern institutions that predated 1789.[5] In any process of regime change, the question of the new state's political legitimacy is crucial. Through a symbolic break with the past, the new power attempts to distance itself from the discredited old regime, yet still maintain its newfound authority. In post-World War I Czechoslovakia, the continuity of the state—partially a result of continuing war conditions in peacetime—undermined the legitimacy of the new Republic in the eyes of the public.

Institutional Continuity and Continuation of War Conditions

As they seized government institutions on 28 October, the National Committee's members' chief concern was to ensure the continuity of the state apparatus.[6] Indeed, the first general law issued with the declaration of independence stated that all the current laws were to remain in effect.[7] To avoid violence and avert the threat of civil war, which was the main concern for the republic's provisional government, many of the civil servants in the army or the police kept their jobs. Only the top-level hierarchy was removed, as well as those who were too obviously linked with the previous regime, such as Prague's Chief of Police. The historian Ivan Šedivý's work on the personnel of the Interior Ministry shows that officials with key functions remained in their posts.[8] Samuel Ronsin's study of the police revealed similar results: despite pressures to incorporate returning soldiers into the police force, the officers remained, for the majority, those who had served under the monarchy.[9] As for local state administrations in Bohemia, 90 percent of the personnel were shielded from cleansing.[10]

With growing unemployment and returning soldiers claiming a position in society, the retention of so-called "Austrians" (former Habsburg civil servants) in their jobs was widely resented by the population. The few Czechs who worked in the Vienna ministries and returned to Prague after the war to work for the new state were often deemed too "Viennese" and accused of having pro-Austrian orientations by other Czech civil servants.[11] The continuity of personnel, necessary for the efficient functioning of the state, appeared to many as a symptom of the unchanged conditions in the new republic. Despite immediate instructions to instill a new vision of the bureaucracy inspired by democratic values, this lack of personnel change influenced policymaking in the new state in the immediate postwar period.[12] Certain liberties like the freedom of assembly were still very limited despite the democratic ambitions of Czechoslovakia.[13] Instead of a violent cleansing in 1918, most state institutions opted for a progressive transformation, such that by the mid-1920s, the situation had somewhat evolved.[14]

In parallel, however, local authorities quickly took initiatives to cleanse public space from references to the monarchy. During the war, renaming streets had been a powerful tool to express Habsburg patriotism. The new Czechoslovak authorities also employed this tool, progressively removing traces of the old regime in Prague's streets. As early as 13 November, the municipal council created a commission to rename streets and public spaces.[15] Avenues and squares took new names to honor such Czechoslovak heroes as the legions who had fought for the country's independence.[16] The main train station was renamed Wilson station for the American president, while Franz Joseph square took the celebratory name of Republic square. Nearby, "Revolution Avenue" was christened.

More neutral names were also changed. The state train station became the Masaryk station, and the Northwest station was named for the French Slavicist Ernest Denis. Two monuments linked to the monarchy were removed in 1919—the statue of Marshall Radetzky, which had been the site of patriotic demonstrations in August 1914, was first veiled and later taken away;[17] and the equestrian statue of Emperor Francis I on the Vltava River was removed in June 1919.[18] The new names either had to refer to a national figure or have a more Slavic connotation (rather than German). Decisions in Prague can be compared to those taken in Bratislava, where the majority of the population was Hungarian- and German-speaking. As Peter Bugge shows, a new name had to be found to emphasize the city's Slavic character. The new name, writes Bugge, "symbolically 'Czechoslovakized' the city."[19] Renaming was not the only strategy for staking out national identity. The Slavic linden tree planted on Wenceslas Square in Prague had become a rallying point during the 28 October street demonstrations celebrating Czechoslovak freedom. Another "linden tree of freedom" was then planted in the courtyard of the army barracks at Pohořelec in June 1919. The festivities organized for the occasion by an army regiment included a procession, reception, and dancing. National costumes were welcome.[20] New symbols were a means to mark public space as part of a new polity.

Yet, even in its most republican aspects, the new system revealed similarities with the old regime. In many ways, the figure of the new president, Tomáš Garrigue Masaryk, came to replace the image of the old emperor Franz Joseph. As Andrea Orzoff has shown, the official portrayal of Masaryk as a benevolent father figure and its direct link to the military borrowed many elements from Franz Joseph's "scenario of power," and contributed to a reassuring sense of continuity.[21] Following the Habsburg custom, his birthday was celebrated as a national holiday.[22] A circular sent by the provincial administration in 1920 indicated that all official buildings in Prague should be decorated with flags for the occasion, and that offices would be closed on that day.[23]

Prague celebrated Masaryk's return from exile abroad in December 1918 in a very official and ceremonious fashion. His automobile journey into the city from the train station to the Prague Castle was similar to a triumphal royal entry. Indeed, it closely mirrors the triumphal entries of the Belgian king and Romanian king in their capital cities in November and December 1918, respectively.[24] The military (legionaries in the Czech case) prominently featured in all these celebrations. When Masaryk arrived at the train station, he was offered bread and salt, an old Slavonic welcoming ritual (which was also performed in Bucharest for the king). Government officials greeted his arrival with speeches. Outside, Masaryk was supposed to ride in the imperial carriage drawn by two pairs of white horses and decorated with blue and white lilac and red roses. However, he preferred to use an automobile (also decorated with flowers and wreaths) and left the carriage to his family who followed behind him in the procession. Masaryk himself might have felt that this mode of transportation was not Republican enough, but the event's organizers had clearly prepared the event according to the old customs.[25] The event drew enormous crowds in the city; not only were buildings decorated with white and red flags of all sizes, but also with portraits of Masaryk and Wilson. A banner "Long live little father Masaryk!" was also visible.[26] Members of various national associations (culture, gymnastics, singing, etc.), political organizations, and of the different clergies lined both sides of the city's main streets. School children were mandated to attend the ceremony, and all the church bells rang out.[27] The ceremony underlined the direct link between the people and the president, as crowds saluted Masaryk with hats and handkerchiefs or songs. Numerous letters sent to the Police Headquarters warned of a potential assassination attempt against the returning "savior."[28] As the new president made a speech in Parliament and met municipal authorities at the Town Hall before making his way to the castle, his itinerary through Prague resembled that of the Belgian king in Brussels and does not really find equivalents among democratically elected leaders.

Insults against the president were taken as seriously by the police as lèse-majesté crimes in the former Empire. In one incident, a woman was arrested for an "impertinent statement about the president," as a deputation of women approached Masaryk in August 1919.[29] In another, a journalist was denounced by a bank clerk for having insulted the president in a bar at 4:00 a.m. during a lively political discussion. He was taken to the police station.[30] Three students were also arrested in July 1919 for having said in a pub that "the president was a zero and they did not give a damn about the republic."[31] The consistency with the numerous arrests for insulting the Emperor in wartime Bohemia is striking.[32] These were minor offenses and the perpetrators were soon released, but they show how the authorities and, to some extent, the population at large could view the new ruler through the lens of the old monarchy's political culture. The continuity between the two states was thus obvious in terms of the personalities in public jobs but, in a more insidious way, it also permeated to the role of the institutions themselves and their perception by the politicians and the public.

This institutional continuity was essential given the battles Czechoslovakia had to fight for its borders.[33] The German nationalist movements were not prepared to be incorporated into a new national Czech state, and they thus pushed for their own independence. Meanwhile, the Hungarians were trying to keep their hold on Slovakia. The disagreement over the Teschen border region with the Poles added to the conflicts faced by the new state. The campaign in Slovakia necessitated the redrafting of war-weary men. Prague's inhabitants had increasingly suffered from the prolonged conflict and had shown their longing for peace, especially during demonstrations in 1917–18, and yet peace did not immediately follow the defeat of Austria-Hungary as new battles were waged to secure the borders of the Czechoslovak state. These border wars necessitated a continuation of the war effort on the home front and of the war discourse by the political elites and the press.

The charity programs for the benefit of soldiers and their widows continued under the guise of benefits for the "legionaries." During the world war, part of the revenues from plays and other entertainment had been transferred to charity organizations connected with the military effort.[34] As early as 3 November, the National Theatre advertised its performances as being "for the benefit of the bereaved families of legionaries," thus extending the wartime functions of the entertainment industry.[35] Similarly, the religious service celebrated in St. Vitus Cathedral for the deceased soldiers simply became a memorial mass for deceased Czech legionaries.[36] Moreover, the new Czechoslovak state also carried on the appeal for war loans to save the states' finances, thus continuing the Austrian policy in this realm.[37]

The Teschen conflict also mobilized the population in Prague. The temporary partition of the region between Poland and Czechoslovakia in November 1918 had been challenged by the Czech occupation in January 1919, following the announcement that Poles from Teschen would vote in Polish legislative elections. Short skirmishes between Czechoslovak and Polish troops followed. Rallies were organized in the city to protest the cession of the region to Poland. Prague's mayor, Karel Baxa, even wrote a letter to the Paris Peace conference to convey "the sentiments of the whole population of Prague" on the subject, and to plead for Teschen to be part of Czechoslovakia.[38]

Volunteers going to fight in Slovakia departed from the city's main train stations accompanied by cheering crowds, just as troops had been sent off to the world war in the preceding years. In June 1919, 150 Sokol volunteers were cheered by an "enormous group of people" on their way to the Masaryk station.[39] Alarming false rumors apparently circulated on the situation in the East as they had in wartime.[40] Refugees from Slovakia arriving in Prague were met at the train stations by the association *České srdce* (Czech Heart) and were eligible to receive state support, just as refugees from Galicia had recently been.[41] The Czechoslovak government reused the former refugee internment camp of Choceň/Chotzen to house them. Even if their numbers were more limited than during the world war, it is nonetheless interesting to see how the authorities pursued their wartime welfare policy. Although the situation in Czechoslovakia was relatively stable compared with the rest of the region, the first two years of "peace" still exhibited a warlike atmosphere, including fears of coups by monarchists or German agents, support for the fight at the borders, and the slow, ongoing process of demobilization.[42]

Finally, and most importantly, independence did not suddenly resolve the deep food crisis inherited from wartime.[43] Shortages persisted through the next winter and, at least, until 1921, and war profiteers were not punished by the new regime, as many had hoped. The rationing system established by the Austrian government during the war and built around central agencies monitoring the purchase of common goods remained in place. According to a German newspaper, Czech circles accused these agencies of functioning exactly as they had in Austrian times, although the Ministry for the population's food supply denied such claims.[44] What could not be denied was that, through 1921, the state's Office for Grain continued to subsidize the market for cereals and paid an inflated price for bread before selling it to the population at a lower price.[45] As a result of these continued food shortages, and despite the foreign aid obtained by the government, the social tensions that had sparked demonstrations and strikes in the last years of the war were still consequential in the first years of the Republic. Between 1919 and 1920, there were some three hundred demonstrations in the streets of Prague, including political rallies (but not including workers' strikes).[46] The number of strikes in the Bohemian lands also increased after 1918—from 184 that year to 242 the next, and 590 in 1920.[47]

Nor were these tensions eased by exaggerated expectations for immediate change. As early as December 1918, people queuing in front of the town hall in the Prague suburb of Žižkov complained about the unchanged conditions of food supply in the new state.[48] The food riots, which had become an almost weekly occurrence in 1917 and 1918, continued throughout 1919, with the crowd sometimes directly plundering shops or requiring merchants to reduce prices. In some cases, they brought out the gallows to scare the "profiteers." In Prague, during protests on 22 May, the gallows bore a sign: "Last warning for the profiteers."[49] Another sign read: "We want a republic without thieves."[50] The hopes that the birth of Czechoslovakia would bring an end to the system of food distribution were disappointed. The common feeling was that peace should not have implied the continuation of the war economy and prices. Workers' representatives in January 1919, following a demonstration in front of a butcher in a Prague suburb, asked for the district office to cover half of the meat's price as current prices were too high for workers.[51] The demands during these protests were thus not much different from what they had been in the previous years. Striking workers wanted higher wages to compensate for the inflation, and all classes protested the high prices and general unavailability of certain goods. In this respect, the founding of a new republic did not fundamentally change the relationship of citizens to the state, or their general impression of the inefficiency of food distribution. As the material conditions clearly did not improve, trust in the authorities did not increase with the regime change. The fact that the authorities themselves had not changed much added to this distrust.

Who Is the State?

In a short pamphlet from 1918, publicist Josef Žemla answered the question "What is a republic?" for his compatriots, as "it might be that our imprecision of concepts could cause many disappointments in the broader sections of the population."[52] The meaning of the word "republic" and the type of state government it should entail was not necessarily clear for people who had lived in a monarchy their whole lives and interpretations could differ. The new democracy gave legitimacy to all sorts of protests. A report from January 1919 described the "widespread opinion that in the republic everybody can do as he pleases and that the political authority, if it asks to be notified about a meeting in order to know what it concerns, has nothing else on its mind other than to 'harass in the Austrian way' the citizens."[53] To the public, state agents seemed at odds with the new ideas and principles of a democratic republic. Reports from the military command in Prague in 1919 mention frequent complaints against the state administration and a very high level of distrust.[54] One of them summed up the general discontent: "there are bitter complaints about the actions of the bureaucracy and their inefficiency, also the rude behaviour of the officials towards the public in offices."[55] Another report later that year noted that many vented their disappointment, "always laying the blame on the republic" and saying that it was "even worse than under Austria."[56]

The general disappointment with the new Czechoslovak regime did not signal a desire to return to the former period, but rather dissatisfaction with how far the society had been transformed. Communist era historians have argued that this longing represented a wish for a Bolshevik revolution along Russian lines. This interpretation ignored the fact that these countries had well-organized socialist parties with their own, non-Bolshevik traditions.[57] But beyond the party rallies, when Prague's inhabitants marched in the streets, their goal was typically vaguer than the establishment of a communist republic. In many protests, workers and women expressed their discontent with a state that had failed to provide them with the social justice they craved or, more basically, with adequate food supplies. They also promoted a purer vision of the new state more in line with their own national or social interpretations of what the Czechoslovak republic should be.

The movement of Hussite women (*husitské ženy*, in reference to the protestant reformer Jan Hus) and the fears that crystallized around it constitutes a good example of these contradictory conceptions of the new state in the uncertain atmosphere immediately after the war. The Hussite women organized demonstrations and printed flyers to voice the complaints of women on the city's material situation. According to the historian Antonín Klimek, the movement was born out of the anger from the Prague "pavlač" (a typical apartment building with a courtyard and balconies, the scene of much gossip).[58] One woman said that she heard about the movement from another woman on the Old Town Square, and then came to a meeting.[59] Another ran into an acquaintance who explained that a meeting was happening in a nearby pub. She found out that the women were wearing a black armband with a red chalice (symbol of the Hussites), which she then went home to fabricate for herself.[60] The reference to Hus and the chalice had been used in prewar street protests and was important in Czech working class culture.[61]

The movement was not composed exclusively of women, and legionaries were often present in their meetings and protests. Their interpretation of the political situation distinguished the positive elements of the Republic (Masaryk and the legionaries) from the civil servants who were the cause of all wrong. In a leaflet calling for a demonstration, the "little father" (*tatíček*) president Masaryk was presented as a hostage of the German Austrians in the ministries. The Hussite women invited both men and women to protest "against the profiteering, the central agencies, the 'Austrianity' (*rakušáctví*) in the administration and in the army."[62] A demonstration they organized in September 1919 saw twenty thousand people gathered on Prague's Old Town Square to demand a new government. Masaryk welcomed a delegation at the Castle announcing that he understood their anger but that "anger [was] not a program."[63]

The varied reactions to these September demonstrations are indicative of the tense climate in this stabilization phase of the Republic. The demonstrators were accused of being manipulated by a monarchist plot to discredit the new regime and restore the monarchy. Bohemian aristocrats were even interrogated as part of the police investigation into the demonstration.[64] Although monarchist restoration attempts were a real threat in East Central Europe after the war, the authorities in Prague seemed to have overestimated their capacity to generate a popular movement.[65] Press commentaries evinced fear of the repercussions of the demonstration on the republic's image abroad, especially while the treaties were still being negotiated. The French press, for example, reported on "incidents in Prague" of a certain gravity, and that the coup's instigators hoped to create pogroms to "discredit the republic [and] . . . proceed to an anti-democratic coup."[66] Members of the "Hussite women" reacted to defend their organization and goals against these accusations. In one newspaper column, the editor Jaroslav Motyčka explained their purpose thus: "Our group was founded according to and follows only humanitarian goals, not at all clerical, Bolshevik or monarchical goals."[67] Such accusations and counter-accusations make it difficult to assess whether there were any links with monarchist agitators. However, the depositions gathered in the police files and the detailed defense published by one of its organizers a year after the September 1919 demonstration seem to indicate that the demonstrators' motives were genuine.[68] The fact that the case was dropped also indicates that not much evidence of a monarchist plot could be found.

The perception that the republic was in danger shaped the Czechoslovak authorities' interpretation of various social movements. In this stabilization phase, the young Czechoslovak government was afraid of foreign agents and Bolsheviks. This fear of agents that would support a Bolshevik or monarchist coup was also visible in broader sections of the population. They could be accused of both simultaneously; Hungarians, for example, represented both the threat of monarchic restoration (with Karl's restoration attempts there) and of Bolshevism. A flyer in March 1919 called for vigilance and accused a few individuals of wanting to organize a coup using "fake promises of a socialist republic." The text explained that they were actually working for the "restoration of the old monarchy."[69] A woman denounced a supposed plot against Masaryk by describing a reported conversation between a priest, a noble high-ranking official, and a military officer where they mocked the legionaries and exchanged information about the president.[70] The conversation probably did not take place, but it reflects the impression that the old pillars of the monarchy were working against the new regime. Anxiety over spies and internal enemies linked the immediate postwar to the wartime period: foreigners, social protesters, and former elites could all be suspected of threatening a precarious new order.

Demonstrators in 1919 and 1920 felt that they had as much of a legitimate claim to represent the state as civil servants. This was especially true for the military veterans who were progressively coming back. The legionaries who had deserted to the legions from the Russian or Italian fronts wanted to control the "new" city and participate in the creation of its Czech identity under the Republic. Having fought for the creation of Czechoslovakia, they felt robbed of their victory by politicians. They also often could not find work given the high unemployment rate in the city, and considered it their role to regulate the new society. In many cases, the veterans acted as surrogate policemen, defending their vision of what was good for the nation, which could coincide or clash with that of the police. On 2 March 1919, legionaries from Russia interrupted a dancing evening in the Prague German House on suspicion that someone had fired at a legionary. They then proceeded to close the nearby cafés and send their guests home.[71] The public sometimes encouraged the legionaries' policing role. For example, in April 1920, a legionary, seeing a long queue for milk, exclaimed: "Is that what we fought five years for?" A woman in the queue suggested he go and slap the saleswoman; a demand the legionary carried out.[72] The government was often ambivalent toward the legionaries, at once treating them as official heroes of the new state and fearing their potential for social upheaval. Martin Zückert has demonstrated the new state's relative success in pacifying its society in comparison to the demobilization process in neighboring countries.[73] Indeed there are no equivalents in the Bohemian lands to the paramilitary units active in Hungary, Austria, or Germany.[74] However, as John Paul Newman has argued for the Croatian case, the absence of an open conflict between Reds and Whites should not prevent us from studying the existing violence that emerged from the Great War.[75] Czech veterans in this period were both instigators of low-level violence in the streets and regulators of citizen-based violence. At times, this meant that the legionaries tried to refrain the outbursts of the mob. When a lieutenant colonel was accused of throwing water from his window on a parade of Sokols and the crowd began breaking into his apartment, some legionaries intervened to get everybody outside.[76] At other times, however, they felt themselves to be above the law, as in the case of a journalist threatened in his office by two legionaries who did not like an article he published.[77] The public was divided over this show of force: some supported the legionaries, while others denounced how "the military [was] turned by incompetent officials into an army of thieves."[78] The legionaries did not form a group with homogenous political affiliations. Some were influenced by Bolshevik ideas, championed radical changes, and desired a socialist revolution. But many others found Czechoslovakia's politics not nationalistic enough and pushed for a dictatorship under Masaryk.

The atmosphere of uncertainty and potential for more upheaval in the first years of the Czechoslovak republic created a blurred notion of who was a legitimate representative of the state. Street protesters claimed to know better than civil servants how the republic should be governed, while legionaries could point to their military record in having fought for Czechoslovak independence.

"De-austrianization"

In the immediate aftermath of the world war, the frustrations expressed by Prague citizens often referenced the continuation of the old order in the new state. The new rallying cry of the Czechs was "de-austrianization" (*odrakouštění*), and even German-language newspapers criticized Czechoslovakia for being too much like old Austria. For example, censorship of the private post continued in the postwar period and was denounced by the *Prager Tagblatt*.[79] As one memoirist recalls, "although no one could say exactly what it was supposed to mean, 'we must de-austrianize ourselves' became a favorite applause-winning formula and an unquestioned appurtenance of platform patriotism."[80] Many publications echoed the debate about this idea in the Czech public.[81] Yet what was actually understood by "de-austrianization" was not always clear or consensual. Certainly it was to encompass the political, cultural, social, and economic domains.[82] Politically, this generally meant the democratization of institutions and habits, and the affirmation of the Czech(oslovak) character of the new state. For example, "Austrianity" (*rakušáctví*) could be found in offices still using German. One newspaper complained that it was alive and well in the trade court in Prague, where a summons exclusively in German had been sent.[83]

But the idea of Austrianity could go deeper, and necessitate a real (self) re-education. One advocate for this internal transformation affirmed that, "willy-nilly we adopted much Austrianity in our opinions and a re-education is necessary, in order to become pure Czechs, that we must all strive for." The enumeration of vices constitutive of Austrianity included corruption, cowardice, lying, and profiteering.[84] The *Prager Tagblatt* additionally accused Czechs of continuing the culture of denunciation that had marked "old Austria" by denouncing Germans for lacking in patriotic attitude.[85] The injunction to cleanse the country of Austrianity led to a number of denunciations for "complicity with Austria" during the war. Again, these were not limited to political circles. The director of the theatre in the suburb of Královské Vinohrady/Königliche Weinberge was accused of Austrianity, feeling thereby attacked in his "artistic and citizen's honor."[86]

The gradual return of the legionaries in 1919 and 1920, who were celebrated as heroes, acted as a kind of barometer of the flaws in the society to which they were returning. Thus, for example, the satirical newspaper *Humoristické listy* published a cartoon following a legionary on a walk around Prague and "reading" his thoughts: in front of the station, he wondered at the line of unemployed men and untended dirty streets; he was shocked to see that the bridge toll was not abolished; looking at prices in a butcher shop, he cursed the owner. He was also surprised to see the monument to Marshall Radetzky still standing (although veiled).[87] In this case, the legionary represents an idealized version of the nation looking upon its current condition and disapproving of the remnants of the old order.

The impression of continuity between the two regimes was so strong that it shaped responses to everyday events. The adjective "Austrian" referred to any behavior seen as restraining individual freedom or tolerating profiteering. In an incident reminiscent of Arthur Schnitzler's *Leutnant Gustl*, a young man who was blocking the exit from the room in a theatre resisted when an inspection officer placed a hand on his shoulder and asked him to "move on." The man cried, "Don't push me!" And after having been controlled by a policeman came back to the officer and told him publicly: "Do you know how you behaved? Like an Austrian corporal." This remark caused a stir among those present, who quickly fell into debating the incident.[88] In many cases, any attempt at authority was resented as being part of the old value system, which did not make the work of the police easy. In another example, two drunken soldiers who had been breaking windows and threatening clients in a pub insulted the policeman trying to stop them by calling him an "Austrian murderer."[89] "Austrian" thus became a popular insult, symbolizing both the desire for distance from the old regime and its persistence in the new order. Ferdinand Peroutka pointed to the increasing misuse of Austrianity as an insult in public life, citing a deputy who accused Alois Rašín (one of the men who organized the 28th of October takeover) of Austrianity in Parliament.[90]

State agents were often portrayed in contemporary satire as foreign elements who tried to pass as loyal Czechoslovak citizens. As so many remained in service from one regime to the next, this was probably not far from the truth. A civil servant recalled the despair of his colleagues in the ministry of commerce in Vienna in October 1918, when getting a job in Prague became one of their only options:

> I found my colleagues silently sitting in their offices, not knowing what to do and avoiding discussion of the catastrophe. . . . Before the war I had worked under two ministers of commerce, Fort and Fiedler, who were Czechs, and the Undersecretary, Dr. Mueller, was a Czech, an assistant secretary a Pole, and in my own department two out of five officials were Czech. They asked me if they should leave the office and I advised them to go to Prague, where they might be needed by the new government.

... Though they had worked in my office during the war, they now belonged to victorious Czechoslovakia and I to defeated Austria.[91]

Prague, which was still a relatively provincial town, was a difficult place to hide a loyal Habsburg past. The newspaper *Národní Politika* complained, for example, of a high placed functionary at the postal service who "put on a new coat and became Czechoslovak."[92] Ivan Olbracht's short story "The Career of Eduard Žak" also portrays a Prague police officer in the transition from monarchy to republic. It conveys the disillusionment with unchanged conditions, as the same people were officials of the new regime.[93]

Several satirical pieces showcased characters speaking a bad Czech, full of German words and expressions, which yet embodied the new state institutions. This use of half German sentences was meant to underline the duplicity of these people, who have to give the appearance of good Czechoslovak patriots, but are revealed as Austrians. In *Drops of Poison*, the Viennese wife of a civil servant in a ministry complains half in German about the Czech patriotic parades she has to attend. In another scene, a young lieutenant explains to a fellow officer that he stupidly reported to his superior in German instead of Czech one day, according to the old custom. These satirized characters are balanced by the background presence of a legionary, who closes the play with the leitmotiv: "And that's what we fought for in faraway places?"[94] The righteous legionary, a stand-in for the nation at large, can only observe and comment upon the parody of the "new" Czechoslovakia. In a more humorous vein, Eduard Bass's cabaret play depicts a censorship officer who speaks Czech with a strong German accent. When he goes to the cinema Konvikt to see the film "Wilson against Wilhelm," the officer decides, out of respect for the German Emperor, to cut the scenes that are too critical of him.[95] This satirical piece refers to an actual event in May 1919, when scenes from this American propaganda film denouncing Wilhelm II's war crimes were deleted by an overzealous censorship officer.[96] During the projection of the film in Prague, the audience booed, shouting: 'Shame on the censorship! We want Czech censorship!' Afterward, a crowd of 120 people went to the nearby police headquarters to complain about the ill-advised cuts in the film.[97]

This extreme example of an administrative apparatus that continues to function as it did under the Habsburg Empire demonstrates the chasm that had developed between state and society during the last years of the world war, and that was not immediately resolved by the new Republic.[98] The continued censorship of both private post and the press generated much anger among the general public. Letters from suspected communist agitators and suspicious German "non-patriots" were seized by the police, just as Czech antipatriotic letters had been during the war.[99] Newspapers, especially German-speaking but not only, often had articles cut by the censor. A parliamentary question to the

Ministry of the Interior inquired about the censorship of an article in *Národní Listy*, which had published testimonies of soldiers fighting in Slovakia. As the article was patriotic, the deputy denounced the censorship practice, explaining that it "remind[ed him] of the worse period of the persecution of newspapers by the Austrian administration." The Defense Ministry, however, believed that the article contained sensitive military information.[100] The surveillance activities continued as they had during the war, though with new targets. For example, reports on "events, currents and movements who could endanger republican thought, democratic principles or the state constitution" followed the same template as those in the wartime period.[101]

This general impression of continuity with the old Austrian system, and disappointment in the expected changes, did not fully disappear with the improved economic conditions of the 1920s. The communist leader and future president of Czechoslovakia, Antonín Zápotocký, alluded to it in a text from 1946, when he addressed "those who . . . know how the promised times looked, when everything went according to the old legal and police order, which did not change from the old Austrian monarchy and which they took over with her bureaucracy."[102] The high hopes for change generated by World War I and upset by the return of the old system would find a repercussion in the following decades.

Conclusion

The end of World War I constituted a moment of acute crisis in Prague, as the economic situation became critical and the traditional relationship of citizens to the state was destabilized by the war conditions. The Czechoslovak declaration of independence and the subsequent creation of a Republic catalyzed expectations that peace would bring about a better world. It soon became clear, however, that economic problems persisted and not much had changed in the Bohemian lands. In order to function efficiently in these unstable times, the young Czechoslovak state kept most civil servants from the previous regime. This necessary continuity was largely resented by the general population, and it thus undermined the legitimacy of the new state. When studying the Great War from this state-building viewpoint, 1918 thus does not appear as a good ending point. In order to understand the disruption created by the military conflict, it is essential to examine this transitional moment, as new governments attempted to forge bonds of citizenship with an old state apparatus. The disappointment with the new conditions in the first years after the war led to an attempt to reclaim the state for its citizens from an administration perceived as alien. The Czechoslovakia of the 1920s, hailed as a model of democracy in the region, appeared to have successfully weathered this difficult postwar phase. More research would nevertheless be needed to determine how much of this discourse of disappointment reemerged with the crisis of the 1930s, and thus can be considered as one of the structural weaknesses of the First Republic.

Claire Morelon is ERC Postdoctoral Research Fellow at the University of Padova. Her research focuses on the interactions between state and society in the late Habsburg Empire and in the immediate aftermath of World War I. She received her PhD from the University of Birmingham and the Institut d'Études Politiques (Sciences Po) in Paris (dual degree). She is currently preparing her first monograph for publication, entitled *Streetscapes of War and Revolution: Prague, 1914–1920*. Before coming to Padova, she was Junior Research Fellow at The Queen's College, University of Oxford.

Notes

1. Jiří Červený and Rudolf Jílovský, *Kapky jedu* (Praha: Josef Springer, 1919), 7.
2. For a more detailed treatment of this question, see Claire Morelon, "Street Fronts: War, State Legitimacy and Urban Space, Prague 1914–1920" (PhD diss., University of Birmingham and École Doctorale de Sciences Po, 2015), chapter 6.
3. Gustav Gratz and Richard Schüller, *Der wirtschaftliche Zusammenbruch Österreich-Ungarns: die Tragödie der Erschöpfung* (Wien: Hölder-Pichler-Tempsky A.G., 1930).
4. Karel Pichlík, "Der militärische Zusammenbruch der Mittelmächte im Jahre 1918," in *Die Auflösung des Habsburgerreiches: Zusammenbruch und Neuorientierung im Donauraum*, ed. Richard Plaschka and Karlheinz Mack (München: R. Oldenbourg, 1970), 249–65.
5. Alexis de Tocqueville, *L'Ancien Régime et la Révolution* (Paris: Gallimard, 1967).
6. Gary B. Cohen, "Nationalist Politics and the Dynamics of State and Civil Society in the Habsburg Monarchy, 1867–1914," *Central European History* 40, no. 02 (2007): 278.
7. "Zákon, vydaný Národním výborem dne 28. října 1918," *Národní listy*, 29 October 1918, 1.
8. Ivan Šedivý, "K otázce kontinuity nositelů státní moci: jmenování vedoucích úředníků v kompetenci ministerstva vnitra v letech 1918–1921," in *Moc, vliv a autorita v procesu vzniku a utváření meziválečné ČSR (1918–1921)*, eds. Jan Hájek, Dagmar Hájková et al. (Praha: Masarykův ústav, 2008), 184–97.
9. Samuel Ronsin, "Police, Republic and Nation: The Czechoslovak State Police and the Building of a Multinational Democracy, 1918–1925," in *Policing Interwar Europe: Continuity and Crisis, 1918-40*, ed. Gerald Blaney (Basingstoke: Palgrave, 2007), 136–58.
10. Aleš Vyskočil, *C.k. úředník ve zlatém věku jistoty* (Praha: Historický ústav, 2009), 296.
11. See Zdeněk Kárník, *České země v éře první republiky (1918–1938)* (Praha: Libri, 2000), 156.
12. Memorandum from the Governor's office to all local civil servants, 5 November 1918, in Alois Kocman, ed., *Boj o směr vývoje Československého státu: Říjen 1918–červen 1919*, vol. 1 (Praha: Nakladatelství Československé Akademie Věd, 1965), 126.
13. On Czech interwar democracy, see Peter Bugge, "Czech Democracy 1918–1938: Paragon or Parody?" *Bohemia* 47 (2006/07): 3–28.

14. Vyskočil, *C.k. úředník*, 321–23.
15. *Národní listy*, 13 November 1918, 3.
16. Václav Ledvinka, "Die Namen von Prager öffentlichen Räumen als Spiegelung des Wandels der politischen Realität im 20. Jahrhundert," in *Die Besetzung des öffentlichen Raumes: politische Plätze, Denkmäler und Straßennamen im europäischen Vergleich,* ed. Rudolf Jaworski and Peter Stachel (Berlin: Frank & Timme, 2007), 338.
17. The monument was not, however, destroyed and is visible today in the Lapidarium of the Národní Muzeum.
18. "Jediný pomník Habsburků v Praze odstraněn," *Národní politika*, 3 June 1919, 3.
19. Peter Bugge, "The Naming of a Slovak City: The Czechoslovak Renaming of Pressburg/Pozsony/Presporok in 1918–19," *Austrian History Yearbook* 35 (2004): 221.
20. Invitation sent to the municipality, Archiv hlavního města Prahy (Municipal Archives of Prague), Magistrát hlavního města Prahy (Prague municipality) I, ka 889, sig. 80/2, no 1461(?), 31 May 1919.
21. Andrea Orzoff, "The Husbandman: Tomáš Masaryk's Leader Cult in Interwar Czechoslovakia," *Austrian History Yearbook* 39 (2008): 121–37; Lothar Höbelt, "Entösterreicherung im Vergleich: die Verfassungsentwicklung dr Tschechoslowakei und (Deutsch-) Österreichs nach 1918," in *České křižovatky evropských dějin. 1, 1918: model komplexního transformačního procesu?,* ed. Lucie Kostrbová and Ivan Šedivý (Praha: Masarykův ústav, 2010), 93–99. On scenarios of power, see Richard Wortman, *Scenarios of Power: Myth and Ceremony in Russian Monarchy; From Peter the Great to the Abdication of Nicholas II* (Princeton: Princeton University Press, 2006).
22. Dagmar Hajková, "'Dokud člověk jí klobásy, tak neumře': Oslavy narozenin T. G. Masaryka," in *Historik nad šachovnicí dějin: K pětasedmdesátinám Jana Galandauera,* ed. Dagmar Hájková, Velek Luboš et al. (Praha: Masarykův ústav, 2011), 218–35.
23. Narodní Archiv (Czech National Archives, hereafter NA), Prezidium policejního ředitelství (Presidium of the Prague police department, hereafter PP), 1916–1920, ka 2931, sig F 13/11, circular from 4 March 1920.
24. See Victor Demiaux, "La Construction rituelle de la victoire dans les capitales européennes après la Grande Guerre (Bruxelles, Bucarest, Londres, Paris, Rome)" (PhD diss., École des Hautes Études en Sciences Sociales, 2013), 182–96.
25. *Návrat presidenta Masaryka do vlasti* (Smíchov: Stanislav Minařík, 1920), 176–91.
26. Ibid.
27. "Slavnostní uvítání presidenta Československé republiky," NA, PP 1916–1920, ka 2931, sig. 13/7, undated.
28. Letter from Otokar Š., NA, PP 1916–1920, ka 2931, sig. 13/7, 15 December 1918. Other letters to be found in the same folder.
29. Alois Kocman, ed., *Souhrnná týdenní hlášení presidia zemské správy politické v Praze o situaci v Čechách 1919–1920* (Praha: Nakladatelství Československé Akademie Věd, 1959), 87.
30. Police report on the events of the day, NA, Prezidium ministerstva vnitra (Presidium of the Interior Ministry, hereafter PMV), ka 179, sig. N, no. 297, 21 March 1920.
31. NA, PMV, ka 179, 1 July 1919.
32. For examples, see the weekly reports in Libuše Otáhalová, ed., *Souhrnná hlášení presidia pražského místodržitelství o protistátní, protirakouské a protivalené činnosti v Čechách 1915–1918* (Praha: Nakl. Československé akademie věd, 1957).

33. Martin Zückert, "National Concepts of Freedom and Government Pacification Policies: The Case of Czechoslovakia in the Transitional Period after 1918," *Contemporary European History* 17, no. 3 (2008): 338.
34. For a description of this practice in Vienna, see Maureen Healy, "Exhibiting a War in Progress: Entertainment and Propaganda in Vienna, 1914–1918," *Austrian History Yearbook* 31(2000): 70–72.
35. *Věstník obecní král. hláv. města Prahy*, 14 November 1918, 307.
36. See an invitation by the Archbishop's consistory with the crossed out mention of "warriors fallen in the present war" and replacement by "Czech legionary soldiers": NA, Archiv pražského arcibiskupství III, ka 1298, no 15733, 16 November 1918.
37. *Národní listy*, 11 September 1919, 1.
38. The National Archives (London), Foreign Office 608/6, 1 September 1919.
39. Deposition from a policeman, NA, PP 1916–1920, ka 3039, sig. M 34/67, 6 June 1919.
40. NA, PP 1916–1920, ka 3039, sig. M 34/67, no 6007, 15 June 1919.
41. NA, PP 1916–1920, ka 3025, sig. M 34/1/III.
42. Rudolf Kučera, "Exploiting Victory, Sinking into Defeat: Uniformed Violence in the Creation of the New Order in Czechoslovakia and Austria, 1918–1922," *The Journal of Modern History* 88, no. 4 (2016): 827–55. For a regional overview, see Robert Gerwarth and John Horne, eds., *War in Peace: Paramilitary Violence in Europe After the Great War* (Oxford: Oxford University Press, 2012).
43. On wartime food shortages in Austria, see Maureen Healy, *Vienna and the Fall of the Habsburg Empire: Total War and Everyday Life in World War I* (Cambridge, UK: Cambridge University Press, 2004).
44. *Prager Tagblatt*, 10 January 1919, 3.
45. Alois Rašín, *Les finances de la Tchécoslovaquie jusqu'à la fin de 1921* (Paris: Éditions Bossard, 1923), 152–53.
46. Alois Kocman, ed., *Souhrnná týdenní hlášení presidia*, 9.
47. After that, the number of strikes started to decrease. See table in Peter Heumos, "'Kartoffeln her oder es gibt eine Revolution': Hungerkrawalle, Streiks und Massenproteste in den böhmischen Ländern 1914–1918," in *Der Erste Weltkrieg und die Beziehungen zwischen Tschechen, Slowaken und Deutschen*, ed. Hans Mommsen, Dušan Kováč, and Jiří Malíř (Essen: Klartext, 2001), 271.
48. Deposition by Zdenka J., NA, PP 1916–1920, ka 2931, sig. F 13/7, 13 December 1918.
49. Ibid., 57.
50. NA, Prezidium českého místodržitelství (Presidium of the Bohemian Governor's Office, hereafter PM), ka 4973, 8/1/16/40, no 17536/19, 23 May 1919.
51. NA, PM, ka 4979, 8/1/25/6, no 594/19, 6 January 1919.
52. Josef Žemla, *Co jest republika?* (Praha: V. Rytíř, 1918), 5.
53. Alois Kocman, ed., *Souhrnná týdenní hlášení presidia*, 18.
54. Examples: NA, PM, ka 5114, no 31905/19, 20 September 1919; no 36140/19, 3 October 1919; no 40981/19, 15 November 1919.
55. NA, PM, ka 5114, no 33318/19, 24 September 1919.
56. NA, PM, ka 5114, no 44847/19, 18 December 1919.
57. Ivo Banac, "The Emergence of Communism in East Central Europe, 1918–1921," in *The Effects of World War I: The Class War After the Great War; The Rise of Communist Parties in East Central Europe, 1918–1921*, ed. Ivo Banac (Boulder, CO: East European Monographs, 1983), 3.

58. Antonín Klimek, *Vítejte v první republice* (Praha: Havran, 2003), 46.
59. Statement by Marta Lenertová, 11 September 1919. NA, PP 1916–1920, ka 2919, sig. D 6/11.
60. Statement by Marie Siglová, 10 September 1919. NA, PP 1916–1920, ka 2919, sig. D 6/11.
61. Jakub S. Beneš, *Workers and Nationalism: Czech and German Social Democracy in Habsburg Austria, 1890–1918* (Oxford: Oxford University Press, 2017), 164.
62. Leaflet for a demonstration on 5 September 1919, NA, PP 1916–1920, ka 2919, sig. D6/5 IX.
63. *Národní listy*, 7 September 1919, 3.
64. Deposition by Erwein Nostitz, NA, PP 1916–1920, ka 2919, sig. D 6/11, 8 September 1919.
65. See Timothy Snyder, *The Red Prince: The Secret Lives of a Habsburg Archduke* (New York: Basic Books, 2008), 121–48.
66. *Le Gaulois*, 8 September 1919, 3.
67. Ibid.
68. F. V. Micka, *Černý pátek: velezrádný pokus o státní monarchistický převrat v Praze dne 5. září 1919* (Praha: Bohemia, 1919).
69. NA, PM 1911-1920, ka 5043, no 8498/19, 15 March 1919.
70. NA, PP 1916-1920, ka 2931, sig. 13/7, deposition by Antonie K., 15 December 1918.
71. Alois Kocman, ed., *Souhrnná týdenní hlášení presidia*, 34–35.
72. NA, PMV, ka 179, sig. N, 1920, č. j. 104, Police report on the events of the day, 13 April 1920.
73. Martin Zückert, "National Concepts of Freedom."
74. Robert Gerwarth, "The Central European Counter-revolution: Paramilitary Violence in Germany, Austria and Hungary After the Great War," *Past and Present* 200 (August 2008): 175–209.
75. John Paul Newman, "Post-imperial and Postwar Violence in the South Slav Lands, 1917–1923," *Contemporary European History* 19, no. 3 (2010): 249–65.
76. 13 June 1920, Alois Kocman, ed., *Souhrnná týdenní hlášení presidia*, 214.
77. NA, PMV, ka 179, sig. N, 1920, č. j. 27, Police report on the events of the day, 27 January 1920.
78. Quote from an anonymous letter to the president, 25 January 1919, NA, PP 1916–1920, ka 2891, sig. A 15/1 1918.
79. NA, PP 1916–1920, ka 3077, sig. P 56/1, no. 328, 24 June 1920, *Prager Tagblatt*, 11 June 1920.
80. Zikmund Konečný, *Changing Fortunes: A Central European Recalls—The Memoirs of Zikmund Konečný* (New York: Columbia University Press, 2000), 27.
81. Some examples of brochures: Alexandr Batěk. *Odrakouštit a převychovat!* (Praha-Břevnov: vl. nákl., 1919); Albert Vojtěch Frič, *Odrakouštěte svoje duše!* (Praha: nákl. vl., 1919); František Joklík, *Jak se odrakouštujeme* (Praha: Hejda & Tuček, 1920), quoted in Jiří Kořalka, *Tschechen im Habsburgerreich und in Europa 1815–1914: sozialgeschichtliche Zusammenhänge der neuzeitlichen Nationsbildung und der Nationalitätenfrage in den böhmischen Ländern* (München: R. Oldenbourg, 1991), 36.
82. Emil Brix, "Die 'Entösterreicherung' Böhmens: Prozesse der Entfremdung von Tschechen, Deutschböhmen und Österreichern," *Österreichische Osthefte* 34, no. 1 (1992): 5–12.
83. *Národní Listy*, 16 May 1919, 4.

84. *Národní Listy*, 17 August 1919, 1.
85. *Prager Tagblatt*, 2 January 1919, 3.
86. *Národní Listy*, 31 August 1919, 5.
87. *Humoristické listy*, 7 February 1919, 54.
88. Police report on the events of the day, NA, PMV, ka 179, sig. N, 1920, no 106, 15 April 1920.
89. Police report on the events of the day, NA, PMV, ka 179, sig. N, 1919, no 159, 8 June 1919.
90. Ferdinand Peroutka, *Budování státu*, vol. 2 (Praha: Lidové noviny, 1991), 952.
91. Jürgen Nautz, *Unterhändler des Vertrauens: aus den nachgelassenen Schriften von Sektionschef Dr. Richard Schüller* (München: Oldenbourg Wissenschaftsverlag, 1990), 216–18.
92. *Národní Politika*, 1 August 1919, 4.
93. The short story was originally published in 1921. Available in Ivan Olbracht, *Bejvávalo: Sedm veselých povídek z Rakouska i republiky* (Praha: Svoboda, 1954).
94. Červený and Jílovský, *Kapky jedu*, 12.
95. Eduard Bass, *Letáky, satiry, verse, písničky*, ed. Adolf Branald and Jarmila Víšková (Praha: Československý Spisovatel, 1958), 221–25.
96. *Národní listy*, 13 May 1919, 5.
97. NA, PMV, ka 179, sig. N, 1919, no. 133, Police report on the events of the day, 13 May 1919.
98. See John Deak and Jonathan Gumz, "How to Break a State: The Habsburg Monarchy's Internal War, 1914–1918," *American Historical Review* 122, no. 5 (2017): 1105–36.
99. For the continued censorship of letters see the letters censored from 1918 to 1920 in the file NA, PP 1916-1920, ka 3077, sig. P 56/1.
100. Parliamentary question, 24 June 1919, NA, PMV ka 169, no. 8407.
101. NA, PM ka 5115, 3949/19 1 February 1919.
102. Antonín Zápotocký, *Naše národní revoluce v roce 1918 a 1945* (Praha: Práce, 1946), 5.

Bibliography

Banac, Ivo, ed. *The Effects of World War I: The Class War After the Great War; The Rise of Communist Parties in East Central Europe, 1918–1921*. Boulder, CO: East European Monographs, 1983.
Bass, Eduard. *Letáky, satiry, verse, písničky*, edited by Adolf Branald and Jarmila Víšková. Praha: Československý Spisovatel, 1958.
Beneš, Jakub S. *Workers and Nationalism: Czech and German Social Democracy in Habsburg Austria, 1890–1918*. Oxford: Oxford University Press, 2017.
Brix, Emil. "Die 'Entösterreicherung' Böhmens: Prozesse der Entfremdung von Tschechen, Deutschböhmen und Österreicher." *Österreichische Osthefte* 34, no. 1 (1992): 5–12.
Bugge, Peter. "Czech Democracy 1918–1938: Paragon or Parody?" *Bohemia* 47 (2006/07): 3–28.
———. "The Naming of a Slovak City: The Czechoslovak Renaming of Pressburg/Pozsony/Prešporok in 1918–19." *Austrian History Yearbook* 35 (2004): 205–27.
Červený, Jiří and Rudolf Jílovský. *Kapky jedu*. Praha: Josef Springer, 1919.

Cohen, Gary B. "Nationalist Politics and the Dynamics of State and Civil Society in the Habsburg Monarchy, 1867–1914." *Central European History* 40, no. 02 (2007): 241–78.

Demiaux, Victor. "La Construction rituelle de la victoire dans les capitales européennes après la Grande Guerre (Bruxelles, Bucarest, Londres, Paris, Rome)." PhD diss., École des Hautes Études en Sciences Sociales, 2013.

de Tocqueville, Alexis. *L'Ancien Régime et la Révolution*. Paris: Gallimard, 1967.

Gerwarth, Robert. "The Central European Counter-revolution: Paramilitary Violence in Germany, Austria and Hungary After the Great War." *Past and Present* 200 (August 2008): 175–209.

Gerwarth, Robert, and John Horne, eds. *War in Peace: Paramilitary Violence in Europe After the Great War*. Oxford: Oxford University Press, 2012.

Gratz, Gustav, and Richard Schüller. *Der wirtschaftliche Zusammenbruch Österreich-Ungarns: die Tragödie der Erschöpfung*. Wien: Hölder-Pichler-Tempsky A.G., 1930.

Hajková, Dagmar. "'Dokud člověk jí klobásy, tak neumře': Oslavy narozenin T. G. Masaryka." In *Historik nad šachovnicí dějin: K pětasedmdesátinám Jana Galandauera*, edited by Dagmar Hájková, Velek Luboš et al., 218–35. Praha: Masarykův ústav, 2011.

Healy, Maureen. "Exhibiting a War in Progress: Entertainment and Propaganda in Vienna, 1914–1918." *Austrian History Yearbook* 31(2000): 57–85.

———. *Vienna and the Fall of the Habsburg Empire: Total War and Everyday Life in World War I*. Cambridge, UK: Cambridge University Press, 2004.

Heumos, Peter. "'Kartoffeln her oder es gibt eine Revolution': Hungerkrawalle, Streiks und Massenproteste in den böhmischen Ländern 1914–1918." In *Der Erste Weltkrieg und die Beziehungen zwischen Tschechen, Slowaken und Deutschen*, edited by Hans Mommsen, Dušan Kováč, and Jiří Malíř, 255–86. Essen: Klartext, 2001.

Höbelt, Lothar. "Entösterreicherung im Vergleich: die Verfassungsentwicklung dr Tschechoslowakei und (Deutsch-) Österreichs nach 1918." In *České křižovatky evropských dějin. 1, 1918: model komplexního transformačního procesu?*, edited by Lucie Kostrbová and Ivan Šedivý, 93–99. Praha: Masarykův ústav, 2010.

Kárník, Zdeněk. *České země v éře první republiky (1918–1938)*. Praha: Libri, 2000.

Klimek, Antonín. *Vítejte v první republice*. Praha: Havran, 2003.

Kocman, Alois, ed. *Boj o směr vývoje Československého státu: Říjen 1918–červen 1919*, vol. 1. Praha: Nakladatelství Československé Akademie Věd, 1965.

———. *Souhrnná týdenní hlášení presidia zemské správy politické v Praze o situaci v Čechách 1919–1920*. Praha: Nakladatelství Československé Akademie Věd, 1959.

Konečný, Zikmund. *Changing Fortunes: A Central European Recalls—The Memoirs of Zikmund Konečný*. New York: Columbia University Press, 2000.

Kořalka, Jiří. *Tschechen im Habsburgerreich und in Europa 1815–1914: sozialgeschichtliche Zusammenhänge der neuzeitlichen Nationsbildung und der Nationalitätenfrage in den böhmischen Ländern*. München: R. Oldenbourg, 1991.

Kučera, Rudolf. "Exploiting Victory, Sinking into Defeat: Uniformed Violence in the Creation of the New Order in Czechoslovakia and Austria, 1918–1922." *The Journal of Modern History* 88, no. 4 (2016): 827–55.

Ledvinka, Václav. "Die Namen von Prager öffentlichen Räumen als Spiegelung des Wandels der politischen Realität im 20. Jahrhundert." In *Die Besetzung des öffentlichen Raumes: politische Plätze, Denkmäler und Straßennamen im europäischen Vergleich*, edited by Rudolf Jaworski and Peter Stachel, 337–44. Berlin: Frank & Timme, 2007.

Micka, F. V. *Černý pátek: velezrádný pokus o státní monarchistický převrat v Praze dne 5. září 1919*. Praha: Bohemia, 1919.
Morelon, Claire. "Street Fronts: War, State Legitimacy and Urban Space, Prague 1914–1920." PhD diss., University of Birmingham and École Doctorale de Sciences Po, 2015.
Nautz, Jürgen. *Unterhändler des Vertrauens: aus den nachgelassenen Schriften von Sektionschef Dr. Richard Schüller*. München: Oldenbourg Wissenschaftsverlag, 1990.
Návrat presidenta Masaryka do vlasti. Smíchov: Stanislav Minařík, 1920.
Newman, John Paul. "Post-imperial and Postwar Violence in the South Slav Lands, 1917–1923." *Contemporary European History* 19, no. 3 (2010): 249–65.
Olbracht, Ivan. *Bejvávalo: Sedm veselých povídek z Rakouska i republiky*. Praha: Svoboda, 1954.
Orzoff, Andrea. "The Husbandman: Tomáš Masaryk's Leader Cult in Interwar Czechoslovakia." *Austrian History Yearbook* 39 (2008): 121–37.
Otáhalová, Libuše, ed. *Souhrnná hlášení presidia pražského místodržitelství o protistátní, protirakouské a protivalené činnosti v Čechách 1915–1918*. Praha: Nakl. Československé akademie věd, 1957.
Peroutka, Ferdinand. *Budování státu*. Praha: Lidové noviny, 1991.
Pichlík, Karel. "Der militärische Zusammenbruch der Mittelmächte im Jahre 1918." In *Die Auflösung des Habsburgerreiches: Zusammenbruch und Neuorientierung im Donauraum*, edited by Richard Plaschka and Karlheinz Mack, 249–65. München: R. Oldenbourg, 1970.
Rašín, Alois. *Les finances de la Tchécoslovaquie jusqu'à la fin de 1921*. Paris: Éditions Bossard, 1923.
Ronsin, Samuel. "Police, Republic and Nation: The Czechoslovak State Police and the Building of a Multinational Democracy, 1918–1925." In *Policing Interwar Europe: Continuity and Crisis, 1918-40*, edited by Gerald Blaney, 136–58. Basingstoke: Palgrave, 2007.
Šedivý, Ivan. "K otázce kontinuity nositelů státní moci: jmenování vedoucích úředníků v kompetenci ministerstva vnitra v letech 1918–1921." In *Moc, vliv a autorita v procesu vzniku a utváření meziválečné ČSR (1918–1921)*, edited by Jan Hájek, Dagmar Hájková et al., 184–97. Praha: Masarykův ústav, 2008.
Snyder, Timothy. *The Red Prince: The Secret Lives of a Habsburg Archduke*. New York: Basic Books, 2008.
Vyskočil, Aleš. *C.k. úředník ve zlatém věku jistoty*. Praha: Historický ústav, 2009.
Wortman, Richard. *Scenarios of Power: Myth and Ceremony in Russian Monarchy; From Peter the Great to the Abdication of Nicholas II*. Princeton: Princeton University Press, 2006.
Zápotocký, Antonín. *Naše národní revoluce v roce 1918 a 1945*. Praha: Práce, 1946.
Žemla, Josef. *Co jest republika?* Praha: V. Rytíř, 1918.
Zückert, Martin. "National Concepts of Freedom and Government Pacification Policies: The Case of Czechoslovakia in the Transitional Period after 1918." *Contemporary European History* 17, no. 3 (2008): 325–44.

Newspapers
Le Gaulois
Humoristické listy
Národní listy
Národní politika
Prager Tagblatt
Věstník obecní král. hláv. města Prahy

Chapter 3

STRANGERS AMONG FRIENDS
Leon Biliński between Imperial Austria and New Poland

Iryna Vushko

In mid-August 1920, Leon Biliński prepared for what would be his last trip from Warsaw to Vienna. While Europe was recovering from the world war, the Polish-Soviet war was raging and Bolshevik armies were approaching Poland's capital. Even the most optimistic Poles feared imminent disaster and prepared to evacuate. The long-serving finance minister was among them.

Ironically, Biliński had moved to Warsaw from Vienna just one year earlier. Raised in the Galician countryside (part of the Polish territories under Austrian rule) and educated at the law faculty of Lwów (Austrian Lemberg/Ukrainian L'viv) University, he started his career as a professor of national economy, rose quickly to dean of the law faculty, and by 1878 was Lwów University's youngest rector. In the early 1880s, Biliński entered politics and moved to the imperial capital where he served until 1918 as deputy to the Austrian parliament, member of the Austrian senate, and eventually as government minister. He also held two tenures as head of the Polish representation in the Austrian parliament, making Biliński one of the most prominent Polish statesmen in the Empire.

His own upbringing, moreover, was symbolic of both the Empire's multinationalism and that of Galicia itself, where Poles and Ukrainians each composed some 45 percent of the population, and Jews made up the rest.[1] From a family of recent converts from Judaism, Biliński was raised as a Roman Catholic Pole who, like many converts, became devoutly Christian. He was also multilingual, learning Ukrainian from the Ruthenian/Ukrainian children he grew up with in Galicia and often speaking German at home.[2] Both served Biliński well in his political career, as did marrying the daughter of a German doctor from Bohemia whom he met while vacationing in Teplitz (today's Teplice, in the Czech Republic).[3]

In 1918, at age seventy-two, Biliński was contemplating retirement. A year later, he moved to a private house near Vienna, thus retreating from high politics in the former Empire's epicenter. However, in July of that year, Poland's provisional head of state, Józef Piłsudski, invited Biliński to join his government as finance minister. The former Habsburg official accepted the offer after some deliberation, and from July to November 1919, became one of only two ministers who held the same position both in the Empire and a successor state.[4] After 1919, Biliński also belonged to the reparation commission that supervised the liquidation of the Austro-Hungarian bank. And in August and September 1920, he headed Poland's propaganda office in Vienna, a diplomatic institution aimed at improving the country's image in Europe. Biliński died in 1923, by which time the new Poland was firmly established in its boundaries and recognized by its neighbors.

Yet Biliński's four final years in Poland were among the most difficult of his life, and not only because of his age. The multinational choices and mixed allegiances that had been the norm in the Empire fell under scrutiny after 1918. Polish nationalists accused Biliński of favoring the Empire and never fully endorsing the Polish republic. Others questioned his knowledge of the Polish language, using his career in German-speaking institutions and his German wife against him. While Biliński's professional record was impeccable and his networks and experience highly valuable for the new state, national ideology often interfered with practical politics. And because Biliński did not fit the ethno-national expectations of Polish nationalists, assimilation became daunting.

Nevertheless, from late 1918 to early 1923, Biliński made a series of decisions that reversed these hostile attitudes and helped launch a remarkably transformative period in new Poland. Through a combination of his nuanced financial knowledge in the division of Austrian gold reserves and his economic decisions as part of the reparation commission, Biliński earned support at home from nationalists who now recognized how his Austrian experience could be used to defend Polish national interests. His former Austrian colleagues in Vienna, on the other hand, were enraged that an "insider" was using his expertise against them.

For Biliński and his many peers from the empire, the years before 1918 were formative in ways that would affect their choices beyond its collapse. All were educated in the same or similar institutions (the law faculty of Vienna University was the alma mater of many of this chapter's protagonists). Even outside of Vienna, men like Biliński were educated in German, the language of all institutions of higher learning (except for select chairs). Educational and political models across the empire were analogous: coffee-shop politics was just as dominant in Vienna as in Lemberg/Lwów, where decisions were often negotiated over a drink in crowded cafés by people who spoke German at work and a variety of languages at home. The tradition of negotiating with political and ideological opponents, and thus a shared understanding of politics based on compromise, was also a constant of imperial politics. And though this form of politics was far from perfect and compromises sometimes failed, violence was rare—after all, these men universally believed in the empire as the best possible political entity both for them personally and for the national and territorial entities they represented.

Through the figure of Leon Biliński and several of his Polish, Ukrainian, and Austrian colleagues, this chapter explores the transition from empire to nation-state in post-World War I Europe. Biliński embodied both the ruptures and continuities of this transition in terms of the expectations the new states placed upon their citizens, and the individual dilemmas many of them faced in either accepting or rejecting that state in light of their previous allegiances. I chose Biliński because of his unique status as having held the same position in the two different governments. Through his work for new Poland, we see the Empire living well beyond its collapse in 1918. At the same time, however, we are witness to the gradual breakdown of imperial networks and the consolidation of new national polities upon their ruins.

A Successful Career in the Late Empire

After the 1867 Austro-Hungarian Compromise, Galicia, which had been part of the Habsburg Empire since 1772, secured autonomy. The Compromise era in which Biliński came of age also inaugurated parliamentarianism and constitutionalism in the Empire. Yet in favoring the Hungarians, the Compromise left most people discontented. In particular, the Poles in Galicia and the Czechs of Bohemia had hoped their provinces would secure status on par with Hungary. When they failed to do so, disappointment only grudgingly gave way to acceptance by most Polish elites (with the significant exception of the radical nationalists). This adaptation was in part the product of geopolitics on the Galician borderland. In 1863–64, Poles in Russia had risen up against their rulers. The Russian army violently suppressed the revolution and repression followed. Thus, it was the failure of radical solutions to their status that made an increasing number of Poles amenable to the terms of the Compromise. Just when the Russian Empire was imposing new limitations upon Polish political and cultural activities, its Austrian neighbor was opening new possibilities in these realms.

Galician conservatism was a product of failed revolution in Russia and the new politics in Austria. Conservatives who endorsed the Austro-Hungarian Empire hoped to use its institutions to promote Polish culture and politics. The conservative movement thus mobilized a large spectrum of statesmen and intellectuals, many of whom lacked clear political allegiances. All, however, were united in their commitment to the Empire. They never entirely abandoned the goal of independence, but neither did they make it their most pressing political aim.

Biliński was one of the leading men in the Galician conservative movement. In 1882, he defined his political views thus: "I have become a moderate conservative—that is, someone who neither intends to wreak havoc nor to call for changes in the name of liberalism, yet who at the same time supports reforms needed for the land (*kraj*)."[5] Before 1914, Biliński concerned himself exclusively with Galicia, considering the Austro-Hungarian Empire to offer Poles the best opportunities among the three partitioning states (Russia, Prussia, and Austria). With the onset of World War I, he extended his Habsburg unification plans to *all* Polish territories from the three partitions (1772, 1793, 1795). Biliński's upbringing and connections favored imperial solutions over national ones. Indeed, he belonged to a generational cohort that could not imagine itself outside the empire.

Biliński's launched his political career in 1881 when he joined the Polish representation in the Austrian parliament. From 1892 to 1918, he resided almost permanently in Vienna. It was during this period that Biliński's Italian colleague in parliament, Alcide de Gasperi, famously described it as a "proverbial tower of Babel."[6] Although the parliament's official language was German, each nation formed its own delegation and conversed in its own tongue. The exception was the Social Democrats, who formed a separate parliamentary representation as part of the pan-imperial party. The Polish national representation was dominated by the Conservatives, with Biliński as one of its leaders. But other political movements and parties were also represented, which helped foster negotiations across ideological divides.

During the 1890s, the National Democrats on the extreme right of Polish politics became increasingly prominent both in Galicia and the imperial parliament. Consolidated in Warsaw under Russian rule, Polish National Democracy spread its political propaganda into Galicia by taking advantage of Austria's constitutional opportunities. Prohibited from publishing their material in Russia, these Polish nationalists simply extended their activities across the border into Austria. Yet this cross-border cooperation notwithstanding, Polish nationalists in Galicia never became as radically exclusive as they were in Russia.[7] Antisemitism, a key party platform in Warsaw, played no major role among Polish nationalists in Galicia, who focused their antagonism on the Ukrainians rather than the Jews.

Polish Liberal Democrats occupied the middle ground between the nationalist right and conservative center. Headed by Florian Ziemiałkowski, they supported the Empire in the expectation of extensive reforms. Unlike Conservatives who aimed chiefly to preserve the status quo, Liberal Democrats demanded universal manhood suffrage, the expansion of schooling to the lower classes, and liberal economic policies. Thus, while conservatives advocated gradual reforms carried out by traditional elites (mostly noble landowners), the democrats favored lower-class participation.[8] The major differences between Conservatives, Liberal Democrats, and Nationalists came down not to their attitudes toward the Empire (which most of them endorsed before 1916), but rather to their views on reform and national minorities. Even the Polish National Democrats favored the Austrian Empire over Russia. And many, including their Galician leader Stanisław Głąbiński, were active in the Austrian imperial parliament and held positions in government.

The relationship between Biliński and Głąbiński at once illustrates the early cooperation and gradually escalating conflict between members of different political movements. Born in Galicia in 1862, Głąbiński did a doctorate in political economy at Lwów University under Biliński's mentorship. And like his mentor as well, he moved from academia to conservative party politics. Yet by the 1890s Głąbiński had shifted rightward, becoming a leader of the Polish Nationalists in Galicia. The two men managed to maintain friendly relations until 1909, when they finally parted ways.

Biliński's major successes were linked to his work as government minister. On 9 January 1892, he was appointed head of the Austrian imperial railways.[9] In principle, the ministry was nonpolitical. However, Biliński was soon torn between his duties to the Habsburg rulers and his commitments to Galicia.[10] The issue at stake concerned where to expand the railways. Despite financial difficulties, Biliński pushed to build a new railway section from Lwów (the provincial capital of Galicia) to one of its regional centers in Złoczów, which would secure a major industrial advancement for his native region. Both his Polish and non-Polish colleagues scrutinized Biliński's every move—the former expecting investment into the Galician or, as some saw it, the national economy; the latter insisting the minister be guided by imperial rather than national interests.

The year 1895 was a political milestone for Poles in Austria-Hungary: the new government included four Polish ministers (Kazimierz Badeni as Prime Minister, Ageonor Gołuchowski as foreign minister, Edward Rittner as minister of education until 1896 and then minister for Galicia, and Biliński as the finance minister).[11] This situation reflected both the Poles' leverage in the Empire and their attitude toward imperial politics, which placed them second only to the Germans in terms of imperial ministers and in notable contrast to the Czechs, who often boycotted imperial governments because of their perceived support for Bohemian Germans. Poles saw things differently, and Biliński belonged to a large cohort that held governmental appointments going back to the 1860s.

The 1895 Polish government resigned a year later in the wake of several controversies, though Biliński himself suffered no major setbacks. He remained active in politics and returned to government soon thereafter. It was during his tenures as finance minister (1905–09 and 1909–11) that new divisions developed between Biliński and Polish colleagues who had again hoped he would use his position to increase investment into Galicia. In particular, Polish leaders were frustrated that Bohemia received priority over Galicia in a major water channel project. With Głąbiński leading the charge, many Polish deputies accused Biliński of putting Austria before Poland when funding for the Dunaj-Odra-Wisła-Dniester connection was postponed. Biliński had acted under intense pressure from the Czechs. Yet Głąbiński's outrage was as much a personal as a political blow for the finance minister, and one likely driven by professional envy: Głąbiński, after all, benefited from Biliński's demise to secure a ministerial position.[12]

Głąbiński, however, was not Biliński's sole Polish adversary. Another was the Galician socialist deputy Herman Diamand, who grew up in an assimilated Jewish family and gained a reputation as a talented economist. There was also the socialist Ignacy Daszyński, who was famous for his eloquent parliamentary speeches and exquisite knowledge of German. Both men opposed the *bourgeois* government on ideological and practical grounds, and both accused Biliński of disregarding the interests of the working classes, favoring the *bourgeoisie*, and misusing his power.[13]

After 1918, Biliński's major critics were former colleagues and even friends who never forgot his decisions dating back to the 1880s. His subsequent confrontation with these men proved to be more severe than among those who had not known one another before 1918, as accusations from the past were often highly personalized. For example, in 1910 tensions among Polish deputies had caused a governmental crisis that precipitated Biliński's resignation. In 1912, the Polish newspaper *Słowo Polskie* published "The End of a Career," which heralded Biliński's political demise.[14] At age sixty-six, Biliński was clearly not the same man who went days without sleep while writing his *Habilitation* (professorial thesis). He was also, in all likelihood, less flexible than during his first tenure as minister of railways, when he traversed the monarchy and beyond on *his* trains. Nevertheless, Biliński disproved his detractors and withstood this crisis of legitimacy, remaining politically active and relevant throughout the war. Biliński simply saw no conflict of interest between nationalism and imperial loyalty. Believing that the Poles could best realize their potential under the Habsburgs, he supported the preservation of the empire through its last days, and almost beyond.

Negotiating with the Ukrainians

Even as Biliński was losing the support of some Polish colleagues, his status in Vienna and relationships with German-Austrian colleagues remained positive.

Moreover, he made several decisions that won him the backing of Ukrainian colleagues, especially as Biliński was one of the few Poles who believed adamantly in national compromise.

In 1908, and with the endorsement of Głąbiński (then head of the Polish parliamentary representation), Biliński organized a meeting with leading Ukrainian deputies, including Mykola Wasylko and Kost' Levytskyi. Held at his office in the Austrian-Hungarian Bank in Vienna, the meeting aimed to resolve the escalating crisis following the assassination of the Polish governor of Galicia, Andrzej Potocki, by the Ukrainian student Myroslav Sichynskyi. The assassination was counterproductive, as Potocki had been willing to make concessions to the Ukrainians. Nevertheless, it had turned many Ukrainians toward political violence, which gave their Polish opponents further pretext for repression. By 1908, compromise between the two peoples seemed impossible. Biliński was one of the few politicians who supported negotiations in order to prevent violence.

The men who shared the table in Biliński's office in 1908 had known one another for years. Mykola Wasylko, originally from Bukovina, was one of the most influential Ukrainian statesmen in Vienna. Although he was almost twenty years Biliński's junior, Wasylko represented an older generation of conservative statesmen who had expressed their loyalty toward Austria. The Austrians treasured his commitment, and in 1906 made Wasylko the only Ukrainian representative on an electoral reform commission.[15] He was also known for being the only Ukrainian deputy who supported Biliński's candidacy in the government.[16]

Although Wasylko never served as a minister, he seemed to have access to many important people in Vienna and was famous for political intrigue. His unique leverage was linked to the government's assessment of Galicia's Ukrainian population as potentially dangerous due to its Russian ties. Vienna had long pursued counter-intelligence against Russia by exploiting these cross-border Ukrainian connections. In fact, many of the Ukrainians used in these operations were Austrian parliamentary deputies who were reimbursed for their work. Wasylko was one of them. In 1912, the Austrian bank *Creditanstalt* paid off his personal debts of 350,000 crowns. The government itself negotiated the pay-off as a reward for Wasylko's services, though what these services entailed exactly has never been entirely clear.[17]

In 1908, the men who met at Biliński's office reached an unprecedented compromise: the Polish representation in the Austrian parliament pledged to coordinate its efforts with Ukrainian deputies. The Ukrainians thus secured a number of important political positions, including vice-president of the provincial administration and vice-head of the provincial diet. Polish deputies also pledged to support Ukrainian candidates for positions in the ministries of education and of Galicia. Once implemented, the agreement gave Ukrainians access to postings they had regularly been denied under the current regimen of Polish obstruction.

It is virtually certain that the compromise was achieved through Biliński's initiatives, especially considering Głąbiński's animosity toward the Ukrainians. Indeed, in 1908, Biliński likely felt greater affinity for Wasylko than Głąbiński. Głąbiński's colleagues from Polish National Democracy responded to the agreement by accusing Biliński of betraying Polish national interests. The leading National-Democrat, Stanisław Skarbek, even remarked that Biliński "should rather have confessed to his Ukrainianess."[18] In 1908, Biliński seems to have embraced politics by compromise wholeheartedly. Skarbek's references to Biliński's "Ukrainianess" should thus be taken with a grain of salt, even if Biliński often did place Ukrainian and Jewish interests above those of many Poles. His decisions in 1908, in any case, would long remain in Polish national memory and thus become an obstacle to his integration into the postwar Polish state.

Wartime Transformations

In 1912, Biliński became head of the joint finance ministry now responsible for both the Austrian and Hungarian parts of the Empire, rather than just the Austrian half. That same year, he was appointed governor of Bosnia and Herzegovina, which had been annexed to the Empire in 1908. In the summer of 1914, Biliński negotiated Vienna's response to the Sarajevo crisis, eventually supporting Austria's entrance into the war against Serbia and Russia. Biliński sincerely believed that the war offered a chance of revival for the Monarchy, as well as an unprecedented opportunity to unify all partitioned Polish territories under Habsburg rule and in federal affiliation with Vienna.

More immediately, however, the war presented profound difficulties for Poles, many of whom found themselves fighting against one another for different countries. Most Galicians rallied behind the Habsburgs. Yet Poles from the Russian Empire were divided between St. Petersburg and the Austro-German coalition. These divisions were influenced by a combination of contrasting geopolitical views and the political status of the Polish territories. Thus Roman Dmowski's radical nationalists in Warsaw considered Russia to be the lesser evil compared to Germany, while Józef Piłsudski's socialists looked to Vienna.[19] During the war, Piłsudski and Biliński allied their efforts toward the creation of a new Poland under Austrian rule.

United Poland actually did become less of a pipedream during the war. In 1915, Germany conquered most of the Polish territories, which meant that the Central Powers controlled nearly all of partitioned Poland. In April 1916, the Austro-Hungarian foreign minister István Burián departed for Berlin to discuss the future of these Polish territories with his German counterpart. "We were certain," Biliński later recalled, "that the Germans would give us the Kingdom of Poland, that they had no other alternative."[20]

Yet the Berlin negotiations did not go as planned. The Germans instead hoped to create a Polish buffer state between themselves and Russia. Highly disappointed, Biliński suspected that Burián had sabotaged the plans because, as a Hungarian, he opposed the transition from dualism to trialism.[21] Burián resigned in December 1916. The new foreign minister, Ottokar Czernin, pledged to support the Poles toward the creation of a new Polish territorial unit under the Habsburgs. Yet he proved no more successful in doing so than his Magyar predecessor. Frustrated with the failures of Austrian diplomacy, Biliński abandoned his plan of a united Poland and focused on securing improved federal status for Galicia.[22]

Biliński's Polish-Austrian schemes suffered further setback during the war's final year. In February, news leaked of the Brest-Litovsk treaty between Germany and Bolshevik Russia, which was eager to exit the war. Known in German as the "peace for bread" (*Brotfrieden*), the treaty was in part designed to secure a steady food supply (mainly grain) from Ukraine to Germany. As such, the Austro-Hungarian and German Empires signed a separate treaty with the emergent government of the Ukrainian republic. Now some eight million Ukrainians from former tsarist Russia were technically citizens of a new Ukrainian state.

These territorial agreements had serious consequences for the Polish nation. The Chełm region (which the Germans conquered earlier in the war) became a self-administered territory. Czernin also consented to the division of Galicia—the western part, centered in Kraków, would remain in Poland, while eastern Galicia around Lwów (Lemberg/L'viv) was turned over to the new Ukrainian republic.[23] Many Poles considered this tantamount to a "fourth partition of Poland."[24]

For Habsburg-true Biliński, Brest-Litovsk entailed the additional frustration of being kept in the dark by his own government. He first learned of the agreement from Mykola Wasylko, who was one of the Ukrainian delegates to the talks appointed by Foreign Minister Czernin. Czernin himself had strived to keep the negotiations secret from the Poles.[25] In his memoirs, Biliński would write that Wasylko proved "more reliable than the emperor and his ministers."[26]

Despite these setbacks, Biliński did not give up on his commitment to the dynasty. In February 1918, he proclaimed the Poles' loyalty to Emperor Karl thus: "We stand by you, we stand and we will always stand!"[27] By then, even some of the most-conservative Poles endorsed independence. Polish journalists accused Biliński of state treason, and derisive images of him plastered the walls of public toilets in Lwów.[28] Over the years, a hurtful narrative took shape in Polish collective memory: at the time of building an independent Poland, Leon Biliński had described himself as "*ein alter Oesterreicher*," an old Austrian.[29] His reputation as someone who supported the Habsburgs through their last days became one of the chief obstacles to the former minister's full assimilation into Poland.

The Transition to the New Polish State

These declarations of dynastic loyalty were indeed untimely: by fall 1918, it was clear that the Empire would not survive the war. Coupled with Woodrow Wilson's call for "an independent Polish state" in his Fourteen Points (January 1918), the founding of modern Poland seemed only a matter of time. In October 1918, the Polish liquidation commission was created in Lublin to supervise the transition of authority from Austrians to Poles. In November, a provisional Polish government was created under the leadership of Ignacy Daszyński. In late 1918, Poland's socialist leader Józef Piłsudski was freed from German imprisonment, and he made his way to Warsaw. In early 1919, he was appointed Poland's temporary head of state and the first free elections took place across Poland, except for Galicia.[30]

In February 1919, during the first parliamentary sessions in Warsaw, the underlying tensions between deputies from different parts of Poland were already apparent. The Polish historian Adam Pragier commented that "socialist deputies from Małopolska could easily find consensus with the *stanczyky* and *podoliaky* (branches of Galician conservatives) because all of them used to meet in the Pucher coffee house in Vienna."[31] But Warsaw knew of no such coffeehouse political tradition, and Poles from the Russian partitions generally had little experience of parliamentary politics. *Russian* Warsaw, *German* Poznań, and *Austrian* Lwów more closely resembled their former metropolises—St. Petersburg, Berlin, and Vienna respectively—than they did each other.[32] And largely agricultural Galicia, with some 20 percent of new Poland's population, was the most backward of all the partitions. Yet of the three former empires, Austria-Hungary provided the best example of political participation for its subject peoples.

Although the proportion of Galicians in the Polish parliament was half that of their overall share of the population (44 out of 432 delegates, or 10 percent of the *Sejm*), the perception that Galicians were overrepresented in Warsaw shaped politics in post-1918 Poland.[33] Poland's radical right had long been hostile to Germany and German-speakers generally. So when Austrian Poles moved to Russian Warsaw, the right readily invented a new adversary—the "Galician Import," the "procrastinators, illiterates, and idlers" arriving from Vienna, Lwów, and Kraków. And if the writer acknowledged the presence of valuable and qualified officials among these foreign masses, he insisted that most were incompetent laggards who could not meet the tasks of a new Poland.[34]

Biliński embodied these tensions between peoples from different regions of Poland. Imperial past was one object of controversy. When Piłsudski invited him to join the government in July 1919, he also warned the finance minister that he would face more than just economic problems—Poland's right fundamentally opposed his political involvement, while Galician nationalists still resented his support of the Habsburgs and attempts to compromise with the Ukrainians during the Empire's last months.³⁵ Then there was the issue of Biliński's mixed family and German ties—a norm in the Empire that became a liability in independent Poland. The statesman would later recall how parliamentary colleagues addressed him in German even when he started the conversation in Polish. As for his German wife, Jósefa Seichs, she faced the additional hardship of seeing her family divided by the Austro-Czech border. But Jósefa, who had learned Polish and moved to Warsaw with her husband, did not allow idle talk about their "Germanness" to intimidate her. Rather, she encouraged Biliński's participation in the government and held doggedly to her routine of travelling between Warsaw and Vienna with a German maid.³⁶

The fact was that Biliński's experience and contacts were badly needed in the new Poland. Despite his complex and compromised national allegiances, he was the only Pole among the partitions ever to have served as finance minister.³⁷ His professional reputation, moreover, was impeccable.³⁸ Thus, the more pragmatic conservative circles in Kraków and Lwów, as well as some of Warsaw's leading periodicals, rallied behind Biliński. As the *Kurier Polski* commented in August 1919, "Dr. Biliński is the only person capable of carrying out such [economic] work."³⁹

Nor did Biliński disappoint his supporters. In August 1919, his professionalism impressed a delegation of the British, Belgian, and French businessmen who had secretly come to Warsaw to negotiate the sale of the Austrian and German oil platforms in Galicia.⁴⁰ Shortly thereafter, Biliński collaborated with the joint Prime Minister/Foreign Minister Ignacy Paderewski to secure foreign credits for Poland. A member of the American delegation negotiating the credits commented on the "efficiency with which the Polish government processed the agreement, [which] reminded me of American methods of arranging matters."⁴¹

Nevertheless, several of Biliński's financial decisions produced domestic political tensions. Perhaps the best example was his insistence on retaining the German mark as a temporary currency rather than too quickly introducing the Polish złoty. While Biliński worried that the new currency could harm the country's feeble economy, his nationalist opponents denounced this as yet another sign of the former Habsburg minister's Germanic affinity.⁴² Only in the early 1920s would Biliński be vindicated by the success of his currency strategy. In some circles, he was even hailed as a national savior.⁴³

In the meantime, more controversies were to come. In September 1919, Biliński ordered a cash payout without parliamentary approval and thus in defiance of the Polish constitution (though not, notably, of the old Austrian constitution). For his increasingly hardened Galician opponent Herman Diamand, this was tantamount to operating "as if he still lived under Franz Joseph, the benevolent emperor." As the socialist Diamand continued in a speech to parliament:

Mr. Biliński cannot rid himself of the instinct of an absolutist minister. How can one sleep not knowing whether tonight the finance minister may initiate another assault and issue several, several thousand, or several thousands of millions of new banknotes?[44]

In the Empire, Diamand had opposed Biliński's ministerial decisions on the grounds that they favored the *bourgeoisie*. After 1919, he argued just as strenuously that Biliński's imperial mindset could inflict serious financial damage on the new state.

Yet if Diamand did not hesitate to question the finance minister's support for Polish republican institutions, he never went so far—or sunk so low—as to accuse Biliński of not being Polish enough. After all, like his antagonist, Diamand too had made a career in imperial Austria and was a Jew raised in a German-speaking household.[45] And while he certainly was a staunch patriot, Diamand also regularly had to defend his allegiance to Warsaw.[46] Thus, when he extolled to parliament in 1920 "the centripetal tendencies" of Galicia–Małopolska, he was interrupted by claims that Galicia was more drawn to Vienna than Warsaw. "To the Polish center," clarified Diamand, who stressed that "all political developments in Małopolska were shaped by the perception of its earlier belonging to the common Polish state."[47]

Diamand's opposition to Biliński provoked questions from other deputies as well. Many perceived that former Habsburg subjects would support each other in difficult situations, and were thus dubious of Diamand's critiques. As one delegate shouted in parliament: "Mr. [Diamand] knew him [Biliński] and supported his nomination!" In response, Diamand calmly explained: "I do not deny knowing Biliński . . . the very fact that I know people does not imply that they make good ministers."[48]

As for the finance minister himself, he justified his decisions by declaring political emergencies in Poland and warning that news of the dire economic situation could cause unnecessary panic.[49] However, when he was dismissed in November 1919, it was neither because of the payout nor the war, but rather due to his unpopular tax program. Nor was the dismissal particularly unusual, as none of Biliński's predecessors and few of his successors managed to retain their offices for more than a few months. In interwar Europe, Poland became famous for its frequent government rotations.

Another deputy who faced regular suspicion because his political ideals were not based on the national principle was Ignacy Daszyński, who actually hailed from Polish nobility. As a socialist educated in German institutions, Daszyński additionally suffered from his accented Polish.[50] When in February 1921, the Galician National Democrat Stanisław Głąbiński accused the Galician socialists of having joined German Social-Democracy, Daszyński retorted: "We had been members of a federation made up of Czechs, Poles, Ukrainians, Italians, and

Germans that constituted an organization of Austrian socialist deputies. And someone calling such an association a German socialist party admits to things that are false."[51]

Pre-1918 principles and connections thus proved a mixed bag in postwar Poland. Early on, people who knew each other from their respective empires were drawn together by a shared past and political legacy. Yet these commonalities began to come apart once Poland's political establishment solidified along party lines rather than regional ones. Thereafter, one's memories of the pre-1918 past could determine whether political leaders worked together constructively or, at the other extreme, developed mutually antagonistic relationships.

In this respect, Daszyński played a key role in Biliński's postwar political life. In the summer of 1920, with Bolshevik armies threatening Poland's capital, the newly appointed prime minister made it possible for several of his most vulnerable colleagues to leave Warsaw. Biliński, because of his "Germanness," was one of them. So too, ironically, was his chief critic, the socialist Herman Diamand. The latter moved to Berlin to manage the propaganda office there. Biliński, of course, resettled in Vienna. Both men, widely criticized for lacking the proper national credentials, were now working toward improving Poland's image abroad.[52]

The timing, moreover, was crucial. The Polish-Soviet war was putting the new state under increasing international pressure for its territorial claims in the east and its treatment of minorities at home. These tensions had first surfaced at the Paris Peace Conference, when the British Prime Minister David Lloyd George called attention to Poland's claims to territories that were not quite Polish, and European diplomats noted that there were more Ukrainians than Poles in Eastern Galicia.[53] Now Daszyński responded to critiques of Poland's colonial ambitions by establishing a propaganda office. Diamand and Biliński thus departed for Berlin and Vienna with the nationalist aim of justifying Poland's expansion.

Return to Vienna

Vienna was a second home for Biliński, as it was for many others from his generation. His return to politics here thus took little effort. Upon arriving in the former imperial capital on 14 August 1920, Biliński immersed himself in the city's active social and political life—meeting with Austrian deputies, interviewing with journalists, and giving talks on Poland's political situation. Biliński later recalled that most Austrians were sympathetic toward Poland, and he had particularly fond memories of meetings with his old acquaintance, the Social Democrat leader Dr. Karl Renner. After the Empire's collapse, Renner became the first chancellor of independent Austria. He later served as Foreign

Minister. Biliński also met with former employees from the imperial finance ministry—divided by national borders, they were now crossing paths in Vienna on financial business related to their new states.

In Poland, the Russian army had suffered surprising defeats. Biliński observed the Miracle on the Wisła (Vistula), which saved Warsaw, from a safe distance. He and his colleagues working to promote Poland abroad were soon recalled to the capital. Under pressure from parliament, Daszyński dissolved the propaganda office in early September. Polish nationalists now considered their claims for territories and strategies for seizing them as fully legitimate, so that no further justifications or propaganda were necessary. Yet Daszyński could not conceal his displeasure with Biliński's conduct at Vienna, which he thought had displayed too much loyalty toward Austria.[54]

A new assignment came along while Biliński was in Vienna, and it had long-term effects. In August, Poland's finance ministry invited Biliński to join the international commission that was supervising the liquidation of the Austro-Hungarian bank. Initiated on 1 January 1920, the liquidation process involved issuing disbursements to the successor states, and this was causing financial complications.[55] Moreover, many members of the liquidation commission had worked under Biliński in the imperial finance ministry. These included the bank's director, the Austrian economist Alexander Spitzmüller, as well as the Italian Giuseppe Luxardo, the Romanian Gregor Hostuc, the Czech Josef Hladký, and the Yugoslav Rudolf Ban. Poland itself was represented by Wilhelm Binder.[56] In fact, the only commission member who had *not* previously worked with Biliński was the American Edward Whitmann. And all of them had by now started careers in their respective states.

Of course, the new national circumstances were bound to cause tension among the former colleagues. Yet it was their relations with the Austrians that were especially complicated. Spitzmüller noted how Czechoslovakia's finance minister, Alois Rašín, unscrupulously used resources and institutions to Austria's detriment. But it was Biliński himself who, ironically, raised the most protests against the Austrians. As Spitzmüller recalled, Biliński "surpassed his colleagues in other delegations by violent procedures against the institution for the sole purpose of gaining favors for his government."[57]

Biliński now found himself in the polar opposite position from that in 1910, when his Polish colleagues charged him with foregoing Poland's national interests in his work as joint finance minister. In 1920, his former imperial colleagues accused Biliński of defending Poland to the point of hurting their own nation-states. Of course, none of these new states could rival the Empire. Yet by seemingly turning against the others in order to secure the best possible financial arrangement for Poland, Biliński damaged whatever friendship had remained after 1918. Indeed, his involvement with the liquidation commission would destroy Biliński's reputation among his former imperial colleagues.

The issue that ultimately led to this break was the division of the Austro-Hungarian gold reserves. According to Article 206 of the Saint-Germain Treaty, Austria was obliged to pay reparations for its role in initiating the war.[58] The gold reserves were to be used for a currency reform in the struggling new state.[59] But in 1920, the liquidation commission voted to divide the 65 million in gold crowns among the successor states, a decision that would have devastating consequences for Austria's fragile economy (worse even than that of Poland and Czechoslovakia).[60] Just as Austria's government was trying to secure credits to pay off old debts, maintain reparation payments, and cover domestic expenditures, the liquidation commission put the state's very survival at stake.[61]

Karl Renner took the lead in defense of Austrian interests, insisting that the commission's claims to the gold were illegitimate:

> On what grounds do these nation-states lay claim to this gold? For starters, we must recognize that this gold is no longer in the possession of the Austro-Hungarian Bank. As a result of currency reforms dating back to 1902 and 1908, the Austrian and the Hungarian governments respectively monopolized the right to 600 million gold crowns. They never renounced these rights, and thus retained ownership of this gold.[62]

In a later passage, Renner did not hesitate to name names: "These measures were enforced by members of the nation-states, such as Mr. Luxardo, who had earlier worked in our finance ministry. The other one among these people is an interesting and distinctive personality, Herr Leon Biliński, a one-time finance minister."[63] The bank director Spitzmüller asked rhetorically: "Who are those people who decided to rob Austria and Hungary of its gold reserves?"[64] Many Austrian deputies also knew that Biliński had not been a neutral party when it came to Austria-Hungary. In March 1921, the Social Democratic leader Otto Bauer reminded his colleagues of Biliński's early endorsement of Austria's entrance into the war with Serbia (and Russia).[65]

It is difficult to assess whether Biliński's choices were driven by political considerations. Before 1918, his Polish colleagues generally regarded him as an entirely apolitical professional. Yet after the war, his Austrian colleagues discovered political aspects to his economic decisions, which led some to assume that Biliński had intentionally inflicted financial damage on Austria in order to improve his image in Poland. The political history of interwar Central Europe has been partially shaped by the perception that the new nation-states emerged out of just such treachery.[66]

Never again would Biliński be welcomed as "an old friend" among his Austrian colleagues. Yet in Poland, his role in the division of the Austro-Hungarian gold reserves was met with acclaim. Even the most radical right-wing periodicals, he recalled, welcomed his participation on the liquidation commission and praised the division of the reserves, part of which would land in Poland.[67] The gold intervention proved detrimental to Austria and somewhat (though not overwhelmingly) favorable for Poland. As for Biliński, it helped to seal his international disgrace.

A good example of this increasing isolation in the international arena came in early 1921, when Czechoslovakia called for an economic conference of the Habsburg successor states. Since 1918, Biliński had participated in several such discussions of the most important financial issues facing Poland and its relations with the other new states. But this time he was not invited to join the Polish delegation to the meeting on tariff and trade agreements, which was held in the Italian (formerly Austrian) town of Portorose, near Trieste.[68] Rumors later leaked that the Italian ambassador to Poland, Francesco Tommasini, had mobilized efforts to prevent Biliński from participating in the economic forum.

Tommasini was one of the few diplomats who served in Poland without interruption between 1918 and 1923, and the only ambassador to remain in Warsaw in August 1920.[69] He thus knew the nuances of Polish politics, as well as the men in power. In 1921, the Austrians had turned to Tommasini in order to prevent Biliński's participation in the Portorose conference.[70] Yet Poland also had good reason to anticipate Italian support. In 1919, the Polish Prime Minister Paderewski had discussed efforts to improve Poland's chances of securing Galicia with Tommasini.[71] And in March 1921, Tommasini promised Italy's support for Polish claims to Galicia under the condition that Poland would agree to join an anti-Habsburg alliance.[72]

Ukrainians in the Postwar Order

Fears of a Habsburg restoration unnerved Europe from 1918 to 1939.[73] Yet despite international conflict and the dire postwar financial circumstances, most Habsburg successors and national statesmen endorsed their new nation-states. Even most Austrians favored building a national republic over a multinational monarchy.

Of course, competing claims to resources, territories, and the people who populated them complicated the nation-state building process and strained relations between former colleagues. This was certainly the case with Biliński and his imperial ally from Ukraine, Mykola Wasylko. Like most Poles, Biliński endorsed the Polish claim to Galicia. Wasylko, meanwhile, advocated the province's division into two parts. In 1916, he informed Biliński that if the Poles insisted on keeping all of Galicia for themselves, the Ukrainians would turn to violence.[74]

In November, the Polish-Ukrainian conflict over Galicia exploded into war. Ukrainian battlefield successes, however, were short-lived. By July 1919, the Polish army reconquered most of Galicia from the Ukrainians, though conflict over the region would persist through 1921.

In 1918, Biliński had come to believe that the political concessions he made to the Ukrainians in 1908, and which had drawn so much ire from the National Democrats, had paved the way for Ukrainian military successes in 1918. As he wrote in his memoir: "Who knows if the blood spilled by our (Polish) brothers was not a consequence of a mistake in 1908; were it not for 1908, would [the Ukrainians] ever have felt themselves so secure and achieved similar positions in Austrian politics and government?"[75] Unsurprisingly, Galicia's Polish Nationalist leader, Stanisław Głąbiński, also attributed Polish problems in the region to Biliński's 1908 concessions to the Ukrainians.[76] During the fights over Galicia, Głąbiński spoke bluntly in parliament on the Ukrainian atrocities and requested help for Polish refugees: "We all know that the Ukrainian armies treat the Poles barbarically."[77]

Wasylko observed these events from a safe distance. From 1919 to 1923, he served in Ukrainian diplomatic representations in Vienna, Berlin, and Bern, working first on behalf of Western Ukraine and later for the Ukrainian People's Republic in Kiev. Although he was one of the few politicians capable of bridging the two Ukraines, his reputation as a political manipulator had not changed.[78] Poles, Austrians, foreign diplomats, and even his Ukrainian colleagues all treated Wasylko with a certain degree of distrust.[79] In early 1919, Wasylko tried to secure weapons for the Ukrainians fighting the Poles in Galicia. In June of that year, Hungary's short-lived communist ruler, Béla Kun, received an anonymous letter from Bern advocating the creation of a West Ukrainian socialist republic possibly centered in Budapest. Wasylko was not known for his leftist sympathies, but speculation soon emerged that he had been involved in this *démarche*.[80] A possible Soviet solution in western Ukraine also raised concerns around Europe.

After 1919, Wasylko represented the Ukrainian People's Republic (centered in Kiev) as concurrent ambassador to Italy, Germany, and Switzerland. By then, he had revised his earlier views on the Republic and come to believe that its only chance for survival lay in an alliance with Poland and Romania against Bolshevik Russia. He renewed contact with Biliński in order to advocate for such an alliance.[81] In September 1919, the Ukrainian diplomat Vasyl Onatsky commented that "Baron Wasylko . . . when he was still an ambassador to Berlin, played a very important role in the reconciliation between the Ukrainian People's Republic and Poland that eventually resulted in Poland's annexation of eastern Galicia and in the Warsaw agreements."[82]

In a letter to Kost' Levytskyi, his former colleague-deputy from the Austrian parliament, Wasylko explained:

> The Ukrainians must give up on everything that now hinders their alliance with Poland and Romania, which [both] have interests similar to that of Ukraine—i.e., to prevent the reconstruction of a great Russia. The sooner we agree to that, the sooner we will have the opportunity to work for the satisfaction of the national rights of our people, who would be left under Poland and Romania.[83]

Any Polish-Ukrainian alliance, Wasylko realized, would force the Ukrainians to cede Galicia to Poland. But he was willing to accept this sacrifice in order to ensure the survival of (any) Ukrainian political entity. In early 1920, Wasylko contacted Biliński and requested an invitation to Warsaw. Biliński refused, citing the reluctance of Poland's central government. In particular, Piłsudski allegedly believed that Wasylko's initiatives and, even, his presence in Warsaw would pose dangers to Poland's security.[84]

Although forbidden to travel to Warsaw, Wasylko could still influence Ukrainian politics. Thus, the idea of Polish-Ukrainian negotiations lived on. In April 1920, the head of the Ukrainian Republic, Symon Petlura, arrived in Warsaw for talks with Piłsudski that resulted in the signing of a Polish-Ukrainian alliance against Bolshevik Russia. In return for military assistance, Petlura renounced Kiev's claim to Western Ukraine (which largely corresponded to Galicia).[85] The treaty of Riga between Poland and Soviet Russia in March 1921 finalized the territorial settlements.[86] Most of Western Ukraine remained in Poland. In December 1922, the Ukrainian's People Republic around Kiev became part of the Soviet Union. Independent Ukraine ceased to exist.

Conclusion

Leon Biliński and Mykola Wasylko died in 1923 and 1924, respectively. By then, Poland and Austria were well ensconced in their new boundaries, with only minor territorial issues left to resolve. Ukraine appeared briefly on the European map between 1918 and 1922, and disappeared again thereafter. The rest of Europe, however, consolidated around new nation-states that remained in place until 1939.

The year 1920 seemed to signal the end of the generation of those who, born between the 1840s and 1860s, had matured politically and otherwise under the empire and now represented a poor fit for Europe's new postwar system. But 1920 did not, in fact, represent some stark break with the past, and continuities between the prewar and postwar periods were more significant than generational or political divides. Like many others, Biliński enjoyed a second career that proved as successful in Poland as it had been in the empire. A Habsburg statesman par excellence; a public servant committed to his government through its last days; a man more at home in Vienna than Warsaw—Biliński not only relocated to Poland late in life, but he eventually won the favor of its nationalist right.

Biliński's dilemmas in transitioning from one system to another—imperial Austria to national Poland—were by no means unique. And while it is true that he represented an older generation of conservatives who had strongly supported the Empire before 1918, the fact is that many of his contemporaries shared similar ideals. The foundational narratives of the successor states that stressed the long-term struggle of their politicians against imperial oppression had, in fact, little to do with the political realities of the Habsburg Empire.

Biliński embodied the viability of the Austrian inheritance and the importance of her institutions. Although they only formed a small group in Poland's parliament, former Austro-Hungarian political leaders played a crucial role in the creation and stabilization of the new Polish state. Practically all of them, including radical nationalists, had previously either endorsed or actively supported the Habsburg Empire. Many, with the exception of socialists, cooperated with the imperial government and held ministerial positions. Some, like Biliński, viewed the Empire's collapse as a personal tragedy. And most, including Biliński, changed their stance soon after the transition from empire to nation-state. Once a stranger in Warsaw who was rejected by Poland's radicals and criticized by his former Austrian colleagues, Biliński integrated into the national political establishment and secured his acceptance at home. This embrace of national politics was not only remarkably quick, it also proved irrevocable.

Throughout his years in Poland, Biliński continued to operate within the framework of his experience under the empire. There was a stark contrast between the sense of alienation and confrontation he experienced in Warsaw and the ease with which he blended in with former colleagues in Vienna. Even his political and financial decisions were made in reference to imperial models. Indeed, he was one of a large cohort of former *Austrians* dispersed across Europe after 1918 who remained true to the imperial legacy and tradition. One's adjustment or nonadjustment to the successor state was not contingent upon age or pre-1918 political/ideological affiliations. Many of Biliński's adversaries in Poland, including the nationalist Stanisław Głąbiński, acted within a similar framework by building their careers upon imperial precedents such as respect for institutions and negotiations. Hundreds of their peers from other countries did too. It was only the renewal of war in 1939 that destroyed their hope that stability and democracy in Europe could be preserved or restored. The beginning of World War II marked the end of an era in European history far more radically than did 1918.

Iryna Vushko is an Assistant Professor of History at Princeton University. She received her PhD in European History from Yale University in 2008. Her first book, *The Politics of Cultural Retreat: Imperial Bureaucracy in Austrian Galicia, 1772–1867*, came out with Yale University Press in 2015. She is currently completing her second monograph, tentatively titled *The Lost Fatherland: Europeans between Empire and Nation States, 1867–1939*.

Notes

1. For the general statistics, see Rudolf A. Mark, *Galizien unter österreichischer Herrschaft: Verwaltung-Kirche-Bevölkerung* (Marburg: Herder-Institut, 1994), 2.
2. In the nineteenth century, the term Ruthenian was commonly used to identify people who today call themselves Ukrainians. The term Ukrainian began to be used regularly in the late nineteenth century. To avoid confusion, I use Ukrainian throughout this chapter.
3. On Biliński's wife, Jósefa Seich, see Kazimierz Chłędowski, *Pamiętniki: Wiedeń, 1881–1901*, vol. 2 (Kraków: Wydawnictwo Literackie, 1957), 117–18.
4. The other was Joseph Redlich, who served as the Empire's last finance minister and later held that position in a government of the postwar Austrian republic. Both of his tenures, however, were short and unremarkable.
5. Leon Biliński, *Znamiona polityki narodowej i krajowej* (Kraków: Nakładem autora, 1882), ix.
6. Paolo Piccoli and Armando Vadagnini, *De Gasperi: un trentino nella storia d'Europa* (Soveria Mannelli: Rubbettino, 2004), 76.
7. Grzegorz Krzywiec, *Szowinizm po polsku: Przypadek Romana Dmowskiego (1866–1905)* (Warszawa: Instytut Historii PAN, Neriton, 2009), 349. On National Democracy (with a focus on Russia), see Brian Porter, *When Nationalism Began to Hate: Imagining Modern Politics in Nineteenth-Century Poland* (New York: Oxford University Press, 2000), chapter 8: "National Egoism," 189–232. On Polish National Democracy in Galicia, see Adam Wątor, *Narodowa Demokracja w Galicji do 1918 roku* (Szczecin: Wydawn. Naukowe Uniwersytetu Szczecińskiego, 2002), 53–55; 173–77 (on Głąbiński); and Roman Wapiński, *Narodowa Demokracja 1893–1939: Ze studiów nad dziejami myśli nacjonalistycznej* (Wrocław: Ossolineum, 1980), 122.
8. Harald Binder, *Galizien in Wien: Parteien, Wahlen, Fraktionen und Abgeordnete im Übergang zum Massenpolitik* (Wien: Verlag der Österreichischen Akademie der Wissenschaften, 2005), 41.
9. See: Hermann Strach, ed., *Geschichte der Eisenbahnen der Österreichisch-Ungarischen Monarchie*, vol. 2 (Vienna: K. Prochaska, 1898), 10. For a contemporary reference to Biliński's appointment: "Parlamentarisches," *Neue Freie Presse*, 11 January 1892, 3.
10. Strach, *Geschichte der Eisenbahnen*, vol. 2, 10.
11. A detailed analysis of the entire tenure of the "Polish government" is Waldemar Łazuga, *"Rządy polskie" w Austrii: Gabinet Kazimierza hr. Badeniego 1895–1897* (Poznań: Wydawnictwo Naukowe UAM, 1991).
12. For Biliński's interpretation of these events, see his memoir: *Wspomnienia: Dokumenty. 1846–1919*, vol. 1 (Warszawa: Nakładem Ksiegarni F. Hoesicka, 1924), 199–202. Głąbiński denied any personal motives: Stanisław Głąbiński, *Wspomnienie polityczne* (Prlplin: Nakładem i czcionkami drukarni i ksiegarni Sp. Z. O. O., 1939), 118, 124.
13. Ignacy Daszyński, *Pamiętniki* (Kraków: Nakładem Z. R. S. S. "Proletarjat," 1926), 38–41, 53–54; Herman Diamand, *Pamiętnik Hermana Diamanda zebrany z wyjątków listów do żony* (Kraków: Nakładem Tow. Uniwersytetu Robotniczego [TUR], 1932), 68.
14. Biliński, *Wspomnienia*, vol. 2, 203.
15. Czesław Partacz, *Od Badeniego do Potockiego: Stosunki polsko-ukraińskie w Galicji w latach 1888–1908* (Torún: Wydawnictwo Adam Marszałek, 1997), 193.
16. See Biliński, *Wspomnienia*, vol. 2, 155.

17. Alexander Spitzmüller Freiherr von Harmersbach, *Memoirs of Alexander Spitzmüller Freiherr von Harmersbach (1862–1953): Former Minister of Trade and Minister of Finance in the Austro-Hungarian Empire, Governor of the Austro-Hungarian Bank, Director-General of the Creditanstalt Bankverein*, translated by Carvel de Bussy (Boulder, CO: East European Monographs, 1987), 173.
18. Biliński, *Wspomnienia*, vol. 2, 156.
19. The choice of allies was shaped by geopolitical considerations. Dmowski believed that Russia's main sphere of expansion lay in the east (toward Central Asia) and that it did not include Poland. Germany, by contrast, was seen as posing a major geopolitical threat to Poland.
20. Bibilioteka Naukowa PAU i PAN w Krakowie, Rękopisy, N 7316 (hereafter BNPPK): Posiedzenia Kola Polskiego dnia 3.X. 1916, Przemówienie Je. Dr. L. Bilińskiego, 12.
21. Biliński, *Wspomnienia*, vol. 2, 64.
22. Ottokar Czernin, *Im Weltkriege*, 2nd ed. (Berlin: Verlegt bei Ullstein & Co, 1919), 280; Biliński, *Wspomnienia*, vol. 2, 159.
23. Chełm had earlier belonged to Russia, and it was occupied by Germany in 1916. Poles hoped that it would become part of Poland after the war.
24. Maciej Janowski, *Inteligencja wobec wyzwań nowoczesności: Dylematy ideowe polskiej demokracji liberalnej w Galicji w latach 1889–1914* (Warzsawa: Instytut Historii PAN, 1996), 74. On the "fourth partition," see also: Torsten Wehrhahn, *Die Westukrainische Volksrepublik: Zu den polnisch-ukrainischen Beziehungen und dem Problem der ukrainischen Staatlichkeit in den Jahren 1918 bis 1923* (Berlin: Weißensee Verlag, 2004), 67.
25. Wasylko's name has been variously transliterated as Vasylko, Wassilko, and Wasylko. On his involvement in Brest-Litovsk, see Czernin, *Im Weltkriege*, 336; Frank Golczewski, *Deutsche und Ukrainer 1914–1939* (Paderborn: Ferdinand Schöningh, 2010), 190; Biliński, *Wspomnienia*, vol. 2, 170; Theophil Hornykiewicz, *Ereignisse in der Ukraine 1914–1922: Deren Bedeutung und historische Hintergründe*, vol. 1 (Philadelphia: W. K. Lypynsky East European Research Institute, 1966), 297.
26. Biliński, *Wspomnienia*, vol. 2, 170.
27. "Oesterreichischer Reichsrat," *Neue Freie Presse*, 28 February 1918, 2.
28. On this episode: Biliński, *Wspomnienia*, vol. 2, 163.
29. Ibid., 176.
30. Galicia was at the time engulfed by the Polish-Ukrainian war. The decision was reached in Warsaw not to hold elections there. Instead, the forty-four Polish deputies to the Austrian parliament secured their seats in the new Polish parliament.
31. Adam Pragier, *Czas przeszły dokonany* (London: Świderski, 1966), 227.
32. For an interesting analysis of different political models in the interwar nation-states, see Hugh Seton-Watson, *Eastern Europe Between the Wars, 1918–1941* (New York: Routledge, 1986), 150. A good overview of the history of interwar Poland is Antony Polonsky, *Politics in Independent Poland, 1921–1939: The Crisis of Constitutional Government* (Oxford: Oxford University Press, 1972).
33. On the first Sejm, the number of deputies, and their party affiliations, see Michał Pietrzak, *Rządy Parlamentarne w Polsce w latach 1919–1926* (Warszawa: Książka i Wiedza, 1969), 87.
34. "Import galicyjski," *Czas*, 5 March 1919.

35. On the National Democratic (Endek) Party's campaign against Biliński, see "Powolanie Dr. Bilińskiego," *Czas*, 1 August 1919; "Biliński w Warszawie," *Kurier Polski*, 29 July 1919, 2; "Dr. Biliński—ministrem skarbu," *Kurier Polski*, 2 August 1919, 1.
36. Biliński, *Wspomnenia*, vol. 2, 147.
37. J. D., "Dr. Biliński," *Kurier Polski*, 2 August 1919, 1.
38. For example, see Joseph Redlich's assessment of Biliński as one of a very few suitable candidates for the position of finance minister in 1909, in Fritz Fellner, ed., *Schicksalsjahre Österreichs: 1908–1919; Das politische Tagebuch Josef Redlichs*, vol. 1: 1908–1914 (Graz: Böhlau, 1953), 5–7.
39. "Dr. Biliński," *Kurier Polski*, 2 August 1919, 1.
40. On this secret meeting, see Archiwum Akt Nowych (hereafter AAN), Akta Juliusza Twardowskiego (hereafter AJT), folder no. 45, p. 80: Telegram Szyfrowy, Nr. 25 (14 August 1919). On the Galician oil, see Alison Fleig Frank, *Oil Empire: Visions of Prosperity in Austrian Galicia* (Cambridge, MA: Harvard University Press, 2005).
41. O'Laughina, "Oświadczenie," *Kurier Warszawski*, 5 December 1919, 2. Paderewski also served as Poland's Foreign Minister in 1919.
42. Biliński, *Wspomnienia*, vol. 2, 307.
43. Guibal-Roland, *La Vie Polonaise: Observations d'un commerçant* (Paris: E. de Boccard, 1921), 143.
44. SSPSP, N 119 (13 February 1920), Poseł Diamand, CXIX/33–34.
45. Diamand regularly corresponded with his father in German. See his letter from 1898: NBSL, Diamand 31, Krakau (2 September 1898), 127.
46. His son, for example, had a typically Polish name that has no equivalent in German: Zdisław. See a letter from Zdisław to his father: NBSL, Diamand 32/1, Fordon (23.VII.1920), 50.
47. SSPSP (14 January 1920), Poseł Diamand, CX/14.
48. SSPSP, N 119 (13 February 1920), Poseł Diamand, CXIX/34.
49. Biliński, *Wspomnienia*, vol. 2, 218.
50. Chłedowski, *Pamiętniki*, vol. 2, 335.
51. SSPSP, 28 (10 February 1921), Poseł Daszyński, p. CCVIII/68.
52. On the offices of propaganda: Walentyna Najdus, *Ignacy Daszyński: 1866–1936* (Warszawa: Czytelnik, 1988), 435–37.
53. See excerpts from the Versailles conference: Klaus Schwabe, ed., *Quellen zum Friedensschluss von Versailles* (Darmstadt: Wissenschaftliche Buchgesellschaft, 1997): Paris (5 June 1919, 11 Uhr), 342.
54. Biliński, *Wspomnienia*, vol. 2, 329.
55. For months, international efforts to stop new emissions led nowhere. See Alois Rašín, *Financial Policy of Czecho-Slovakia During the First Year of Its History* (Oxford: Oxford University Press, 1923), 19–22. On the negotiations between the Czechoslovak government and the bank, see Karel Leopold, *Vzpomínky: z prvých dob ministerstva financí. Díl I. Část revuální*. V červnu 1928, 28, available on the Czech Ministry of Finance website: http://www.mfcr.cz/cs/o-ministerstvu/sluzby-verejnosti/odborna-knihovna/z-historie-mf/2013/historicke-publikace-o-ministerstvu-fina-13236.
56. AAN, PUL, no. 93: An Seine Exzellenz Herrn Vizegouverneur des österreichisch-ungarischen Bank von PAP in Wien 20. Dezember 1919; AAN, PUL, N 93, Likwidacja banku austro-węgierskiego: Sprawozdanie z posiedzeń Komitetu dyrektywnego i Rady Generalnej Banku austrowęgierskiego z 31 sierpnia 1920.

57. Spitzmüller Freiherr von Harmersback, *Memoirs of Alexander Spitzmüller*, 247.
58. The Saint-Germain agreements were signed in September 1919 between the victorious powers and Austria. On the treaty's relevant provisions, see Hanns Leo Mikoletzky, *Österreichische Zeitgeschichte vom Ende der Monarchie bis zum Abschluss des Staatsvertrages 1955* (Vienna: Austria-Edition, 1964), 76–81; Fritz Fellner, "Der Vertrag von St. Germain," in *Österreich, 1918–1938: Geschichte der Ersten Republik*, ed. Erika Weinzierl and Kurt Skalnik (Graz: Styria Verlag, 1983), 85–106.
59. Jerzy Michalski, *Traktat pokojowy w Saint-Germain a obciążenie Polski* (Kraków: nakł. Krakowskiej Spółki Wydawniczej, 1920), 13.
60. At the end of November, the bank's entire gold reserve was calculated at 239.5 million crowns in gold coin (*Goldmünze*) and 49.5 million crowns in gold change (*Goldwechseln*). "Die Nationalstaaten und der Goldschatz der Österreichisch-ungarischen Bank," *Neue Freie Presse*, 23 February 1921, 2.
61. On Austria's debt, see Sitzungen der Konstituierenden Nationalversammlung der Republik Österreich (hereafter SNRÖ) 73 Sitzung (20 April 1920), Seipel, 2118. See also Mikoletzky, *Österreichische Zeitgeschichte*, 43.
62. SNRÖ (1 March 1921), Renner, 467.
63. Ibid., 468.
64. On the emotional aspects of the liquidation, see: Spitzmüller Freiherr von Harmersback, *Memoirs of Alexander Spitzmüller*, 247.
65. SNRÖ (1 March 1921), Dr. Bauer, 468.
66. One book that expresses such views is G. E. R. Gedye, *Heirs to the Habsburgs* (Bristol: Arrowsmith, 1932).
67. Biliński, *Wspomnienia*, vol. 2, 342.
68. On Portorose, see Rawi Abdelal, "Purpose and Privation: Nation and Economy in Post-Habsburg Europe and Post-Soviet Eurasia," *East European Politics and Societies* 16, no. 3 (Fall 2002): 898–933. See also American and Austrian newspaper reports from 1921: "Mögliche Verschiebung der Konferenz von Portoroße," *Neue Freie Presse*, 23 February 1921, 1; and "Porto Rosa Conference Postponed," *The New York Times* 27 October 1921, 20.
69. Francesco Tommasini, *La Risurrezione della Polonia* (Milano: Fratelli Trevers, 1925). On Tommasini, see also Stanisław Sierpowski, *L'Italia e la ricostituzione del nuovo stato polacco, 1915–1921* (Wrocław: Ossolineum, 1979), 24.
70. Biliński, *Wspomnienia*, vol. 2, 357.
71. Mariapina Di Simone, ed., *Documenti per la storia delle relazioni italo-polacche, 1918–1940* (Roma: Ministero per i Beni Culturali e Ambientali, 1998), no. 39: Il ministro a Varsavia, Tommasini, al ministro degli esteri, Scialoja (Varsavia, 9. Dicembre 1919), 178–79.
72. Ibid., no. 85: Il ministro a Varsavia, Tommasini, al ministro degli esteri, Sforza (Varsavia, 31. maggio 1921), 310–11. On Italy's support of Poland as a buffer state against Russia, see also Domenico Caccamo, "Governi e partiti italiani di fronte alla Guerra russo-polacca (aprile-ottobre 1920)," in *"Polonia Restituta": l'Italia e la ricostituzione della Polonia 1918–1921*, ed. Marta Herling (Milano: Centro di studi sull'Europa orientale, 1992), 35–53.
73. On postwar restoration attempts in Hungary, see Gordon Brook-Shepherd, *The Last Habsburg* (London: Weybright and Talley, 1968), 256–86. On Habsburg restoration plans, particularly surrounding Poland and Ukraine, see Timothy Snyder, *The Red Prince: The Secret Lives of a Habsburg Archduke* (New York: Basic Books, 2008).

74. Biliński, *Wspomnienia*, vol. 2, 185.
75. Ibid., 165.
76. Głąbiński, *Wspomnienia polityczne*, 166.
77. SSPSP (1 July 1919), Poseł Głąbiński, *Wspomnienia*, LIII.
78. Cited after Felix Höglinger, *Ministerpräsident Heinrich Graf Clam-Martinic* (Graz: Böhlau, 1964), 203.
79. On Ukrainians' distrust of Wasylko, see Isaak Mazepa, *Ukraïna v ognì j burì revolûciï, 1917–1921* (Kyiv: Tempora, 2003), 248.
80. Ibid., 198.
81. Dmytro Doroshenko, *Moi spomyny pro nedavnie mynule, 1914–1920* (Kyiv: Tempora, 2007), 236; Mazepa, *Ukraïna v ognì*, 287.
82. Ievhen Onatskyi, "Pid omoforom barona V. Vasylka," *Ukrainskyi istoryk* 65–68, no. 1–4 (1980): 122.
83. Ibid., 123: Wasylko to Kost Levytskyi (6 November 1919).
84. Biliński, *Wspomnienia*, vol. 2, 299.
85. On the treaty of Warsaw, see Timothy Snyder, *Sketches from a Secret War: A Polish Artist's Mission to Liberate Soviet Ukraine* (New Haven: Yale University Press, 2005), 8. For an overview of the Polish-Soviet war in English, see Norman Davies, *White Eagle, Red Star: The Polish-Soviet War 1919–1920* (London: Macdonald, 1972).
86. A fine analysis of the Treaty of Riga is Jerzy Borzęcki, *The Soviet-Polish Peace of 1921 and the Creation of Interwar Europe* (New Haven: Yale University Press, 2008).

Bibliography

Abdelal, Rawi. "Purpose and Privation: Nation and Economy in Post-Habsburg Europe and Post-Soviet Eurasia." *East European Politics and Societies* 16, no. 3 (Fall 2002): 898–933.

Biliński, Leon. *Wspomnienia: Dokumenty. 1846–1919.* 2 vols. Warszawa: Nakładem Ksiegarni F. Hoesicka, 1923–24.

———. *Znamiona polityki narodowej i krajowej.* Kraków: Nakładem autora, 1882.

Binder, Harald. *Galizien in Wien: Parteien, Wahlen, Fraktionen und Abgeordnete im Übergang zum Massenpolitik.* Wien: Verlag der Österreichischen Akademie der Wissenschaften, 2005.

Borzecki, Jerzy. *The Soviet-Polish Peace of 1921 and the Creation of Interwar Europe.* New Haven: Yale University Press, 2008.

Brook-Shepherd, Gordon. *The Last Habsburg.* London: Weybright and Talley, 1968.

Chłędowski, Kazimierz. *Pamiętniki: Wiedeń, 1881–1901*, vol. 2. Kraków: Wydawnictwo Literackie, 1957.

Czernin, Ottokar. *Im Weltkrieg.* 2nd ed. Berlin: Verlegt bei Ullstein & Co, 1919.

Daszyński, Ignacy. *Cztery Lata Wojny: Szkice z dziejów poliyki polskiej partyi socjalno-demokratycznej.* Kraków: Nakładem Posła Zygmunta Klemensiewicza, 1918.

———. *Pamiętniki.* Kraków: Nakładem Z. R. S. S. "Proletarjat," 1925.

———. *Teksty,* edited by Jerzy Myśliński. Warszawa: Czytelnik, 1986.

Davies, Norman. *White Eagle, Red Star: The Polish-Soviet War 1919–1920.* London: Macdonald, 1972.

Diamand, Herman. *Pamiętnik Hermana Diamanda zebrany z wyjątków listów do żony*. Kraków: Nakładem Tow. Uniwersytetu Robotniczego [TUR], 1932.
Di Simone, Mariapina, ed. *Documenti per la storia delle relazioni italo-polacche, 1918–1940* Roma: Ministero per i beni culturali a ambientali, 1998.
Doroshenko, Dmytro. *Moi spomyny pro nedavnie mynule, 1914–1920*. Kyiv: Tempora, 2007.
Fellner, Fritz. "Der Vertrag von St. Germain." In *Österreich, 1918–1938: Geschichte der Ersten Republik*, edited by Erika Weinzierl and Kurt Skalnik, 85–106. Graz: Styria Verlag, 1983.
———, ed. *Schicksalsjahre Österreichs: 1908–1919; Das politische Tagebuch Josef Redlichs*. 2 vols. Graz: Böhlau, 1953.
Frank, Alison Fleig. *Oil Empire: Visions of Prosperity in Austrian Galicia*. Cambridge, MA: Harvard University Press, 2005.
Gedye, G. E. R. *Heirs to the Habsburgs*. Bristol: Arrowsmith, 1932.
Golczewski, Frank. *Deutsche und Ukrainer 1914–1939*. Paderborn: Ferdinand Schöningh, 2010.Głąbiński, Stanisław. *Idea samodzielności a finanse Galicyi*. Lwów: Nakładem autora, 1902.
———. W*spomnienie polityczne*. Prlplin: Nakładem i czcionkami drukarni i ksiegarni Sp. Z. O. O., 1939.
Guibal-Roland. *La Vie Polonaise: Observations d'un commerçant*. Paris: E. de Boccard, 1921.
Herling, Marta, ed. *"Polonia Restituta": l'Italia e la ricostituzione della Polonia 1918–1921*. Milano: Centro di studi sull'Europa orientale, 1992.
Höglinger, Felix. *Ministerpräsident Heinrich Graf Clam-Martinic*. Graz: Böhlau, 1964.
Hornykiewicz, Theophil. *Ereignisse in der Ukraine 1914–1922: Deren Bedeutung und historische Hintergründe*. Philadelphia: W. K. Lypynsky East European Research Institute, 1966.
Janowski, Maciej. *Inteligencja wobec wyznań nowoczesności: Dylematy ideowe polskiej demokracji liberalnei w Galicji w latach 1889–1914*. Warszawa: Instytut Historii PAN, 1996.
Krzywiec, Grzegorz. *Szowinizm po polsku: Przypadek Romana Dmowskiego (1866–1905)*. Warszawa: Instytut Historii PAN, Neriton, 2009.
Łazuga, Waldemar. *"Rządy polskie" w Austrii: Gabinet Kazimierza hr. Badeniego 1895–1897*. Poznań: Wydawnictwo Naukowe UAM, 1991.
Leopold, Karel. *Vzpomínky: z prvých dob ministerstva financí. Díl I. Část revuální*. V červnu 1928, p. 28, available on the Czech Ministry of Finance website: http://www.mfcr.cz/cs/o-ministerstvu/sluzby-verejnosti/odborna-knihovna/z-historie-mf/2013/historicke-pu blikace-o-ministerstvu-fina-13236.
Mark, Rudolf A. *Galizien unter österreichischer Herrschaft: Verwaltung-Kirche-Bevölkerung*. Marburg: Herder-Institut, 1994.
Mazepa, Isaak. *Ukraïna v ogni j burì revolúcìï, 1917–1921*. Kyiv: Tempora, 2003.
Michalski, Jerzy. *Traktat pokojowy w Saint-Germain a obciążenie Polski*. Kraków: nakł. Krakowskiej Spółki Wydawniczej, 1920.
Mick, Christoph. *Kriegserfahrung in einer multiethnischen Stadt: Lemberg 1914–1947*. Wiesbaden: Harassowitz, 2010.
Mikoletzky, Hanns Leo. *Österreichische Zeitgeschichte vom Ende der Monarchie bis zum Abschluss des Staatsvertrages 1955*. Vienna: Austria-Edition, 1964.
Najdus, Walentyna. *Ignacy Daszyński: 1866–1936*. Warszawa: Czytelnik, 1988.
Onatskyi, Ievhen. "Pid omoforom barona V. Vasylka," *Ukraïnskyi istoryk* 65–68, no. 1–4 (1980): 122.
Partacz, Czesław. *Od Badeniego do Potockiego: Stosunki polsko-ukraińskie w Galicji w latach 1888–1908*. Torún: Wydawnictwo Adam Marszałek, 1997.

Pasvolsky, Leo. *Economic Nationalism of the Danubian States*. New York: The Macmillan Company, 1928.
Piccoli, Paolo and Armando Vadagnini. *De Gasperi: un trentino nella storia d'Europa*. Soveria Mannelli: Rubbettino, 2004.
Pietrzak, Michał. *Rządy Parlamentarne w Polsce w latach 1919–1926*. Warszawa: Książka i Wiedza, 1969.
Polonsky, Antony. *Politics in Independent Poland, 1921–1939: The Crisis of Constitutional Government*. Oxford: Oxford University Press, 1972.
Porter, Brian. *When Nationalism Began to Hate: Imagining Modern Politics in Nineteenth-Century Poland*. New York: Oxford University Press, 2000.
Pragier, Adam. *Czas przeszły dokonany*. London: Świderski, 1966.
Rašín, Alois. *Financial Policy of Czecho-Slovakia During the First Year of Its History*. Oxford: Oxford University Press, 1923.
Rawi, Abdelal. "Purpose and Privation: Nation and Economy in Post-Habsburg Europe and Post-Soviet Eurasia." *East European Politics and Societies* 16, no. 3 (Fall 2002): 898–933.
Schwabe, Klaus, ed. *Quellen zum Friedensschluss von Versailles*. Darmstadt: Wissenschaftliche Buchgesellschaft, 1997.
Seton-Watson, Hugh. *Eastern Europe Between the Wars, 1918–1941*. New York: Routledge, 1986.
Sierpowski, Stanisław. *L'Italia e la ricostituzione del nuovo stato polacco, 1915–1921*. Wrocław: Ossolineum, 1979.
Singer, Bernard. *Od Witosa do Sławka*. Paris: Instytut Literacki, 1962.
Snyder, Timothy. *The Red Prince: The Secret Lives of a Habsburg Archduke*. New York: Basic Books 2008.
———. *Sketches from a Secret War: A Polish Artist's Mission to Liberate Soviet Ukraine*. New Haven: Yale University Press, 2005.
Spitzmüller Freiherr von Harmersbach, Alexander. *Memoirs of Alexander Spitzmüller Freiherr von Harmersbach (1862–1953): Former Minister of Trade and Minister of Finance in the Austro-Hungarian Empire, Governor of the Austro-Hungarian Bank, Director-General of the Creditanstalt Bankverein*, translated by Carvel de Bussy. Boulder, CO: East European Monographs, 1987.
Strach, Hermann, ed. *Geschichte der Eisenbahnen der Österreichisch-Ungarischen Monarchie*, 2 vols. Vienna: K. Prochaska, 1898.
Tommasini, Francesco. *La Risurrezione della Polonia*. Milano: Fratelli Trevers, 1925.
Wapiński, Roman. *Narodowa Demokracja 1893–1939: Ze studiów nad dziejami myśli nacjonalistycznej*. Wrocław: Ossolineum, 1980.
Wątor, Adam. *Narodowa Demokracja w Galicji do 1918 roku*. Szczecin: Wydawn. Naukowe Uniwersytetu Szczecińskiego, 2002.
Weinzierl, Erika and Kurt Skalnik, eds. *Österreich, 1918–1938: Geschichte der Ersten Republik*. Graz: Styria Verlag, 1983.
Wehrhahn, Trosten. *Die Westukrainische Volksrepublik: Zu den polnisch-ukrainischen Beziehungen und dem Problem der ukrainischen Staatlichkeit in den Jahren 1918 bis 1923*. Berlin: Weißensee Verlag, 2004.

Archives
Biblioteka Naukowa PAU i PAN w Krakowie, Rękopisy (BNPPK): Leon Biliński. N 7315, 7817, N 7316, 8125, 12090.

Chapter 4

IDEOLOGY ON DISPLAY
Continuity and Rupture at Exhibitions in Austria-Hungary and Czechoslovakia, 1873–1928

Marta Filipová

On the tenth anniversary of the founding of the Czechoslovak Republic in 1928, the Exhibition of Contemporary Culture was held in Brno: "the center of the republic . . . where all nations shake hands in an effort to cooperate on cultural matters." Brno was not the only city celebrating the allegedly peaceful communion of peoples in Czechoslovakia—that year, the entire country became a place where, at least in the minds of state and local officials, "national minorities [i.e., Germans, Hungarians, Poles, and the citizens in Sub-Carpathian Russia] have no reason to complain that anyone was obstructing their intellectual life and cultural/economic needs."[1]

The author of these upbeat assertions was Brno's deputy mayor, Jan Máša. Writing for the exhibition catalogue, Máša boasted that the Republic's various ethnic groups now "have their [own] schools and are free to pursue their [unique] economic development."[2] Touting such achievements was part of the ideology on display at the Brno exhibition—an idealized vision of ethnic autonomy in which "mutual tolerance and respect for fellow citizens" were proud features of postwar Czechoslovakia. What Máša may not have realized, however, was that this means of showcasing the state had direct parallels to official proclamations on ethnic acceptance made at similar exhibitions during the imperial era.

This chapter explores these and other correspondences between the 1928 exhibition in Brno and other exhibitions on either side of the World War I divide.

Beginning with an overview of European exhibitions in the late nineteenth century, the chapter then narrows its purview to the Austro-Hungarian Empire and, in particular, the Bohemian crown lands and postwar Czechoslovakia. These national and international exhibitions before and after World War I were crucial for recreating and affirming identity for their respective state, city, or ethnic group. Moreover, in competing to become recognized events in the regional and international exhibition circuit, many of the same aims and elements of the earlier exhibitions persisted into the postwar Czechoslovak nation-state.

Yet, in addition to the continuities with the prewar "exhibition complexes," interwar politics and events made important new contributions to the exhibitionary culture.[3] This chapter will thus explore these as well. Whether regional, national, or even international, the exhibitions considered here all served as important microcosms of the political, cultural, and economic realities of the day. Condensed in the confined space of a temporary exhibition ground, they can help shed crucial light on the much larger issues affecting the nation-state in its transition from the imperial era.

Exhibiting Progress and Identity

The standard literature on exhibitionary cultures often calls the late nineteenth to the early twentieth century the golden era of great exhibitions and large-scale international fairs in European and American metropolises.[4] Such events sought to promote trade by showcasing the best products of contemporary manufacturing from the exhibiting nations or groups. Yet underlying these economic motivations were the political and ideological ambitions of the organizers and/or exhibitors. The so-called great exhibitions, in short, were also used to proclaim political ideas about the states and nations that were displaying or displayed, whether in the exhibits themselves or at the events organized alongside them. Through their direct connection to industry, progress, and consumer culture, exhibitions served as both vehicles for the spread of modernity and the construction of ethno-national identity.[5]

More modest exhibitions held in such cities as Melbourne (1854), Edinburgh (1886), Barcelona (1888), and Osaka (1903) found their models in the Great Exhibition in London (1851), the Parisian *expositions universelles* (1855, 1867, 1878, 1889, 1900), and several of the United States world's fairs (particularly those in Philadelphia in 1876 and Chicago in 1893). Yet it would be wrong to assume that these events merely replicated the structural and organizational schemes of the larger *expositions universelles*.[6] Certainly their intention to secure international standing by showcasing technological achievements was consistent with the era's exhibitionary trend. Yet the smaller-scale exhibitions were invariably also linked to the local and national politics of the region's ethnic groupings.

In Central Europe, the tradition of large, ambitious exhibitions dates back to at least the 1840s. The 1844 All German Exhibition in Berlin showcased "German national identity" well before "Germany" was a political reality.[7] Moreover, by requiring exhibitors to be members of the German Customs Union that had been founded a decade earlier, Austria was excluded. The All German Exhibition may have been officially focused on technical education and trade expansion, but it already "showed signs of the propaganda of industrialization and modernization, [as well as] the historicism of industrial development."[8]

The importance of displaying the "best of" the constructed past and presenting it at large exhibitions of arts and industries was widely accepted in Austria-Hungary. Indeed, the multinational Monarchy nurtured numerous exhibitions of all sizes and purposes. Some, like the *Weltausstellung* in Vienna (1873) or Budapest's 1896 Millennium Exhibition, conformed to or, at least, did not contest the notion of a shared imperial identity. By contrast, exhibitions with closer ties to local communities in places like Prague (1891), Lemberg (Lviv/Lwów, 1894), and Reichenberg (Liberec, 1906) had more nationalist undertones. In these cases, organizers often emphasized the uniqueness of whichever ethno-national group's history, culture, and industries were on display.

In Bohemia, the first recorded exhibition predates the industrial and trade exhibitions that became popular from the mid-nineteenth century. Held in Prague's Klementinum Library on the occasion of Czech King Leopold II's coronation in 1791, this exhibition had both economic and educational aims.[9] Later exhibitions in Bohemia followed suit. In 1842 and 1852, the important northern textile town of Reichenberg held reasonably successful exhibitions both in terms of the number of visitors and exhibitors.[10] The early fairs that took place in Eger (Cheb, 1871,1881), Leitmeritz (Litoměřice, 1877), Teplitz (Teplice, 1875, 1879, 1884), and in Aussig (Ústí nad Labem, 1874, 1880) in northern and northwestern Bohemia aimed mainly to promote local industries, education, and tourism.

Unsurprisingly, the major Central European exhibitions took place in Vienna, with their own defined political dimensions. The 1873 *Weltausstellung* was foremost an immense display of science and industry. Yet it also privileged contemporary culture and modern civilization by promoting the Monarchy's powerful economic, cultural, and political position in Europe.[11] The approximately twenty-six thousand exhibitors in pavilions spread throughout the Prater displayed the industries and technologies, agriculture, science, arts, and "arts and crafts" (national domestic industries) of thirty-five nations including the "exotic"—the British colonies, as well as Japan, China, Persia, and Egypt. Austria-Hungary herself presented its new dual political identity (dating to the 1867 Compromise following the Empire's defeat to Prussia a year earlier) as a "bridge between East and West"—Budapest and Vienna.[12]

A further element of the Habsburg Empire's self-construction in 1873 was that of a peaceful and contented union of diverse peoples. This thematic spectacle, however, could be hotly contested. The Czechs, for instance, refused to take official part in the event because they were denied their own exhibition space. Indeed, some of the Czech press—particularly the nationalist newspapers *Moravská orlice* and *Národní listy*—dismissed the exhibition as "merely a German business based on a German idea." The paper went on to assert that "the impression it gives to all unbiased visitors is one of embarrassment, because the displayed items do not reflect the true . . . conditions and it is the truth that will suffer most because only a single German element is celebrated and glorified here."[13]

The Czechs were not the only Habsburg nationality whose participation in the *Weltausstellung* was partial and problematic. Romanians, Hungarians, Slovaks, and Moravians were mainly represented as peasants in displays on rural lifestyles, their "simple" wooden homes juxtaposed with the more richly decorated stone dwellings of ethnic Germans.[14] In thus displaying different levels of "civilization," the exhibits highlighted the need for a Germanic cultural and economic presence in the "backward" regions of rural Austria-Hungary.

The *Weltausstellung* was not a financial success. Although more than seven million people visited Vienna in 1873, it left the city with a nineteen million guilder debt due to a combination of economic crisis, cholera and chicken pox epidemics, and the general elections.[15] Yet the exhibition did have a significant impact on subsequent such events in Austria-Hungary and its successor states. In particular, the ethnographic village, a street of rural houses from various parts of the monarchy, inspired displays exploring the relationship between folk culture and national heritage/identity. The 1894 Universal Exhibition in Lemberg and Budapest's Millennium Exhibition in 1896 included reconstructions of rural dwellings intended to highlight the importance of autochthonous cultures in relation to the heritage of nations in the making. And despite their dismissals of the *Weltausstellung* as too German, Czechs also found much that was useful for their own exhibitionary nation-building endeavors.

Exhibiting the Czechs in Prague

It did not take long for Austro-Hungarian state and municipal governments, local patriots, and enterprising industrialists to recognize the nationalistic potential of large-scale exhibitions. In 1891 and 1895, Prague alone hosted two such events, both of which were forceful proclamations of Czech nationalism. The Chamber of Commerce, Czech Diet, and City Hall organized the Jubilee Exhibition (1891) to commemorate the centenary of Leopold II's coronation (Figure 4.1). Yet their goals were far grander than imperial pomp: the event sought to support international trade; establish new business links; familiarize local manufacturers with the competition and new production technologies;

Figure 4.1. The Palace of Industries, Prague, 1891. Postcard. Author's collection.

and, even, to increase Prague tourism. The Jubilee Exhibition thus featured numerous pavilions, newly commissioned artworks, and cultural events highlighting the industry, agriculture, and culture (both folk and high art) of Bohemia and Moravia.[16]

The idea of organizing an exhibition of this scope was largely inspired by the Paris *exposition universelle* of 1889. The Club of Czech Tourists, a patriotic organization founded by the collector, politician, and journalist Vojtěch Náprstek (1826–94), dispatched some four hundred people to visit the *exposition*.[17] They returned with plans for a downscaled Czech version complete with a miniature Eiffel tower on the Petřín hill. As it happened, the sixty-meter lookout tower became the exhibition's indelible *clou*—an eye-catching structure that dominated the fairgrounds and would be imitated in numerous other exhibitions. The exception in Prague's case was that the tower stood outside the main fairground in the Royal Game Preserve (today's Stromovka Park) and was accessed by a funicular.

The exhibition's other *clou* was an illuminated fountain designed by the Czech inventor and electrification advocate František Křižík (1847–1941). *Fontaines lumineuses* were quite common at international arts and industry exhibitions, including those in London (1884), Barcelona (1888), Paris (1889), Glasgow (1889), and Vienna (1873 and 1890). Typically viewed as emblems of modernity for their elaborate electric lighting, the official catalogue for the Prague exhibition gave another, more nationalistic reason for this fountain's uniqueness: "while 210 hectoliters of water per minute sprang up from the Parisian fountain [and] 70 hectoliters from the Viennese one, our own fountain shot up 440 hectoliters," the catalog proudly emphasized.[18]

The Czech national character of the Jubilee Exhibition was already taking shape during the preparatory works. Although the planners had hoped the event would unite *all* ethnic groups in Bohemia, Moravia, and Silesia (including Bohemian Germans), the German minority declined to take part for political reasons, mainly the failed compromise of 1890 that was an attempt to find a solution to the nationalist problems in Bohemia. Official exhibition publications thus reflected Czech indignation over the German withdrawal, and the six-month event turned into a celebration of Czech identity with immense consequences for national self-awareness.[19] For one, the Czech organizers and exhibitors realized that they were able to stage an event of such size and importance without the Germans and inform local and foreign visitors of what they understood as Czech economy, history, and culture.

Indeed, the elevation of Czech culture was evident on virtually every exhibitionary corner. The "purely Czech" style was readily identifiable in the fine art displays, as well as those on folk art/culture in the "Czech Village House." This exhibit, as was common for Czech ethnography at the time, presented the country folk as curious, bizarre, and primitive, but also as embodying the prototypical forms of Czech cultural and artistic life. Much like the ethnographic village at the Vienna *Weltausstellung*, the Village House was designed as both a fusion and imitation of actual village structures. It also included figurines representing the diverse types of Slavic peoples and attributes such as facial features, body postures, and "peculiar costumes."[20]

Yet in contrast to Vienna, where folk culture from different parts of the Monarchy appeared as diverse and supranational, the exhibitors in Bohemia stressed cultural homogeneity and its connection to the nation. Their appreciation for the uniqueness and authenticity of folk art and culture thus gave pride of place to peasants—the main purveyors of Czech traditions and heritage. This highly nationalistic perspective carried over into several exclusively ethnographic exhibitions in Bohemia and Moravia, the largest of which also took place in Prague. The 1895 Czechoslovak Ethnographic Exhibition introduced the regional cultures of Bohemia, Moravia, and Slovakia, and presented folk art as both a static display in the vitrines of the Ethnographic Palace and live exhibits in the Exhibition Village. According to the organizers, the Ethnographic Exhibition aimed to explore "the entire original life of the Czech people and to preserve its image." It additionally sought to present the genuine and historical national culture independent of German influences; as well as to educate Czechs and the "world about the nation's originality, character and strengths."[21]

The grounds consisted of various buildings typically found in a village—a smithy, mill, school, church, and, of course, a pub and distillery. These were designed by contemporary architects, including Dušan Jurkovič (1867–1947), Jan Koula (1855–1919), and the ethnographer Josef Klvaňa (1857–1919), who had actively collected and preserved aspects of folk culture before the exhibition.

At the Ethnographic Exhibition, these elements were modified to suit the motivations of the organizers and the needs of the visitors. Such was the case, for instance, with the smithy designed by Koula. "Practical requirements forced him to design a special doorway on the left [of the house], through which the numerous visitors, who entered through the main door, could leave. Also, for practical reasons, the usual position of the smith's flat in the house was transformed into an exhibition room, in which the smith's old tools and products were displayed."[22]

Such ethnographic exhibitions were, thus, simplified versions of the village reality, meant to allow the local bourgeoisie to identify their origins in a peasant and folk art that also symbolized the increasingly cultured middle-class civilization to which they now proudly belonged. In their depictions of vernacular culture, the Prague exhibitions conformed to the pattern established by the *Weltausstellung* and repeated around the Monarchy at the end of the nineteenth century. In Vienna, Central European peasants appeared in "ageless tradition" alongside the most current technical and scientific advancements. What distinguished the Prague exhibitions was their increased emphasis on national identity preserved in folk culture.

The Ethnographic Exhibition was both a national *and* international success. Of the many foreign journalists and scholars who visited Prague, the Polish writer Adolf Strzelecki came away with a better understanding of the importance of history and culture for the nation's future development.[23] He also favorably compared the exhibition village in Prague to a similar display at the Lemberg Universal Exhibition a year earlier. According to Strzelecki, "the small village at our Lemberg exhibition was pretty, without comparison much prettier as regards its composition, and—in our opinion—nicer also because it was ours, local and native; but at the Prague exhibition, the illusion was more complete."[24] Strzelecki credited this to the inclusion of live exhibits in the houses that showed such ordinary activities as daily chores and field labor, and depicted customs like weddings, dances, and singing.[25]

Exhibitions outside Prague

The Provincial Universal Exposition that Strzelecki referred to opened in Lemberg in 1894. Its purpose, in part, was to distract people from the political "misery" in Galicia, which was one of the reasons the event did not overemphasize profit-making goals. Instead, it concentrated on educating the visitors through the displays of over five thousand exhibitors ranging from trade and agriculture to the Austrian aristocracy, fine arts, and folk culture.

Nevertheless, the exposition was politicized by mere virtue of the fact that it was held in Galicia. Its greater aim, in other words, was to strengthen popular sentiment for the province's union with Austria. This was made especially plain by Emperor

Franz Joseph's visit to the exposition, which many Austrian politicians and Polish leaders viewed as an acknowledgment of Austrian political supremacy and the increasingly close ties between the Habsburg dynasty and Polish Galician leaders. Of course, there was opposition to this portrayal of the Poles and the Empire. In particular, Polish Social Democrats, Ukrainian nationalists, socialists, and much of the urban intelligentsia used the exposition to mobilize nationalist sentiments and highlight their national heroes.[26] One of the most egregious examples of this was an enormous panorama commemorating the 1794 Battle of Racławice, part of the Kościuszko insurrection against Russia. Painted by numerous artists of Polish and German origin—foremost Wojciech Kossak (1856–1942), who was assisted by Ludwik Boller, Tadeusz Popiel, Zygmunt Rozwadowski, and Teodor Axentowicz, among others—the display became something of a pilgrimage site for local peasants calling for a new uprising.

Unsurprisingly, local elites throughout Austria-Hungary took advantage of exhibitions held outside the main capitals to defend, or oppose, political ideas concerning such issues as the use of Czech and German as administrative languages in Bohemia. Ethnic Germans excluded from the Czech exhibitions in 1891 and 1895 focused on organizing their own events in German-majority cities in north and northwest Bohemia. These regional exhibitions often incorporated the terms "German" or "German Bohemian" into their titles in order to highlight their exclusivist ethno-political orientation.[27] A good example is the 1906 German-Bohemian exhibition in Reichenberg (Figure 4.2). From the end

Figure 4.2. The German-Bohemian exhibition, Reichenberg/Liberec, 1906. Postcard. Author's collection.

of the nineteenth century, as ethnic Germans lost their prominence in Prague and many started moving to the border regions, the northern city of Reichenberg increasingly became the unofficial capital of the Bohemian Germans. The 1906 exhibition thus offered a good opportunity "to demonstrate the significance of German work in Bohemia, thereby legitimizing the political and national claims of the Bohemian Germans."[28] They did so with more than 1,500 exhibitors representing local industries, crafts, the industrial arts, agriculture, the fine arts, education, health care, social services, the military, and cultural history.

Participation of the Czechs in this and in other exhibitions organized by the Bohemian Germans was limited, and Czech exhibitors were not invited unless they were involved in joint enterprises. This was one of the reasons the Czech press was generally critical of the exhibition. An article in *Lidové noviny* went so far as to call it proof of the "all-round cultural impotence of Bohemian Germans."[29] The article questioned the exhibition's actual "Germanness" by insisting that "all [the] works that required more than craftsmanship were commissioned by Germans of the Reich or, at best, from Vienna, therefore—if one also excludes all the work that the Czechs carried out—nothing much of the [Bohemian] German contribution is in fact left here."[30] Thus did the era's nationalist tensions between the two main ethnic groups in Bohemia play out not only in the political arena, but on the exhibition grounds as well.

Continuity or Rupture? The Ongoing Importance of Exhibitions

World War I meant a break in plans to stage these costly and ideologically complex exhibitions across Europe. Thus the detailed proposals for the 1917 Budapest Universal Exhibition—which was to celebrate fifty years since the Compromise (*Ausgleich*) that created the Dual Monarchy and spurred Hungarian economic and cultural advancement—were shelved by the war, after which Hungary had more pressing issues than hosting an expensive international exhibition. By the same token, the new political composition of postwar Central Europe created the need to present one's country as not only economically and politically independent, but also historically and culturally justified. Exhibitions provided an excellent means to do that, both for the domestic population and for a larger, international audience.

In particular, participation at international exhibitions was a practical (and more affordable) way to validate national identity and garner international acceptance. Bohemia and later Czechoslovakia had been represented by single exhibits or whole sections at a number of world's fairs, including the Great Exhibition in London (1851), the Paris *exposition universelle* (1889), the Louisiana Purchase Exposition of 1904, and even in Launceston, Tasmania, where a Bohemian section was part of the International Exhibition held there in 1891–92. In

1922, Czechoslovakia took part in the Centenary Exhibition to celebrate Brazil's independence from Portugal. Held in Rio de Janeiro, the exhibition gave Czechs the opportunity to promote their country's modernity, republican government, economic recovery, and trading potential.[31]

In Rio, Czechoslovakia was one of thirteen states that built their own pavilions and showcased their products for what were officially advertised as "purely economic" reasons.[32] Yet as the "only state from Central Europe," boasted *Národní listy*, the Czechoslovak government clearly had national motives for building a pavilion amidst the limited foreign exhibitors from countries the likes of Great Britain, France, Japan, and the United States.[33] It did so, moreover, with a building designed by the esteemed modernist architect Pavel Janák, who integrated popular vernacular motifs into a space rented out to some seventy companies. Most of these businesses exhibited industries that had the potential for competing in the new markets of the Americas. In this way, economic and political aims combined to help put Czechoslovakia on the world map.[34]

If we consider the staging of exhibitions of arts and industries to be an indicator of a stable economic environment, then it was at least a decade before such a favorable atmosphere was reached in post-Habsburg Central Europe. Following the 1928 Exhibition of Contemporary Culture in Brno, the Polish National Exhibition in Poznań (1929) commemorated the tenth anniversary of Poland's independence. According to the official guidebook, the exhibition was a "symbol of the work of the entire Polish nation, a symbol of the peaceful efforts of the Polish state."[35] The event thus focused on Polish achievements in industry, trade, agriculture, education, hygiene, sport, culture, and the arts over the previous decade. In this and other respects, the Poznań exhibition strove to dissociate the city from its Prussian past.[36]

Reinvention and/or reinterpretation of the past were common to exhibitions both before and after 1918. In 1891 in Prague, for instance, few historical displays related to the Bohemian Germans, let alone to other ethnic groups in Bohemia and Moravia. Yet "the mutual tolerance and respect for fellow citizens" announced by Brno's deputy mayor during the 1928 Exhibition of Contemporary Culture signaled a sea change in terms of the recognition of ethnic minorities in Central Europe. At the very least, it indicated intent to adapt to the post-imperial political framework and the increasing democratization of society since Czechoslovakia declared its independence on 28 October 1918.

Despite being a parliamentary democracy, Czechoslovakia, in certain respects, resembled a reincarnation of Austria-Hungary in terms of the internal national problems it inherited and failed to address.[37] This largely stemmed from competing claims for autonomy. Under Habsburg rule, Czech political leaders had typically grounded their national identity and quest for independence in the historic existence of the Bohemian crown lands. This strategy was modeled on that of Hungarian nationalists, whose claims to national legitimacy deriving from the historic Hungarian kingdom were largely met by the 1867 Compromise (*Ausgleich*) with Austria.[38] Yet Slovaks in the Dual Monarchy and postwar Czechoslovak Republic had no prior tradition of political sovereignty. They had to argue for their *natural* right to form a state on the basis of ethnic self-determination.

After 1918 and, in particular, the union of Czechs and Slovaks in the Czechoslovak constitution of February 1920, the Slovaks' precarious position was exacerbated by conflict with the German and Magyar minorities in the new Czechoslovak territories. While the Germans strove to establish national provinces *within* Bohemia and Moravia, the Hungarians went to war with Romania in part over Slovakia, or "Upper Hungary" as it was then known. The Trianon Treaty of June 1920 resolved the issue by ceding Slovakia, with its large Hungarian population, to Czechoslovakia. Yet this only prolonged nationalist resentments among all three groups. For example, the Prague government did not recognize Slovak claims to greater ethnic autonomy in Czechoslovakia for fear that this would encourage the Bohemian Germans to make similar requests.[39] Thus, the transformational year 1918 did not bring the radical restructuring of domestic political and cultural arrangements that many had hoped for in the Czechoslovak state. In many respects, in fact, the Czechoslovak political program prolonged the ethnically convoluted situation.

When the Exhibition of Contemporary Culture opened in Brno on 26 May 1928, it was apparent that, despite being held outside the contentious capital, it was a product of the Czechoslovak Republic's new political and ideological configuration. While the event's chief aim was—as usual for such exhibitions—to celebrate the cultural, technical, economic, and social achievements of the past decade, the political changes in the country over that period required that the event also confront the ongoing tensions between Czechs, Slovaks, Germans, and Magyars. In this regard, the organizers' effort to showcase contemporary culture (with a rather careful presentation of the past) seemed logical, especially given the success of the Prague national exhibitions of the 1890s and the fact that until 1918, Brno (Brünn) had been dominated by German cultural organizations. Indeed, the city's first Czech society—The Association of the Friends of Art—was not established until 1900. And in 1907, the founding members of the Association of Moravian Fine Artists chose the southern Moravian town of Hodonín for their headquarters. Brno, they felt, was too German.[40]

In 1928, exhibiting Czechoslovakia as a modern democratic nation was thus accompanied by a celebration of Brno's own modernization and Czechization. This was not difficult considering the city's remarkable expansion from 1890, when its population was approximately 95,000 mostly Germans, to 1921, when Brno and its surrounding administrative area had 604,000 Czech-Slovak inhabitants and 135,000 ethnic Germans.[41] This rapid Czechization was accelerated by the opening of several Czech universities after 1918, including Masaryk University, the University of Agriculture, and the University of Veterinary Studies. It also helped that Brno was made seat of the Czechoslovak Supreme Court. But the most important factor for the city's postwar Czechization was economic growth. Thus while the exhibition catalog paid token homage to the old town's historic monuments, it also devoted substantial space to the description of the rows of factory chimneys stretching out from the railway intersection. And if most of these "symbols of the renowned industries of Brno" dated to Habsburg times, in 1928 they helped bolster the city's image as "the Manchester of Moravia."[42]

Hosting an international exhibition and building a large permanent exhibition ground was like "opening a window onto the world," said Brno Mayor Karel Tomeš.[43] In this respect, geography also played an important role in introducing the new state's second largest city to a broader audience. As part of Austria-Hungary, Brno had been more closely linked to Vienna than to Prague based both on physical proximity and historic/cultural affinity (i.e., the city's largely ethnic German population). The Exhibition of Contemporary Culture could thus highlight the city's reorientation toward the Czechoslovak capital and, consequently, separation from its Austrian heritage. Moreover, Brno's central location between the country's Czech and Slovak regions made it symbolically suited as "a bridge between East and West," just as Austria-Hungary had advertised itself at the 1873 *Weltausstellung*. Nor was this merely a bridge between the two Slavic groups. According to event organizers, the Brno exhibition aimed to "emphasize the excellent position of the young Czechoslovak state in the center of European culture and civilization."[44] If attendance figures are any measure of whether it achieved this, then the exhibition was a big success—over 2.5 million people visited Brno from May to September 1928, which was more than each of the previous two Prague exhibitions.

Modernization and Modernity

The Exhibition of Contemporary Culture was designed to fit into the character of Brno not only as a modern city, but also as a modernist one. Art and architectural scholars recognize interwar Brno as an important hub of functionalism and internationalism. And while it is most famous for Mies van der Rohe's Villa Tugendhat (commissioned in 1928 and completed in late 1930), Brno can actually boast of numerous modernist structures in the city center and residential neighborhoods. The design of the fairground and its pavilions for the 1928 exhibition would well reflect this.[45]

Indeed, the very architects in the process of giving Brno its modernist image designed the main exhibition building (the Palace of Trade and Industry)—a central rotunda with arched aisles in reinforced concrete and glass. This functionalist form contained exhibits ranging from technology, the sciences, and applied arts to education, fine art, and religion. Other structures built according to international trends for functionalist architecture included the pavilions housing urban exhibits (like Brno and Prague), a Moravian pavilion, the tower and hall of the Brno fairs company, and a pavilion dedicated to the work of the Czech paleontologist Karel Absolon (entitled "Man and Mankind"). Renowned architects from Prague and Brno also designed the more modest buildings in which various firms and manufacturers displayed their wares. Thus Bať'a shoes, a bakery, gas company, newspaper publishers, and even the food and drink vendors were housed in pavilions meant to become "landmark[s] in our modern architecture . . . a manifest" of modernism.[46]

In an effort to address contemporary socioeconomic problems like the housing crisis in Czechoslovakia, several model homes were set up on the exhibition premises. A house built by *Svaz díla* (the "Association of Arts and Crafts," which was similar to the German *Werkbund*), for example, was conceived as a small and inexpensive yet comfortable apartment building with shared laundry and other facilities. Its design followed the current trend in Germany and Belgium of collective, functional, and hygienic living that was also affordable.[47] Another way in which architects exhibited their solutions to the housing dilemma was the so-called New House colony: an extensive development adjacent to the main exhibition ground.[48] The inspiration for this project came from the Weissenhoff estate in Stuttgart, which had been built a year earlier by Mies van der Rohe, Le Corbusier, and Walter Gropius, among others, for the exhibition "Die Wohnung" ("The Apartment").[49] This development consisted of sixteen family homes with open spaces and terraces, thus subscribing to the functionalist ideals that were already so ubiquitous at the Brno exhibition.

By showcasing practical solutions to contemporary problems like housing, Brno and other post-1918 exhibitions were more attuned to their modern environments than parallel prewar events in Central Europe, which tended to create idealized visions of the future. The Poznań Exhibition that took place a year later thus also strived to symbolize the new era as embodied by the Polish state. And though Poznań had belonged to the prewar German rather than Austro-Hungarian Empire, exhibition organizers, like their counterparts in Brno, still sought to display their city's modernity and separation from the imperial past through the exhibition's content and political orientation. In this respect, the fairground architecture was again crucial to reviving the "Polish" spirit and highlighting the Polish identity of the new state.[50] This time, however, "classicizing Modernism," which was based on principles of classical architecture and therefore familiar to the public, was assigned the role of "transforming the past rather than rejecting it, [thus] making use of [the past] in a new, more individual yet disciplined manner."[51]

The exhibition organizers in Poznań and Brno turned their backs on narrowly national and ethnographic objectives in their efforts to reinterpret the past and, thereby, shape the future. In so doing, they sought a place for their respective states in a contemporary European (that is, West European) political and cultural contexts. For Brno and, by extension, Czechoslovakia as a whole, this entailed trying to prove their political and cultural reorientation by breaking free from the legacy of dissension between Czechs and Germans that characterized the earlier exhibitions. The Germans were thus not excluded from the 1928 Exhibition—on the contrary, they took an active part as both organizers and exhibitors. Yet, as I will mention shortly, the exhibition failed to create an accurate picture of the current ethnic composition of the state.

This break with nineteenth-century events in favor of a more pragmatic and less disputatious approach was on display in several exhibits and pavilions in Brno. Potentially conflictual references to religion, for instance, were overshadowed by greater attention to science and technology. At the *Weltausstellung* in Vienna, there had been a section on religious art, and the 1895 Prague exhibition devoted considerable space to the Catholic and Evangelical churches, as well as religious art objects and literature, famous church leaders, and statistical surveys of the religious activities of Czechs living abroad. In Brno, by contrast, religion was incorporated into a section entitled "The Spiritual Life of Man," where it coexisted with exhibits on sociology, philosophy, linguistics, and psychology. The focus, moreover, was more historic and institutional than spiritual.[52] This new postwar worldview was perhaps also epitomized by a replica of a five-meter tall mammoth, a symbol of evolution reconstituted by Professor Absolon and financed by the shoe manufacturer Tomáš Baťa. The mammoth corresponded to the image of an empirically oriented and pragmatic state.[53]

Nations on Display

Even as it aimed to be modern, futuristic, and all-embracing, the Brno exhibition continued the trend going back to the *Weltausstellung* of presenting an idealized unity for the state's ethnic groups. This was foremost visible in displays that included the participation of German schools, companies, or simply individuals, as in the pavilion of the Association of German Artists *Werkbund*. Founded in Liberec in 1926, this group paralleled German and Austrian associations established in 1907 and 1912, respectively. According to the exhibition catalogue, both branches survived the war and the 1918 revolution because "elementary cultural ideals are independent of changing political circumstances."[54] In Brno, the *Werkbund* presented these ideals through traditional techniques of craft making and displays of "high quality" objects that were "true to [their] material, formal beauty and functionality." Its exhibits also emphasized the distinctive German culture in the Czechoslovak state—"the great German artists and architects . . . who are active in our lands in such an excellent way." The exhibition catalogue supported this, citing these craftsmen as further proof that "our [German] nation is a substantial participant in our [Czechoslovak] state."[55]

Yet if German integration could be presented as part of the Czechoslovak state's larger cultural fabric, other ethnic minorities were more easily marginalized in 1928. Slovaks in particular were underrepresented among the event's organizers and, apart from a small pavilion on Bratislava and a handful of exhibits by artists linked with Slovakia, there was little to be seen of Slovak contemporary culture in Brno generally. Both on the exhibition grounds and in the city at large, Slovak culture was overwhelmed by that of the Czechs and subsumed into the larger Czechoslovak culture.

There are historical reasons for Slovak marginalization at the exhibition that go beyond sheer numbers. When Czechs and Slovaks were united into one state for the first time in history (alongside Polish, German, Hungarian, and Ruthenian minorities), not only did a political reality emerge, but a sociocultural one as well.[56] For many, a new identity had to be devised for Czechoslovak citizens in order to justify their joint existence and to secure claims to their shared territory. Above all, it became crucial to create a Slavic majority in the new state to top the German and Hungarian minorities, and it is in this context that the press and politicians began promoting the idea of a *Czechoslovak* people and language. Moreover, as with any nation-building undertaking, it was necessary to emphasize a common cultural tradition.[57] Thus did Czechs and Slovaks in the new Czechoslovakia find themselves in a classic situation in terms of national development—searching for historical relics of political autonomy, recovering memories of earlier independence, and reconnecting with a medieval written language all in order to legitimize their joint political sovereignty.[58]

A unified *Czechoslovak* culture, the natural product of *Czechoslovak* nationality and statehood, was emphasized at Brno from the opening speeches to the many individual exhibits. For example, when the chair of the exhibition organizing committee, Ladislav Pluhař, stressed the originality of the "Czechoslovak culture," he also noted that "each nation has a specific soul, a specific character, and only on the basis of such authenticity can it create its own culture and contribute to the universal [cosmopolitan] culture."[59] Pluhař added that only a nation with firm roots in its history could "grow and overgrow" other nations, which was why the cultural display in Brno could compete with the global culture. In this way, Pluhař announced the international ambitions of the exhibition in terms of authenticating Czechoslovak identity and distinguishing it from the more nationalistic, inward-focused Czech exhibitions of the 1890s.

Another reason for this universal presentation of "national" cultures in Brno had to do with a more fluid understanding of the nature of culture. In 1928, "culture" referred to the material and spiritual achievements of the past decade of national independence. This lent itself to an emphasis on the uniqueness of Czechoslovak culture on one hand, and its international character and competitiveness on the other. Moreover, this modern, post-1918 culture was mainly that of cities and towns, industry, and the middle classes. The countryside and villages were secondary in this modern cultural construct. Since Czechs generally saw the less industrialized Slovak regions of the country as rural and backward, Slovaks themselves slipped out of the exhibition's main focus.

Of course, Czech notions of cultural superiority and historical longevity were nothing new—they had long served to justify Czech claims to the Bohemian territory. Yet rather than denying their "backwardness," Slovak social and political elites used their rural image to their advantage—cultivating close ties between the Slovak people, agriculture, and peasant life in order to stress their rootedness in the land. Milan Hodža (1878–1944), an influential nationalist Slovak politician and historian who in 1918 became leader of the Czechoslovak Agrarian Party, was fond of making the distinction between "the naturally practical and collaborative Slovak people," skilled in hand and simply dressed, and the "arrogant, fainéant, reactionary, factious aristocrats" of Hungary.[60] For Hodža, Slovak national awareness derived from the humble virtues of traditional peasantry. He thus maintained that Slavic connections, which were retained in the core of the nation and formed the basis for the new union with the Czechs, survived among the Slovaks.

Notwithstanding the Slovaks' own appreciation of their peasant heritage, the dearth of exhibits from Slovakia in Brno meant that earlier such representations of the region were not part of the ideological orientation at the 1928 exhibition. Despite being located in Moravia, with all that region's rural associations (which had been well on display at the 1890s Prague exhibitions), the city now sought to distance itself from a culture often depicted as feminine and naive. Instead, the urban modernity associated with Prague was foremost.[61] Thus, the farmhouse displayed in Brno was electrified from floor to ceiling and featured automated milking machines, a heated poultry house, and its own meteorological station, phone exchange, and distillery—the very vision of futuristic agriculture. Missing in 1928 were the figurines and *tableaux vivants* of daily peasant life and folk culture/costume. Those artifacts from a fast-disappearing premodern society were now only to be found in photographs of the Moravian Regional Museum exhibit.

The interspersal of traditional presentations of national identity with modern (and modernist) ones lent the Brno exhibition a multilayered narrative. This strategy, and in particular the turn toward cosmopolitanism and internationalism, was directly related to Czechoslovakia's western political orientation as it emanated from the Prague Castle toward France, Britain, and the United States. This no doubt reflected a conscious effort by Czechoslovak political leaders to present their new state in the most forward-looking light possible. Thus, besides the Brno Exhibition's clear contribution to that image, the government produced a wealth of official data by leading academics on topics including the country's history, ethnic composition, democratic vision, and, of course, cultural richness.[62]

This political direction can be traced back to the negotiations with the Allies during the world war and, in particular, the roles played in those talks by Edvard Beneš (Minister of Foreign Affairs from 1918–35) and Tomáš Garrigue Masaryk (the first Czechoslovak president). The latter would become the country's most prominent politician and a key symbol of the democratic state. Less well known is that Masaryk served as protector (guardian) of the Brno exhibition. His statue stood in the most prominent place of the main exhibition hall, where it oversaw the opening and closing ceremonies (Figure 4.3). Masaryk himself helped to promote the exhibition, and his three visits to the fairgrounds were closely documented and widely commented upon in the press.[63]

And herein lies one final, important parallel between the prewar and postwar, imperial and national exhibitions: at Prague in both 1891 and 1895, the Emperor Franz Joseph was the official patron, with his own statue in the central exhibition area. Moreover, just as the survey of the 1891 exhibition praised the Kaiser as the "bright, fatherly and kind head of state"—a patron of St. Wenceslas' crown—who visited the Jubilee Exhibition personally, post-1918 Masaryk was also depicted as a fatherly figure.[64] Indeed, "tatíček" (Papa) Masaryk was regularly referred to as caring, charitable, and modest—traits which, evidently, appealed to people in both eras. So too, official pomp and ceremony surrounded both men—much like Emperor Franz Joseph, President Masaryk's birthday, name day, and everyday encounters with common people were both fêted and fawned over in Czechoslovakia.[65] In this way, the ruptures with the past that were so assiduously cultivated at the Exhibition of Contemporary Culture still left room for continuity when it came to the higher political level of national theater.

Conclusion

The presence of the head of state, whether a monarch or a president, conferred official sanction on exhibitions organized on the international, national, or regional levels. Typically, the types of exhibitions examined in this chapter were closely linked to the dominant state ideology—the exhibition projecting a miniature, idealized version of the state or locality accessible to a mass audience. Such exhibitions therefore told the story of the ruling ideology in which minorities were often under- or misrepresented. The exhibitions in Brno and Vienna functioned as what the cultural theorist Tony Bennett calls "exhibition complexes," where the various displays, pavilion designs, and even the flow of the crowd were aligned with the official ideological system of the ruling class—a system supported by the exhibition itself.[66]

Figure 4.3. The Exhibition of Contemporary Culture in Czechoslovakia, Brno, 1928 (statue of President Masaryk in the center). Postcard. Author's collection.

At the same time, however, the late nineteenth-century events in Prague and northern Bohemia consciously contested the dominant state ideology in order to raise the visibility of ethnic minorities and their growing national awareness. In Prague, ethno-nationalism was thus on display, for example, in the form of folk exhibits and their connection with authentic traditional Czech culture. In Reichenberg, the Bohemian Germans were showcased as the economic driving force in Bohemia and the city as the new regional capital of the German minority.

In this respect, the postwar Brno exhibition sought to break free from the narrowly defined nationalism of previous events in Prague and elsewhere by presenting a modern, modernist, and cosmopolitan image of state and society. The romanticized folk culture was removed as an archaic remnant of the premodern past, often associated with Austria-Hungary, and turned into a museum exhibit. It was replaced by a utilitarian and forward-looking image of a modern village that could actively contribute to the state's prosperity. Similarly, religion and, especially, the Catholic faith that were so closely linked with the Habsburg monarchy were marginalized in favor of the more pragmatic orientation of Prague and the Castle.

The deliberate attempt by the organizers of the 1928 Brno exhibition to disassociate it from the legacy of the Habsburg monarchy resulted in an image of contemporary culture with new values, traditions, and identities. Yet in order to claim the status of a nationally and internationally significant exhibition, and to connect it with the global exhibition network generally, the events held in such places as Prague, Brno, and northern Bohemia had to replicate many features—formal and ideological alike—of their larger, more famous predecessors. Thus next to the significant ruptures with the imperial past, one also finds much continuity between the Viennese *Weltausstellung* and the exhibitions organized in the Czech-speaking lands from the late nineteenth through early twentieth centuries.

Marta Filipová, PhD, Research Fellow, University of Birmingham, is an art and design historian interested in identity construction in the visual arts of modern Central Europe, in the politics of displays at national and international exhibitions, and, more generally, in the relationship between the global and local in art. She has published a number of articles on these topics in journals including the *Austrian History Yearbook*, the *Journal of Design History*, and the *RIHA journal*. She is the editor of *Cultures of International Exhibitions 1840–1940: Great Exhibitions in the Margins* (Farnham: Ashgate, 2015) and is currently completing a monograph for Routledge on theoretical and historical debates about Czech modern art and the construction of identity.

Notes

1. Jan Máša, "Deset let československé republiky," in *Výstava soudobé kultury v Československu Brno 1928: Hlavní průvodce*, ed. Vladimír Úlehla, Jaroslav B. Svrček, and František V. Vaníček (Brno: Výstava soudobé kultury v ČSR, 1928), 44.
2. Ibid.
3. Tony Bennett, "The Exhibitionary Complex," *New Formations* 4 (Spring 1998): 73–102.
4. Bibliographies related to international and universal exhibitions can be found in: Alexander C. T. Geppert, Jean Coffey, and Tammy Lau, *International Exhibitions, Expositions Universelles and World's Fairs, 1851–2005: A Bibliography* (Berlin: Freie Universität Berlin, 2006); John Allwood, *The Great Exhibitions, 150 Years* (London: Exhibition Consultants Ltd., 2001); Christian Beutler, *Weltausstellungen im 19. Jahrhundert: Ausstellung Katalog* (Munich: Staatliche Museen, 1973); Robert Bordaz and Marc Vellay, *Le Livre des Expositions Universelles 1851–1989* (Paris: Herscher, 1983); John E. Finding and Kimberley D. Pelle, eds., *Encyclopedia of World's Fairs and Exhibitions* (Jefferson, NC: McFarland & Company, 2008); Robert Goehlert, Kira Homo, John Russell, Jason Schultz, Claudia Silverman, and Skye Thomsen, *World's Fairs: A Guide to Selected English-Language Resources* (Bloomington: Indiana University Press, 2005).
5. Paul Greenhalgh, *Ephemeral Vistas: History of the Expositions Universelles, Great Exhibitions and World's Fairs* (Manchester: Manchester University Press, 1990).
6. Marta Filipová, ed., *Cultures of International Exhibitions 1840–1940: Great Exhibitions in the Margins* (Farnham: Ashgate, 2015).
7. John R. Davis, "A Marginal Exhibition? The All-German Exhibition in Berlin, 1844," in *Cultures of International Exhibitions*, 69–90.
8. Ibid.
9. *Výstava Klementinum 1791: dvousté výročí první průmyslové výstavy na evropském kontinentě* (Prague: Národní knihovna, 1991), 3–4.
10. Johann Slokar, *Geschichte der österreichischen Industrie und ihrer Förderung unter Kaiser Franz I* (Vienna: F. Temsky, 1914), 236.
11. Matthew Rampley, "Peasants in Vienna: Ethnographic Displays at the 1873 World's Fair," *Austrian History Yearbook* 42 (2011): 111.
12. Ibid.
13. Anon, "Světová Výstava ve Vídni," *Národní listy*, 3 May 1873, 1.
14. Rampley, "Peasants in Vienna," 122.
15. Anon, "K otevření světové výstavy," *Moravská orlice*, 2 May 1873, 1; Rampley, "Peasants in Vienna," 129.
16. Catherine Albrecht, "Pride in Production: The Jubilee Exhibition of 1891 and Economic Competition between Czechs and Germans in Bohemia," *Austrian History Yearbook* 24 (1993): 106.
17. Vilém Kurz, *Lanová dráha a rozhledna na Petříně* (Prague: Pražská informační služba, 1891).
18. *Jubilejní výstava zemská Království českého v Praze 1891* (Prague: V. Šimáček, 1894), 156.
19. Albrecht, "Pride in Production," 101–18.
20. F. V. Vykoukal, "Lidové umění," in *Jubilejní výstava zemská*, 742.
21. Emanuel Kovář, ed., *Národopisná výstava českoslovanská v Praze* (Prague: Výbor Národopisné výstavy Českoslovanské, 1891), 532.

22. Čeněk Zíbrt, "Národopisná výstava českoslovanská," *Český lid* 1 (1896): 307.
23. Adolf Strzelecki, *Wystawa etnograficzna w Pradze* (Krakow: Czasu, 1896), 4.
24. Ibid., 21.
25. Marta Filipová, "Peasants on Display: The Czechoslavic Ethnographic Exhibition of 1895," *Journal of Design History* 24, no. 1 (March 2011): 15–36.
26. Daniel Unowsky, *The Pomp and Politics of Patriotism: Imperial Celebrations in Habsburg Austria, 1848–1916* (West Lafayette: Purdue University Press, 2005), 164.
27. Tomáš Okurka, "'Witness to the Momentous Significance of German Labour in Bohemia': Exhibitions in the German-Speaking Regions of Bohemia Before the First World War," in *Cultures of International Exhibitions*, 91–112.
28. *Katalog der Deutschböhmischen Ausstellung Reichenberg 1906* (Liberec: Selbstverlag, 1906), 44–45.
29. Anon, "Výstava Němců v Čechách," *Lidové noviny*, 17 May 1906, 2.
30. Ibid.
31. Livia Rezende, "Nature and the Brazilian State at the Independence Centennial International Exhibition in Rio de Janeiro, 1922," in *Cultures of International Exhibitions*, 163–82.
32. Ladislav Turnovský, "Československo na světové výstavě v Rio de Janeiro," *Národní listy*, 10 February 1923, 6.
33. Ibid.
34. Ibid.
35. František Krajna, *Průvodce po výstavě: Všeobecná zemská výstava roku 1929 v Poznani*, (Prague: Reklamní Kanceláře "Par," 1929), 7.
36. Krajna, *Průvodce po výstavě*, 7; Hanna Grzeszczuk-Brendel, "Architecture of the Polish National Exhibition (1929) and Architecture in Poznań of the 1930s: Transfer of Modern Movement Ideas," in *Modernism in Europe. Modernism in Gdynia: Architecture of 1920s and 1930s and Its Protection*, ed. Maria Jolanta Sołtysik and Robert Hirsch (Gdynia: Gdynia City Hall, 2009), 115–24.
37. Mary Heimann, *Czechoslovakia: The State That Failed* (New Haven: Yale University Press, 2009).
38. Jan Rychlík, "Czech-Slovak Relations in Czechoslovakia, 1918–1939," in *Czechoslovakia in a Nationalist and Fascist Europe, 1918–1948*, ed. Mark Cornwall and R. J. W. Evans (Oxford: Oxford University Press, 2007), 14–15.
39. Ibid.
40. Ladislava Horňáková, *100 SVUM: 100. výročí založení Sdružení výtvarných umělců moravských* (Hodonín: Galerie výtvarného umění v Hodoníně, 2007), 10.
41. František Šujan, "Jak rostlo Brno," in *Výstava soudobé kultury v Československu Brno 1928: Hlavní průvodce*, ed. Vladimír Úlehla, Jaroslav B. Svrček, and František V. Vaníček (Brno: Výstava soudobé kultury, 1928), 51–52. At this time, one-quarter of the Moravian population declared German ethnicity.
42. Alois Kožíšek, "Brněnské pozoruhodnosti," in *Výstava soudobé kultury*, ed. Úlehla et al., 62. These industries included textiles, heavy machinery, and leather manufactures.
43. Anon, "Karel Tomeš, rozhovor," *Pestrý týden* 5 (1928): 4.
44. Ladislav Pluhař, "K zahájení výstavy soudobé kultury v Československu," *Příloha Národních listů*, 26 May 1928, 1.
45. For a history of the Villa Tugendhat, see Iveta Černá and Dagmar Černoušková, *Tugendhat: Ludwig Mies van der Rohe's Commission in Brno* (Brno: Brno City Museum, 2014).

46. The architect Jan Koula quoted in Vladimír Šlapeta, "Funkcionalismus na Výstavě soudobé kultury 1928," in *Výstava soudobé kultury Brno 1928: Exhibition of Contemporary Culture*, ed. Zdeněk Müller (Brno: Veletrhy Brno, 2008), 15.
47. See: Hubert Guzik, "The Diogenes Family: The Collectivization of Accommodation in Bohemia 1905–1948," *Art in Translation* 1, no. 3 (2009): 381–417.
48. Oldřich Starý, "Kolonie 'Nový dům,'" *Stavba* VII (1928–29): 97–103; Bedřich Václavek and Zdeněk Rossmann, *Katalog výstavy moderního bydlení Nový dům* (Brno: F. Uherka and Č. Ruller, 1928); Zdeněk Kudělka and Jindřich Chatrný, *O nové Brno: brněnská architektura 1919–1939* (Brno: Muzeum města Brna, 2000).
49. Ivan Ruller, "The 'New House in Brno' Development," in *Výstava soudobé kultury*, ed. Úlehla et al., 16.
50. Grzeszczuk-Brendel, "Architecture of the Polish National Exhibition," 117.
51. Ibid., 118.
52. Nevertheless, in 1930, the number of members of the Catholic Church in the Czech lands exceeded 78 percent of all inhabitants. This included the ethnic Germans and Poles. Zdeněk Kárník, *České země v éře první republiky (1918–1938) I: Vznik, budování a zlatá léta republiky (1918–1929)* (Prague: Libri, 2003), 324.
53. Vladimír Úlehla, "Člověk a příroda živá," in *Výstava soudobé kultury*, ed. Úlehla et al., 96.
54. František Kubelka, "Werkbund," in *Výstava soudobé kultury*, ed. Úlehla et al., 161.
55. Ibid., 162, 163.
56. See: Andrzej Szczerski, *Modernizacje: Sztuka i architektura w nowych państwach Europy Środkowo-Wschodniej 1918–1939* (Łódź: Muzeum Sztuki w Łodzi, 2010), 311–15.
57. Rychlík, "Czech-Slovak Relations," 15.
58. Miroslav Hroch, *Social Preconditions of National Revival in Europe: A Comparative Analysis of the Social Composition of Patriotic Groups Among the Smaller European Nations* (Cambridge, UK: Cambridge University Press, 1985). Cited in Umut Özkirimli, *Theories of Nationalism: A Critical Introduction* (Basingstoke: Palgrave Macmillan, 2000), 159–60.
59. "Slavnostní zahájení výstavy," *Národní politika*, 2nd supplement, no. 147, 27 May 1928, 2.
60. Milan Hodža, "Šviháci," *Slovenský týždenník* V, no. 19 (10 May 1907); reprinted in Milan Hodža, *Články, reči, štúdie I* (Prague: Novina, 1930), 141–45.
61. Jindřich Chylík, "Brněnská jubilejní výstava," *Příloha Národních listů* 28 (May 1928): 2.
62. Andrea Orzoff, *Battle for the Castle: The Myth of Czechoslovakia in Europe, 1914–1948* (New York: Oxford University Press, 2009), 8.
63. Jiří Rak, "Stařičký mocnář a tatíček Masaryk," in *19. století v nás: modely, instituce a reprezentace, které přetrvaly,* ed. Milan Řepa (Prague: Historický ústav, 2008), 267.
64. Rudolf Jaroslav Kronbauer, *Naše Jubilejní výstava* (Prague: Josef Vilímek, 1892), 279.
65. Rak, "Stařičký mocnář", 269.
66. Bennett, "The Exhibitionary Complex."

Select Bibliography

Albrecht, Catherine. "Pride in Production: The Jubilee Exhibition of 1891 and Economic Competition between Czechs and Germans in Bohemia." *Austrian History Yearbook* 24 (1993): 101–18.

Bennett, Tony. "The Exhibitionary Complex." *New Formations* 4 (Spring 1998): 73–102.
Filipová, Marta, ed. *Cultures of International Exhibitions 1840–1940: Great Exhibitions in the Margins*. Farnham: Ashgate, 2015.
———. "Peasants on Display: The Czechoslavic Ethnographic Exhibition of 1895." *Journal of Design History* 24, no. 1 (March 2011): 15–36.
Greenhalgh, Paul. *Ephemeral Vistas: History of the Expositions Universelles, Great Exhibitions and World's Fairs*. Manchester: Manchester University Press, 1990.
Grzeszczuk-Brendel, Hanna. "Architecture of the Polish National Exhibition (1929) and Architecture in Poznań of the 1930s: Transfer of Modern Movement Ideas." In *Modernism in Europe. Modernism in Gdynia: Architecture of 1920s and 1930s and Its Protection*, edited by Maria Jolanta Sołtysik and Robert Hirsch, 115–24. Gdynia: Gdynia City Hall, 2009.
Guzik, Hubert. "The Diogenes Family: The Collectivization of Accommodation in Bohemia 1905–1948." *Art in Translation* 1, no. 3 (2009): 381–417.
Heimann, Mary. *Czechoslovakia: The State That Failed*. New Haven: Yale University Press, 2009.
Hodža, Milan. "Šviháci." *Slovenský týždenník* V, no. 19 (10 May 1907); reprinted in Hodža, Milan. *Články, reči, štúdie I*. Prague: Novina, 1930, 141–45.
Horňáková, Ladislava. *100 SVUM: 100. výročí založení Sdružení výtvarných umělců moravských*. Hodonín: Galerie výtvarného umění v Hodoníně, 2007.
Hroch, Miroslav. *Social Preconditions of National Revival in Europe: A Comparative Analysis of the Social Composition of Patriotic Groups Among the Smaller European Nations*. Cambridge, UK: Cambridge University Press, 1985.
Jubilejní výstava zemská Království českého v Praze 1891. Prague: V. Šimáček, 1894.
Kárník, Zdeněk. *České země v éře první republiky (1918–1938) I: Vznik, budování a zlatá léta republiky (1918–1929)*. Prague: Libri, 2003.
Katalog der Deutschböhmischen Ausstellung Reichenberg 1906. Liberec: Selbstverlag, 1906.
Kovář, Emanuel, ed. *Národopisná výstava českoslovanská v Praze*. Prague: Výbor Národopisné výstavy Českoslovanské, 1891.
Krajna, František. *Průvodce po výstavě: Všeobecná zemská výstava roku 1929 v Poznani*. Prague: Reklamní Kanceláře "Par," 1929.
Kronbauer, Rudolf Jaroslav. *Naše Jubilejní výstava*. Prague: Josef Vilímek, 1892.
Kuděłka, Zdeněk and Jindřich Chatrný. *O nové Brno: brněnská architektura 1919–1939*. Brno: Muzeum města Brna, 2000.
Kurz, Vilém. *Lanová dráha a rozhledna na Petříně*. Prague: Pražská informační služba, 1891.
Máša, Jan. "Deset let československé republiky." In *Výstava soudobé kultury v Československu Brno 1928: Hlavní průvodce*, edited by Vladimír Úlehla, Jaroslav B. Svrček, and František V. Vaníček, 7–9. Brno: Výstava soudobé kultury v ČSR, 1928.
Müller, Zdeněk, ed. *Výstava soudobé kultury Brno 1928: Exhibition of Contemporary Culture*. Brno: Veletrhy Brno, 2008.
Orzoff, Andrea. *Battle for the Castle: The Myth of Czechoslovakia in Europe, 1914–1948*. New York: Oxford University Press, 2009.
Özkirimli, Umut. *Theories of Nationalism: A Critical Introduction*. Basingstoke: Palgrave Macmillan, 2000.
Pluhař, Ladislav. "K zahájení výstavy soudobé kultury v Československu." *Příloha Národních listů*. 26 May 1928, 1.
Rak, Jiří. "Staříčký mocnář a tatíček Masaryk." In *19. století v nás: modely, instituce a reprezentace, které přetrvaly*, edited by Milan Řepa, 267–73. Prague: Historický ústav, 2008.

Rampley, Matthew. "Peasants in Vienna: Ethnographic Displays at the 1873 World's Fair." *Austrian History Yearbook* 42 (2011): 110–32.
Rychlík, Jan. "Czech-Slovak Relations in Czechoslovakia, 1918–1939." In *Czechoslovakia in a Nationalist and Fascist Europe, 1918–1948*, edited by Mark Cornwall and R. J. W. Evans, 13–26. Oxford: Oxford University Press, 2007.
Slokar, Johann. *Geschichte der österreichischen Industrie und ihrer Förderung unter Kaiser Franz I*. Vienna: F. Temsky, 1914.
Starý, Oldřich. "Kolonie 'Nový dům.'" *Stavba* VII (1928–29): 97–103.
Strzelecki, Adolf. *Wystawa etnograficzna w Pradze*. Krakow: Czasu, 1896.
Szczerski, Andrzej. *Modernizacje: Sztuka i architektura w nowych państwach Europy Środkowo-Wschodniej 1918–1939*. Łódź: Muzeum Sztuki w Łodzi, 2010.
Úlehla, Vladimír, Jaroslav B. Svrček, and František V. Vaníček, eds. *Výstava soudobé kultury v Československu Brno 1928: Hlavní průvodce*. Brno: Výstava soudobé kultury, 1928.
Unowsky, Daniel. *The Pomp and Politics of Patriotism: Imperial Celebrations in Habsburg Austria, 1848–1916*. West Lafayette: Purdue University Press, 2005.
Václavek, Bedřich and Zdeněk Rossmann. *Katalog výstavy moderního bydlení Nový dům*. Brno: F. Uherka and Č. Ruller, 1928.
Výstava Klementinum 1791: dvousté výročí první průmyslové výstavy na evropském kontinentě. Prague: Národní knihovna, 1991.
Zíbrt, Čeněk. "Národopisná výstava českoslovanská." *Český lid* 1 (1896): 1–17; 97–128; 193–214; 289–311; 385–415.

Journals and Newspapers
Lidové noviny
Moravská orlice
Národní politika
Národní listy
Pestrý týden
Příloha Národních listů

Part II

THE HABSBURG ARMY'S FINAL BATTLES

Chapter 5

REFLECTIONS ON THE LEGACY OF THE IMPERIAL AND ROYAL ARMY IN THE SUCCESSOR STATES

Richard Bassett

By mid summer 1918, after four years of constant warfare on never fewer than two and often three fronts, the armed forces of the multinational Habsburg Empire still largely held firm. Since the opening of hostilities in August 1914, they had fought against Serbia, Italy, Russia, Romania, and in Palestine. Now they faced unrelenting assault from British and French units as well. And yet they fought on.

Despite initial setbacks in Serbia and Russia, Habsburg armies had demonstrated formidable powers of recovery and perseverance. Indeed, the "imperial and royal"—*kaiserlich und königlich*, or *k. (u.) k.*—army had fought with such determination the previous year that by December 1917, with Russia, Romania, and Serbia defeated and out of the war, it had achieved all of its major objectives: Serbia, against whom the Dual Monarchy had entered the war in the first place, had been liquidated as a factor in Balkan politics; tsarist Russia, Serbia's powerful protector, had been overthrown and the tenuous Bolshevik government was about to cede significant territory in a peace settlement; and Italy, which had cost the Habsburgs two crown lands in the late nineteenth century and declared war on its nominal ally in 1915, had been crushed at Caporetto. By December 1917, not a single enemy soldier stood on Habsburg territory.

These multifront victories, even if only temporary, made the Austro-Hungarian armed forces unique among the belligerents. Even from the viewpoint of morale, the k. (u.) k. army was arguably in better condition than the others, which without exception had either failed to achieve their objectives (e.g., the German, French, and British forces on the Western Front; the Russians in the East) or had been comprehensively defeated in the course of 1917 (e.g. the Italian and Romanian armies). In a year that saw serious mutinies in France and revolution in Russia, the Habsburg Army displayed such discipline and fighting power that a vigorously negotiated peace and the federalization of the Austro-Hungarian Empire might well have prevented its disintegration.

Nor did the wave of mutinies that began spreading across the Empire in the spring of 1918 bring down the Monarchy the way it had in Russia, and as many had expected it to. When some elements of the Imperial and Royal Navy mutinied in Cattaro (Kotor, Montenegro), it was the prelude to several acts of insubordination: Slovenes revolted in Styria; Czechs mutinied in northern Bohemia; Hungarians refused to accept orders in Budapest; and a largely Serbian unit from the old military frontier in Pécs, together with Bosnian recruits at Mostar and some Slovak reservists in Kragujevac (occupied Serbia) began questioning orders. Habsburg military authorities responded with severe suppression and the reimposition of iron discipline.[1] Yet the imperial structure held together, and by summer, order had been fully restored. To the great consternation of Austria-Hungary's opponents, the long hoped for collapse of the k. (u.) k. armies had once again failed to materialize.[2]

This was all the more remarkable given that allied propaganda sought to sow disaffection among the army's non-Austrian elements. For example, on 9 August 1918, London issued a proclamation recognizing the Czechoslovaks as "an allied nation."[3] This appeal to Czechs and Slovaks fighting for the Habsburgs closely followed a concerted campaign to undermine the morale of Croats and Slovenes by persuading them that their fate lay in the formation of a South Slavic (i.e., Yugoslav) state. Likewise, the "German" Austrians were subjected to a barrage of enemy propaganda that aimed to drive a wedge between the empire's different nationalities. London-based intellectuals like the journalist Henry Wickham Steed and the historian Robert Seton-Watson, both of whom had wide experience of the Slav problem in the Habsburg Monarchy during the years immediately preceding the war, encouraged such tactics.[4]

Support for the war in Austria-Hungary was further eroded by the increasingly poor condition of military supplies and equipment, not to mention the dire food shortages on both the military and home fronts. Many uniforms were now made of artificial fabrics derived from such exotic (and cheap) materials as stinging nettles, which barely survived a day in the rain and sleet of the Alps. Similarly, ersatz fabrics for footwear quickly fell apart. Coupled with the aforementioned anti-Habsburg propaganda, such conditions prompted the *Arbeiter Zeitung* in Vienna to abandon its slogan of "patriotic socialism" and declare, as early as March 1918, that "enthusiasm for the war has sunk below zero. It no longer has even the slightest support among the masses; the people desire only peace."[5] Nevertheless, the k. (u.) k. army—frozen, exhausted, hungry, and menaced from all sides—preserved a united front and forged on.[6]

It actually achieved more than this. In early August 1918, as French, Italian, and Serb forces gathered in Albania to drive two divisions of the k. (u.) k. army out of that country, the Austro-Hungarian supreme command proved it was still capable of reacting swiftly and effectively by replacing the rather unenterprising General Hozak in Albania with the energetic and accomplished General Pflanzer-Baltin. Arriving in Albania after an epic journey by ship, rail, and air, Pflanzer-Baltin quickly marshaled his troops to force the French and their allies to evacuate Fier and Berat in a brilliantly coordinated counter-offensive against materially and numerically superior opponents. This was no mean achievement for an army supposedly on the brink of disintegration. As late as 20 October, Pflanzer-Baltin safely led his men out of Albania in a series of dazzling rearguard actions over the Mati River and on to the Adriatic coast, after which he prepared them for evacuation by ships of the Imperial and Royal Navy. When a powerful British naval task force led by the HMS Weymouth attempted to intercept Pflanzer-Baltin's army just as it was embarking, an Austrian submarine torpedoed the Weymouth and the remaining task force scattered. Pflanzer-Baltin was thus able to complete his troop transfer to Austrian naval ships undisturbed.[7] Today, this action is perhaps best remembered as the last time the celebrated Order of Maria Theresa was awarded to an Imperial and Royal officer in action. But in 1918, it also demonstrated that the Habsburg Monarchy was still a factor in military and naval circles, despite four years of uninterrupted fighting.

The tenacity and courage demonstrated by the Imperial and Royal Navy in assisting Pflanzer-Baltin's withdrawal underlined its formidable training and history. As the British Admiral Sir Ernest Troubridge commented, "Iron discipline and tremendous keenness of spirit [has] made the Austrian Navy, small as it is, ship for ship, perhaps the most efficient of modern times."[8] One reason for this was the impressive esprit and morale of both the navy's and the army's multilingual, multinational, and multiconfessional officer corps. Although by no means multicultural in the modern sense (German, after all, was the language of command with the exception of the Hungarian *Honvéd* units), the ethnically diverse officers were deeply loyal both to military tradition and to the Habsburg dynasty.[9] This loyalty persevered, moreover, despite huge combat losses.

The second factor for the Monarchy's military persistence was summed up by General Edmund Glaise-Horstenau, when he referred to Habsburg forces as "a living, active, historically evolved body upon which only the greatest storms could make any impression."[10] Thus as late as September 1918, it was still possible to deploy two Habsburg divisions (the 106th and the 39th *Honvéd*) to the Western Front to support the German army. This was the first time that Austro-Hungarian infantry had been deployed to that horrific war zone. And it successfully took place even as different parts of the Empire, including Hungary herself, were actively seeking autonomy from the Habsburg crown.

Nevertheless, by this time the writing was on the wall, and quite literally so—one morning, a famous Hungarian regiment (Szekler no. 82) deserted its trenches, leaving a note pinned to the trench wall that read: "Up to now none of us has deserted, but we cannot resist hunger any longer."[11] Clearly these were receptive conditions for Bolshevist propaganda. And obviously such evidence for why the Monarchy ultimately disintegrated is anecdotal. But it is important to stress that right up to the end of the war, neither the nationalist nor socialist factors that historians typically attribute to the Empire's breakup were determinative. In many cases, and at least as far as the army was concerned, material needs proved more decisive in the military and state's disintegration than ideological (i.e., nationalist) aspirations.[12]

When the Allies launched their final offensive on 24 October 1918 (the anniversary of their great defeat at Caporetto), the Austro-Hungarian army went into battle for the last time. As one contemporary observed: "The world had never before beheld such a spectacle: an army fighting on behalf of a country that to all intents and purposes had ceased to exist."[13] The allies massed twenty-two divisions, with nineteen in reserve and some 4,750 guns. For more than four days, they attacked unsuccessfully, despite massive material advantages and nearly 3:1 numerical superiority. Against them stubbornly fought Czechs, Slovaks, Magyars, Ukrainians, Slovenes, Poles, and Austrians. By now, every tenth officer on this front was of Jewish origin, while another 10 percent were Serbs.[14] It is impossible to say what combination of factors inspired this diverse collection of troops so late in the war. Perhaps their spirits were raised upon hearing, on 24 October 1918, the last proclamation a Habsburg Emperor would ever address to his men in uniform:

> Soldiers! Your duty is as clear and simple as your oath! That is an unalterable fact. All peoples of the Monarchy have found a common home in the army. For that reason it has been able to accomplish so much. The army will overcome the present dangers in the same spirit in which it marched to war—calm, determined, loyal and honorable—for the protection of *all* its peoples. God be with you![15]

Beneath its Horatian oratory, these words betrayed a simple truth: the Imperial and Royal army signified a compact between the dynasty and all the peoples over which the Emperor ruled. This compact included Jews and Muslims (both fiercely monarchist and patriotic), as well as Catholics, Protestants, Orthodox, and Lutherans. As defeat turned into revolution, the question arose as to what, if anything, of this compact could survive.

One positive and telling answer was delivered shortly thereafter by the Croatian Field Marshal Svetozar Boroević von Bojna, the "Lion of the Isonzo" whose dynastic loyalty was as unflinching as that of his forefathers on the old

Austrian military frontier.[16] In a memorandum published by the historian Friedrich Funder, Dr. Adam Hefter (then Bishop of Klagenfurt) recalled meeting the Field Marshal during the first week of November 1918. It was a precarious time—just days earlier, Austria-Hungary had fought and lost its final battle of the world war, and the Italians, by unilaterally manipulating the hour of the ceasefire, had "captured" Habsburg armies around Vittorio Veneto without firing a shot. Meanwhile, Austrian regiments from Styria, Carinthia, and Upper Austria had withdrawn to defend the frontier against (correctly) anticipated territorial demands on behalf of the emerging Yugoslav state.[17] According to Hefter, the Field Marshal confided in him the following:

> I have twice telegraphed the Emperor offering my troops to form a force which could, fulfilling its traditional obligations to the dynasty, occupy Vienna and thus provide His Majesty with the freedom of maneuver in negotiations which he appears to have lost but desperately needs. But I can only do this on his command. Only his orders can invest me with the powers I need to command an army. I am, after all, someone who was born in Croatia which now belongs to Yugoslavia.[18]

Boroević added that he planned to transport unreliable units away from Wiener Neustadt, outside of Vienna, from where his troops would advance on the capital and take control of it within twenty-four hours. Everything, he stressed, was prepared, but twice the Emperor—who knew Boroević well and was familiar with his efficiency—had appeared to ignore his offer. On 11 November, less than forty-eight hours after this exchange, Emperor Charles issued the following declaration:

> I have not hesitated to restore constitutional life and I have opened up for the peoples the paths of their development as independent states. Filled now as ever with unwavering devotion to all my peoples, I do not wish to oppose the free government with my own person. I recognize in advance whatever decisions that German Austria may make about its future form. I renounce all participation in the affairs of state. . . . The happiness of my peoples has from the beginning been the object of my most ardent wishes. Only an inner peace can heal the wounds of this war.[19]

This last sentence, which was characteristic of the Emperor's sensibility and deeply held Christian beliefs, can be read as the formal public reply to Boroević's telegrams. The Field Marshal stood down and contemplated with his soldiers their uncertain future, as did thousands of other k. (u.) k. officers.

Despite being the only wartime leader to have served as a regular officer both before and during the world war, the Emperor Charles understood his foremost duty to preserve the lives of his subjects rather than risk everything for the sake of the dynasty. He had served with Boroević before and knew that his arrival in Vienna would mean yet more bloodshed and perhaps even civil war, an eventuality the Emperor was determined to avoid. Yet by the same token, the army did not let the dynasty down in its supreme moment of crisis. Instead, the sovereign exhibited an altruism and statesmanlike realism that was rare among monarchs and rather unusual, though not unheard of, for Habsburgs, when he broke the compact which bound the House of Austria to its army for three hundred years.

This decision was, of course, rich in historic irony. In June 1619, Ferdinand II was besieged in the *Hofburg* by a Bohemian Protestant mob. When he fell to his knees and implored the Almighty to send soldiers to rescue him, D'Ampierre's dragoons appeared almost miraculously to force the mob back, a real turning point in the history of the Thirty Years' War. In seemingly answering the Emperor's prayers, those few score dragoons sealed an understanding between the military and dynasty that would last for centuries. Indeed, the fact that subsequent Habsburgs never forgot this was ensconced in the tradition of allowing the colonel commanding the dragoon regiment that succeeded D'Ampierre's cavalry unit "unrestricted access to the Hofburg and the Emperor at any time."[20] This may seem like irrelevant symbolism, but such traditions were exactly what contributed to the Monarchy's longevity.

Three hundred years later, Ferdinand II's successor also devoutly prayed for help, though he flinched from deploying the one factor that might have saved his House. As Charles's penultimate Foreign Minister, Count Ottokar Czernin observed rather waspishly in his memoirs: Charles, unlike his uncle Franz Ferdinand, was not someone to die "sword in hand" for the Empire.[21] That may have been true, but Charles was also capable of thinking differently. When his adviser Polzer-Hodel suggested Max Wladimir von Beck as a suitable candidate for prime minister because "he was in the line of logical development" for the post, Charles rounded on him and said: "Why are you so obsessed with the line of logical development? The line of logical development is the collapse of this monarchy."[22] Charles' motivation in 1918 arose from the same sort of independent thinking and dynastic devotion toward "all his peoples," regardless of whether that ultimately doomed the Habsburg Empire.

The imperial proclamation of 11 November thus formally closes the history of the k. (u.) k. army. Its culture and ethos made it incapable of functioning effectively without the support, guidance, and leadership of the dynasty. It could never have assumed control of the government in the way the German army increasingly did under Generals Ludendorff and Hindenburg, who had turned the country into a war machine by 1916.[23] Nor could the army become the instrument of one particular nation or religion. In this sense, it was spiritually, mentally, and practically ill-adapted to the modern era, when the most powerful movements of the day—socialism and nationalism—were about to meld. Once the compact with the dynasty was broken, the k. (u.) k. army was incapable of discharging its traditional functions, as Boroević's dilemma made clear.

So what, if anything, of the Habsburg military's remarkable fabric, professionalism, and ethos survived in the successor states? In many cases, the trauma of military disintegration was intense, especially among senior officers. Worn out and aged well before their time, a large proportion of these career officers died within years of the war's end. Field Marshal Boroević might have honored his Croatian origins, but as the prestigious former commander of a Habsburg army, Yugoslav authorities—Croat and Serb alike—made it clear that he was not welcome in their new country. They quickly confiscated his property and possessions, including all his personal effects, as they passed through Slovenia en route to Klagenfurt.[24] For all his mastery of the battlefield against the Italians, British, and French, Boroević was persona non grata in the land of his birth, now the newly constituted Kingdom of the Serbs, Croats, and Slovenes.

Sadly, Boroević's fate was not untypical of k. (u.) k. officers who remained in Austria proper. His pension was largely worthless in a republic ravaged by financial and social dislocation, and he died virtually penniless. Indeed, one of the only things keeping him alive were the modest sums bestowed by the former Emperor—an echo, perhaps, of the generous sense of obligation that Franz Joseph had shown just a few years earlier toward the impoverished composer Anton Bruckner. When Boroević died in Klagenfurt in May 1920, he was already an anachronism even in Austria. His magnificent grave in Vienna's *Zentralfriedhof* was paid for personally by the ex-Emperor Charles.

The political dislocation in postwar Central and Eastern Europe made it particularly difficult for the k. (u.) k. officer class to find a stable basis for their lives. Nor did it help that everywhere, the old supranational values were under siege by nationalists. In the new Austrian Republic, for example, political leaders on the socialist left favored unification with Germany. They even went so far as to introduce military uniforms based on the German *Reichswehr*, symbolically replacing the Habsburg Black and Gold insignia with the "new" Austrian colors (Red, White, Red) and consigning the old collar patches and *Farbenkastl* ("paint-box" of colors) to history. However, the Austrian Republic's true conservative/Catholic orientation under Engelbert Dollfuß, a politician who actively encouraged Austrian patriotism, was best demonstrated during the 1934 leftist insurgency, sometimes portentously referred to as "Austria's Civil War." When communist and socialist activists took refuge in the large blocks of Vienna's new social housing, regular army units shelled them. All across the capital, the insurgency was easily put down.[25]

Many quickly forgot the values of the Habsburg army as German pressure increased in the run-up to the *Anschluß*. By 1938, when the Wehrmacht incorporated the small Austrian army (limited by the Allies to thirty thousand troops), the traditional Habsburg methods of multinational and multiconfessional militarism had largely died out. Their brief return, hinted at in the form of the old k. (u.) k. uniforms that Dollfuß revived, only served, like Austria's economic recovery in the late 1930s, as a poignant echo of a seemingly distant past, one vividly described in Alexander Lernet-Holenia's novel *Die Standarte*.[26]

In that best-selling work, the hero, Ensign Herbert Menis, suddenly encounters the old Habsburg uniforms while walking through the Volksgarten on a sunny afternoon in the early 1930s.

For the German nationalist professional officer class, the Wehrmacht offered a seductive alternative. More than two hundred of Hitler's generals were former k. (u.) k. officers. But many others were persecuted (including the Walderdorff family, to name just one prominent example), and many who had been devout Catholics were disinherited and even imprisoned. Jewish officers, of course, suffered the most. Irrespective of rank, they were cashiered in 1938 after the *Anschluß*. Even Jews of "mixed" origins (i.e., just one Jewish grandparent) were dismissed in 1940 when, together with Jesuit priests and members of dynastic families, they were formally pronounced "unworthy of military service."[27]

Not all officers who remained were entirely won over by the new order. Hitler appointed General Edmund Glaise-Horstenau, the Habsburg army historian after World War I, as General Plenipotentiary to the newly formed Croatian Ustasha state, which the Nazis established after a British-Soviet coup deposed the accommodationist Yugoslav regent, Prince Paul, and the Wehrmacht invaded Yugoslavia.[28] Like many Austrian Nazis, Glaise-Horstenau initially naively thought that Germany's revival would restore the values and ethos that were lost when the Austro-Hungarian Empire collapsed. But he was swiftly disillusioned by the murderous behavior of the Ustasha, whom he memorably reported to his Wehrmacht seniors as having "gone quite raging mad."[29] Glaise-Horstenau realized rather late that the old army of the Monarchy was not being recreated before his eyes, but rather something far more intolerant and barbaric. He would later commit suicide.

Austrian Wehrmacht officers on the whole fought willingly for the new order, though there were other exceptions as well.[30] One was a young Croat-Slovene who had attracted attention during World War I on account of his discipline, smartness, and courage. But the NCO Josip Broz had digested the lessons of the old Habsburg army far too well to fight for the new Nazi one. Instead, "Tito"—the communist party pseudonym he adopted in the mid-1930s—led one of the most effective Partisan insurgencies in Nazi-controlled Europe, succeeding in part by incorporating integrative aspects of the k. (u.) k. army. After the war, Marshal Tito would unify socialist Yugoslavia by employing all of the old Habsburg techniques of divide and rule in a yet more authoritarian manner, and above all by creating a crude version of the imperial army in miniature.

The Yugoslav National Army (JNA), which through the late 1980s was a dominating element of socialist Yugoslavia and one of Europe's most powerful military forces, was officered mostly by Serbs with impeccable communist partisan credentials. But it also openly embraced elements of both the multinational Habsburg army and the old Austrian eighteenth-century Military Frontier, which had united subjects of varying religions and ethnicities into a loyal but irregular force. The language of command, for example, was based on sixty-eight words, just as in imperial times (though now in Serbo-Croat rather than German). Furthermore, the authorities took great pains to garrison units of a single nationality away from their recruiting areas, something familiar to imperial army regiments after the Napoleonic Wars.[31] Thus, well through the 1980s, Macedonians and Serbs would be sent to the Julian Alps, while Slovenes would find themselves in barracks near Kosovo, all in an effort to show each minority that they were part of a multiethnic national fabric.[32] That this integrative instrument fell apart after Tito's death in 1980 can be ascribed both to the lack of comparable stature among the Marshal's successors, as well as to the politicization of the JNA, factors which had already eroded the legacy of the k. (u.) k. army in the other successor states as well.

Conscious attempts to replace the role of the dynasty with that of a political party or particular ethnic group that was loyal to the national government met with almost universal failure. It is worth noting that, with the exception of Poland, none of the successor states created an army that was capable of cohesively fighting a war after 1918. Poland was unique. Already in 1914, the Austrian high command had realized that it needed to grant some privileges to the Poles in order to seal their loyalty. Thus, the Archduke Frederick, commander of the Austro-Hungarian army in Galicia, recruited two Polish k. (u.) k. generals to command Polish units. Additionally, these units were permitted to use Polish as the language of command, and they were not required to wear the standard Habsburg cap-badge or the imperial cockade.

The regiments under József Piłsudski's command, which became known as "the legions," also became increasingly autonomous, resisting attempts by the Austro-Hungarian high command to integrate them into the k. (u.) k. *Landsturm* or comparable reserve units. Indeed, the legions would form the backbone of the new Polish army that Piłsudski led to victory against Soviet Russia in 1921. More than two decades later, during World War II, the commander of the 1944 Warsaw Uprising, General Bór-Komorowski, was himself a former k. (u.) k. officer who had learned his profession in the service of Emperor Charles.

In nearby Hungary, still nominally a kingdom ruled by a regent, the situation appeared rather different. The former Imperial and Royal admiral, Miklós Horthy, betrayed his oath to Emperor Charles and denied him the opportunity to return to Budapest to claim his crown. Yet he also kept his naval rank (despite the fact that Hungary had lost its coastline in the Treaty of Trianon) and, moreover, kept the old Habsburg uniforms for the new Hungarian army. Thus was Hungarian national military spirit embodied in the uniform of the Imperial and Royal hussar (as it still is to this day).[33] The English illustrator and writer Osbert Lancaster, who witnessed a St. Stephen's Day procession in the late 1920s, glowingly described the ironic, postwar survival of these Habsburg uniforms:

Immediately behind the crowd of bishops, monsignori and censer-swinging acolytes marched the Regent, Admiral Horthy, together with members of the government among whom the tail-coated representatives of the bourgeoisie were, I noted, in a marked minority. Close on their heels followed all the rank and nobility of Hungary, some traditionally booted and be-furred . . . others wearing the full-dress uniforms of the old k.(u)k. Armee, but all ablaze with the forgotten orders of a vanished chivalry. As they passed, one was conscious of a slight smell of formaldehyde. . . . With what excitement and satisfaction did I identify the cap-badges of the Deutschmeister regiment and the Radetzky Hussars! . . . What pleasure I derived from the recognition of the insignia of the Golden Fleece![34]

In 1919, Hungary had finally achieved what she had long struggled for against Vienna: an "independent army" in which Magyar was the exclusive language of command. Thus, with the fiction of a "kingdom" preserved, the Hungarian army maintained its taproot while providing Horthy with several years of "freedom of maneuver," enabling him to keep the country out of the Nazis' clutches and, until relatively late in the war, its Jewish population safe from the death camps. But Hungary's army would never play a significant role as an independent military force.

In postwar Czechoslovakia, the struggle against the "German Austrians," who made up almost a third of the country's population, entered a new and unfortunate phase.[35] The Republic's first president, Tomáš Garrigue Masaryk, had long wanted to eliminate the Habsburg inheritance. In November 1918, a Czech mob took this even further by destroying the venerated Marian Column in Prague's Old Town Square (one of the city's most important public spaces). Since 1650, the Column had symbolized the Counter-Reformation and the Austrian/Habsburg presence in the city—meaning which was further heightened when it was scarred during the Prussian siege of the city in the War of the Austrian Succession (1740–1748). Likewise, the old statue of Field Marshal Joseph Radetzky, which adorned the "Little Quarter" (*Malá Strana*) of the city, was carted off, while uniforms of a distinctly American cut replaced the old Habsburg cloth (although some "Austrian wave" was incorporated into the sleeve facings and has survived to this day).

In terms of the new Czechoslovak officer class, most "German" personnel were replaced by Czechs and approximately 30 percent of all former Habsburg officers were cashiered.[36] Of those erstwhile k. (u.) k. officers who did enter the Czechoslovak army, it is possible to see in photographs how several maintained the bearing and elegance of their Wiener Neustadt training, though, as elsewhere in the former empire, the traditional multinational tolerance of the imperial army had vanished.[37] Additionally, the Czechoslovak army, unlike the Habsburg army, was now consciously politicized, its upper ranks dominated by the so-called "Legionaries" who had been in Siberia during World War I. Considered more loyal to the "Slavic state," the Legionaries were romanticized in Czech literature of the period. This highly politicized military force, the twentieth anniversary of which was ostentatiously celebrated with publications and festivities in late 1938, fell to pieces a few months later when confronted with the threat of the German Wehrmacht.

And what of other places that had known the *Doppeladler*? We have already noted General Pflanzer-Baltin's brilliant campaign in Albania. A few years earlier, his predecessor had been presented with an Albanian named Ahmed Zogu who led the tribes around Kruja, a small but significant hill town outside of modern Tirana. So impressed were the Austrians by Zog—to use his familiar name—that he was sent to Vienna to meet the Emperor Franz Joseph, who promptly made him an honorary aide-de-camp for three months. According to the late King Zog's descendants (notably relations of his wife Geraldine, a Hungarian from the aristocratic Apponyi family), Zog had picked up many useful lessons in "divide and rule" at the Habsburg court. When he became King of Albania in 1928, he allowed the Italians to organize his army while insisting that an elite force of gendarmes be trained by the British. The uniforms Zog selected for his ceremonial guard, however, owed much to a production of Franz Lehár's *The Merry Widow* and the coronation of King Charles in Budapest in 1916, film clips of which Zog had viewed and studied.[38]

In Trieste, once the fourth city of the Habsburg Empire and its commercial hub, Baron Geoffrey (or Gottfried, or later Goffredo) Banfield quickly learned that his cosmopolitan home's new Italian masters had little patience for the Habsburg legacy. The "Eagle of Trieste," as the World War I flying ace Banfield was known, had commanded the city's naval air station, from where he and a handful of other pilots had denied the Italian air force any undisputed penetration of imperial airspace. For his valor, Banfield was honored with the Habsburgs' highest military award—the Order of Maria Theresa. Yet, soon after the war and despite his fluent Italian (not to mention German, French, and English), the new Italian authorities made Banfield painfully aware that Trieste would no longer be his home. Arrested and incarcerated in 1918, the "Eagle of Trieste" was only released through the intervention of the British Consul—his father had been an English subject, though also a senior officer in the k. (u.) k. navy at the turn of the century. Thus, after two days in prison, Banfield was given just twenty-four hours to leave Italian soil. He moved to England where he found work as a draughtsman in Newcastle and married his teenage sweetheart from Trieste, Maria Tripcovich, at Brompton Oratory. Banfield's pitiful war pension, however, did not follow him. Indeed, the paperwork mysteriously turned up in Rome decades later. Eventually, Banfield was able to return to Trieste, where he was venerated as "*il nostro barone*." He served as Honorary French Consul in 1977. After five changes of passport during his lifetime, Banfield felt only the keenest of skepticism toward European nationalism. When he died in 1985, he was one of the last survivors of the truly supranational officer class that had ruled the Habsburg Empire.

It is perhaps fitting that Trieste, the multinational Monarchy's city par excellence, should have had in Banfield such a vivid reminder of the old order. In no part of former Habsburg Europe did the ghosts of empire return in more macabre fashion than to what had once been the Austrian littoral. After Italy surrendered to the allies in 1943, South Tyrol and the areas around Trieste were subjected to a bizarre return to the status-quo ante 1866.[39] Austrian officials and former k. (u.) k. officers, many of whom had served the Habsburg Empire in the region twenty years earlier, resurfaced in Nazi uniforms in Trieste and Carniola (Slovenia) to serve the German government, the Wehrmacht, and the SS. Indeed, the entire administrative apparatus of Trieste appeared to have reverted to people who had worked there in 1914 for the Austrians. Mussolini sent his personal representatives to attempt to reincorporate the area into "Italy," but they were politely shown the door. The city's oligarchy, which in 1918 had swiftly ditched the Austrians to form an alliance with the fascist *squadristi*, now effortlessly adapted to the new (old) order.[40]

Yet while many of the old Austrian military administrative personnel may have returned to Trieste in the guise of the new Nazi order, the multinational/confessional k. (u.) k. army was light years from the German Wehrmacht. One need only think of Kaiser Franz Joseph's intervention to ensure that Jewish officers were deemed "*satisfaktionfähig*" when one was blackballed at the Vienna Jockey Club.[41] And when an Austro-German nationalist in Graz greeted Franz Joseph in 1888 with the words "Heil Kaiser," he chose never again to visit the city.[42] During the Third Reich, it was wholly in keeping with Franz Joseph's (and later Emperor Charles's) values that the last Crown Prince of Austria, Otto von Habsburg, consistently refused to meet Adolf Hitler in Berlin, where Otto was a student in the 1930s. Moreover, as the decade progressed and Hitler solidified his power, a movement favoring a Habsburg restoration emerged in Austria. In the summer of 1933, another new uniform was introduced that was virtually identical to the Habsburg attire. The old "paint-box" (*Farbenkastl*) of colors was rebranded as *Egalisierungsfarben* (leveling colors), and the collar stars were brought back to distinguish rank. Not for nothing was Germany's annexation of Austria code-named "Operation Otto" in reference to the Nazis' greatest potential rival for Austrian affections, the Archduke Otto von Habsburg.

Unfortunately, however, the fracture of interwar domestic politics, culminating in the 1934 "civil war," had so split the country along "Black/Red" lines that it was impossible to achieve a nationally cohesive response to the *Anschluß*. The army, which fully embraced the Black (i.e., Catholic, anti-socialist) side, contended with pan-German elements that had been working toward *Anschluß* well before 1914. These political pressures made it psychologically difficult for Austrians to resist the Germans in 1938. Moreover, as the Archduke Otto later recalled, there was little anyone in Austria could do given England's support for the *Anschluß*, articulated most memorably, and crassly, by Anthony Eden's comment to a colleague at the Foreign Office who had lamented the German annexation: "What is Austria? Five Habsburgs and a hundred Jews?"[43]

Tragically, if unsurprisingly, many former imperial and royal officers from Austria fought in the Wehrmacht (the elite *Gebirgs-Divisions* were often officered by Austrians), joined the SS, and committed war crimes. One was Alfred Richter, whose diary describes how his mainly Bavarian Alpine units massacred thousands of Italian troops on the Ionian island of Cephalonia.[44] The fate of those Italians was sealed by the so-called "*Scharfes Befehl*" (harsh command) issued by the former k. (u.) k. officer General Alexander Löhr, who was born in present-day Romania. After the war, Löhr was tried and shot as a war criminal in Belgrade. Perhaps Löhr, like Glaise-Horstenau, naively believed that he was acting as a professional German officer who had been schooled in Austria, and that the Third Reich would restore some of the old imperial luster. In 1984, the far right Austrian Freedom Party erected a memorial tablet to General Löhr in Vienna. It rightly provoked much outrage.[45]

Other k. (u.) k. officers responded more humanely to the challenges of the Third Reich. Colonel Erwin Lahousen-Vivremont, the trusted lieutenant of Admiral Canaris, was described by his German contemporaries as "the purest example of the old k. (u.) k. officer type" largely because of his efforts to save lives and preserve certain standards of decency in the *Abwehr* (German military intelligence).[46] Canaris approached Lahousen shortly after the *Anschluß* in order to secure reliable personnel for the *Abwehr* station that was to be reinforced in Vienna, and because he felt that Lahousen represented the old values of the Monarchy. Indeed, Canaris implicitly trusted him enough to say: "Bring me real Austrians, I do not want any Austrian Nazis in my service."[47]

Unfortunately, however, not all serving Austrian officers had such luck. The highly decorated Field Marshal Johann Friedländer, for example, was dismissed from his post for failing to disown his Jewish wife. He was subsequently sent with her to Theresienstadt and, eventually, Auschwitz, where he was murdered barely two months before the war's end. Apparently, the SS Guard insisted on shooting him twice through the head because, "after all, he is a Field Marshal."[48]

In 1939, the *Reichsbund jüdischer Frontsoldaten* (Association of Jewish World War I Soldiers, or RjF) counted thirty-nine thousand members in Austria. Shortly after the *Anschluß*, German authorities outlawed the organization and a terrible persecution began. Of the few Jewish officers who had trained in the old imperial and royal army and survived the Holocaust, many went on to successful careers in the armed forces of the fledgling state of Israel. Rudolf Loew (Rafael Lev) and Sigmund (Edler von) Friedmann both played important roles on the command staff of the Haganah, the precursor to today's Israeli Defense Forces (IDF). Along with Wolfgang von Weisl, they recalled after the 1948 Israeli-Arab War how their military training had been "simply the finest" in the old imperial and royal army.[49] They also all noted that they had never encountered any antisemitism in the old k. (u.) k. army. Ironically, Emperor Franz Joseph had once countered an antisemitic remark with the comment that the Jews in his military performed such excellent service that they could "alone furnish a smaller state with its own army."[50]

If we look for echoes of the k. (u.) k. army in today's successor states, one hundred years after the Monarchy's collapse, we will surely be disappointed. And yet lately there have been signs of a heightened awareness of and appreciation for the legacy of the Kaiser's army. Archduke Otto's remarkably well-attended funeral in Vienna in the summer of 2011, for example, saw the uniformed presence of the modern Austrian *Bundeswehr*, as opposed to the many other historical reenactors.[51] This would have been unheard of just twenty years earlier. In fact, I well remember the soul-searching debates in Austrian government circles in 1989 over whether to grant permission for Empress Zita (Charles's wife) to be buried in the Capuchin Crypt, let alone for her to be honored with a traditional funeral procession through the Austrian capital. The government, and in particular the conservative People's party (ÖVP), spent hours in tortuous wrangling before finally assenting to the burial with a significant caveat: no members of the armed forces could attend the funeral in uniform. Inevitably, however, they all did—from the Chief of the Austrian General Staff down, the Austrian officer corps disobeyed the Federal Chancellor's order and turned out in parade dress. This brief disciplinary blip, it should be added, had no "unfortunate" consequences for the officers involved.

Otto's funeral more than two decades later proved that even politicians could learn from their mistakes—this time the army was allowed to show its respect in "*grossen Stil*" (great fashion). Nevertheless, the Habsburg legacy is still a sensitive one for the modern Austrian state, where its ceremonial units do not wear a Habsburg style uniform (the same is true in the Czech Republic, though not in modern Hungary, as we have seen). A sure sign of political maturity for today's Second Austrian Republic will only come when it can attire these official corps in uniforms that draw upon its long and distinguished imperial history.

On the other hand, perhaps the paranoid Austrian republicans know what they fear. Oskar Kokoschka, the famous fin-de-siècle Viennese painter who fought the 1914–18 war in a smart dragoon uniform (made for him by Goldman and Salatch), later recalled a telling anecdote from his time working as a Hollywood extra to supplement his meager earnings as a painter. He and other destitute Austrians had found themselves on the set of Erich von Stroheim's film *The Wedding March* (1928), during a scene in which an actor playing Emperor Franz Joseph briefly appears. And "as this actor in his uniform and whiskers walked slowly towards us," recalled Kokoschka,

> we all without a sound completely involuntarily stiffened our backs and stood to attention before the director had even uttered a word. It was as if the old Kaiser

had been brought back to life. I felt in that moment, and I think the others who had served in the army also did, that we were no longer in America, but somehow powerfully transported back in time to Vienna. It was as if we were still serving k.(u) k. officers.[52]

What von Stroheim achieved with film, the writers Stefan Zweig, Joseph Roth, Lernet-Holenia, and Robert Musil did in literature. The obituary of the old k. (u.) k. army has been penned in such classics as Roth's *The Radetzky March* and Musil's *The Man Without Qualities*.

The Radetzky March, which today is required reading in many Austrian schools, was originally, of course, the title of perhaps the most famous march composed by Johann Strauss—the martial hymn of the Habsburg Empire. Today, this "Marseillaise of Reaction," as it was known due to its association with the 1848 revolution, still unfailingly brings the Vienna Philharmonic's annual New Year's concert to a rousing close. Indeed, the k. (u.) k. army lives on in all the armed forces of the successor states through their military music. The marches of Strauss, Lehár, Komzák, Wagnes, and Blümel, to name but a few of the truly great composers who wrote for the old Habsburg army, continue to resound internationally. Even during the communist era in East-Central Europe, and much to my surprise and delight, President Gorbachev's state visit to Prague castle in April 1987 was greeted by a Czechoslovak military band playing the famous Habsburg march *Unter dem Doppeladler* (Under the Double Eagle) with tremendous gusto.[53] Fittingly and poignantly, it is in the strains of these celebrated pieces of music that the old imperial and royal army endures, impervious to political currents just as this once truly European army was beholden neither to nationalism nor religious fanaticism.[54]

Richard Bassett is a Bye-Fellow of Christ's College Cambridge, where he studied Law, and author of the groundbreaking and internationally acclaimed history of the Habsburg Army—*For God and Kaiser* (New Haven: Yale University Press, 2015). Following fifteen years in Central Europe working first as a musician and then as the Eastern Europe Bureau chief of *The Times*, he worked for twenty-five years in the City of London for several European banks. His memoir of his time in Central Europe will be published next year by Penguin Random House.

Notes

1. Peter Feldl, *Das Verspielte Reich: Die Letzten Tage Österreich-Ungarns* (Vienna: Zsolnay, 1968), 145–51.
2. See, for example, British Admiral Sir Ernest Troubridge's report in Alexander von Randa, *Österreich in Übersee* (Vienna: Herold, 1966), 139.

3. Cited in Edmund Glaise-Horstenau, *Die Katastrophe: Die Zertrümmerung Österreich-Ungarns und das Werden der Nachfolgestaaten* (Vienna: Almathea, 1928), 47.
4. See Henry Wickham Steed, *Through Thirty Years: 1892–1922* (London: Heinemann, 1924). For the French contribution to this propaganda, see François Fejtö, *Requiem für eine Monarchie: die Zerschlagung Österreich-Ungarns* (Vienna: ÖBV, 1991), 306–30. See, too, Mark Cornwall, *The Undermining of Austria-Hungary: The Battle for Hearts and Minds* (Basingstoke: Palgrave Macmillan, 2000). Cornwall is particularly strong on the anti-Habsburg propaganda emanating from Italy.
5. "Angenommen!" *Arbeiter Zeitung*, 8 March 1918, 1.
6. Glaise-Horstenau, *Die Katastrophe*, 22ff.
7. Richard Bassett, *For God and Kaiser: The Imperial Austrian Army 1619–1918* (New Haven: Yale University Press, 2015), 530–31.
8. Cited in von Randa, *Österreich in Übersee*, 139.
9. For a precise breakdown of the ethnic origins of the Habsburg officer body, see: István Deák, *Der k. (u.) k. Offizier, 1848–1914* (Vienna: Böhlau, 1991), 219–21; and Erwin Schmidl, *Juden in der k. (u.) k. Armee, 1788–1918* (Eisenstadt: Österreichisches Jüdisches Museum, 1989).
10. Glaise-Horstenau, *Die Katastrophe*, 154.
11. Ibid.
12. This point is made in Svetozar Boroević's memoir, *O vojni proti Italiji od Feldmaršala Boroevića* (Ljubljana: [s.n.], 1923), 26. See also: Feldl, *Das Verspielte Reich*, 285–334.
13. Glaise-Horstenau, *Die Katastrophe*, 158.
14. Schmidl, *Juden in der k. (u.) k. Armee*, 144ff.
15. Glaise-Horstenau, *Die Katastrophe*, 168.
16. Ernest Bauer, *Der Löwe vom Isonzo: Feldmarschall Svetozar Boroević de Bojna* (Graz: Styria, 1985). Boroević was baptized in the Orthodox Church, but later acknowledged Croatia as his homeland. Today he is widely perceived to have been the finest defensive commander of World War I. See, for example, John Keegan and Andrew Wheatcroft, *Who's Who in Military History: From 1453 to the Present Day* (London: Routledge, 1976), 48.
17. For the long saga of Slovene-Austrian tensions in the first half of the twentieth century, see Albert F. Reiterer, *Kärntner Slowenen: Minderheit oder Elite? Neuere Tendenzen der ethnischen Arbeitsteilung* (Klagenfurt: Drava, 1996).
18. Bauer, *Der Löwe vom Isonzo*, 126.
19. Ibid., 103–12; Feldl, *Das verspielte Reich*, 335–37; and Glaise-Horstenau, *Die Katastrophe*, 284.
20. See Johann Christoph Allmayer-Beck and Erich Lessing, *Die kaiserlichen Kriegsvölker: Von Maximilian I bis Prinz Eugen 1479–1718* (Munich: C. Bertelsmann, 1978), 14–15; and Wilhelm Guilielmus Germaeus de Lamormaini, *Ferdinand II: Romanorum Imperatoris, Virtutes* (Antuerpiæ: apud Ioannem Meursium, 1638).
21. Ottokar Czernin, *In the World War* (New York: Harper & Bros, 1919), 48–49.
22. Cited in Feldl, *Das verspielte Reich*, 79ff.
23. Norman Stone, *The Eastern Front, 1914–1917* (London: Hodder and Stoughton, 1975). Also see Jonathan Gumz's excellent study, *The Resurrection and Collapse of Empire in Habsburg Serbia 1914–1918* (Cambridge, UK: Cambridge University Press, 2009).
24. Bauer, *Der Löwe vom Isonzo*, 103.

25. The controversial events of March 1934 remain highly sensitive for Austrian historians, as they can still fracture opinion along "red-black" lines. See G. E. R. Gedye, *Betrayal in Central Europe: Austria and Czechoslovakia; Fallen Bastions* (London: Harper, 1939), for a slightly partisan, if vivid, description of the civil war.
26. Alexander Lernet-Holenia, *Die Standarte* (Berlin: Suhrkampf, 1942).
27. Schmidl, *Juden in der k. (u.) k. Armee*, 148.
28. The coup carried out in March 1941 while the Soviet Union was nominally still allied to Germany is well described in Cecil Parrott's memoir *The Tightrope* (London: Faber & Faber, 1975).
29. The Ustasha Leader Ante Pavelić famously told Glaise-Horstenau that he would "expel a third, convert a third and kill a third of the non-indigenous population," by which he mainly meant ethnic Serbs living in the newly independent Croatian state. See Fitzroy Maclean, *Eastern Approaches* (London: Jonathan Cape, 1949), 233ff.
30. Cited in Arnold Suppan, *Hitler-Beneš-Tito: Konflikt, Krieg und Völkermord in Ostmittel- und Südosteuropa*, vol. 1 (Vienna: ÖAW, 2014), 743.
31. Scholars have recently questioned the degree to which regiments were stationed away from their recruiting depots. See David Laven's study of conscription, *Venice and Venetia under the Habsburgs, 1815–1835* (Oxford: Oxford University Press, 2002), which notes that the eight Venetian regiments were often stationed on Venetian or Italian speaking territory. The details of the orders for the Vienna "Haus" Regiment (Nr 4 Hoch und Deutschmeister) between 1849 and 1866 suggest, however, that many regiments served long spells miles away from their homes. See Herbert von Patera with Gottfried Pils, *Unter Österreichs Fahnen* (Graz: Styria, 1960).
32. Richard Bassett, *Balkan Hours: Travels in the Other Europe* (London: John Murray, 1990).
33. Even in 1988, under communist rule, an international Hussar "congress" was organized with units from NATO countries participating: See Richard Bassett, "Stylish Hussars stir memories of Habsburg glory," *The Times*, 27 October 1988, 9.
34. Osbert Lancaster, *With an Eye to the Future* (London: J. Murray, 1967), 95–96.
35. Although they had long been Habsburg subjects, the "German Austrians" of Czechoslovakia, unlike those in other former crown lands, are in many cases more accurately described as "Austrian Germans," as German nationalists often felt greater affinity toward Germany than Austria.
36. See Martin Zückert, *Zwischen Nationsidee und Staatlicher Realität: Die Tschechoslowakishe Armee und ihre Nationalitätspolitik 1918–39* (Munich: Oldenbourg, 2006), 96–113. Also see Swejda Family album (private collection), Prague.
37. Swejda Family album.
38. Author's conversation with the late Ihsan Bey Toptani, 21 March 1998.
39. In his masterly study *Italy's Austrian Heritage, 1919–1946* (Oxford: Clarendon Press, 1969), Dennison Rusinow mordantly styles this the "Habsburg Revenge."
40. Ibid., chapter 12ff.
41. Schmidl, *Juden in der k. (u.) k. Armee*, 125ff.
42. Hans-Georg Behr, *Die Oesterreischische Provocation: Ein Mahnruf für Deutsche* (Frankfurt: Fischer, 1973), 25.
43. Cited in Otto von Habsburg, *Zurück zur Mitte* (Vienna: Almathea, 1991), 75.
44. Cited in Hermann Frank Meyer, *Blutiges Edelweiss* (Berlin: Links, 2008), 289–95.
45. "Nazi Memorial Plaque Stirs Controversy," *The Times*, 3 April 1983, 12.
46. Karl Bartz, *Die Tragödie der Deutschen Abwehr* (Salzburg: Pilgram, 1955), 24.

47. Richard Bassett, *Hitler's Spy Chief: The Wilhelm Canaris Mystery* (London: Pegasus Books, 2005), 149.
48. Heeresgeschichtliches Museum (HGM) Exhibition Catalogue, *Feldmarschalleutnant Johann Friedländer (1882–1945): ein vergessener Offizier des Bundesheeres* (Wien: BMLV, 1995).
49. Schmidl, *Juden in der k. (u.) k. Armee*, 148.
50. Ibid.
51. Austrian National Radio (ÖRF, 4 July 2011) estimated that one hundred thousand people attended the funeral ceremonies.
52. I am indebted to the late Professor Georg Eisler, a pupil of Kokoschka and the son of the composer Hans Eisler—himself a former k. (u.) k. officer—for this anecdote.
53. Ironically, the Czechoslovak military school of music, lovingly preserved under Soviet occupation, was the first casualty of cuts imposed on the Czech military budget when it joined NATO. The school, housed in the Lobkowitz castle of Roudnice, was closed down in the early twenty-first century.
54. Austrian military engagements of the 1860s, notably Översee and Könnigrätz, are full of eyewitness accounts of Imperial and Royal Infantry being rallied mid-battle by the regimental band striking up *Radetzky March*. For General Ludwig Freiherr von Gablenz deploying this tactic in a hail of enemy fire, see Wilhelm Gründorf, *Memoiren eines österreichischen Generalstäblers 1832–1866* (Stuttgart: R. Lutz, 1913).

Select Bibliography

Allmayer-Beck, Johann Christoph and Erich Lessing. *Die kaiserlichen Kriegsvölker: Von Maximilian I bis Prinz Eugen 1479–1718*. Munich: C. Bertelsmann, 1978.
Bartz, Karl. *Die Tragödie der Deutschen Abwehr*. Salzburg: Pilgram, 1955.
Bassett, Richard. *Balkan Hours: Travels in the Other Europe*. London: John Murray, 1990.
———. *For God and Kaiser: The Imperial Austrian Army 1619–1918*. New Haven: Yale University Press, 2015.
———. *Hitler's Spy Chief: The Wilhelm Canaris Mystery*. London: Pegasus Books, 2005.
Bauer, Ernest. *Der Löwe von Isonzo: Feldmarschall Svetozar Boroevič de Bojna*. Graz: Styria, 1985.
Behr, Hans-Georg. *Die Oesterreichische Provokation: Ein Mahnruf für Deutsche*. Frankfurt: Fischer, 1973.
Bobič, Pavlina. *War and Faith: The Catholic Church in Slovenia 1914–18*. Boston: Brill, 2012.
Boroevič, Svetozar. *O vojni proti Italiji od Feldmaršala Boroeviča*. Ljubljana: [s.n.], 1923.
Brixel, Eugen, Gunther Martin, and Gottfried Pils. *Das ist Oesterreichs Militärmusik: Von der "Türkischen Musik" zu den Philharmonikern in Uniform*. Graz: Kaleidoskop im Styria Vlg., 1982.
Cornwall, Mark. *The Undermining of Austria-Hungary: The Battle for Hearts and Minds*. Basingstoke: Palgrave Macmillan, 2000.
Czernin, Ottokar. *In the World War*. New York: Harper & Bros, 1919.
Deák, István. *Der k. (u.) k. Offizier: 1848–1918*. Vienna: Böhlau, 1991.
de Banfield, Goffredo. *L'Aquila di Trieste*. Trieste: LINT, 1984.
de Lamormaini, Wilhelm Guilielmus Germeus. *Ferdinand II: Romanorum Imperatoris, Virtutes*. Antwerp: apud Ioannem Meursium, 1638.

Fejtö, Francis. *Requiem für eine Monarchie: die Zerschlagung Oesterreich-Ungarns*. Vienna: ÖBV, 1991.
Feldl, Peter. *Das Verspielte Reich: Die Letzten Tage Oesterreich-Ungarns*. Vienna: Zsolnay, 1968.
Forstner, Franz. *Przemyśl: Oesterreich-Ungarns bedeutende Festung*. Vienna: Österreichischer Bundesverlag, 1987.
Gedye, G. E. R. *Betrayal in Central Europe: Austria and Czechoslovakia; Fallen Bastions*. London: Harper, 1939.
Glaise-Horstenau, Edmund. *Die Katastrophe: Die Zertrümmerung Österreich-Ungarns und das Werden der Nachfolgestaaten*. Vienna: Almathea, 1928.
Gründorf, Wilhelm. *Memoiren eines österreichischen Generalstäblers 1832–1866*. Stuttgart: R. Lutz, 1913.
Gumz, Jonathan. *The Resurrection and Collapse of Empire in Habsburg Serbia 1914–1918*. Cambridge, UK: Cambridge University Press, 2009.
Heeresgeschichtliches Museum (HGM) Exhibition Catalogue. *Feldmarschalleutnant Johann Friedländer (1882–1945): ein vergessener Offizier des Bundesheeres*. Wien: BMLV, 1995.
Keegan, John, and Andrew Wheatcroft. *Who's Who in Military History: From 1453 to the Present Day*. London: Routledge, 1976.
Lancaster, Osbert. *With an Eye to the Future*. London: J. Murray, 1967.
Laven, David. *Venice and Venetia under the Habsburgs, 1815–1835*. Oxford: Oxford University Press, 2002.
Lernet-Holenia, Alexander. *Die Standarte*. Berlin: Suhrkamp, 1942.
Maclean, Fitzroy. *Eastern Approaches*. London: Jonathan Cape, 1949.
Meyer, Hermann Frank. *Blutiges Edelweiss*. Berlin: Links, 2008.
Parrott, Cecil. *The Tightrope*. London: Faber & Faber, 1975.
Reiterer, Albert F. *Kärntner Slowenen: Minderheit oder Elite? Neuere Tendenzen der ethnischen Arbeitsteilung*. Klagenfurt: Drava, 1996.
Rusinow, Dennison. *Italy's Austrian Heritage, 1919–1946*. Oxford: Clarendon Press, 1969.
Schmidl, Erwin A. *Juden in der k. (u.) k. Armee, 1788–1918*. Eisenstadt: Österreichisches Jüdisches Museum, 1989.
Steed, Henry Wickham. *Through Thirty Years: 1892–1922*. London: Heinemann, 1924.
Stone, Norman. *The Eastern Front, 1914–1917*. London: Hodder and Stoughton, 1975.
Suppan, Arnold. *Hitler-Beneš-Tito: Krieg und Völkermord in Ostmittel-und Südosteuropa*. Vienna: ÖAW, 2014.
von Habsburg, Otto. *Zurück zur Mitte*. Vienna: Almathea, 1991.
von Patera, Herbert, with Gottfried Pils. *Unter Oesterreichs Fahnen*. Graz: Styria, 1960.
von Randa, Alexander. *Oesterreich in Übersee*. Vienna: Herold, 1966.
Zückert, Martin. *Zwischen Nationsidee und Staatlicher Realität: Die Tschechoslowakische Armee und ihre Nationalitätspolitik 1918–19*. Munich: Oldenbourg, 2006.

Private Papers
Papers of the late Baron Gottfried von Banfield, Trieste.
Max Thurn Nachlass (Bequest), Vienna.
Swejda family papers, Prague.

Newspapers
The Times Archive 1934–35 and 1988–89. London.
Arbeiter Zeitung 1918–19. Vienna.

Chapter 6

IMPERIAL INTO NATIONAL OFFICERS
K. (u.) k. Officers of Romanian Nationality before and after the Great War

Irina Marin

Postwar transitions are notoriously difficult. On both the winning and losing sides, there are both winners and losers, and change affects people in many ways. The breakup of the Austro-Hungarian Empire in 1918 and the ensuing transition to nation-states and federations blurred the lines between winners and losers, especially when the population of the same ethnicity had been divided among empire and nation-state. This was the case of the Empire's Romanians, who, ever since a Romanian state emerged in 1859, had a nation-state to look to and in some—though by no means all—cases, gravitate toward.

Yet rather than examining Romanian irredentism in the Empire, this chapter maps the transition from empire to nation-state for those Romanians whose lives and careers were deeply embedded in and dependent upon the Empire— career officers who swore professional allegiance to the Habsburg emperor. By 1918, there were at least fifteen generals of Romanian nationality in the Austro-Hungarian army, and commensurate lower-ranking officers. The literature on these men is scant and uneven, with some of them better researched and documented and others merely figuring as names in military records. On the other hand, the literature on the Austrian Military Border, where many of the officers came from, is more substantial. Moreover, high-ranking officers from this region are particularly well represented in these works.[1]

In following the trajectory of Austro-Hungarian officers of Romanian nationality from the Habsburg into the Romanian army, this chapter focuses on the dual—imperial and national—nature of their allegiance and its transformation after World War I. It argues that this transformation did not presuppose a switching of allegiances, but rather the continuation of old loyalties in a new guise. My contribution thus examines the formation of a Romanian military elite in the Austro-Hungarian Empire; its relations with the Romanian state; the role these officers played in Romanian cultural politics inside the Empire; their allegiance and behavior during World War I; and their role in combatting postwar anarchy and restoring order. Finally, the chapter explores individual careers in the new state.

The Making of Imperial Officers

By the late nineteenth century, a pyramid of military schools was available in the Habsburg Empire as career pathways to high rank for gifted students of non-noble origin. The Romanian imperial officers considered in this article all studied in such schools. The lowest level of Habsburg military education had three tiers. The first—the *Militär Unter-Erziehungshäuser* (later known as *Militär Unterrealschulen*)—prepared students for the *Militär Ober-Erziehungshäuser* (*Militär Oberrealschulen*). This was followed by the *Schul-Compagnien* (known as *Kadettenschulen* from 1866), which trained noncommissioned officers, or *Unteroffiziere*.[2] These institutions, whose names and location varied during the nineteenth century, formed a recruitment pool for the academies, which constituted the second level of military training. The Military Academy at Wiener-Neustadt furnished lieutenants to the infantry, cavalry, and riflemen units (*Jäger*). The Artillery Academy at Mährisch Weißkirchen (Hranice) prepared officers for artillery and sapper units, as well as for the railway and telegraph regiments.[3]

The more famous of these two academies, the *Wiener-Neustädter Akademie* (or *Theresianische Militär-Akademie*), was founded by Empress Maria Theresa in 1752. Joseph II's donation letter (*Stiftsbrief*) of 1786 stipulated that of the four hundred places in the Academy, 304 were to be reserved for the sons of those who had served faithfully as superior officers. The letter took special account of orphans and the children of worthy parents (or of parents who served in regions where there were no educational opportunities).[4] The institution was famed for producing an elite officer corps. The historian Alan Sked describes its lavish lifestyle (including four-course dinners) and strict rules, which encouraged segregation from family and, even, the outside world.[5]

The Wiener-Neustädter officer was easily recognizable in society and often found it difficult to integrate. Theoretically superior to other officers, he could be socially inadequate after so many years of secluded military instruction.[6] Yet the Theresien Military Academy also held unexpected opportunity for the professional and social advancement of pupils from humbler backgrounds. As the archivist Michael Hochedlinger writes, "the Military Academy did not serve to discipline the nobility, unlike the Prussian cadet schools, but primarily provided a welcome opportunity for impecunious subaltern officers who had risen from the ranks to have their sons educated at public expense and then commissioned into some regiment, again without having to pay for it."[7]

Although Wiener-Neustadt was the more famous of the two military academies, the *Fachanstalt* (technical academy) was the more rigorous when it came to military proficiency. This was, above all, because the latter's skills-based admissions criteria were largely meritocratic, whereas the *Theresianische Militär-Akademie* was restricted to the sons of impoverished nobility, imperial officers, and clerks. This ensured the *Fachanstalt* a socially broader student body.[8]

Yet not all officers' sons could enter the military academies due to the small number of available places. The so-called cadet schools (*Kadettenschulen*, known until 1866 as *Schulcompagnien* and after 1875 as *Infanterieschulen*) made up for this shortage.[9] These schools were less restrictive than the academies and privileged practical over theoretical subjects.[10] There was a cavalry cadet school in Mährisch-Weißkirchen (Hranice), an artillery cadet school in Vienna, and a *Pionnier-Kadettenschule* in Hainburg, which also trained officers for the railway and telegraph regiments.[11]

The third level of military instruction was the *Kriegsschule* (War Academy), with its advanced artillery and engineering courses for outstanding officers who had already served three years.[12] These schools of higher military education and specialization contributed to the erosion of the aristocratic promotion system in the Habsburg army.[13] They constituted a meritocratic means of advancement and, in the case of the *Kriegsschule*, a gateway to high command.[14] Highly skilled and professionally versatile officers were employed by the *Generalstab* (General Staff), which by the nineteenth century had become a vital military institution tasked with the army's strategic, tactical, and administrative organization. As the historian Allmayer-Beck shows, the General Staff officers formed a special elite within the officer corps.[15]

The officers produced in these schools wielded what Heinz Hartmann called "functional authority," or authority based on specialized knowledge and skills which are achieved rather than ascribed.[16] In other words, they are arrived at meritocratically. It's thus no surprise that the *Kenntnisse* (knowledge) and *Geschicklichkeiten* (skills) sections of high-ranking officers' *Qualificationslisten* (CVs) are impressive by any measure. These men were truly the gray matter of the Habsburg military establishment.

Imperial and National Allegiance among Romanian Officers

In his classic work *Beyond Nationalism: A Social and Political History of the Habsburg Officer Corps, 1848–1918*, the historian István Deák argues that the education received by imperial officers was blind to all nationalism and predicated upon loyalty to the Emperor. This is confirmed by the military papers of the time, which omitted nationality from its personnel descriptions. The fact that the army as an institution was nationality-blind does not, however, mean that its individual members did not nurture a sense of national belonging, or that national identity was institutionally repressed. In the case of Romanian officers, various army institutions and organizations helped to instill both a sense of imperial loyalty *and* national awareness. Some, like in the Austrian Military Border (from which most of the officers discussed below came), did so directly. Yet others used such indirect opportunities as religious services provided in the mother tongue to encourage expressions of national pride that were consistent with imperial allegiance.[17]

Far from inhabiting an ivory tower that made them oblivious to their national background, imperial officers of Romanian nationality, especially the high-ranking ones, were often involved in cultural projects initiated by the Empire's Romanian community. They were among the most important subscribers to Romanian periodicals; donated funds for Romanian schools and cultural organizations/activities; and they used their military status to strengthen petitions for cultural and linguistic rights. Such initiatives may have been circumscribed by injunctions against political involvement by active officers, but they were not at variance with their imperial allegiance or military status. On the contrary, a recurrent argument in support of this cultural activism was that it strengthened the Empire by satisfying the reasonable claims of all nationalities. In other words, there was no inherent conflict between the equitable treatment of the nationalities and loyalty to the Monarchy.

Brigadier General Trajan Doda (1822–95), a graduate of the Wiener-Neustadt Military Academy and recipient of the *Militär Verdienst-Kreuz* (Military Merit Cross, or MVK), was perhaps the era's most famous Romanian general in the imperial army. He had seen action in 1848–49, 1859, and 1866, and proved to be an excellent commander and administrator. General Doda entered politics after his retirement in 1872, and was repeatedly elected to the Hungarian Parliament as an independent who supported a national-imperial program. As he stressed in the political platform he presented to his constituents in Karánsebes (Caransebeș) in 1873:

> Each nationality has the right to educate and develop its youth in their mother tongue. On this premise, the Germans should have German schools, the Romanians

Romanian schools, the Serbs Serbian schools, the Slovaks Slovakian schools; in short, each nationality should have schools in its language. National education and development should not, however, be confined to popular and civil schools—they should be extended to higher institutions, including universities. . . . If a nationality does not have the necessary means to maintain these schools, it is the State's duty to provide [them] out of the State treasury. For if we are liable to support the State with our entire wealth and being, then the State, in turn, is duty-bound to give us the necessary means for our cultural national development.[18]

General Doda further argued that the national languages "be introduced and used in public life," while also recognizing Hungarian as "the language of the government and legislation." In 1889, his criticism of the Hungarian electoral system incurred charges of incitement against the Hungarian nation. Doda rejected these accusations as wholly incompatible with his military ethos, writing in his petition for grace to the Emperor (July 1889): "An imperial general inciting hatred against a nationality! I, who have always upheld the principle that only brotherly communion and the collaboration of all peoples that make up Austria-Hungary can preserve this monarchy! I should laugh at such an allegation if its consequences were not so terribly sad."[19]

General Doda was hardly alone among Romanian imperial officers in terms of his national-imperial agenda. Brigadier General Michael Trapsia, a graduate of the Technical Military Academy who like Doda hailed from the Banat Military Border, supported Romanian newspapers and bequeathed funds to establish a Romanian-language girls' school in Karánsebes (Caransebeș). As with other imperial officers, Trapsia maintained close ties with leaders of the Romanian national movement in the Empire.[20] Another officer and MVK holder who promoted Romanian cultural activities in the Monarchy was David Urs, Baron of Margina (1816–97) and Knight of the Theresian Order. Urs was a founding member of the *Asociația Transilvană pentru Literatura Română și Cultura Poporului Român* (Transylvanian Association for Romanian Literature and the Culture of the Romanian People, or ASTRA), which many Austro-Hungarian generals of Romanian nationality joined. In a 1902 ASTRA report, General Alexander Lupu is listed among the donors to a fund for establishing the first historical and ethnographical museum of Romanians under the Crown of St. Stephen.[21] Urs himself bequeathed his wealth to the Romanian Uniate Church and regularly sponsored cultural projects, for example scholarships for Romanian students. One beneficiary of his patronage was the future General Ioan Boeriu, who, as we will see, played a central role in the transition from empire to national state in 1918.[22]

An examination of the activities and network of *România jună* (Young Romania), a Vienna-based Romanian literary and cultural society, shows that active officers of Romanian nationality were regularly, if most often indirectly, involved with it as well. For example, in 1896 Major General Theodor Seracsin was listed as having attended the religious service dedicated to departed members of the society and occasioned by its twenty-five year jubilee.[23] Twelve years later, General Lupu spoke at a commemorative meeting of *România junǎ* held on the twenty-fifth anniversary of the Romanian composer Ciprian Porumbescu's untimely death.[24] In the society's annual report for 1891, Aurelia Trapsia-Kron, General Michael Trapsia's wife, figures among its honorary members.[25]

Orthodoxy provided another convergent point between life in the Austro-Hungarian army and Romanian cultural politics. Romanian regiments in Vienna had long celebrated the New Year and Christian holidays in the garrison church, each confession having its own priest.[26] Likewise, the Romanian Orthodox community in Vienna shared a church with the Greeks on the basis of a late eighteenth-century imperial privilege. Eventually, a Romanian Orthodox chapel was established in the capital thanks largely to the efforts of General Lupu.[27] When the chapel was consecrated in January 1907, two Romanian generals from the former Austrian Military Border, Michael Sandru and Daniel Materinga, were in attendance.[28]

General Lupu (1838–1925) had risen from the ranks. According to his *Qualificationsliste*, he spent his first eight years of service in the Romanian Banat Border Regiment No. 13. It took him almost twenty years to be promoted to captain, another nine to reach major, and eight years to become a colonel. Twelve years after retiring in 1896, Lupu received his Brigadier General rank as *Titel und Charakter*, that is, upon retirement, without actually discharging this function in active service.[29] General Lupu's national allegiance manifested itself through active involvement with the Romanian Orthodox community in Vienna. In his autobiographical notes, he recorded his endeavors toward establishing the aforementioned Romanian Orthodox chapel:

> After ascertaining that the parishioners of the Viennese Greek-Orthodox churches, namely the Greek, Russian, and Serbian church, spoke Romanian more than any other language, I decided to draw up a list of all the Romanians in Vienna. In 1898 I extracted all the Romanian addresses from the Lehmann dictionary; I then sent the young people from *România junǎ* throughout Vienna to verify the Romanian identity of these families. I personally went to Catholic monasteries to find out how many Romanian girls were there; I then requested from the *Schulrat* the name of all the Romanian Greek-Orthodox female students enrolled at secondary and national [*poporale*] schools in Vienna.[30]

For Lupu, Romanian identity was defined by language and Orthodoxy (hence his worry that Romanian girls were being educated as Catholics). His informal census constituted the first step toward the creation of a Romanian Orthodox Society in Vienna. After building the centrally located chapel (8 Löwelstraße), the Society went on to establish a parish church.[31]

These endeavors to solidify the Romanian community in Vienna represented an integrationist assertion of national identity. The resulting society—*Asociaţia română greco-orientală jubiliar imperială pentru zidirea bisericii şi întemeierea comunităţii bisericeşti din Viena* (roughly translates as: the Greek Orthodox Romanian Association which was founded on the occasion of the Imperial Jubilee for Building a Romanian Church and Parish in Vienna)—affirmed its imperial loyalty by timing its church-building project with the jubilee celebrations of Emperor Franz Joseph's sixty-year reign (1908). This assertion of national and religious identity thus presupposed a *reaffirmation* of Romanians' monarchical allegiance. It also sought to dispel suspicion of secessionist intentions implicit in Lower Austrian officials' 1892 refusal to permit the foundation of a Romanian national colony on the grounds that, as citizens of the Austro-Hungarian Empire, the applicants did not require one.[32] Further, Lupu resolved the problem of obtaining a Romanian priest for the chapel by directly asking the War Minister to permit the military priest, Dr. Virgil Ciobanu, to perform religious rites outside of his regimental duties.[33] Lupu's action again demonstrates how high military rank and national activism were by no means incompatible in the Empire. Indeed, careful and resourceful officers profited from their prestige and connections to become leading patrons of national culture.

Relations with the Romanian Kingdom

With the founding of a modern Romanian state in 1859 (albeit still under Ottoman suzerainty until 1878), there was a steady flow of manpower and military knowhow from the Habsburg army to the new Romanian one.[34] Although the first Romanian military academies had been established in the 1840s–50s, the fledgling army vitally needed expertise from abroad, and families like the Brătianus (doyens of the Romanian National Liberal Party) were keen to attract it in the form of high-ranking Romanian nationals in the Habsburg army. Thus, in 1868, during a controversy over the use of Prussian army instructors, Dumitru Brătianu wrote:

> I believe that we absolutely need at least three or four of the most distinguished Romanian officers in Austria, even if this means that the Prince will have to guarantee their position until it can be regulated by Parliament; and as an incentive, it would be good if they could be promised a higher rank than the one they held or are holding in the Austrian army. . . . I do not see any pressing need for foreign instructors; on the contrary, it is a weakness on our part to show the world that, just like the Turks, we are in perpetual need of foreign leaders. We do, indeed, need several experienced officers, but [let them be] Romanian.[35]

The 1877–78 Russo-Turkish war boosted efforts to draw Romanian officers from the Austro-Hungarian army. Apart from volunteers who enthusiastically crossed the Carpathians from the Monarchy's Hungarian half to join Romania's campaign for independence from the Porte, Romanian authorities conducted informal and eventually abortive negotiations to secure an experienced Chief of General Staff and other high-ranking military officers. This was part of a strategic plan for Romania to strengthen its postwar claim on independence by entering the war under its own command, rather than merely providing auxiliary troops to the Tsar. Various Romanian political leaders thus went to Austria-Hungary to sound out high-ranking Romanian officers. Retired Brigadier General Trajan Doda, an MP in Hungary, was the main target of these overtures. Inquiries were also made for Colonel David Urs Baron of Margina, Colonel Michael Trapsia, and Brigadier General Alexander Guran, all of whom came from Romanian regiments in the former Austrian Military Border.[36]

These recruiting efforts were unprecedented only insofar as they were directed at the highest echelons of the Austro-Hungarian military. Voluntary emigration from the Habsburg into the Romanian army had been encouraged before and proven its worth to the new force's battlefield performance. Indeed, two of the army's ablest and most famous generals, Moise Groza (1844–1919) and Ioan Dragalina (1860–1916), had transferred from the Austro-Hungarian army as lieutenants and made their marks in Romania as wartime officers. Groza, who immigrated in 1873, at the urging of the War Minister Ioan Florescu (they had met two years earlier during a cartographical mission on the Transylvanian border), disregarded orders during the 1877–78 Russo-Turkish war, brought his cartographical expertise to bear on its conduct, and helped break the military deadlock. His action not only saved lives, it made Groza into a hero of the Romanian officer corps. Later in peacetime, he founded Romania's first military-geographical institute.[37]

Ioan Dragalina graduated from the Wiener-Neustadt Military Academy, where, like his father, he specialized in geodetic engineering. His itinerant childhood between Karánsebes (Caransebeș) and Râmnicu-Vâlcea (southeastern Romania), coupled with his experience as a young lieutenant serving in Line Regiment No. 43 (in Karánsebes), likely influenced Dragalina's decision to emigrate and join the Romanian army. In a biography by his son Virgil, there is an episode that sheds light on the young officer's loyalties. During the Hungarian parliamentary elections of June 1884, two candidates were competing for MP in Boksánbánya (Bocșa Română), southern Hungary: the future Hungarian prime minister István Tisza; and Coriolan Brediceanu, a lawyer who belonged to the Romanian National Party in Hungary. Lieutenant Dragalina was commanding the troops assigned to maintain order during the elections. When local civilian authorities instructed him only to allow voters supporting the Hungarian candidate to pass, Dragalina refused. In response, he was publicly insulted to the point of demanding satisfaction. His son documented the episode with a copy of the official report the Lieutenant submitted to his superiors.[38] On 1 December 1887, the Austro-Hungarian army approved his resignation, and ten days later, Dragalina joined the Romanian army with the same rank. Upon leaving for the Romanian Kingdom, he met with retired General Trajan Doda who reportedly told him: "The oppressed Banat loses a brave fighter; free Romania wins a brilliant officer. Which will be more fateful for our nation?"[39]

In Romania, Dragalina embarked upon a successful military career thanks to the skills and qualifications he had acquired in Austria-Hungary. As Captain Dragalina, he served under Colonel Constantin Prezan, a Romanian general in World War I who eulogized him in 1936: "to his teachings I owe the tactics and strategy and all I knew and applied during the war and as Chief of the General Staff."[40] General Dragalina died of his wounds in 1916 while commanding the 1st Romanian Army, depriving the country of one "of its most dynamic and inspiring field commanders" just months after it had entered World War I.[41]

Another successful military émigré from Austria-Hungary, Traian Moșoiu (1868–1932), joined the Romanian army in 1891 and was quickly promoted to colonel during the Balkan wars. In World War I, he served in the 1st Romanian Army, which pushed into Transylvania in 1916. By the war's end, Moșoiu was a brigadier general with a central role in administering Transylvania and organizing the Romanian troops deployed against the communist regime in Budapest.[42]

As the historian Glenn Torrey points out, such examples of military migration were not "uncommon during the early years of Romania's membership in the Triple Alliance."[43] Moreover, contact between officers in the Austro-Hungarian and Romanian armies regularly took place through military exchanges, invitations to maneuvers, social occasions like the celebration of King Carol of Romania's birthday, and informal cross-border relations between Romanian officers in Austria-Hungary and their conationals in the Kingdom of Romania. Indeed, on the eve of the outbreak of war in 1914, retired Major General Nikolaus Cena was receiving two high-ranking Romanian officers as part of a "courtesy call."[44] And in September 1914, Austrian Chief of the General Staff Conrad von Hötzendorf cites an exchange of letters between officers in the Romanian and Austro-Hungarian armies.[45]

World War I and the Test of Allegiances

When World War I broke out, Austro-Hungarian officers of Romanian nationality were both well-integrated and nationally conscious. Some, particularly among retired officers, were highly regarded in their local communities and active promoters of Romanian language and culture. There is even evidence that they collaborated with prominent members of the Romanian National Party and had contacts with officers in the Romanian Kingdom. During the war, however, such intermingling got some of these officers into trouble. In August 1914, retired Major General Nikolaus Cena spent nearly a month in prison on suspicion of espionage deriving from his support for the Romanian Orthodox Church and Romanian culture in Mehadia (southern Hungary) where he was president of the Orthodox parish. Cena was keenly interested in the region's Roman past and had contacts with officers in the Romanian army. Yet when interrogated about these liaisons, he insisted that whenever the subject of taking sides in a war came up, he told the Romanian officers: "I would be very sorry about that, but in that case the war would find us on opposite sides."[46] The espionage charges were eventually dropped.

Similarly, in early 1918, retired General Alexander Lupu was tried by a Vienna military court for providing "support through occasional monetary contributions and the procurement of salaried positions . . . at several Romanian institutions" to two persons accused of espionage. He was also alleged to have supplied them with "an ethnographic map of the Monarchy extracted from a military work and annotated with information on the number of people of Romanian nationality in the regiments," as well as other useful military knowhow.[47] Since no indication of the trial's outcome has been forthcoming, one may assume that, as with General Cena, the evidence was either too tenuous to produce a conviction or the Monarchy's dissolution rendered the case irrelevant. But the point is that these two legal actions involved retired officers who, by virtue of their rank and status, were highly regarded by Romanians both in the Empire and the Romanian Kingdom. Both also turned out to be wartime misinterpretations of cultural networking.

In virtually all cases, active imperial officers of Romanian nationality executed their duties faithfully throughout the war. Indeed, there were no egregious cases of defection among officers. Some were even decorated and promoted for their military accomplishments. And if this were partially abetted by an imperial policy that strove to avoid sending troops to a front where they would be fighting their conationals, this alone cannot explain the Romanian officers' impressive service record. The three officers considered below—Domaschnian, Boeriu, and Bacsilla—illustrate how successful careers in the Habsburg military and exemplary wartime performance did not preclude retaining connections with the national community in the Empire. Two of these men, as we shall also see, were to be equally successful in the post-World War I Romanian state.

One of the few sources for officers' military performance is the *Qualificationsliste*, those generally dry and pragmatic CVs with basic information on skills, training, and career path. Seldom does the superior officer's notation rise above a formulaic appraisal. Yet this is exactly what makes the assessment of General Georg Domaschnian (1868–1940) so useful to scholars. Domaschnian's 1918 military referees sang his praises: "distinguished, chivalrous character, noble-minded and enthusiastic, full of ideals; generous and of a lucid and broad mind; quick on the uptake and accurate, with sharp judgment and rapid decisions." According to his *Qualificationsliste*, Domaschnian possessed all the characteristics of an exceptional troop leader: courageous, coldblooded, decisive. One of the referees even recommended him for commander of the prestigious *Kriegsschule* in Vienna. Another called him "a complete man, an exceptional general."[48] Two years earlier, in 1916, the Imperial War Minister Alexander Freiherr von Krobatin summed up his portrait of Domaschnian on an equally superlative note: "one of the most outstanding officers, in character and spirit that I have ever met in my long military career."[49]

Domaschnian was an ethnic Romanian of Greek Orthodox faith who, like other officers we have encountered, hailed from the former Austrian Military Border. His peacetime military career—*Militär-Unterrealschule*, *Militär-Oberrealschule*, Wiener-Neustadt, War Academy in Vienna—and outstanding wartime performance mixed naturally with his concern for his fellow nationals in the Empire. Taking advantage of his elevated position in the War Ministry in 1914 (Domaschnian was working in the ministry's fourth department when the hostilities broke out), he interceded on behalf of his colleague, General Cena, who sought satisfaction for moral injury sustained during his wrongful imprisonment in the aforementioned espionage case:

> I feel duty bound to inform you that I have known FMLt Cena since I was a child, that I respect and consider him a model officer who is highly regarded by everyone in his community, Hungarian chauvinists excepted. If sufficient satisfaction is not granted to FMLt Cena, this would give the impression that the officer in general—the first class in the Monarchy—has been abandoned to the whims of the civil administration, which could have detrimental effects on the loyal population of the former Border.[50]

Ioan Boeriu (1859–1949) and Traian Bacsilla (1867–1931) also pursued successful military careers in the Austro-Hungarian army. Like his mentor and scholarship sponsor Colonel Urs de Margina, Boeriu was awarded both the Knight Cross of the Maria Theresa Order and the Knight Cross of the Leopold Order for his distinction in World War I. He was also promoted to major general. Injuries eventually forced Boeriu from the frontline, though he served the Empire to the very end at the War Ministry in Vienna.[51]

As for the Wiener-Neustadt graduate Bacsilla (1867–1931), he reached the rank of Brigadier General (*Generalmajor*) in 1917. Described in his CV as lively and sociable, Bacsilla seems to have gotten the best of both worlds: a flourishing military career *and* a family. Bacsilla was one of the lucky few officers whose fiancée's family could guarantee the *Heiratskaution* necessary to obtain permission to marry.[52]

For the Habsburg officer corps, the final weeks of the world war were the swan song of their careers. Despite war weariness and social upheaval, their imperial loyalty shone brightest just as the Empire was unraveling fastest. In a moving depiction of those days, the Transylvanian Hungarian aristocrat Miklós Bánffy, who became Minister of Foreign Affairs in 1921 in rump Hungary, reminisced about Habsburg officers guarding the *Hofburg*:

> [I] was told that a few hundred officers, of their own free will and dressed as common soldiers, had occupied the palace and the museums and in uninterrupted shifts, guarded the place so strictly that no one was allowed in or out. Deeply loyal, in spite of all that had been happening in the last weeks, they felt it their duty to guard what they considered imperial property. There, right in the centre of the city, the *Hofburg* was like a warship alone at sea, hopelessly battling against a raging storm and yet, manned by a loyal crew still faithful to their duty, still fighting on despite the fact that the leader to whom they owed that duty had abandoned them. . . .
> All the same it was beautiful to see and touching. It was the last time that there was to be seen the true spirit of *Mannestreue*, that ray of moral sunshine such as had been sung in the *Nibelungenlied*.[53]

The Austrian journalist Friedrich Funder similarly recalled how the Transylvanian Romanian lieutenant Iuliu Maniu reported to the War Ministry in Vienna in order to offer his troops to protect government buildings and institutions. He made good on the offer—his final imperial duty before returning to Transylvania. There, as a political leader of Transylvanian Romanians, Maniu took part in the National Assembly that resolved to unify Transylvania with the Romanian Kingdom.[54]

Postwar: The Transfer of Allegiance and Careers to the New State

What became of Romanian officers in the Austro-Hungarian army after 1918? Their paradoxical situation was more pronounced than that of the civilian population, since the officers had not only fought to defend the Empire, but since 1916 they had been at war with Romania itself. Moreover, their entire personal and professional ethos centered upon duty to the Habsburg dynasty and preservation of its Empire. More than any other professional class, Austro-Hungarian imperial officers were children of the Empire.

Nevertheless, many of them chose to join the enlarged Romanian state after 1918, including high-ranking officers like General Boeriu. Boeriu himself even had an important role in the negotiations that brought Transylvania, the Banat, and Bukovina into the Romanian Kingdom. Was this "switching sides" at odds with their status as imperial officers? Did it amount to suppressed irredentism that betrayed their imperial devotions? Correspondingly, how did their peers in the Romanian army respond to this apparent change in loyalties? Did they receive the new officers warmly, as long-lost brethren; or rather, did friction and even animosity lurk behind the facade of national reunion?

Tracing the former Austro-Hungarian officers into the post-1918 Romanian army poses problems both orthographic and bibliographic. In his *Liste aller aus der österreichisch-ungarischen Armee hervorgegangenen Offiziere, die 1930/1931 in der rumänischen Armee noch aktiv waren* ("List of all officers originating in the Austro-Hungarian army, who in 1930–31 were still active in the Romanian Army"), Franz Kuschniriuk noted that, "once included in the Romanian army yearbook, several names were orthographically altered. First names were, for the most part, Romanianized and sometimes replaced by Romanian equivalents (for instance, Rudolf became Radu)."[55] Some of these alterations predated the empire's collapse. General Michael Trapsia initially spelled his name "Trapscha," in the German fashion. But in 1879, he requested the Romanian spelling be used instead.[56] General Cena's first name varied from Nicolai in autograph documents to Nikolaus in official documents. After 1918, one finds still more variations, including Trapșa/Trapcea and Nicolai/Nicolae. Trajan Bacsilla would henceforth be Traian Băcilă, and Georg Domaschnian became Gheorghe Domășneanu.

The second, more crucial problem with following officers from the imperial into the national army is the dearth and fragmentary nature of the sources. The bibliography on the post-1918 period is more diffuse than that for Austria-Hungary, in part because Romanian historiography has traditionally concentrated on 1918 as a moment of national apotheosis and thus viewed the transition from empire(s) to nation-state as a natural, even teleological one. What follows in terms of the personal and professional destinies of former k. (u.) k. officers has by necessity been pieced together from sources ranging from newspapers, prosopographic articles, memoirs, and diaries.

Before the collapse of Austria-Hungary at the end of the world war, Emperor Franz Joseph's death in 1916 had already eliminated a powerful imperial symbol and vital cohesive force for the nationalities. His young and inexperienced successor, Karl I, was unequal to the enormous task of rebuilding this bond with his various peoples. Moreover, Karl was too dwarfed by his great uncle's mighty stature to command widespread respect and loyalty amid such an unprecedented crisis. The flight of the imperial family from the Hofburg in 1918 not only confirmed the victory of the republic—it was the final act in the life of the Habsburg Monarchy.

It was in this context that Romanian soldiers and officers gradually made their way back to their home provinces, which now de facto belonged to the enlarged Romanian state. At the end of the war and before the Treaty of Trianon came into effect, Transylvania and much of eastern Hungary were occupied by Romanian troops. From his position at the War Ministry, General Boeriu was well placed to take charge of the fluid situation and organize the Romanian troops of the disintegrating k. (u.) k. army. He thus liaised with the Governing Council

(*Consiliul dirigent*) the Romanians had established in Transylvania, and later went there to serve in the National Assembly at Alba Iulia as part of the Council's military section. On 1 December 1918, the Council decided that Transylvania would join the Romanian Kingdom. In an order issued in February 1919 and signed by Boeriu himself, the Military Command in Sibiu began forming a Transylvanian army from active Romanian nationals in the Austro-Hungarian armed forces. General Boeriu's signature was also on the circular—disseminated in both German and Romanian—that delineated the terms by which each recruit would be sworn into the new army.[57]

Like Boeriu, the retired general Nikolaus Cena spent the better part of the war in Vienna, though in his case it was a condition of the Hungarian authorities for his release from prison rather than a consequence of combat injuries. He returned home to Mehadia, in the Banat, at the conclusion of hostilities. His friend and Mehadia's Orthodox priest, Coriolan Buracu, wrote in his memoirs that Cena received the Romanian troops with open arms and tear-filled eyes.[58] Likewise, he was welcomed into the Romanian army at the same rank at which he had retired from the k. (u.) k. army. His collection of Roman artifacts—which attracted so much suspicion in 1914—was turned into a museum visited by military and civilian grandees from Bucharest. An old man at war's end, Cena appears to have remained a local personality, though his correspondence also indicates that he gradually withdrew from positions of power.[59]

Immediately after the war, General Domaschnian (after 1918, Romanian sources refer to him as Domășneanu) took charge of the military division in Temesvár (Timișoara). In 1929, he entered politics as a member of the Romanian National Peasant Party and was elected Mayor of Timișoara. He even ran for the Romanian Parliament, though he seems to have been sidelined by political machinations.[60] Iosif Iacobici (1884–1952) also entered politics after transferring into the Romanian army (as a lieutenant-colonel) in 1918. By World War II, he had risen to Major General and served as both the War Minister and Chief of Staff in Ion Antonescu's government. Iacobici was replaced in 1942 for opposing Antonescu's plan to advance into Soviet territory with German troops.[61]

Other former k. (u.) k. officers also went into Romanian politics. Officers had traditionally maintained connections with the Romanian National Party in the Monarchy's Hungarian half, so some, such as Domășneanu, joined the Romanian Peasant Party (created out of the merger in 1926 between the Romanian National Party of Transylvania and the Peasant Party of the Romanian Kingdom). Others supported more nationalist parties. Colonel Romulus Boldea, the son of a Romanian Orthodox priest in southern Hungary, founded the Christian National Party, which fused Octavian Goga's Agrarians with A. C. Cuza's League of National-Christian Defense.[62] After transferring into the Romanian army, he acted as Prefect of Severin County and eventually became an MP. Traian Moșoiu, by contrast, had liberal leanings, though he also served several governments in key functions: War Minister (1920), Minister of Communications, and Minister of Public Works (1922–26).[63]

Although the outcome of retired General Lupu's trial in late 1918 remains unclear, we do know—from documents related to his wife's *Heiratskaution*—that he stayed in Vienna after the war. According to Victor Lăzărescu, Lupu applied for Romanian citizenship even though it cost him his Austrian army pension. Lăzărescu also indicates that Lupu acted as synod and congress representative (*deputat sinodal și congresual*) of the Caransebeș eparchy in Vienna until his death in 1925, and that he and his wife were founding members of ASTRA in Lugoj.[64] Judging from the place of death in their military records, Generals Trajan Bacsilla (Traian Băcilă) and Daniel Materinga, among others, also remained in Vienna after the war.

How were Romanian nationals from the k. (u.) k. army received by the Romanian state and military? While no comprehensive study of this integration yet exists, it is possible to hypothesize based on the lives of individual officers. For example, despite the successful careers of Moise Groza, Ioan Dragalina, and Traian Moșoiu, one still finds evidence of animosity from some of their Romanian Kingdom superiors. A long-unpublished letter from 1906 testifies to Groza's difficulties with certain members of the Romanian War Ministry, who tried forcing him into early retirement. Although their decision was ultimately vetoed by King Carol I, the archivist Valer Rus views the incident as part of a wider campaign by the Romanian Kingdom military establishment to marginalize emigré officers.[65] This would include, for example, Ioan Dragalina and his brother Alexandru's posting to remote poverty-stricken regions shortly after their immigration to Romania and enrollment in the army.[66] Still more egregiously, Traian Moșoiu was blamed for the failure of Romanian troops to take the poorly defended city of Hermannstadt (Sibiu) in August 1916. According to the accusing commanding general, Moșoiu had refused to bomb the city in order to protect family property. Yet General Moșoiu had no relatives in Hermannstadt (Sibiu). In fact, the military debacle was due to the endemically poor lines of communication between Romanian troops and the commanding general's own indecision.[67]

This antagonism was likely rooted in resentment—after all, the former k. (u.) k. officers were not only outsiders (*venetici*), they were better qualified and trained than most of their Romanian Kingdom counterparts. Groza made a name for himself during the 1877–78 war by blatantly disobeying orders and proving his superiors incompetent in the process. He also contributed cartographical skills sorely needed by the young Romanian army. As for Dragalina, his military records are full of superlative assessments. Yet unlike many of his Romanian colleagues, he was opposed to corporal punishment on the grounds that it attested to an officer's poor knowledge and incapacity to train his troops properly. Such a civilizing attitude toward military leadership was also evident in General Moşoiu's command. Traveling through Hungary shortly after the withdrawal of Romanian troops in autumn 1919, Miklós Bánffy was surprised to see that looting had impoverished the inhabitants in some areas, while in others the troops had not even touched the local property: "I asked in Nagykigyos why this was, and they told me that, south of the desolate area I had noticed, the Romanian general Moşoiu had been in command and that he had not only forbidden all looting but had also punished it severely."[68]

Conclusion

World War I and the dissolution of the Habsburg Monarchy were inevitably life-changing events for Austro-Hungarian officers of Romanian nationality. Yet while their loyalties underwent a fundamental metamorphosis, this was not in the straightforward sense of forsaking old allegiances and embracing new ones. For most of these men, the imperial strand of loyalty was tightly interwoven with the national one, and the two together determined their identity. Thus, as the former unraveled and lost meaning, these officers still had a national sense of self that they had acquired by virtue of their very military background—reinforced by the fact that many, as we have seen, came from the former Austrian Military Border—and elite status, which enabled them to socialize and collaborate with political representatives of the Romanian national community in the Empire. In other words, the transformation of the officers' loyalties was quantitative rather than qualitative—their national allegiance continued into the postwar period, but one component of it was lost with the Empire itself.

Irina Marin is Assistant Professor in Political History at Utrecht University in the Netherlands. She gained her PhD at University College London and is the author of two books: *Contested Frontiers in the Balkans: Ottoman and Habsburg Rivalries in Eastern Europe* (London: I. B. Tauris, 2012), and *Peasant Violence and Antisemitism in Early Twentieth-Century Eastern Europe* (Basingstoke: Palgrave Macmillan, 2018).

Notes

1. Antoniu Marchescu, *Grănicerii bănăţeni şi Comunitatea de Avere (Contribuţiuni istorice şi juridice)* (Caransebeş: Tiparul Tipografiei Diecezane, 1941); Liviu Maior, *In the Empire: Habsburgs and Romanians, From Dynastic Loyalty to National Identity* (Cluj-Napoca: Romanian Academy, Center for Transylvanian Studies, 2008); Liviu Groza, *Contribuţii la cunoaşterea culturii grănicerilor bănăţeni* (Lugoj: Fundaţia Europeană Drăgan, 1993);

Günter Klein, "Die rumänischen Offiziere in der k. (u.) k. Armee: Sozialer Aufstieg ohne Verlust der nationalen Identität," *Revista istorică. Serie Nouă* VII, no. 3–4 (1996): 175–89; Liviu Maior, Nicolae Bocşan, and Ioan Bolovan, eds., *The Austrian Military Border. Its Political and Cultural Impact* (Iaşi: Editura Glasul Bucovinei, 1994).
2. Anton Bolz, *Erziehungs- und Bildungs-Anstalten: 35 jährige Wiedersehensfeier d. Jahrgange 1918* (Vienna: Selbstverlag, 1953), 4.
3. Gustav Bancalari et al., *Unter den Fahnen: Die Völker Österreich-Ungarns in Waffen* (Wien: Buchändler der kaiserlichen Akademie der Wissenschaften, 1889), 418.
4. Ibid., 419.
5. Alan Sked, *The Survival of the Habsburg Empire. Radetzky, the Imperial Army and the Class War, 1848* (London: Longman, 1979), 3.
6. Ibid., 7.
7. Michael Hochedlinger, *Austria's Wars of Emergence* (London: Longman, 2003), 306.
8. Erwin Schuster, "Die österreichischen Militärschulen und ihre Zöglinge bis 1918 (eingeschränkt aus Cisleithanien)," Österreichisches Staatsarchiv (henceforth OeStA), Kriegsarchiv (henceforth KA), Wien, MS/All, 327: 71.
9. Bancalari, *Unter den Fahnen*, 449; Boltz, *Erziehungs- und Bildungs-Anstalten*, 4.
10. Sked, *Survival of the Habsburg Empire*, 8.
11. Bancalari, *Unter den Fahnen*, 450.
12. Ibid., 453.
13. For an evaluation of the ratio between aristocracy and service nobility in the Habsburg army, see also Gunther E. Rothenberg, "Nobility and Military Careers: The Habsburg Officer Corps, 1740–1914," *Military Affairs* 40, no. 4 (1976): 182–86.
14. Ibid., 184.
15. Johann Christoph Allmayer-Beck, *Militär. Geschichte und Politische Bildung. Aus Anlaß des 85. Gerburtstages des Autors*, ed. Peter Broucek and Erwin A. Schmidl (Wien: Böhlau Verlag, 2003), 417.
16. Jacques van Doorn, *The Soldier and Social Change: Comparative Studies in the History and Sociology of the Military* (London: Sage Publications, 1975), 29.
17. Irina Marin, "Reforming the Better to Preserve: A K. u. K. General's View on Hungarian Politics," in *Eliten im Vielvölkerreich: Imperiale Biographien in Russland und Österreich-Ungarn (1850–1918)*, ed. Tim Buchen and Malte Rolf (Berlin: De Gruyter Oldenbourg, 2015), 159, 169, 176.
18. OeStA, KA, Kriegsministerium (henceforth KM), Präs 1874, Aktenzahl 9–2/2.
19. Marchescu, *Grănicerii bănăţeni şi comunitatea*, 357–61; Irina Marin, "The Formation and Allegiance of the Romanian Military Elite Originating from the Banat Military Border" (PhD Diss., University College London, 2009), 207–8.
20. George Cipăianu, *Vincenţiu Babeş, 1821–1907* (Timişoara: Facla, 1980), 133–34; Arhivele Naţionale Sibiu (The National Archives in Sibiu), Fond Astra, Acte, Nr. 188/1893; Biblioteca Astra (Astra Library Sibiu), Colecţii Speciale, Manuscrise, Inventar 483.
21. *Analele Asociaţiunii pentru Literatura Română şi pentru Cultura Poporului Român*, no. IV, July–August, (Sibiu, 1902), 60, accessed 25 August 2013, http://documente.bcucluj.ro/web/bibdigit/periodice/transilvania/1902/BCUCLUJ_FP_279996_1902_Anale_004.pdf.
22. Simion Retegan, *George Bariţ şi contemporanii săi. Corespondenţă trimisă*, vol. X (Bucureşti: Editura Enciclopedică, 2003), 451, footnote 4; OeStA, KA, KM Präs, 1877,

Aktenzahl 47 11/1–40, Report No. 33, p. 3 recto and p. 7 verso; Ioan Părean, *Orlat: File de istorie* (Sibiu: Editura Constant, 1999). Urs had served in the First Transylvanian Border Regiment.
23. I. Grămadă, *Societatea Academică Socială Literară România jună din Viena (1871–1911): Monografie istorică* (Arad: Editura Societății România Jună, 1912), 106.
24. Ibid., 83.
25. *Raportul anual al Societății academice social-literare "România jună"* (Vienna, 1891), 17.
26. Iuliu Moisil, "Viața studenților români din Viena în a doua jumătate a sec. al XIX-lea. Amintiri,"*Arhiva Someșană* 18 (1936): 374.
27. Nicolae Dura, *Biserica trăită departe: Viața religioasă a românilor din Austria* (București: Editura Institutului Biblic și de Misiune al Bisericii Ortodoxe Române, 2005), 178–79.
28. Ibid., 225–26.
29. OeStA, KA, Qualificationslisten 1842 (Luoni-Luria), Alexander Lupu.
30. Marin Braniște, "Comunitatea ortodoxă română din Viena: 200 de ani de la recunoașterea ei de către Împăratul Iosif al II-lea și 80 de ani de la întemeierea actualului său lăcaș de închinare," *Almanahul Parohiei Ortodoxe Române din Viena*, XXVI (Viena, 1987), 64.
31. Trințu Măran and Liviu Groza, *Documente vieneze referitoare la Banatul grăniceresc* (Lugoj: Editura Dacia Europa Nova, 2005), 75.
32. Victor Lăzărescu, "Un bănățean promotor al vieții sociale românești din Viena: Generalul Alexandru Lupu," *Almanahul Parohiei Ortodoxe Române din Viena*, XXVI (Viena, 1987), 90.
33. Măran and Groza, *Documente vieneze referitoare*, 74–75.
34. Modern Romania was created by the union of the Danubian Principalities of Wallachia and Moldavia.
35. Arhivele Naționale Istorice Centrale București (The National Historical Central Archives, Bucharest, henceforth ANIC), Fond familial Brătianu Nr. 1286, Dosar 155, p. 1/recto, Letter from Paris dated 23 September 1868, from Dumitru Brătianu to his brother, Ion C. Brătianu; Dosar 157, p. 5/recto, Letter from Paris dated 26 October 1868, from Dumitru Brătianu to his brother, Ion C. Brătianu.
36. ANIC, Fond familial Brătianu Nr. 1286, Dosar 22/1877.
37. Valer Rus, "O scrisoare inedită din corespondența lui Moise Groza cu Aurel Mureșanu: Dimensiunea negativă a mentalităților din Vechiul Regat în viziunea unui bănățean," *Țara Bârsei*, 25–32, accessed 25 August 2013, http://tara-barsei.ro/wp-content/uploads/2008/11/rus2003.pdf; Gh. Preda and Liviu Groza, *Un erou bănățean al independenței: Generalul Moise Groza* (București: Editura Militară, 1977), 13–14.
38. Nicolae Popescu, *Generalul Ion Dragalina* (București: Editura Militară, 1967), 11–12; Virgil Alexandru Dragalina, *Viața tatălui meu: Generalul Ioan Dragalina* (București: Editura Militară, 2009), 59–65.
39. Dragalina, *Viața tatălui meu*, 75: "Banatul subjugat pierde un luptător viteaz, România liberă câștigă un strălucit ofițer. În balanța neamului nostru, care va cântări mai greu?"
40. Popescu, *Generalul Ion Dragalina*, 17.
41. Glenn Torrey, *The Romanian Battlefront in World War I* (Lawrence, KS: University Press of Kansas, 2011), 129.
42. General Traian Moșoiu, *Memorial de Război (August–Oct. 1916)*, ed. Al. Dragomirescu and Marius Pop (Cluj-Napoca: Editura Dacia, 1987), 6; Torrey, *The Romanian Battlefront*, 56–57.
43. Torrey, *The Romanian Battlefront*, 346 (endnote no. 18).

44. Irina Marin, "World War One and Internal Repression: The Case of Major General Nikolaus Cena," *Austrian History Yearbook* 44 (2013): 202.
45. Conrad von Hötzendorf, *Aus Meiner Dienstzeit*, vol. 4 (Wien: Rikola Verlag, 1924), 757–58.
46. Marin, "World War One and Internal Repression," 202.
47. OeStA, KA, KM Ministerial Kommission, 1917, (1731–2320), Karton 218, Aktenzahl 2196, Report to the "Ministerialkommission im k.u.k. Kriegsministerium in Wien" dated 8 March/ 4 April 1918.
48. OeStA, KA, Qualificationslisten, 479, Domansky—Döme, Vormerkblatt für die Qualificationsbeschreibung für die Zeit vom 22./4. 1917 bis 15./2. 1918.
49. OeStA, KA, Qualificationslisten, 479, Domansky—Döme, Vormerkblatt für die Qualificationsbeschreibung für die Zeit vom 27. Juli 1915 bis 31. Mai 1916, Fasz. 528, page 1/ recto, Begutachtung, Krobatin Generaloberst, 31/12 1916.
50. OeStA, KA, KM Präs, 1914, Karton 1583 (40/1–41/3), Aktenzahl 40–19/5–2, 5. Abteilung des k.u.k. Kriegsministeriums, Bemerkung, Folio 18/verso.
51. Ioan Părean, "Slujitori ai ASTREI: Generalul Ioan Boeriu (1859–1949), primul comandant al Corpului VII Armată şi membru marcant al Asociațiunii ASTRA," accessed 16 July 2013, www.asociatiunea-astra.ro/site/fp/d18nr8182.doc; Ioan Părean, "Generalul Ioan Boeriu (1859–1949), fiu al Ţării Făgăraşului," *Revista Academiei Forțelor Terestre* 4 (2001).
52. OeStA, KA, Trajan Bacsilla, Qualificationsliste 72; OeStA, KA, Verzeichnis der Generale und Flaggenoffiziere (1911–1918), Seite 143: Trojan Bacsila.
53. Miklós Bánffy, *The Phoenix Land: The Memoirs of Count Miklós Bánffy* (London: Arcadia Books, 2003), 91–92.
54. Friedrich Funder, *Gestern ins Heute: aus dem Kaiserreich in die Republik* (Vienna: Herold, 1952), 535, 586. I am grateful to Trevor Thomas for pointing out this reference to me.
55. OeStA, KA, Manuscripte/Allgemeine Reihe, MS Allg. 509, p. 20.
56. OeStA, KA, Qualificationslisten 3532 (Trappl-Traun), Unterabtheilungs-Grundbuchblatt 1893.
57. Alexandru Baboş, "Constituirea armatei ardelene, parte componentă a armatei României Mari, apărătoarea Marii Uniri din 1 decembrie 1918," *Apulum* XXXIII (1996): 172–73.
58. Coriolan Buracu, *Muzeul General Nicolae Cena în Băile Herculane şi Cronica Mehadiei* (Turnu-Severin: Tipografia şi Libraria Ramuri, 1924), 6.
59. Cluj-Napoca National Archives, Fond personal Valeriu Branişte.
60. Cluj-Napoca National Archives, Fond personal Valeriu Branişte, Newspaper cutting: "O ruşine nemaipomenită."
61. Dennis Deletant, *Hitler's Forgotten Ally* (Basingstoke: Palgrave Macmillan, 2006), 92.
62. Nicolae Danciu Petniceanu, "Părintele Protopop Pavel Boldea (1861–1920)," *Vestea*, accessed 23 July 2013, http://vestea.wordpress.com/istorie-prin-evenimente-si-chipuri/nicolae-danciu-petniceanu- percentE2 percent80 percent9Eparintele-protopop-pavel-boldea-1861-1920 percentE2 percent80 percent9C/.
63. Moşoiu, *Memorial de Război*, 51.
64. Lăzărescu, "Un bănăţean promotor al vieţii sociale româneşti," 94; ANS, Fond Astra, Inv. 23b, VIII/11: "Membrii Astrei, Registru membri fondatori ai despărţămintelor, Despărţământul Lugoj," 87.
65. Rus, "O scrisoare inedită din corespondenţa lui Moise Groza cu Aurel Mureşanu," *Ţara Bârsei*, 25, accessed 25 August 2013, http://tara-barsei.ro/wp-content/uploads/2008/11/

rus2003.pdf. Rus is director of the Mureșanu archive in Brașov, Romania, which holds Groza's correspondence.
66. Dragalina, *Viața tatălui meu*, 85–87.
67. Moșoiu, *Memorial de Razboi*, 79; Torrey, *The Romanian Battlefront*, 56–57.
68. Bánffy, *The Phoenix Land*, 209.

Bibliography

Allmayer-Beck, Johann Christoph. *Militär. Geschichte und Politische Bildung. Aus Anlaß des 85. Gerburtstages des Autors.* Edited by Peter Broucek and Erwin A. Schmidl. Wien: Böhlau Verlag, 2003.
Baboș, Alexandru. "Constituirea armatei ardelene, parte componentă a armatei României Mari, apărătoarea Marii Uniri din 1 decembrie 1918." *Apulum* XXXIII (1996): 171–83.
Bancalari, Gustav, Alfons Danzer, and Franz Rieger. *Unter den Fahnen: Die Völker Österreich-Ungarns in Waffen.* Wien: Buchändler der kaiserlichen Akademie der Wissenschaften, 1889.
Bánffy, Miklós. *The Phoenix Land: The Memoirs of Count Miklós Bánffy.* London: Arcadia Books, 2003.
Bolz, Anton. *Erziehungs- und Bildungs-Anstalten: 35 jährige Wiedersehensfeier d. Jahrgange 1918.* Vienna: Selbstverlag, 1953.
Buracu, Coriolan. *Muzeul General Nicolae Cena în Băile Herculane și Cronica Mehadiei.* Turnu-Severin: Tipografia și Libraria Ramuri, 1924.
Cipăianu, George. *Vincențiu Babeș, 1821–1907.* Timișoara: Facla, 1980.
Deletant, Dennis. *Hitler's Forgotten Ally.* Basingstoke: Palgrave Macmillan, 2006.
Dragalina, Virgil Alexandru. *Viața tatălui meu: Generalul Ioan Dragalina.* București: Editura Militară, 2009.
Dura, Nicolae. *Biserica trăită departe: Viața religioasă a românilor din Austria.* București: Editura Institutului Biblic și de Misiune al Bisericii Ortodoxe Române, 2005.
Funder, Friedrich. *Gestern ins Heute: aus dem Kaiserreich in die Republik.* Vienna: Herold, 1952.
Grămadă, I. *Societatea Academică Socială Literară România jună din Viena (1871–1911): Monografie istorică.* Arad: Editura Societății România Jună, 1912.
Groza, Liviu. *Contribuții la cunoașterea culturii grănicerilor bănățeni.* Lugoj: Fundația Europeană Drăgan, 1993.
Hochedlinger, Michael. *Austria's Wars of Emergence.* London: Longman, 2003.
Klein, Günter. "Die rumänischen Offiziere in der k. (u.) k. Armee: Sozialer Aufstieg ohne Verlust der nationalen Identität." *Revista istorică. Serie Nouă* VII, no. 3–4 (1996): 175–89.
Măran, Trințu, and Liviu Groza. *Documente vieneze referitoare la Banatul grăniceresc.* Lugoj: Editura Dacia Europa Nova, 2005.
Maior, Liviu. *In the Empire: Habsburgs and Romanians, From Dynastic Loyalty to National Identity.* Cluj-Napoca: Romanian Academy, Center for Transylvanian Studies, 2008.
Maior, Liviu, Nicolae Bocșan, and Ioan Bolovan, eds. *The Austrian Military Border: Its Political and Cultural Impact.* Iași: Editura Glasul Bucovinei, 1994.
Marchescu, Antoniu. *Grănicerii bănățeni și Comunitatea de Avere (Contribuțiuni istorice și juridice).* Caransebeș: Tiparul Tipografiei Diecezane, 1941.

Marin, Irina. "The Formation and Allegiance of the Romanian Military Elite Originating from the Banat Military Border." PhD Diss., University College London, 2009.

———. "Reforming the Better to Preserve: A K. u. K. General's View on Hungarian Politics." In *Eliten im Vielvölkerreich: Imperiale Biographien in Russland und Österreich-Ungarn (1850–1918)*, edited by Tim Buchen and Malte Rolf, 155–77. Berlin: De Gruyter Oldenbourg, 2015.

———. "World War One and Internal Repression: The Case of Major General Nikolaus Cena." *Austrian History Yearbook* 44 (2013): 195–208.

Moisil, Iuliu. "Viața studenților români din Viena în a doua jumătate a sec. al XIX-lea. Amintiri." *Arhiva Someșană* 18 (1936): 369–97.

Moșoiu, Traian. *Memorial de Război (August–Oct. 1916)*. Edited by Al. Dragomirescu and Marius Pop. Cluj-Napoca: Editura Dacia, 1987.

Părean, Ioan. "Generalul Ioan Boeriu (1859–1949), fiu al Țării Făgărașului." *Revista Academiei Forțelor Terestre* 4 (2001).

———. *Orlat: File de istorie*. Sibiu: Editura Constant, 1999.

Popescu, Nicolae. *Generalul Ion Dragalina*. București: Editura Militară, 1967.

Preda, Gh. and Liviu Groza. *Un erou bănățean al independenței: Generalul Moise Groza*. București: Editura Militară, 1977.

Retegan, Simion. *George Bariț și contemporanii săi: Corespondență trimisă*, vol. X. București: Editura Enciclopedică, 2003.

Rothenberg, Gunther E. "Nobility and Military Careers: The Habsburg Officer Corps, 1740–1914." *Military Affairs* 40, no. 4 (1976): 182–86.

Sked, Alan. *The Survival of the Habsburg Empire: Radetzky, the Imperial Army and the Class War, 1848*. London: Longman, 1979.

Torrey, Glenn. *The Romanian Battlefront in World War I*. Lawrence, KS: University Press of Kansas, 2011.

van Doorn, Jacques. *The Soldier and Social Change: Comparative Studies in the History and Sociology of the Military*. London: Sage Publications, 1975.

von Hötzendorf, Conrad. *Aus Meiner Dienstzeit*. Wien: Rikola Verlag, 1924.

Chapter 7

SHADES OF EMPIRE
Austro-Hungarian Officers, Frankists, and the Afterlives of Austria-Hungary in Croatia, 1918–1929

John Paul Newman

It is testimony to the many layers and contradictions of late Habsburg history that the scope of responses to Austria-Hungary's end encompasses everything from apocalyptic dejection to euphoric triumphalism, via indifference.[1] And it is testimony to the shifting sands of twentieth-century European history that perceptions of ruptures and continuities are frequently changing as well. What once seemed like a radical departure at war's end is now revealed as merely a dormant line of continuity, and vice versa. Habsburg history in East-Central Europe has frequently been animated by presentist concerns: at times an anchor providing ballast in political storms; at others an albatross portentously hovering above the new ships of state.

This chapter focuses on those dispossessed by the empire's end in 1918. But this is an end with a dynamic rather than a static spectrum, as fates often drastically alter over the course of the interwar period. Moreover, the dispossession of 1918 can only be understood when framed by the contrasting moods of euphoria that, at least officially, celebrated the death of Austria-Hungary in the successor states of interwar Central and Eastern Europe. It was a contrast that generated considerable tension between the minority "cultures of defeat"— isolated, marginalized, but nevertheless present in the successor states—and the larger "cultures of victory," which lauded the monarchy's passing and sought to consolidate their break with the imperial past, yet which lived with a melancholy sense of their victory's human cost and a lingering fear that the "triumph" was incomplete.² This worry was well grounded, as the categories of victor and vanquished rose and fell with the fortunes of the post-imperial state makers.

To illustrate this point, I would offer an epigram and an anecdote. In the 1930s, Tomáš Garrigue Masaryk, the philosopher-president of the First Czechoslovak Republic, spoke of how the post-Habsburg "New Europe" of successor states resembled "a laboratory built over the great graveyard of the world war."³ Masaryk, a political visionary who lived to see his vision realized, had come to bury rather than praise Austria-Hungary. Yet he understood the great challenge the "victors" now faced, as state-forming in Central and Eastern Europe would be conducted over a topography of mass death and collapsed states. Indeed, Masaryk was more prescient than he appreciated: his sepulchral epigram could serve for the entire century. Those parts of Europe ruled by the Habsburgs became, after 1918, a laboratory wherein toiled successive political alchemists: democratic, authoritarian, fascist, communist, democratic again. Nor was this the last time the region would serve as a vast burial ground for people and ideas. This is a history strewn with ruptured and aborted political projects. Like the colossal wreck of Shelley's "Ozymandias," the monuments of failure and political hubris are patently apparent to the casual observer. The continuities, by contrast, are buried deeper.

This brings us to the anecdote, which is set in the Hungarian People's Republic established after World War II—yet another laboratory and, later, graveyard. In the 1950s, the celebrated Croatian author and staunch Yugoslav socialist Miroslav Krleža traveled to Budapest to accept a prize from the Hungarian Writers' Association. A former Habsburg subject like Masaryk, Krleža knew the country well, spoke Hungarian, and had once been a reluctant cadet at Budapest's prestigious Ludoviceum Military Academy.⁴ The wheel of history had turned several revolutions since then, but Krleža knew how the past still echoed around Central Europe's new corridors of power. Retracing his youth along the journey, Krleža visited a military cemetery in which were buried several officers he knew from his time at the Ludoviceum or as an undistinguished soldier in the Great War (before aborting his military career). Earlier, Krleža had ferociously satirized Habsburg army officers in his collection of short stories set during World War I—*The Croatian God Mars* (1922).⁵ Now he adopted a more decorous—if elegiac—tone. Standing in the Hungarian cemetery, Krleža imagined a thread running from one war to the next—the *mentalité* of the officer corps, once the pride of Habsburg heraldry. Not only had the officers' outlook ostensibly survived the Monarchy, but it had also been drawn into the folds of the region's radical-right politics in the 1930s.

Fascism, in short, appealed to many former Habsburg officers by offering the chance to redeem the humiliating defeat of 1918 and, thereby, restore the pomp of imperial power. The ideology's trappings, moreover, were similar to those of the empire, despite fascist claims to a radical rupture with that recent past. Krleža sensed this connection and wondered whether the whole history of Central European fascism (Austrian, Hungarian, and, of course, Croatian) could be told through the biographies of these departed officers. Yet even if this were possible, the link had been decisively ruptured by fascism's fiery death in World War II.

Krleža thus went to Budapest to put the past's discredited pieties to rest and escape the shades of a dead empire. This trajectory likely suited the communist's teleological sense of history, wherein all forms of political organization must eventually give way to the prerogatives of the working class. And it probably suited his literary sensibility as well. After all, this was a poetic story of Habsburg military officers, the tinder of empire, burning incandescently in the fires of fascism until there was nothing but embers by the end of World War II.

Did Krleža's trajectory also possess analytic content? One can certainly trace a thread from Austria-Hungary through the labyrinths of interwar history and on into World War II. Habsburg military officers of various nationalities shared with their Italian and, above all, German counterparts a *revanchist* fury against Europe's postwar political order. In fact, for many officers, the sense of rupture and disorientation was yet more profound, since the very state idea for which they had fought was now extinct. The defeat and disintegration of Austria-Hungary in 1918 is thus the traumatic "primal scene" of the various right-wing political movements in interwar Central Europe—the unhealed wound that at once rouses the outcasts, incites the territorial and political revisionists, and galvanizes the rest of the war's resentful survivors.

Moreover, there was no pause between the death of Austria-Hungary and the quickening of these disaffected forces—the postwar civilization was barely formed before its first discontents took up arms. Like masterless *Rōnin* of a realm passed into extinction, many former Habsburg officers roamed the violent milieus of 1920s Europe.[6] Before long, they perceived their chance for redemption and regeneration in the right-wing politics of the following decade.[7] By presenting his military and economic exploitation of Europe as a triumphal reversal of the failed Paris peace settlements (i.e., a "New Order"), Hitler and other fascist leaders preyed upon these dispossessed parties in interwar Europe.[8] The alchemist thus announced his success: leaden defeat was transformed into gilded victory; rupture replaced continuity.

The Croat case is a particularly good fit for this template. After all, Austria-Hungary's defeat was also that of a small number of *kaisertreu* Croatian military officers who rejected the new south Slavic state (the Kingdom of Serbs, Croats, and Slovenes) and went into exile at the end of the world war. These officers were part of a larger network of right-wing paramilitary groups across Central Europe.[9] By the late 1920s, they had moved into the ranks of the *Ustaša*—the Croatian Revolutionary Organization, a small gang of mainly exiled paramilitaries who adopted the fascist program under Italian tutelage.[10]

The Ustaše were thrust into political prominence with Hitler's creation of the Independent State of Croatia (*Nezavisna država Hrvatska*, or NDH) following Nazi Germany's defeat of Yugoslavia in 1941. They conceived of their state as no less than a triumphant rupture with Serb/Yugoslav subjugation in the interwar period, and in glorious continuity with the Habsburgs. As we will see below, this was in part the Ustaše's backlash against the anti-imperial, anti-Habsburg national culture of the Serb-dominated interwar state. But it was above all an effort to cut out the interwar period in toto as an unwanted offshoot of Croatia's national caudex. The Ustaše thus travestied Croatia's imperial past by exploiting Habsburg symbols and history (especially those having to do with the military) and constructing former k. (u.) k. officers of south Slavic descent as Ustaše *alte Kämpfer*, or original/old fighters. At least initially, the Ustaše placed these old guard officers prominently within the NDH's military formations, in particular its homeguard *Domobran* units.[11] According to official Ustaša genealogy, Croats were proud Habsburg descendants with absolutely no biological ties to interwar Yugoslavia's ruling (and Serbian) Karađorđević dynasty.

This chapter charts the passage of ex-Habsburg officers at the end of World War I into the paramilitary/terrorist Ustaša formations of the early 1930s. Beginning with the chaotic postwar period, it then focuses on the first decade of state-building in the south Slavic kingdom, nearly two-thirds of whose citizens had recently been subjects of Austria-Hungary.[12] It is a story of both rupture and continuity, as well as of disorientation and defeat transformed into a regenerated sense of purpose by the promise of victory—a victory, however, that would ultimately prove hollow. The ex-officers whose stories are told here represent the afterlife not only of a dead empire, but of a defunct idea as well.

The Two-Headed Eagle: Nationalism and Imperialism in Austria-Hungary

In order to understand these officers, it is necessary to comprehend the nature of the Empire and the imperial idea they served, as well as to confront a misconception about Austria-Hungary's binding ideologies. Traditional histories posit a dichotomy between dynastic state loyalty and the "centrifugal" forces of nationalism that would eventually bring down the Empire.[13] This antagonism was circumvented by the historian István Deák's work on the Habsburg officer corps, which argued that institutional loyalties and the Empire's "bureaucratic charisma" pushed its subjects "beyond nationalism." In other words, the officers' national identity was largely supplanted by a dynastic alternative.[14]

More recent scholarship has fine-tuned and broadened Deák's thesis by showing how the Monarchy nurtured a form of national identity that accepted, and was acceptable to, the Empire.[15] According to this argument, dynastic loyalty and national awareness were mutually enhancing within the imperial framework. Yet not all nations were amenable to this process. Serbs, who had wrested de facto independence and later de jure statehood from the Ottomans in the nineteenth century, were one of them. Indeed, Serbian political and, especially, military elites pursued nationalism in contradistinction to the Habsburg compromise—as a ceaseless drive to emancipate their perceived conationals (South Slavs including Serbs, Croats, Slovenes, Bosnians, and Macedonians) from the yoke of empire, be it Ottoman or Austro-Hungarian.

Worsening political relations between Austria-Hungary and Serbia in the early twentieth century sharply delineated the differences between the Habsburg and Serbian solutions to the "national question." The historian Alexander Watson recently argued that Austro-Hungarian leaders willed a local war in order to halt the momentum of the Serbian "nationalizing state," particularly as it threatened their Bosnian subjects.[16] The war between the Habsburg Empire and Serbia was thus in part a battle of peoples mobilized behind antithetical ideas about the nature of the state and international order. It was also a chance for the Dual Monarchy to assert and legitimize its multinational *Staatsidee*, not least of all to its own people. Yet this ideological duel, turned deadly with the assassination of the heir to the Austro-Hungarian throne in 1914, became an existential showdown in the context of the larger European conflict.[17] And this tension was acutely felt in the Habsburg army whose high-ranking officers were tightly bound to the institutions and symbols of the Habsburg state, and who often saw no contradiction between their national interests and the imperial raison d'état.

Enter the Frankists

The Habsburg war against Serbia had enthusiastic supporters among South Slavs, though perhaps none more so than those in the Pure Party of Right (*Čista stranka prava*) in Croatia. Commonly known as the Frankists (*Frankovci*) after its founder Josip Frank, this relatively marginal political faction in the Zagreb *Sabor* (Assembly) embraced Austria-Hungary's hybrid national and imperial fealty in hopes of advancing Croatian interests. In particular, the Frankists held out for a reorganization of the Dual Monarchy along trialist lines, with a third Croat-dominated political entity in the Empire's south Slavic lands.[18] The Habsburg war thus offered the prospect of a reversal of fortunes for the Frankists, as the taming of Serbian nationalism would neutralize a formidable obstacle on the path to trialism. Moreover, it would strengthen the Croat political component by integrating a cowed Serbia into Austria-Hungary.

Yet military victory has a way of normalizing itself in the historical record. The national histories of Austria-Hungary's successor states—Czechoslovakia, Poland, a vastly expanded Romania, and the Kingdom of Serbs, Croats, and

Slovenes (later Yugoslavia)—have thus tended to assert that the war's outcome and their emergence were both inevitable and conclusive.[19] Of course, neither was the case. Indeed, it is too easily forgotten that other serious alternatives for postwar Europe were regularly put forward during the conflict. The military defeat, in short, also meant the apparent annihilation of a political idea, including any plans for reform and/or reconstruction. The Frankists' trialism was one such plan, though as long as there were still Frankists, the political aspirations of Croats would outlive Austria-Hungary.

"Liberation and Unification"

The Kingdom of Serbs, Croats, and Slovenes, ostensibly a new country constituting a decisive rupture with the past, was in fact closely connected to the Kingdom of Serbia. The state's army, political institutions, bureaucracy, money, and dynasty were all inherited essentially unchanged from the prewar state.[20] Serbia, moreover, had already greatly expanded during the Balkan wars before it again emerged victorious in 1918. Thus through the new Kingdom's international and domestic identification with the previous one, its leaders could justify the large south Slavic state to its wartimes allies, France and Britain. Nor was this merely a Serbian geopolitical victory—1918 became a key totem of the south Slavic kingdom's national culture. According to this interpretation, the Balkan wars and World War I represented an existential clash in which the nationalizing Serbian state, born in revolution against the Ottomans in the early nineteenth century, had consummated its struggle to liberate South Slavs by successively vanquishing the Ottoman and Habsburg Empires. And just as those empires perished in the world war, the Serbian nation-state idea was validated through victory. The years 1912–18 were thus constructed as the final stage of this long process of "liberation" from empire and "unification" of the nation.

This created a kind of cultural schizophrenia in Yugoslavia, as the state's birth in a "new Europe" was also the end phase of the Serbian national revolution. As we will see below, the 1920s do not attest to the success of this "liberation and unification" trope in fusing the diverse ethnoreligious groups of the south Slavic state. The decade is rather characterized by prolonged military conflict, political paralysis, national dissension, and, ultimately, failure. Moreover, continuity with victorious Serbia typically entailed the marginalization or outright suppression of other wartime experiences and national histories. For the Frankists and their supporters in the Austro-Hungarian army, for example, "liberation and unification" could not have sounded more ironic and empty. After all, everything they had fought for—the imperial state and dynasty, Serbia's political and military subordination, and the advancement of their own concept of Croatian national interest—had evaporated at war's end. The revolutionary attainment of a Serb dominated south Slavic state seemed more like the passive realization of their own worst fears.

Unsurprisingly then, resurrectionary hopes flickered in the ashes of the destroyed empire. Well into the 1920s, the Serbian/Yugoslav army and its paramilitaries fought a low intensity war against oppositional groups from Macedonia, Montenegro, Kosovo, and Croatia.[21] Many Frankists and their ex-officer supporters joined these insurgencies not only in the south Slavic Kingdom, but also in the ranks of such central European groups as the Austrian *Heimwehr* and the Szeged counterrevolutionaries in Hungary.[22] Yet their contribution to this resistance was relatively negligible—perhaps a few hundred diehards who formed the Croat Legion paramilitary organization and its political manifestation, the Croat Committee. The latter, made up largely of émigrés, lobbied internationally for Croatian independence from the south Slavic Kingdom.[23]

Immediately after the war, many South Slavs were transfixed by the possibility of a Habsburg restoration. Like the Cheshire Cat's disembodied grin, the Frankists leered out at their new rulers even as their Austrian body had vanished—an uncanny reminder of the high domestic cost of the Empire's defeat. Official reports on the Croat Legion and Committee exaggerated their numbers (the Frankists themselves contributed to this by claiming to have mass support for their cause) and overemphasized their continuity with the Habsburg dynasty, typically presenting the Frankists as a conspiracy of "Habsburg officers."[24] When news of the Legion and Committee was leaked by the Belgrade press in 1919, it stirred deep passions, especially when Serbia's leading daily, *Politika*, stoked fears of a reincarnation of their recent foe. In 1921, the Zagreb trial of domestic and émigré Frankists who had supported the Legion and the Committee became a *cause célèbre* in the new state. The lawyer who defended them, the future Ustaša *Poglavnik* (leader) Ante Pavelić (himself a figure of increasing stature in the party), attempted to dismiss the affair as the playacting of political amateurs caught up in the disorientation of the postwar era.[25] Yet he knew there was much more to it.

There was something tragicomic about the counterrevolution as conceived by the Frankists, whose supporting players strutted and fret—without lines or direction—across a barren postwar stage. The Frankists may have felt less stranded by the Monarchy's defeat when they mixed with counterrevolutionary groups from Austria and Hungary. And the instability of the new order likely also sustained their faith in imminent change.[26] Yet whether they knew it or simply could not admit it, the cause for which the Frankists had gone to war was extinguished by 1918. This became increasingly obvious when Croatia's enlarged electoral franchise turned Stjepan Radić's once marginal Peasant Party into the sole mass political force of the interwar period and, correspondingly, the very center of Croatian national life. The labyrinthine electoral structures of Austria-Hungary had held the Frankists aloft. The Empire's defeat was thus theirs as well.

This was above all true because the Frankists' relentless assertion of the Croatian national cause was now encumbered by their legacy of Habsburg affinity in a country directly identified with the dynasty's defeat. The term "Frankist" became increasingly synonymous with any manifestation of extreme Croat nationalism that had also opposed Serbia (and Serbs generally) during the war. Indeed, it became an epithet conveniently deployed in parliament, the press, and the public sphere in order to denounce someone as unpatriotic or even subversive. In time, the Frankists would wear the title as a badge of honor to the point of sarcastically complaining that their opponents' generous use of the term was diluting its meaning.[27] In Yugoslavia, there thus developed a strange symmetry between the raising up of Serbia's military victory and the laying low of the Frankists' "Austrophile" (or Serbophobe) wartime behavior. In the moral schema of "liberation and unification," few insults were more demeaning than that of "Frankist."

A Troubled Decade

Meanwhile, the new state's rulers followed the lodestar of Serbia's military victory, which was stubbornly set, it appears with hindsight, on the wrong course. The first postwar decade is a history of comprehensive political failure starting with the adoption of the so-called Vidovdan Constitution on 28 June 1921—an exclusively Serb Orthodox holiday (St. Vitus's Day) as well as the anniversary of the much mythologized Kosovo battle between medieval Serbia and the oncoming Ottoman Turks (not to mention the Sarajevo assassination). This was neither an auspicious nor a conciliatory start, and the broad opposition—including Radić's Peasant Party and the tenuous Frankists—reacted by boycotting the ratification outright. Yet it was not merely the insensitive timing that offended Radić and his followers—more substantively, they objected to the constitution's centralization of power in Belgrade. They thus abstained from the National Assembly during the new state's critical early years.

Throughout the 1920s, the Yugoslav National Assembly operated in a state of near permanent crisis. It was often incapable of passing the laws essential to unifying the country's disparate currencies, legal codes, social policies, and, it follows, peoples.[28] Especially severe was the political crisis of 1924–25, which was in part an attempt by Serbian leaders of the Democratic Party to break down the political and psychological barriers that persisted from the war years and had been reinforced by the Vidovdan Constitution. The architect of this initiative was party leader Ljubomir Davidović, who spoke openly of the need to erase the divisions in the country between the war's "victorious" and "defeated" peoples.[29] Yet not only did Davidović's efforts fail to heal the national war wounds and bring the abstaining Stjepan Radić back into government, they spurred a new spasm of violence in many parts of the country. And for the most part, the armed militias lashing out at their perceived enemies were made up of war veterans.[30]

On the other side, there was staunch Serbian resistance to any sign that their cult of victory would be undermined by the state. Many Serbs continued to assert their political rights as first among equals specifically because of their role in winning the war. And many also—including, it should be noted, Serbs from the formerly Habsburg parts of the country—became increasingly resentful of the fact that commemorations of their military sacrifices and victory had limited resonance beyond the borders of prewar Serbia. Initiatives toward the construction of authentically "Yugoslav" war narratives, such as the official emphasis on south Slavic volunteers, also failed to take hold in a meaningful way.[31]

Yugoslavia's many problems in the 1920s cannot, naturally, be attributed solely to the Great War's legacy—the vexed "national question," the lack of political vision and flexibility, the ongoing agrarian crisis, and socioeconomic woes have all been emphasized by historians.[32] Yet it was important in Yugoslavia, as it was throughout the Austro-Hungarian successor states, to forge an authentic and inclusive sense of citizenship in order to sustain statehood after the divisive military conflict and traumatic disintegration of the Habsburg Empire. The emphasis on Serbia's military victory as a key source of Yugoslav identity failed to achieve this. Instead, the "liberation and unification" narrative, with its emphasis on continuity with Serbia's national revolution since the nineteenth century and its veneration of the nation's war dead, had quite the opposite effect—it pushed out many of the new state's subjects, while pushing many others into increasingly radical forms of national resistance.[33]

The Frankists' "Culture of Defeat"

The Frankists offered an alternative narrative to "liberation and unification," and one which was diametrically opposed to the Serbian culture of victory. By accepting the period from 1912 to 1918 as one of defeat and death, they constructed what the historian Wolfgang Schivelbusch called a "culture of defeat."[34] This allowed the Frankists to stress the moral superiority of their own military sacrifices and, thereby, to look forward to future redemption. Thus, for example, during the millennial celebrations of the founding of the Zagreb bishopric in 1925, Gustav Perčec, a former Austro-Hungarian officer and leading Frankist, spoke of the Croatian war sacrifice and dissatisfaction with the postwar order. He denied that Croat soldiers had been worn down by the fighting, but rather that they had laid down their weapons as an act of faith—that is, they fully expected that the Croats' right to self-determination would be realized:

> Returning to their homes in disorganized fashion from the battlefield, Croat soldiers had to look tearfully at how every traitor, degenerate, and *naif* betrayed the thousand-year-old right of the Croat homeland. . . . The Croat people still seek and will continue to seek the fulfilment and implementation of the promised self-determination; if this is not realized, Europe will come to resemble a powder keg.[35]

Far from being liberated, the Frankists claimed that Croats had more in common with the defeated nations of World War I. They further argued that the decennial of Serbia's victory at Kumanovo in the first Balkan war (October 1922) was no reason for celebration. According to the Frankist narrative, the Croats had enjoyed good relations with the Turks and the Bulgarians. Why celebrate their defeat?[36]

The Frankists beat the revisionist drum throughout the 1920s, hoping to connect their struggle to the larger revisionist cause in Europe. In a 1927 article entitled "On War" in the Frankist journal *Hrvatsko Pravo* (*Croatian Right*), the author argued that while the consequences of the world war had been terrible for all, the so-called winners were now in worse shape than the losers: "States which were created as a result of the war spread dissatisfaction across half of Europe. The best testament to this is their miserable economic conditions. And not only are the victorious nations dissatisfied with their fate, they are actually in a more chaotic state than they can handle."[37] As for the Croats themselves, the article challenged the assumption that the South Slav state's enemies were, *ipso facto*, their own. Italy, after all, had negotiated during the war on behalf of Croatian independence; and Hungary, though guilty of mistreating the Croats in the days of dualism, had since realized its errors. Furthermore, the author argued, Bulgaria—Serbia's enemy from both the second Balkan war and the world war—had never wronged the Croats:

> Head into a village and ask a Croatian peasant what he thinks of Bulgarians. Each one will answer in the same way. Why should they be our enemies? They have done nothing wrong to us, so should we then provoke them into having an unfriendly stance towards us? . . . Croatians are pacific, but robust, patient, and sober. That is why the nation cannot fall, even if a war greater than the last were to arrive.[38]

A particularly important date in the Frankist calendar was the Catholic holiday of All Souls' Day (November 2), which commemorates the faithful departed and, conveniently, is close to Armistice Day (November 11).[39] The Frankists thus took it as an opportunity to reenact the Golgotha of military defeat in Zagreb's Mirogoj cemetery—offering up their own heroes, ritualizing their war dead, and reminding supporters of the betrayals and violence that Croats had suffered in the conflagration. It was also an occasion to imagine their imminent resurrection. Instead of the Serbian rulers Lazar, Obilić, and Karađorđe, the Frankists sacralized their own political leaders by visiting the gravesites of the likes of Ante

Starčević and Josip Frank. And rather than honoring the dead of Serbian battles such as Kajmakčalan and Cer, they prayed for the Croatian soldiers who were killed while resisting south Slavic unification, including "those who had fallen for Croatian liberation on 5 December [1918]," during a protest at South Slav liberation on Jelačić Square. In 1924, a Frankist speech at the graves of these soldiers promised to redeem their sacrifice:

> One night when our wishes and struggles are realized, we will come, not just those of us here now, but the whole of the Croat people, to call out to you that the idea for which the Party of Right has fought for sixty-three years has finally been brought to life, the idea for which you fell, namely, that only God and the Croats rule in Croatia.[40]

The sacrifice was meaningful because it had been made for the Croat nation. But the Frankists also felt that they could only adequately honor it through further struggle and eventual victory. They thus "called out" to the "December Victims," promising to return as a national whole when their idea was finally "brought to life."

A Black Decennial: The Birth of the Ustaše

The Yugoslav state-building project was dealt a deadly blow on 20 June 1928 when, on the floor of parliament in Belgrade, a Montenegrin deputy of the Serbian People's Radical Party, Puniša Račić, shot five deputies of the Croatian Peasant Party. He killed three of them, including party leader Stjepan Radić who died of his wounds some seven weeks later. Unfortunately, this violent act was neither out of character for the times or its perpetrator. Račić was a veteran of the irregular "Chetnik" military auxiliaries who after the armistice had continued fighting against the Albanian insurgency in his native Montenegro. He was also a leading member of the paramilitary Chetnik associations in the 1920s, and the most vocal opponent of Davidović's proposed 1924 rapprochement with Radić. Račić's mere presence on the chamber floor demonstrates how undertones of war and violence were always close to the country's politics. Indeed, it was a disparaging remark from a Peasant Party deputy about Račić's wartime record that provoked his ire. The attack put an exclamation point at the end of a decade of resentment and division in the country, no small part of it due to the failure to move on from the war.

The prominent Frankist Ante Pavelić, since 1927 also a parliamentary deputy, was quick to condemn Račić's actions as emblematic of Serbian aggression against the Croat nation.[41] At a party meeting in Zagreb held one week after the shootings, Pavelić reminded his colleagues that Frankists like him were merely reiterating what they had been saying since 1918: that Croatia should be the independent master of her own affairs.[42] In a shift welcomed by the Party, the parliamentary shootings helped foster a broader and more vocal rejection of the "liberation and unification" narrative, as well as other emblems of Serbia's war victory. Moreover, the fact that this critical juncture coincided with the decennial celebrations of "liberation and unification" gave newfound confidence to the Frankists and revitalized urgency to their calls for separation. In past ceremonies, the Party had established a narrative of Croat suffering in Yugoslavia. In 1928, during the annual All Souls' Day ceremony at Mirogoj cemetery, the writer and former Austro-Hungarian officer Mile Budak implicitly told the crowd: "The graves of our fathers teach us many truths." He then condemned the Serbian celebrations more forthrightly:

> You [all] will personally hear the great voices of the victims of the past ten years, who are these days gathering around the canton of Ante Starčević, under the leadership of the newest and greatest victim: Stjepan Radić; listen to them and you will hear the deadliest song of Croatian pride and the most enduring celebration—of a black decennial.[43]

Like Pavelić, Budak also stressed the continuity of the Frankists' goals, boasting that all political parties in Croatia now sought that for which they had been fighting the past decade.[44] Gustav Perčec added that the November holiday provided an "alternative" to Belgrade's 1 December ceremonies, since "these heroes were the first who gave their lives for the honor of the Croat people."[45] Pavelić himself called 1 December 1918 "the blackest day in Croatian history," and promised: "when Croatia is free, it will be outlined in a responsible fashion to Croat children, the manner in which they should interpret the dark pages of that day."[46] The Frankists' message was, indeed, the same as it had always been. The crucial difference now was that numerous Croats in the capital shared their goals for an independent state.

The official celebrations at Zagreb Cathedral were sabotaged when unknown persons unfurled three large black flags along the front of the building. One had the date "1 December" sewn in large white letters; another read "20 June 1928"; and the third was covered with black and red squares—the coat of arms of medieval Croatia and Slavonia.[47] Violent clashes between police and demonstrators resulted in the deaths of four Croats and, accordingly, a further deterioration in relations between Zagreb and Belgrade. Branimir Jelić, the leader of the Frankist youth organization, expressed the urgent need for young Croats to organize themselves into "units" that could put aside party differences and factional interests in the battle for "Croatian freedom." Such groups would not know "equivocation, [but] rather discipline."[48] Jelić further noted the "false epoch on Kajmakčalan, the Balkan-Serbian lie about Kajmakčalan-liberation achievements, [is] an infection that will not plague us."

The National Assembly never recovered from the assassinations. During the second half of 1928, King Aleksandar Karađorđević tried to reconfigure various political party formations, including offering the office of prime minister to the Croat Peasant Party leader, Vladko Maček. He declined, and instead the leader of the Slovene People's Party, Anton Korošec, became the first and last non-Serb to hold the office. It was to no avail. As we have seen, the parliamentary crisis played out against the contested decennial celebrations, which only served as reminders of how little had actually been achieved toward an authentic national liberation and unification. On 6 January 1929, barely a month after Serbs celebrated 1 December with ticker-tape parades, while others around the country protested the occasion's Serb-centered symbolism, King Aleksandar suspended parliament and declared his royal dictatorship. This was supposedly a temporary measure to clear the path toward "national oneness." For the King and his supporters (especially in the army and among war veterans), however, the dictatorship was a welcome step toward an authentic realization of "liberation and unification." It thus remained in place until Aleksandar's assassination in 1934, though meaningful parliamentary politics never returned to the interwar Kingdom.

The dictatorship also quickly ended the brief period of Frankist ascendancy, including all talk of Croatian separation. Indeed, Frankist expectations for a full-scale revolt now proved misplaced, as most Croats appeared to accept the dictatorship as a necessary solution to the parliamentary paralysis that had made the country so ungovernable. Pavelić and his long-term collaborator Perčec, however, did not surrender so easily. Along with Branimir Jelić, they fled the country shortly after the King's announcement. Both Perčec and Pavelić were sentenced to death *in absentia* for their cooperation with the Internal Macedonian Revolutionary Organization (*Vnatrešna makedonska revolucionerna organizacija*, or VMRO), an independence movement founded in Salonika in the late nineteenth century. In Italy in the early 1930s, they went on to found their own organization—the Ustaše.

Before settling in fascist Italy, however, Pavelić's first port of call was Vienna, where he visited the coterie of ex-officers gathered around Stjepan Sarkotić (including Ivan Perčević and Stjepan Duić).[49] Sarkotić, the wartime governor-general of Habsburg Bosnia, was practically deified by Frankists for his long-held opposition to Yugoslavia.[50] Other Frankist/ex-officers who joined the ranks of the Ustaša paramilitary units were Mirko Puk, Slavko Štancer, Manko Gagliardi, and Johann von Salis-Sewis. Vilim Begić was frequently arrested in 1929–30 for crossing the border into Hungary in order to assist Pavelić and Perčec, the latter of whom served as the military commander of the Ustaša training camp in Janka Pustza.[51] Slavko Kvaternik joined the movement in 1933 at Pavelić's personal request. And Jelić served as the organization's most senior representative in Berlin, directing a center for Ustaša propaganda in the German capital. All these ex-Habsburg officers filled the highest ranks of the Ustaše in the 1930s. And those who survived its internal power struggles were rewarded plum positions in Pavelić's independent Croatian state.

Conclusion

Throughout the 1920s, a number of former Austro-Hungarian officers, along with members of the Frankist political party, remained unreconciled to the south Slavic state. Resentful of their loss of status after 1918, the Frankist leader Ante Pavelić and his Ustaše paramilitary gave these officers the chance to "remobilize" and, thereby, to recover the relevance they had lost during parliamentary rule in Yugoslavia. The Frankists who graduated into the ranks of the Ustaše were masters of historical reformulation, searing a "culture of defeat" into the very foundations of an organization that promised to revenge the humiliations of 1918. The ritualization of the war defeat by Frankists at Mirogoj and the implacable hostility to Yugoslavia and its "liberation-unification" narrative drew a thread of continuity through this small group during the decade prior to King Aleksandar's establishment of a royal dictatorship. The dictatorship itself then ignited a new phase in this resistance, "remobilizing" these disgruntled and largely forgotten one-time supporters of Austria-Hungary into a resurgent radical right movement. In its origins, the Ustaše was the product of a Croatian "culture of defeat" nursed by former officers of the Austro-Hungarian army and their allies in the Frankist political party.

John Paul Newman is Senior Lecturer in Twentieth-Century European History at Maynooth University. He is the author of *Yugoslavia in the Shadow of War: Veterans and the Limits of State Building, 1903–1945* (Cambridge, UK: Cambridge University Press, 2015), and the coeditor (with Mark Cornwall) of *Sacrifice and Rebirth: The Legacy of the Last Habsburg War* (Oxford: Berghahn Books, 2016), and (with Julia Eichenberg) *The Great War and Veterans' Internationalism* (London: Palgrave Macmillan, 2013). Until September 2011, he was an ERC Postdoctoral Research Fellow working on the project "Paramilitary Violence after the Great War," to which he contributed a case study of violence in the Balkans.

Notes

1. For a survey of these responses, see Adam Kożuchowski, *The Afterlife of Austria-Hungary: The Image of the Habsburg Monarchy in Interwar Europe* (Pittsburgh: Pittsburgh University Press, 2013).
2. "Culture of Defeat" is coined by Wolfgang Schivelbusch in *The Culture of Defeat: On National Trauma, Mourning and Recovery* (New York: Picador, 2003); on cultures of victory, see John Horne, "Beyond Cultures of Victory and Defeat? Interwar Veterans' Internationalism," in *The Great War and Veterans' Internationalism*, ed. Julia Eichenberg and John Paul Newman (London: Palgrave Macmillan, 2013), 207–22.

3. Tomáš Garrigue Masaryk, *President Masaryk Tells His Story* (recounted by Karel Čapek) (London: G. Allen and Unwin, 1934), 299.
4. On this period of Krleža's life, see Djordje Zelmanović, *Kadet Krleža: školovanje Miroslava Krleže u mađarskim vojnim učilištima* (Zagreb: Školske novine, 1987).
5. There is still no English language translation of this work.
6. See Robert Gerwarth, "The Central European Counter-Revolution: Paramilitary Violence in Germany, Austria and Hungary after the Great War," *Past and Present* 200 (August 2008): 175–209.
7. On this topic, see Mark Cornwall and John Paul Newman, eds., *Sacrifice and Rebirth: The Legacy of the Great War in East-Central Europe* (Oxford: Berghahn Books, 2016).
8. See Mark Mazower, *Hitler's Empire: How the Nazis Ruled Europe* (New York: Penguin Books, 2008).
9. See Gerwarth, "The Central European Counter-Revolution."
10. See Mario Jareb, *Ustaško-domobranski pokret od nastanku do travnja 1941. godine* (Zagreb: Školska knjiga, 2006); and James Sadkovich, *Italian Support for Croatian Separatism, 1927–1937* (New York: Garland, 1987). The word "*ustaša*" literally means "insurgence."
11. Fikreta Jelić-Butić, *Ustaše i Nezavisna država Hrvatska 1941–1945* (Zagreb: Liber, 1977), 114. The use of the term *Domobran* was itself a reference to the territorial units set up in Croatia after the *Nagodba*, or Compromise, with Hungary in 1868.
12. By approximating a figure derived from populations living in the state's "historic units" according to the 1921 census, the populations of the former Habsburg territories of Dalmatia, Bosnia-Herzegovina, Croatia-Slavonia, Slovenia, and Vojvodina totaled some 64 percent of the new state's citizens. See Joseph Rothschild, *East-Central Europe between the Two World Wars* (Seattle: University of Washington Press, 1998), 204.
13. See, e.g., Oszkár Jászi, *The Dissolution of the Habsburg Monarchy* (Chicago: University of Chicago Press, 1929). For a recent historiographical outline of late Habsburg history and the demise of Austria-Hungary, see John Deak, "The Great War and the Forgotten Realm: The Habsburg Monarchy and the First World War," *Journal of Modern History* 86, no. 2 (June 2014), 336–80.
14. István Deák, *Beyond Nationalism: A Social and Political History of the Habsburg Officer Corps, 1848–1918* (Oxford: Oxford University Press, 1990).
15. See, for example, Laurence Cole, *Military Culture and Popular Patriotism in Late Imperial Austria* (Oxford: Oxford University Press, 2014); Laurence Cole and Daniel L. Unowsky, eds., *The Limits of Loyalty: Imperial Symbolism, Popular Allegiances and State Patriotism in the Late Habsburg Monarchy* (Oxford: Berghahn Books, 2007); Timothy Snyder, *The Red Prince: The Secret Lives of a Habsburg Archduke* (New York: Basic Books, 2008); Robin Okey, *Taming Balkan Nationalism: The Habsburg "Civilizing Mission" in Bosnia 1878–1914* (Oxford: Oxford University Press, 2007).
16. Alexander Watson, *Ring of Steel: Germany and Austria-Hungary in World War One* (New York: Basic Books, 2014), 11; Rogers Brubaker, *Nationalism Reframed: Nationhood and the National Question in the New Europe* (Cambridge, UK: Cambridge University Press, 1996).
17. Watson, *Ring of Steel*, 14.
18. An exposition of the "trialist" solution in the Croats' favor is offered by Ivo Pilar, (writing under the pseudonym L. V. Südland) in *Die südslawische Frage und der Weltkrieg* (Vienna: Manz, 1918).

19. Deak, "The Great War and the Forgotten Realm."
20. See Ivo Banac, *The National Question in Yugoslavia: Origins, History, Politics* (Ithaca: Cornell University Press, 1988), esp. 141–53.
21. See Banac, *National Question*; Dmitar Tasić, *Rat posle rata: vojska Kraljevine Srba, Hrvata i Slovenaca na Kosovu i Metohiju u Makedoniji 1918–1920* (Belgrade: Utopija: Institut za strategijska istraživanja, 2008).
22. See Gerwarth, "The Central European Counter-Revolution."
23. On the Committee and the Legion, see Banac, *National Question*, 264–66.
24. Hrvatski državni arhiv (Croatian State Archives), Fond "Politička situacija", 1363–65.
25. Bosiljka Janjatović, *Politički teror u Hrvatskoj 1918–1935* (Zagreb: Dom i svijet, 2002), 218.
26. See Robert Gerwarth and John Horne, eds., *War in Peace: Paramilitary Violence in Europe after the Great War* (Oxford: Oxford University Press, 2012).
27. Gustav Perčec, "Frankovci," *Hrvatsko pravo*, 19 December 1924.
28. On the political history of interwar Yugoslavia, see Dejan Djokić, *Elusive Compromise: A History of Interwar Yugoslavia* (New York: Hurst and Company, 2007).
29. See Branislav Gligorijević, "Uloga vojnih krugova u 'rešavanju' političke krize u Jugoslaviji 1924. godine," *Vojnoistorijski glasnik* 1, godina XXIII (January–April 1972): 161–86.
30. Nadežda Jovanović, *Politički sukobi u Jugoslaviji 1925–1928* (Belgrade: Rad, 1974).
31. See Andrew Baruch Wachtel, *Making a Nation, Breaking a Nation: Literature and Cultural Politics in Yugoslavia* (Stanford: Stanford University Press, 1998), 99–100.
32. See, for example, Banac, *National Question*; and Djokić, *Elusive Compromise*.
33. It should also be added, in line with Maria Bucur's arguments about war and twentieth-century Romania, that the official, national commemoration of victory was frequently at odds with the local, microcommemorations people practiced in towns and villages throughout the country. See Maria Bucur, *Heroes and Victims: Remembering War in Twentieth-Century Romania* (Bloomington: Indiana University Press, 2010).
34. Schivelbusch, *The Culture of Defeat*.
35. Gustav Perčec "Pravo samoodredjenja," *Hrvatsko Pravo*, 13 August 1925.
36. Ibid.
37. "S", "On War," *Hrvatsko Pravo*, 21 May 1927.
38. Ibid.
39. The holiday is celebrated on November 3 if November 2 happens to fall on a Sunday.
40. "Na grobovima hrvatskih velikana," *Hrvatsko Pravo*, 4 November 1924.
41. See Branislav Gligorijević, *Parlament i političke stranke u Jugoslaviji 1919–1929* (Belgrade, 1979), 258.
42. Ante Pavelić, "Govor narodnog zastupnika dra. Ante Pavelića," *Hrvatsko Pravo*, 4 August 1928.
43. Mile Budak, "Dan svih Svetih i svih Mrtvih," *Hrvatsko Pravo*, 3 November 1928.
44. Ibid.
45. Mile Budak, "Dan svih Svetih i svih Mrtvih," *Hrvatsko Pravo*, 3 November 1928
46. Ibid.
47. *Novo Doba*, 3 December 1928.
48. Branimir Jelić, "Kajmakčalan," *Hrvatski domobran-omladinski list*, 16 October 1928.
49. Bogdan Krizman, *Ante Pavelić i Ustaše* (Zagreb: Globus, 1978), 53.

50. In 1924 in an article in *Slobodni dom,* Stjepan Radić derided Sarkotić as the "spiritual leader" of the Frankists, cited in Milan Šufflay, *Izabrani politički spisi* (Zagreb: Matica hrvatska, 2000), 67.
51. Krizman, *Ante Pavelić i Ustaše,* 60.

Bibliography

Banac, Ivo. *The National Question in Yugoslavia: Origins, History, Politics.* Ithaca: Cornell University Press, 1988.
Brubaker, Rogers. *Nationalism Reframed: Nationhood and the National Question in the New Europe.* Cambridge, UK: Cambridge University Press, 1996.
Bucur, Maria. *Heroes and Victims: Remembering War in Twentieth-Century Romania.* Bloomington: Indiana University Press, 2010.
Cole, Laurence. *Military Culture and Popular Patriotism in Late Imperial Austria.* Oxford: Oxford University Press, 2014.
Cole, Laurence, and Daniel L. Unowsky, eds. *The Limits of Loyalty: Imperial Symbolism, Popular Allegiances and State Patriotism in the Late Habsburg Monarchy.* Oxford: Berghahn Books, 2007.
Cornwall, Mark and John Paul Newman, eds. *Sacrifice and Rebirth: The Legacy of the Great War in East-Central Europe.* Oxford: Berghahn Books, 2016.
Deák, István. *Beyond Nationalism: A Social and Political History of the Habsburg Officer Corps, 1848–1918.* Oxford: Oxford University Press, 1990.
Deak, John. "The Great War and the Forgotten Realm: The Habsburg Monarchy and the First World War." *Journal of Modern History* 86, no. 2 (June 2014): 336–80.
Djokić, Dejan. *Elusive Compromise: A History of Interwar Yugoslavia.* New York: Hurst and Company, 2007.
Eichenberg, Julia and John Paul Newman, eds. *The Great War and Veterans' Internationalism.* London: Palgrave Macmillan, 2013.
Gerwarth, Robert. "The Central European Counter-Revolution: Paramilitary Violence in Germany, Austria and Hungary after the Great War." *Past and Present* 200 (August 2008): 175–209.
Gerwarth, Robert and John Horne, eds. *War in Peace: Paramilitary Violence in Europe after the Great War.* Oxford: Oxford University Press, 2012.
Janjatović, Bosiljka. *Politički teror u Hrvatskoj 1918–1935.* Zagreb: Dom i svijet, 2002.
Jareb, Mario. *Ustaško-domobranski pokret od nastanku do travnja 1941. godine.* Zagreb: Školska knjiga, 2006.
Jászi, Oszkár. *The Dissolution of the Habsburg Monarchy.* Chicago: University of Chicago Press, 1929.
Jelić-Butić, Fikreta. *Ustaše i Nezavisna država Hrvatska 1941–1945.* Zagreb: Liber, 1977.
Jovanović, Nadežda. *Politički sukobi u Jugoslaviji 1925–1928.* Belgrade: Rad, 1974.
Kożuchowski, Adam. *The Afterlife of Austria-Hungary: The Image of the Habsburg Monarchy in Interwar Europe.* Pittsburgh: Pittsburgh University Press, 2013.
Krizman, Bogdan. *Ante Pavelić i Ustaše.* Zagreb: Globus, 1978.
Masaryk, Tomáš Garrigue. *President Masaryk Tells His Story* (recounted by Karel Čapek). London: G. Allen and Unwin, 1934.

Mazower, Mark. *Hitler's Empire: How the Nazis Ruled Europe*. New York: Penguin Books, 2008.
Okey, Robin. *Taming Balkan Nationalism: The Habsburg "Civilizing Mission" in Bosnia 1878–1914*. Oxford: Oxford University Press, 2007.
Rothschild, Joseph. *East-Central Europe between the Two World Wars*. Seattle: University of Washington Press, 1998.
Sadkovich, James. *Italian Support for Croatian Separatism, 1927–1937*. New York: Garland, 1987.
Schivelbusch, Wolfgang. *The Culture of Defeat: On National Trauma, Mourning and Recovery*. New York: Picador, 2003.
Šufflay, Milan. *Izabrani politički spisi*. Zagreb: Matica hrvatska, 2000.
Snyder, Timothy. *The Red Prince: The Secret Lives of a Habsburg Archduke*. New York: Basic Books, 2008.
Südland, L. V. *Die südslawische Frage und der Weltkrieg*. Vienna: Manz, 1918.
Tasić, Dmitar. *Rat posle rata: vojska Kraljevine Srba, Hrvata i Slovenaca na Kosovu i Metohiju u Makedoniji 1918–1920*. Belgrade: Utopija: Institut za strategijska istraživanja, 2008.
Wachtel, Andrew Baruch. *Making a Nation, Breaking a Nation: Literature and Cultural Politics in Yugoslavia*. Stanford: Stanford University Press, 1998.
Watson, Alexander. *Ring of Steel: Germany and Austria-Hungary in World War One*. New York: Basic Books, 2014.

Part III

CHURCH, DYNASTY, ARISTOCRACY: THE POSTWAR FATE OF IMPERIAL PILLARS

Chapter 8

"ALL THE GERMAN PRINCES DRIVEN OUT!"
The Catholic Church in Vienna and the First Austrian Republic

Michael Carter-Sinclair

The central focus of this chapter is on how Catholic Church leaders in Vienna publicly presented their views on the end of World War I, the collapse of the Habsburg Empire, and the formation and consolidation of the Austrian Republic, from November 1918 through the parliamentary election in October 1923. Its premise is that these views can only be properly understood in the context of the long-term political thinking of the upper Church hierarchy, both under the Empire (before and during the war) and into the 1930s, when the Republic collapsed and was replaced by the authoritarian Corporate State (*Ständestaat*) in 1934. Moreover, since the Church in Vienna was part of a much larger organization, its views were often an extension of, or a local variation on, the political views of the Church in Rome. This chapter will therefore also analyze them in the context of political thinking in Church circles elsewhere in Europe after World War I.

This *longue durée* approach to understanding Church responses to the advent of republican democracy in Austria directly questions the argument put forward in 1959 by the political scientist Alfred Diamant: that while some Catholics had only "contempt" for the First Republic and were antidemocratic in principle, the upper Church hierarchy was initially prepared to accept the Republic and work within its frameworks.[1] Diamant's argument derives in part from the fact that, as will be seen, within days of the armistice, Vienna Church leaders announced that, as far as they were concerned, the form of the new Austrian Republic was insignificant. What mattered in determining Church attitudes toward the democracy was the state's "content"—that is, the policies the Republic sought to implement. At one level, this suggests that the Church had no firm views on republican democracy, which would support Diamant's conclusions that, at the end of the war, the Church was prepared to try to live with the state. Taken at another level, however, the Church was saying that it might oppose the state if it acted against Church wishes. While this would have been perfectly acceptable if such opposition were expressed democratically, the Church's stance toward politics and the state in the modern world—the product of a long-term and deeply deliberated process—was marked by a history of closeness to authoritarian regimes and opposition to democratic principles. How this history played out in the early postwar period is the main theme of this chapter.

Its main relevance lies in the fact that the Catholic Church was a key actor in the transition from Empire to Republic, and it remained politically and socially consequential throughout the interwar period. Despite the image of these years as the onset of "Red Vienna," when the Church's archenemies, the Social Democrats, emerged as the dominant political force on the Vienna City Council, the Church played an important role in shaping public opinion in the capital and the country at large. Parish priests, for example, sat at the heart of a city-wide network of charitable and social organizations that controlled much needed resources and provided patronage for those who conformed with Church teachings.[2] They also used these networks to mobilize support for the Christian Social Party, to which the Church had close ties and through which it accessed political power and influence, as the Party regularly participated in coalition governments. Moreover, support from parish level activists ensured that the Christian Socials, whose voting strength was primarily in rural areas, maintained a sizeable base in the capital.[3] It was also not exclusively the case that access to power in the Republic passed through the Party, as leading Church figures served at the highest levels in national governments.[4]

The Church additionally controlled a range of publications that disseminated its views at the city, district, and parish levels. For the purposes of this chapter, the focus is on the communications of the upper hierarchy and senior clergy in Vienna as presented in the *Wiener Diözesanblatt* (Vienna Diocesan Journal). This publication appeared fortnightly and was aimed squarely at the clergy of the archdiocese, with articles in Latin and German. It counted as an official voice of the Church, bearing on its front-page banner that it was published by the office of the Archbishop of Vienna.[5] While no publication is representative of the entire Austrian Church, the *Diözesanblatt* provides an important window onto the thoughts emanating from the highest Church levels in Vienna. These thoughts found echo in other Church sources, such as parish newsletters (*Pfarrblätter*) and the annual record (*Chronik*, or *Gedenkbuch*) that priests were expected to maintain on important parish matters.⁶

The public stances adopted by the Church toward the Republic in the first years after the war can be broken down into four stages. The first stage, which ran through November and December 1918, brought the aforementioned call for loyalty to the new Republic. During the second stage covering the month of January 1919, this loyalty turned into defiance in a series of press statements. Then in the third stage, after elections to the constituent assembly and the parliament in February 1919 and October 1920 failed to produce a Social Democratic majority, the Church displayed relief that the new world was not the catastrophe it had feared. In the fourth and final stage, after national elections in October 1923, the Church was free to redirect its fire from the Republic toward the Social Democratic stronghold of Vienna. As we will see in this chapter, these publicly evolving positions were the expressions of well-developed and long-held conceptions of the modern world and the republican state.

Entrenched Church Attitudes toward the Modern World and Democracy

Despite giving the appearance of reacting to events as the Empire collapsed and the Republic took shape, the Church had a long history of opposition to democracy. After the 1848 revolutions, it had enthusiastically endorsed the authoritarian neo-absolutism through which the dynasty suppressed political freedoms in Austria.⁷ Shortly thereafter, the Church's staunchly antidemocratic orientation was evident in the 1855 Concordat between the Vatican and the Habsburg Empire, which rewarded Church support with a range of privileges.⁸ From the 1860s onward, the Church was also a dogged enemy of the limited electoral and governmental participation that emerged in the Monarchy. Finally, Church antipathy toward democracy can be seen in the role priests played from the late 1880s in the development of political antisemitism as, above all, an instrument to attack the secularizing force of liberalism. It is only in light of this history that the conciliatory Church writings published at the onset of the Austrian Republic should be read.⁹

This opposition to democracy and modernity generally was put on display before the world war even ended. In a pastoral letter published on 24 August 1918, Austrian bishops and archbishops (that is, from the non-Hungarian parts of the Empire) expressed shock that, "for the first time in history," the peoples of the world were "united in one mind: the will to make war"—indeed, "the bloodiest of all wars."¹⁰ The letter then sought to absolve Austria-Hungary of all blame for the war. The bishops asserted that the war's causes lay not in the desire for reparations for Franz Ferdinand's murder, nor in efforts by the Empire to enhance security against revolutionary activity within its borders. Rather they pointed to what they believed were the political causes of the war—those internal and external enemies who had long aimed to splinter the Habsburg Monarchy.

They pointed, too, at another culprit—the bishops blamed those "familiar secret societies, whose participation in this war has repeatedly been demonstrated." These enemies, through "unscrupulous accomplices," had sought to create "a movement in our Empire that is like a spark in a powder barrel," exploding the ties between the Emperor and his people. Even in peacetime, "disruptive efforts" were being made via "radical demands."[11] When this pastoral letter was published, four years of war had taken a huge toll, and not just on those in the military—the Empire's civilian population was suffering terribly.[12] In a last-ditch effort to rally support for the war, the bishops optimistically declared that the so-called agitators had failed to instill their "radical demands" in the larger population. Moreover, they maintained, the fact that it was "incumbent upon the threatened fatherland [to win the war] had sidelined hitherto competing national disputes and . . . created a united front."[13]

The pastoral letter then turned to what might be called the moral causes of the war. Asserting that humanity had dared to imagine it could turn away from God during the long, pre-1914 peace, the bishops argued that the war's origins lay in modern human vanity: "A God-excluding science [that] believed in inexorable progress and rejected all other-worldly truths. . . . Universal care, which insured everyone against accident, sickness, [and] old age . . . stands as a substitute for Godly providence." Despite these social welfare measures, the bishops also believed that unfettered competition in business and in relations between nations meant that "survival of the fittest" applied to everyday life. Wars, in short, were inevitable in the modern world and the Empire had been forced to fight for its existence.[14]

Furthermore, according to the bishops, the Empire bore no responsibility for the war's undue length, since when "the 'peace pope' Benedict XV . . . made his proposals on 1 August 1917, our noble Emperor was the first, as a true son of Christianity, to send him obedience."[15] In this interpretation, these peace efforts had encouraged similar such initiatives in enemy lands, though they were all crushed by their respective governments. Yet foreign enemies were not the only culprits—the bishops made clear that responsibility for the war's prolongation also lay with people for whom war was "a fortunate opportunity" in terms of profiteering and usury. The bishops boasted that while they had been mocked for exposing the evils of large-scale usury, the war had proven them right, and now everywhere people were unmoved by "bitter need and the sight of poverty."[16] The bishops would have found support for this view among other Catholic circles in which blame for such matters as profiteering, usury, and alleged Jewish avoidance of army service was frequently expressed in explicitly antisemitic terms.[17]

The world war provided the bishops with the opportunity to draw attention to the alleged fallacies of the modern world that had brought on the war in the first place. They offered their views in August 1918 in order to pave the way for a postwar period in which such conflicts could be avoided. Yet in the process, the bishops also revealed the depth of antidemocratic sentiment in the Austrian Church, as their pastoral letter amounted to an indictment of contemporary political and social thought not just for causing the world war, but for a total breakdown in the social fabric. In attacking the liberal emphasis on individual rights, the bishops claimed that the "basic evil of our time" is the "feverish search" for independence, since modern man wished only to rely on internal guidance, not that from God. They used these arguments to denounce "false ideas" such as the "sovereignty of the people, the majority of the people as the source of law, [and] the self-determination of peoples," all of which allegedly sought "to undermine the basis of a social order founded according to Christian legal wisdom."[18] For the Austrian bishops, only "reverence for and obedience towards God-ordained authority" could constitute "the basis for all order in human society."[19]

In his encyclical *Ad beatissimi Apostolorum* (*To the Most Blessed Apostles*) of 1 November 1914, Pope Benedict XV had declared that an important cause of the "general turmoil" was that "the authority of those who hold power in their hands is no longer holy to the mass of the people." Benedict attributed this to the emerging belief that "the origin of all human authority [comes] not from God, but from the free resolution of people." In a statement that reveals the extent to which, in late 1914, the Church still understood society in terms of rigid hierarchies, Benedict lamented the arrival of a world in which the bonds of duty between "superiors" and "subordinates" had loosened to the point that they appeared to be broken.[20] The pastoral letter reaffirmed this.

Several scholars have downplayed the significance of the August 1918 pastoral letter. Ernst Hanisch, for instance, argues that the emotional links between the bishops and the Monarchy, combined with the effects of the Russian Revolution, distorted official Church perspectives. Moreover, the fact that the bishops' average age was sixty meant that these men's formative experiences had taken place under the Monarchy.[21] Hanisch therefore argues that this pastoral letter was an aberration brought on by contemporary circumstances. Yet the evidence that will be presented in this chapter indicates that the letter was part of a carefully conceived, long-term analysis of democracy rather than the panicked thoughts of a gerontocracy. Moreover, the fact that the bishops cite Benedict XV on the failings of the modern world, including democracy itself, suggests that they were channeling the equally long-held and well-conceived opinions of those at the highest levels of the Catholic Church.

The bishops employed the pastoral letter in order to reject publicly the principles that underpin democracy. They did so, as will be seen, mere months before a November 1918 letter counseled unconditional loyalty to the Republic. The bishops gave no credence to the concept that sovereignty rested with the people and, therefore, democratically elected majorities had a mandate to govern. Their world was one in which sovereignty resided in divine "authority" rather than individual or collective rights. This makes it hard to imagine how the Church could respect democratic processes and decision-making. It is equally hard to conclude that the bishops had experienced a complete change of heart by the end of the war.

November 1918: The Initial Public Response of the Church to the Republic

Right up to the collapse of the Empire, the Catholic Church was one of the staunchest supporters of the Habsburg Monarchy. In an alliance of "throne and altar," it had represented and promoted as "normal" a raft of what it called "traditional values."[22] These included deference toward "authority" and the hierarchical nature of society, respect for property, and a religious basis for morality and social institutions such as the family. Through its ties with the Habsburgs and its role as a quasi-public body engaged in such state matters as census-taking, the Church enjoyed a privileged position in society.[23] It had guaranteed access to educational institutions and high social visibility through its participation in state and pseudo-state occasions, such as royal processions and ceremonials. The Church was also close to political power. It engaged in a mutually beneficial relationship with the antisemitic Christian Social Party, which, thanks to a franchise that included the upper and lower bourgeoisie but left out most of the working-class population, controlled the Vienna City Council from 1896 to 1918. The Party was also, from 1907 onward, the largest in the Austrian parliament.[24]

It is therefore understandable that when the Empire collapsed between October and November 1918, the Church recognized that its privileges were under threat. The last Emperor, Karl, and those close to him, including Church figures, had hoped that the dynasty might retain some power. They even discussed the possibility of a constitutional monarchy centered on the Empire's German-speaking territories.[25] Revolutionary protests in Vienna and within parliament, however, put paid to these plans. In a typical Habsburg fudge, Karl, rather than abdicating, announced on 11 November 1918 that he was giving up his rights to a role in government.[26] The next day, following an agreement between the major parties, the Republic of German Austria was proclaimed from the Vienna parliament as a constituent part of the new German Republic to the north, which had replaced the Hohenzollern Empire. Details of how this arrangement would work, however, were scarce. For the time being, a temporary coalition government was put together and crowds cheered as over six hundred years of Habsburg rule in Austria came to an end.[27]

The new Republic was the Austro-German remnant of a multinational empire that had frequently been shaken by nationality disputes. Once Czechs, Slovaks, Hungarians, South Slavs, and other ethnic groups began forming their own so-called nation-states, however, the nationality issue was no longer relevant for a rump Austria overwhelmingly populated by German-speakers.[28] Instead, two questions dominated politics: Should Austria be an independent republic or part of the new Germany; and, if it were to remain independent, what sort of constitution should it have? The Church was outspoken on the former issue: simply put, the vast majority of Austrian clergy favored independence from Germany. This was no doubt due in part to the fact that *Anschluß* meant annexing Austria to a majority Protestant country where Catholics had historically been treated as an "enemy within."[29] Since Austria required its independence in order for the Church to maintain its political influence, Church leaders concerned themselves with the form and purpose of the new state.

In the revolutionary atmosphere of late 1918, the Church was at once looking back at the past and toward the future. Representative of this dilemma was a note left by one parish priest in the north of Vienna: "All the German princes driven out!" he wrote, in a lament for a past which, it seemed, had been suddenly and permanently swept away.[30] This was not just a reference to the loss of princes, but also to the social hierarchies, order, and the respect for order that the princes embodied. The quotation goes on to express fear for the future: "Jews everywhere. Jews at the head of the government."[31] Again, this is not just a reference to antisemitism—Catholic priests and Christian Socials had, after all, built a political and social movement that was in large part held together by antisemitism.[32] For decades, they had based their antisemitism on imagined conspiracies of Jews, Freemasons, liberals, socialists, and any others who stood in opposition to so-called traditional values.[33] "Jews" had become shorthand for a collection of enemies of the Church and its allies. That some of these alleged enemies were now in the government, and that they might be in a position to implement significant change in Austrian society, was a tremendous shock for most clergy. The worry was that, since Austria was on its way to becoming a bourgeois republic as Russia had been, briefly, in 1917, it might also be on the path to becoming a Bolshevik state. In any case, the Grinzing parish priest added anxiously, "What will come of this?"[34]

The Church's immediate reaction to the fall of the Monarchy came in an address issued on 12 November 1918 and published in the *Diözesanblatt* on 18 November. In it, Archbishop of Vienna, Cardinal Friedrich Gustav Piffl, called on clergy to help prevent the revolutionary situation from worsening: "The present political re-ordering ... presents the Catholic clergy with new, far-reaching tasks," said Piffl, adding that priests needed to set a calming example for the agitated population through their cautious and prudent advice.³⁵ After all, he continued, on 11 November, the Emperor had "handed the government to the people." All rights previously held by Karl and the parliament of the Empire's Austrian part (Cisleithania) passed to the German Austrian Council of State until a constituent assembly could be elected and a constitution settled. Piffl also made explicit reference to the new state form, recognizing the Empire's demise and the advent of the Austrian Republic as *"faits accomplis* that were to be acknowledged by the faithful." Piffl was directly addressing those who had desired a different political outcome for Austria at the end of the war. He did so, moreover, by urging "the faithful" to offer the "now lawful" state of German Austria "unconditional loyalty" until the election of the constituent assembly.³⁶

Further support for the Republic came from Monsignor Ignaz Seipel, a minister in the final imperial government. As the war drew to a close, Seipel had spoken publicly in Vienna on such topics as "Empire and Democracy" and "The role of religion teachers in the new times."³⁷ He had also written about the nature of the nation and state, and served as an intellectual commentator on politics and ethics for such venues as the *Reichspost*, the main voice for the Christian Social Party.³⁸ About a week after Piffl's address, Seipel published a series of articles in the *Reichspost* in which he argued that since the old regime could no longer be rejuvenated, it had to be replaced. This, he explained, was not the Emperor's fault, but was brought on by the militarism of those who had advised him on the defense of the realm. He also attributed the regime's downfall to the pettymindedness of the Empire's German politicians, as well as to the lack of justice that non-German parties subsequently showed the Germans of the Habsburg state. Old Austria, he said, could have been saved if a spirit of "true democracy" had taken hold. Seipel would use the phrase "true democracy" repeatedly over the next decade, without ever really defining it.³⁹

Seipel also supported Piffl's acceptance of the new state's legitimacy, since there had been no revolution against divinely held authority and the Emperor himself had given the people the right to self-determination.⁴⁰ He therefore called on all parties in the coming elections to recognize that while there would be victors and losers, there should be no oppressed or oppressors.⁴¹ In an article entitled "The People and the Future State Form" (November 23), Seipel went on to explain how he expected the Republic to develop. For example, he pointed to comments by President Wilson's advisers that there would be "no peace and no bread" for dictatorship, whether militarist or revolutionary, in arguing that America would maintain its promise only to sign treaties with "free peoples." He took further comfort that Wilson was siding with "civilization and bourgeois order" against "class domination" and "Russian methods."⁴²

Where Seipel's message diverged from Piffl's, however, was in his explanation of the Monarchy's end. Gone is the rhetoric about how the Emperor freely handed state authority to the people. Instead, Seipel depicts socialist "revolutionaries" in Berlin and Vienna taking power. He even adds an implicit warning against possible developments: "Only a free, truly democratic state ensures future peace and order. A monarchy would no longer be tolerated by the people; but neither would it tolerate an undemocratic republic, nor one that only appears democratic."[43] Seipel goes on to assert that a truly free state could neither be shaken from above—that is, by those in power—nor below, which implies the working classes.

Scholars have offered varying interpretations of the position that Seipel and the upper Church hierarchy adopted with regard to the Republic. C. Earl Edmondson suggests that Seipel was reaching an accommodation with democracy that "may have been sincere."[44] Diamant, on the other hand, argued that the upper hierarchy was prepared to accept the Republic as the "lesser of two evils" compared with a Bolshevik state.[45] Diamant may have been correct in this, but it is a lenient judgment on the Church, whose "acceptance" is best described as a highly conditional tolerance. When Seipel stated that the people would not "tolerate an undemocratic republic nor one that only appears democratic," he leaves open the question as to what "the people" might actually do in such a situation.[46]

January 1919: Defiance Toward the Republic

Piffl and Seipel made their November statements as people were only just beginning to absorb the reality and ponder the implications of the war's end, and within days of the Emperor Karl's relinquishment of his official responsibilities. Taken together, the statements are double-edged. Both Piffl and Seipel seemed to present a pragmatic response to events as the Monarchy fell, but Seipel went further by formulating a Church position on the possibilities for change that a republic offered. This hardening public position comes through strongly in a pastoral letter from "the bishops of German Austria" published in the *Diözesanblatt* in January 1919, a month before the elections to the constituent assembly. Beginning with the sentiment "God be thanked, the war is over. Peace is near," the letter voiced bitter disappointment that this was "not the peace we had expected . . . it is a peace the world has given." In an almost despairing tone, the letter refers to "the disastrous exit from the war, [which] fills us all, but especially our unbeaten brave soldiers, with great sorrow, because we love our people and our fatherland." For the bishops, this was not the peace that God had wanted since it unfairly punished Austria and her allies. Their letter argued that *all* governments, diplomats, and parliaments must take responsibility for the war, and it expressed anger at the victors for seeking damages from their former adversaries.[47]

The letter soon turned away from the war and toward the future in the new Austria. As with Cardinal Piffl's November 1918 statement, the initial tone is calm, almost reassuring. In an in-depth analysis of the democratic foundation of the new state, the bishops raise no objections to democracy as a concept. Instead, they describe it merely as a "foreign word" meaning the power of the people, and dismiss the notion that democracy in and of itself is dangerous. After all, they add, "everything in the world is dangerous if misused."

The problem for the bishops lies in how such misuse might come about: "if democracy detaches itself from Christianity, then [it is] the tyranny of parties that have seized power for themselves." They go on to express the firm "conviction that the new state will only endure if it is based upon the Ten Commandments and the Sermon on the Mount. The foundations of the state—religion, family, property—must remain unshakeable."[48] The bishops did recognize that traditional virtues like individual charity could not solve all the problems of the modern world. They even made proposals for social welfare reform, a legally enshrined family wage, social insurance, and, more vaguely, "effective protection against usury and exploitation." However, it was also clear that the bishops opposed democracy in the parliamentary, secular form taking shape in postwar Austria. Fundamentally, they were concerned about the potential for social change that democracy represented.

Their proposed measures, laudable as they may seem, were not therefore purely altruistic; rather, they were means to retain the kind of hierarchical and paternalistic social and political order that had existed under the Habsburgs, and which supported traditional property and family structures. This comes through most clearly in the bishops' views of the political form and purpose of the Republic, and, in particular, their support for voting rights based upon character rather than property. This, they argued, would ensure the "fair representation" of various layers of society in parliament and government.[49] Under the Empire, the varied voter qualification systems at the local, regional, and national levels often carried earnings, taxation, or property requirements.[50] The Church now rejected these qualifications, but did not come out in support of a "one person, one vote" democratic system. If character were to determine voting rights and society was to be based upon traditional concepts of morality and social relations, it could be inferred that the Church saw itself as an appropriate institution for deciding voter eligibility, especially since it had long favored structuring any state along corporatist lines.[51] This corporatist orientation, which allocated individuals a place in society along occupational or business lines, and which produced a "top-down" organization of social relationships, was crucial to the bishops' understanding of what the transformation from Empire to Republic should bring in terms of democracy.

In order to ensure that the state took the "correct" course, the pastoral letter emphasized the duty of all Catholics to vote for the "right" candidates in the elections to the constituent assembly. Whoever failed to do so would be guilty of a public sin if the Church were harmed in this new democracy. The bishops used the January 1919 pastoral letter to announce that the prospect of such harm was very real: "a new war is beginning," they wrote, and it was being heralded by "a new . . . cry . . . [for the] 'Separation of State and Church,'" which would mean that the Church would cease being a "public-legal entity" and become a "private society like any other."[52]

The pastoral letter was premised on the notion that the Church had not lost its influence among the people: "the state needs the Church!" the bishops declared, "for it lives from the obedience of its subjects. Public order cannot be maintained by bayonets. Only the Church can teach the people to be loyal to the State, as they were to God, through inner belief rather than compulsion."[53] In seeking to rally Catholics against "free schools" and "free marriage," the letter sought an accommodation between the Church and the Republic: "Should this state turn out to be a true Christian democracy, only one motto will stand for us: 'We are all a people of brothers (sic) who . . . want to attain a happy eternity.'"[54] The pastoral letter does not say what its motto would be if the state did not develop into a "true Christian democracy." Nevertheless, it was clear that a refinement, at the very least, of the Church's position toward the Republic had taken place over the two months since the November statement by Cardinal Piffl. Back then, he had offered unconditional loyalty; now Piffl and the other bishops were setting conditions for their relationship with the state. In order to ensure that the rank and file faithful also understood the importance of the pastoral letter, priests were instructed to read and explain it at Sunday mass in all parishes on 26 January, and 2 and 9 February 1919.[55]

The National Elections of 1919 and 1920 and Their Impact

The dates for the readings of the pastoral letter were chosen carefully. A week after the final reading, elections to a constituent assembly for German Austria were to take place. When the pastoral letter was published, the outcome of these elections was unclear. The bishops' fears about how the state would develop must have been at their peak. They would have been especially concerned at the consequences of a victory for the well-organized and avowedly Marxist Social Democratic Party. In the event, the Social Democrats did emerge as the largest party, but with only 40 percent of the participating electorate, which gave them seventy-one representatives in the 170-seat assembly. The Christian Socials won seventy seats, while the remainder was distributed among various parties, including the German Nationalists.[56] The Social Democrats, whatever the Church may have feared, were unable to govern alone and so entered into a grand coalition, first with the Christian Socials and German Nationalists, then solely with the Christian Socials. Karl Renner, the leading representative of the Social Democratic Party, became chancellor. This was to be the high point of

Social Democratic involvement in national government in Austria, since Renner stepped down in July 1920 after relations broke down between the coalition partners. He was succeeded by Christian Social Michael Mayr, who took over the leadership of the coalition pending elections for a permanent parliament.⁵⁷

Church relief at the Social Democrats' failure to perform better can be inferred from the *Diözesanblatt*. While the newspaper continued to protest what many now termed "a dictated peace" (*Diktat*), it paid less attention to the Republic as a political form after February 1919.⁵⁸ There is no mention, for instance, of how, in September 1919, the victorious allies forced German Austria to rename itself the Republic of Austria, and stipulated that its constitution drop the pretense that it was part of Germany. *Anschluß*, in other words, was expressly forbidden, and this was by no means antithetical to Church opinion.

In October 1920, elections took place for the new parliament that would replace the constituent assembly. For the Catholic Church, the outcome was again encouraging: the Social Democratic vote fell and the Christian Socials advanced enough to enter into a coalition with the German Nationalists (again under Mayr).⁵⁹ These results may not have produced a government of Christian Socials alone, which the bishops desired, but the Republic was by no means becoming a Bolshevik state either. Rather, it seemed to be evolving into less of a threat to the Church, as witnessed by the fact that the *Diözesanblatt* was so devoid of political content throughout 1920 that the paper did not even mention the constitution adopted by the Austrian Republic in November of that year.⁶⁰

By 1921, the content of the *Diözesanblatt* made it plain that Church leaders no longer saw the Republic as their main enemy in Austria. The paper's only overt political reference that year came in March, when it published a vehemently antisocialist speech that Pope Benedict XV gave in Rome in July 1920.⁶¹ Benedict declared that the "most corrupt" were "ardently" waiting for a world republic based upon the complete equality of people, and in which common ownership of property and lack of respect for public or parental authority would be the rule. Referring obliquely to the Soviet Union, he indicated that parts of Europe had already experienced such "horror," and that some wanted to spread revolution to the rest of Europe by inciting "the masses," which could only lead to disorder. The Pope concluded by cautioning against the "contagion" of socialism, "the utmost enemy of Christian thought."

The publication of this speech on the front page of the *Diözesanblatt* signaled just how much the Church wished to convey its antisocialist message to the Vienna faithful. So, too, the instruction to priests to read the speech to their parishioners during the weeklong festival of St. Joseph in April 1921. Church leaders were not completely turning away from the dangers of democracy that they still perceived in the Republic, and they continued to agitate against national legislation that conflicted with their core values, like the Sever marriage law that permitted the civil remarriage of Catholics.⁶² But now the Church was focusing on a political opponent that more directly embodied socialism in Austria—the Social Democratic stronghold of the Vienna City Council.

In the May 1919 elections, Social Democrats had won a commanding majority of seats on the Council.[63] And they were prepared to use that majority to introduce real change in such areas as housing, health provisions, and education, even if their plans outran their resources.[64] The Church was likewise prepared to use the *Diözesanblatt* to attack the Council on everything from its attempts to reform religious education to the new municipal crematorium (this latter attack also having a quasi-religious component, since some priests in Vienna taught that cremated Catholics could lose their souls).[65] Parish priests were broadly supportive of these issues. Father Leopold Lojka of Weinhaus in northwest Vienna, for example, was particularly upset that the City Council was seating boys next to girls in classrooms—an "American" practice, which, he warned, would lead to sexual arousal between classmates. He used the abusive term "*Sozilehrer*" (socialist teacher) to indicate whom he blamed.[66] Father Lojka was also concerned by the new crematorium, fearing that the Viennese would provide "much business" for this facility.[67] There can be little doubt that he would have shared these opinions—which appeared in his parish chronicle (*Chronik*)—with his parishioners.

The Church had other reasons to fear socialism as well. In particular, it was angered by a Social Democratic Party campaign to reduce the number of state-registered Catholics. Hanisch estimates that by the early 1920s, thousands of people were leaving the Church annually. The peak came in 1922, when more than twenty-two thousand Viennese took this difficult step.[68] Abandoning confessional allegiance—that is, becoming *konfessionslos*—did not simply entail renouncing Church membership, but also registering the decision with authorities, for which there was an administration fee.[69] Unsurprisingly, priests were quick to suggest that people were leaving the Church because of pressure from the Social Democrats, whom they accused of using municipal resources—from their control over education and welfare establishments to their patronage of jobs and housing—to wage war on the Church.[70]

In the very year that applications to become *konfessionslos* peaked, the Church received a major boost in its effort to prevent the Republic from being used as a tool to undermine the values on which it believed the state should be based. In May 1922, Seipel, as chair of the Christian Social Party, became Chancellor of Austria, a position he would occupy for five of the next seven years. The elections of October 1923 consolidated his position and that of his party, even as the Social Democrats recovered from their poor showing in 1920. The Christian Social Party ended with eighty-two seats, one short of an overall majority in the now 165-seat strong parliament. The Republic, for the time being, was no longer to be feared. Some in the Church even expressed pride in Austria. In 1923, Father Lojka wrote that Seipel, the "savior of 'little Austria,'" was steering the country "between the Scylla and Charybdis of bankruptcy and revolution."[71]

The Church and Authoritarian Tendencies, 1923–1934

Despite the Church's historical rejections of democracy, it managed to reach an accommodation with the new Austrian state and, even, to work within its rules. It did so for several reasons, not the least of which was that the Church had no feasible alternative to the Republic immediately after the war. The political form of the state was outside its control, and any attempt to change it would have been unacceptable internationally. The British and French, for instance, paid close attention to Austria's domestic and foreign affairs. As late as 1928, France, backed by its Czechoslovak ally, was prepared to go to war in order to prevent unacceptable alterations to the peace settlement.[72] At the same time, the electoral success of the Christian Socials helped the Church through the early years of the first Austrian democracy. As long as the Republic produced results to its liking, then the Church's position could stay accommodating.

However, events were difficult to predict, since the political atmosphere in postwar Austria was anything but stable and often convulsed by violence from both sides of the political spectrum. Moreover, the Church was not alone in rejecting the principles of democracy. While Seipel took the lead in pushing for constitutional changes that would move the Republic in an authoritarian direction, those on the paramilitary right were prepared to take action outside of the constitution. The Church leaned in their direction, and even more so in response to events in 1927. That January, Social Democratic demonstrators at Schattendorf, in Burgenland, were shot and killed by members of a right-wing veterans group. Their trial in Vienna that July returned verdicts of not guilty. As a result, suspicions of a rigged jury led to violent protests in the city, which the army suppressed with such extreme force that more deaths resulted.[73] Church members showed little sympathy for the Social Democratic losses. In his parish at Weinhaus, Father Lojka even recorded that, in his view, the disturbances had resulted from leftist agitation because demonstrators were shot by those legally defending their property.[74]

Some scholars have presented the 1927 events as a turning point in the attitude of the political right toward the Republic.[75] Diamant writes that, for the Church in particular, they marked the moment that "Catholic criticism of democracy became especially intense. . . . [The] most significant fact about the period 1918–1934 was the abandonment by Austrian Catholics of their initial pro-democratic position." Diamant attributes this to the right's frustration with a constitutional system that, he claims, "perpetuated the dominant position" of the Social Democrats.[76] Yet this argument is problematic on several levels, not least because there was no socialist dominance of the national government to begin with, as we have already seen for the early 1920s. Moreover, with the limited exception of the Social Democratic housing program in Vienna, significant social change had not been effected in Austria.

In national elections held in April 1927, Christian Socials and German Nationalists stood together on a "Unity List" (*Einheitsliste*), which won eighty-five seats. Granted, this was down from the ninety-two seats that the constituent parties had tallied in the previous election (1923)—the Social Democrats still won fewer total seats (eighty-three). The anticlerical Agrarian League, which won nine seats in 1927, put aside its differences with the Christian Socials to create a common bourgeois front. Monsignor Seipel remained head of government.[77] The Social Democrats may have been the largest single party in parliament, but they were still out of power.

Considering this national political reality, why might Diamant and other scholars construct 1927 as a crucial turning point for the political right vis-à-vis the Republic? One possible reason is that the electoral trend favored the Social Democrats, and this was a frightening prospect for the right. Yet there is another way of reading this "especially intense" shift in Catholic criticism of democracy in 1927, which is that there was no shift at all in terms of *opinions*—the Church, after all, had long rejected democratic principles. A more plausible argument is that the suppression of the Social Democrats by the army and police prompted a shift in perspective, as it gave antidemocrats reason to believe that something tangible could be done to counter democracy. In this view, 1927 was the year that signaled how the state and its organs could be used effectively to thwart Social Democratic attempts at radical change. Seipel, as the democratically empowered chancellor, began to lay the foundations for this by bringing leaders of the rightist paramilitary group *Heimwehr* (literally: home army) into government.[78] The few Church leaders who protested against political dealings with such groups had little backing.[79] Some senior clergy even called on the faithful to join the militias.[80]

In 1929, Seipel stepped down as Chancellor. A year later, the governing coalition attempted to distance itself from the militias by introducing temporary bans to prevent paramilitary marches and the display of weaponry. But this did not signal a change of heart with regard to forming political alliances with such groups. Instead, it was a practical measure, as militia parades and demonstrations were affecting the lucrative tourist business. Church members, moreover, helped the militias to circumvent the bans. Some priests permitted the *Heimwehr* to participate in church events. Others blessed the banners of right-wing militias in their parish churches.[81] In 1930, Father Lojka recorded with delight the *Heimwehr*'s announcement rejecting democracy and parliamentarianism.[82] He greeted "with an open heart" the paramilitary organization's goal of building a society based on fascism.[83]

Father Lojka likely also shared his views with his parishioners, just as other Church leaders often did. In this respect, they were well aligned with Monsignor Seipel, who had been stepping up pressure for change in the Austrian constitution since 1927. In an echo of the January 1919 pastoral letter, Seipel made manifest that his opinion of what a democracy should be was different from that which underpinned the Republic. Along with promoting the *Heimwehr* as the kind of movement that could "liberate democracy from the rule of parties," Seipel advocated that the government be run by a directly elected president with extensive powers and supported by a Parliament structured along corporate lines.[84] This assault against democracy was so open that Western governments threatened to withhold loans necessary to keep the economy running. In the end, Seipel was unable to implement such constitutional changes.[85] Nevertheless, the chancellor had laid the foundations for the advent of authoritarianism in Austria through democratic means.

Subsequent developments only confirmed the antidemocratic sympathies of the upper Church hierarchy. In 1933, Christian Social Chancellor Engelbert Dollfuß took advantage of legal procedures to suspend parliamentary government and rule by decree. The Catholic Church became one of his first allies in the authoritarian set-up; and by July, a new church-state Concordat had materialized.[86] The government was in the midst of making plans to replace Austrian democracy with a "corporate state" based on the different estates, or corporations, in society when, in February 1934, Austrian workers rebelled against Dollfuß. They were quickly crushed by government forces, who shelled working-class quarters in Vienna. At the St. Laurenz-Gertrud parish in Währing, not far from Father Lojka's Weinhaus parish, Father Albert Schubert proclaimed the defeat of the revolt "a second wonderful Gospel": Vienna and Austria, he wrote, had been freed from the threat of "Austro-Bolshevism" and the state was now a "stronghold of Christian-German culture."[87] This statement makes clear that the liberation was from Social Democracy, but for some priests, it would have been seen as the first step toward "freedom" from democracy in general. It was not uncommon for priests like Father Lojka to write and speak approvingly of how Dollfuß had been gathering in government "the right people around him," in the form of leading figures from right-wing militia. For them, the next logical step would be to end democracy.[88] Seipel, as stated earlier, had set them an example with his authoritarian tendencies.

Father Schubert benefited from the church-state relationship emerging under Dollfuß. As part of a broad-based church building program, his own structure in Währing—henceforth known as the "Memorial church for re-liberated Vienna"—was to be extended.[89] Cardinal Theodor Innitzer, who had succeeded Piffl as Archbishop of Vienna in 1932, laid the foundation stone for the new church. Chancellor Dollfuß, who was well aware of the symbolism of such events, attended the ceremony and spoke on the significance of church building for building the new state.[90]

Most priests recorded the February 1934 uprising in their *Chroniken*, but not necessarily in much detail. One of them felt that events had passed his parish "without a trace," though also noted that several arrests had been made and some schoolteachers dismissed, presumably for their Social Democratic allegiances.[91] Priests paid more attention to the fall of republican democracy on 1 May 1934, when Austria was proclaimed a federal state ordered on corporate lines.[92] More precisely, it became a fascist-leaning corporate state in which the 1933 Concordat was now incorporated into a new constitution.[93] For Father Lojka, this made 1 May a "day of rebirth."[94] The *Diözesanblatt* itself celebrated by printing the full text of the Concordat, as well as other declarations that would form the basis for church-state relations.[95] Chancellor Dollfuß wrote to Cardinal Eugenio Pacelli (later Pope Pius XII) that the Concordat would "contribute to the well-being of our country." Pacelli, for his part, thanked Dollfuß for his "statesmanlike wisdom" in achieving the Concordat such that Austria could be rebuilt "on the grounds of traditional loyalty to Christ and his Church."[96]

Another event well noted by priests in their *Chroniken* was Dollfuß's assassination on 25 July 1934, when small groups of Austrian Nazis seized several official buildings in Vienna, including the chancellery. Although the coup failed, the Corporate State survived. Cardinal Innitzer paid tribute to Dollfuß by consecrating the rebuilt parish church in Währing (the recently renamed "Memorial church for re-liberated Vienna") as the Engelbert Dollfuß Memorial Church.[97] This was just the start of a "state cult" that included the direct association of the "martyr chancellor" with Christian martyrdom.[98]

The continuance of the Corporate State and the religiosity of the Dollfuß cult assured the Church of further benefits. In the Neulerchenfeld parish in working-class Ottakring, for instance, the government turned buildings it had seized from the Social Democrats after the February revolt over to the Church.[99] In 1934, the *Chronik* for Neulerchenfeld recorded how Austria was being brought back to Christianity with a "massive reverse current" of Church membership. In that parish alone, four hundred people had reconverted, while across the capital, the figure was around thirty thousand. Numerous state marriages were now also being "consolidated" through the Church. And even older children were choosing to be baptized.[100] The Church would have considered the recovery of these "souls" to be a greater reward than any material possessions, though perhaps nothing was so gratifying ideologically as the belated publication (4 September 1934, in the *Diözesanblatt*) of the texts of the new constitution and laws for the transition to the Corporate State. Dollfuß and other government leaders had proclaimed the constitution in language that directly echoed that of the bishops of German Austria in 1919: "In the name of God the almighty, from whom all justice emanates, the Austrian people receive this constitution, on a corporate basis, for its Christian, German federal state."[101]

The Church Abroad: Austria in Comparative Perspective

In November 1918, the Vienna Church seemed to be sending a message that it was ready to accept the Republic. Yet shortly thereafter, the Church also explained that there were limits to this acceptance, and that these amounted to a wholesale rejection of democracy. This position was not confined to the upper ecclesiastical hierarchy. In the interwar era, the Catholic Church supported authoritarian regimes in Portugal and Hungary, and was a close ally of fascist Italy.[102] Yet perhaps the best parallel to the Church's democratic antipathies can be found in Spain, which had not fought in the world war but was fighting its own, long-running colonial war in Morocco. It was also suffering from Europe's postwar economic and social malaise. These difficulties brought great disorder to Spanish society.

Tensions first peaked in 1923, when sections of the Spanish army rose against the parliament, although they declared their loyalty to the constitutional monarch, Alfonso XIII. Alfonso, in turn, named General Miguel Primo de Rivera as head of government. Presenting himself as an anticommunist who would strengthen Spain, Primo de Rivera suspended the constitution and assumed dictatorial powers, a move met with "ecclesiastical rejoicing." Several bishops issued prayers for the "regeneration" of the country.[103]

Yet Primo de Rivera's dictatorship lasted only as long as Alfonso supported him. By 1930, several factors—including repressive measures taken against the working classes, the global economic depression, and internal unrest—prompted the King to dismiss Primo de Rivera. A year later, on 14 April 1931, the discredited King abdicated and the monarchy gave way to the Second Spanish Republic. As in Austria in 1918–1919, the Church responded with an article in its leading Catholic daily (*El Debate*) arguing that the form of the state was irrelevant—what mattered was what those in control did with their powers. In an editorial published on 15 April 1931, Church officials called upon the faithful to respect the new regime.[104] The degree and nature of this respect, however, was an open question. Just one day earlier, the newspaper had referred to the "negative barbarism" the Republic represented. In reference to popular protests against the King, it declared that "the sewers [had] opened their sluice gates and the dregs of society inundated the streets and squares." Shortly after issuing these insults, *El Debate* carried its main message: since the Republic had so far changed nothing, those on the right should unite to make sure this remained the case and, thereby, to protect the bases of society—"religion, fatherland, order, family and property."[105] Instructions to the effect that the newspaper should disseminate this message reached the editor of *El Debate*, Angel Herrera, via the papal nuncio in Spain, whose own orders originated in Rome from none other than Cardinal Pacelli.

Herrera was a key figure among a group of Catholic thinkers and politicians who formalized their approach to the Republic in the doctrine of "accidentalism." According to this doctrine, the state's form was immaterial compared to its socioeconomic orientation, which would directly determine whether a state should be opposed.[106] This line of thinking reached its logical conclusion when a center-left government tried to use the institutions of the Spanish Republic to implement significant reforms in such areas as land ownership and the civil privileges of the Spanish Church.[107] The ecclesiastical response was quick and clear: in 1933, José María Gil Robles, head of the *Confederación Española de Derechas Autónomas* (Spanish Confederation of the Autonomous Right, or CEDA), the principal consortium on the Catholic political right, wrote in *El Debate* that democracy was a means to an end, which in this case meant the protection of such traditional interests as those of the Church. Gil Robles further asserted that parliament would either be forced to respect the views of political Catholicism, or it would be "eliminated." In language that would have been familiar to the Catholic right in Austria, he called upon parishioners to "purge the fatherland of judaizing freemasons."[108]

Much like the Austrian First Republic, the Spanish Second Republic never achieved prolonged stability. Political power swung from left to right, and the short-lived governments were rocked by numerous attempts to overthrow them. When in 1936 the political right and much of the military rose up against the Republic, a civil war broke out in which the Church unhesitatingly sided with the army.[109] From Vienna, Cardinal Innitzer expressed his sympathies for lay and ordained Catholics who suffered at the hands of their enemies. Citing Pope Benedict, he blamed these events on the godlessness in the world. Certainly, Catholic citizens suffered atrocities. But Innitzer was in no mood to offer reconciliation, let alone to express sympathy for the many more victims of the military.[110] Nor did he recognize the role the Church played in maintaining a social order that had created some of the worst poverty and oppression in Europe, and which was a root cause of social disorder.[111] The right won the Spanish Civil War, and some of those who had promoted accidentalism received their rewards. *El Debate* editor Angel Herrera dropped out of politics in Spain in the mid-1930s and became an ordained priest in 1940. He returned to the country as Bishop of Malaga in 1947. In 1965, the antirepublican ideologue became a cardinal.[112]

The Church in Spain received far greater rewards for its support for authoritarianism than did the Austrian Church. The Franco regime that was established after the Civil War endured into the 1970s. The Austrian Corporate State collapsed in 1938. The actions of the Church in both countries, however, support the historian Peter Pulzer's statement that, "where [the Church's] chief enemy is not heresy but secularism, it will incline to the support of absolute authority."[113]

Conclusion

When the world war ended in late 1918, Church members in Vienna metaphorically lamented the sweeping away of the German princes as the ultimate destruction of a "divinely decreed" social and political order linked with the

Monarchy. The war as well as the collapse of the Habsburg Empire and advent of the Austrian Republic were understood as the consequences of a modern world that privileged the secular over the religious, and which disregarded the true bases of human society. Civil marriage, secular education, and the gradual elimination of Church privileges had all pointed in this false direction. Unless the Church could accept modern democratic principles and accede to popular sovereignty, church-state conflict was unavoidable in the postwar period.

Early Church proclamations gave the suggestion of just such a willingness to reach such an accommodation with democracy. From 1918 to 1923, the Church appeared to have reconciled itself to the new state, and all the more so when its allies and own representatives controlled the government. This changed with the repression of leftists in 1927, which freed the Church up to discard its conciliatory rhetoric and display its true antidemocratic colors by sanctifying the overthrow of the Austrian Republic. Perhaps nothing proves this better than Church leaders' post-1927 calling of right-wing militias into the government, as well as their consistent support for authoritarian governments in other predominantly Catholic European countries. In short, appearances were deceiving when it came to Church declarations that it was comfortable with the new democratic order in Austria. Examined in its proper historical context, such language reveals an upper Church hierarchy that never fully accepted the secular republic.

Whether the Church fostered outright "contempt" for democracy is more difficult to prove. Clearly its core, consistent, and long-standing position was antithetical to democratic values, which explains why the Church only tolerated the Republic for as long as it satisfied Church requirements for the continuation of the kind of social order that had existed under the Monarchy. In other words, the upper Church hierarchy never really was prepared to give the Republic a chance, as Diamant argued it was. Rather it played a democratic game provided the outcome preserved its political and social prerogatives. In so doing, the Church in Vienna was a crucial component of a larger political movement that did not want the democratic Republic to succeed. Once all the German princes had gone, the Church was anxious for the democracy that had ended the old order to be gone as well.

Michael Carter-Sinclair earned a BA in European Studies from the University of Hull. He then pursued a career in the IT business before taking a PhD in history from King's College, University of London (2012), where he studied antisemitism and extreme German nationalism in Vienna from the mid nineteenth to the mid twentieth centuries. He has taught at King's on World War II and on wider European history from the 1790s onward, and is currently developing a book on Vienna from 1850 to 1950. An accomplished linguist, fluent in English,

German, French, and Spanish, Carter-Sinclair is learning Czech to broaden his research capacities.

Notes

1. Alfred Diamant, *Austrian Catholics and the First Republic* (Princeton: Princeton University Press, 1959), 104–6, 286–87.
2. For a survey of Catholic societal life, see Walter Sauer, *Katholisches Vereinswesen in Wien: zur Geschichte des christlichsozial-konservativen Lagers vor 1914* (Salzburg: Neugebauer, 1980).
3. In elections to Vienna City Council in 1923, Christian Socials polled over 330,000 votes. See Maren Seliger and Karl Ucakar, *Wien: Politische Geschichte 1740–1934*, vol. 2 (Vienna: Jugend & Volk, 1985), 1139.
4. On the relationship between Church and party in the 1920s, see John W. Boyer, *Culture and Political Crisis in Vienna: Christian Socialism in Power, 1897–1918* (Chicago: University of Chicago Press, 1995), 165–68.
5. A number of newspapers were published by or in close affiliation with the Church. See *Die Katholische Presse Österreichs* (Vienna: Das kleine Volksblatt, 1934). This supplement to *Das kleine Volksblatt* provides a directory of the range of Catholic newspapers during the First Republic.
6. *Chroniken* (parish chronicles) were meant to be objective, but priests sometimes included their opinions on political and social developments. *Chroniken* from the following parishes in the capital city can be found in the archive of the Archdiocese of Vienna (Diözesanarchiv Wien, hereafter DAW): Grinzing, Neulerchenfeld, St. Anton von Padua, Schottenfeld, Weinhaus.
7. John W. Boyer, *Political Radicalism in Late Imperial Vienna: Origins of the Christian Social Movement, 1848–1897* (Chicago: University of Chicago Press, 1981), 17–21.
8. Peter Leisching, "Die römisch-katholische Kirche in Cisleithanien," in *Die Habsburgermonarchie 1848–1918*, vol. 4, ed. Adam Wandruszka and Peter Urbanitsch (Vienna: Österreichische Akademie der Wissenschaften, 1985), 25–34, gives details on the Concordat.
9. Boyer, *Political Radicalism*, 122–83.
10. The Archbishops and Bishops of Austria, "I: Hirtenbrief," *Wiener Diözesanblatt*, hereafter *Diözesanblatt*, 24 August 1918, 97 (front page).
11. Ibid., 99.
12. See Maureen Healy, *Vienna and the Fall of the Habsburg Empire: Total War and Everyday Life in World War I* (Cambridge, UK: Cambridge University Press, 2004), 31–86, for the heavy toll that the lack of food took on the population of Vienna during the world war.
13. The Archbishops and Bishops of Austria, "I: Hirtenbrief," *Diözesanblatt*, 24 August 1918, 98–99.
14. Ibid., 97. The complaint of the bishops against unrestrained competition should not be taken as anticapitalist. Catholic and Christian Social protests against capitalism were often thinly disguised attacks on what was termed "Jewish" capitalism and alleged Jewish "political dominance." See Diamant, *Austrian Catholics*, 122; and Boyer, *Culture and Political Crisis*, 253.

15. The Archbishops and Bishops of Austria, "I: Hirtenbrief," *Diözesanblatt*, 24 August 1918, 98.
16. Ibid., 102.
17. For examples, see *Währinger Bezirksnachrichten*, 2 December 1918, 3; *Währinger Bezirksnachrichten*, 24 December 1918, 1; and Boyer, *Culture and Political Crisis*, 427.
18. The Archbishops and Bishops of Austria, "I: Hirtenbrief," *Diözesanblatt*, 24 August 1918, 99, 101.
19. Ibid., 99
20. Ibid., 99–100.
21. Ernst Hanisch, *Die Ideologie des politischen Katholizismus in Österreich, 1918–1938* (Salzburg: Geyer, 1977), 5.
22. John W. Boyer, "Silent War and Bitter Peace: The Revolution of 1918 in Austria," *Austrian History Yearbook* 34 (2003): 1–56.
23. Leisching, "Die römisch-katholische Kirche," 1–247, 96.
24. Boyer, *Culture and Political Crisis*, 111–63, 236–68.
25. Hanisch, *Ideologie des politischen*, 5–7.
26. "Grosse Entscheidungen," *Reichspost*, 12 November 1918, 1.
27. "Feierliche Ausrufung der Republik vor dem Parlament," *Reichspost*, 13 November 1918, 1.
28. For discussion of the nationalities problems of the Empire, see, for example, Pieter M. Judson, *Guardians of the Nation: Activists on the Language Frontiers of Imperial Austria* (Cambridge, MA: Harvard University Press, 2007).
29. See Keith H. Pickus, "Native Born Strangers: Jews, Catholics and the German Nation," in *Religion und Nation, Nation und Religion: Beiträge zu einer unbewältigten Geschichte*, ed. Michael Geyer and Hartmut Lehmann (Göttingen: Wallstein Verlag, 2004), 141–56.
30. DAW, parish chronicle (*Chronik*) of Grinzing, 1918. The original German is: "Alle deutsche Fürsten vertrieben!"
31. Ibid.
32. On the role of the clergy in the development of political antisemitism, see Boyer, *Political Radicalism*, 122–83.
33. DAW, parish chronicle of Grinzing, 1883.
34. DAW, parish chronicle (*Chronik*) of Grinzing, 1918. In German: "*Was soll daraus werden?*" The writing was hardly legible, but clearly the priest was expressing anxiety about the political situation in Austria.
35. Cardinal Friedrich Piffl, "An den hochw. Seelsorgerklerus der Erzdiözese Wien!," *Diözesanblatt*, 18 November 1918, 123.
36. Ibid.
37. *Reichspost*, 12 November 1918, 5; and *Reichspost*, 3 December 1918, 6.
38. Ignaz Seipel, *Nation und Staat* (Vienna: Braumüller, 1916). For a review of the book, see "Nation und Staat," *Reichspost*, 1 June 1917, 2.
39. Ignaz Seipel, "Das Recht des Volkes," *Reichspost*, 19 November 1918, 1; and Ignaz Seipel, "Die demokratische Verfassung," *Reichspost*, 21 November 1918, 1. As late as 1928, Seipel decried what he saw as a sham democracy in Parliament, rather than a true democracy. See "Seipels Diktaturpläne über das Parlament," *Vorarlberger Wacht*, 4 December 1928, 2.
40. Ignaz Seipel, "Das Recht des Volkes," *Reichspost*, 19 November 1918, 1–2.
41. Ignaz Seipel, "Die demokratische Verfassung," *Reichspost*, 21 November 1918, 1.

42. Ignaz Seipel, "Das Volk und die künftige Staatsform," *Reichspost*, 23 November 1918, 1.
43. Ibid.
44. C. Earl Edmondson, *The Heimwehr and Austrian Politics 1918–1936* (Athens, GA: University of Georgia Press, 1978), 15.
45. Diamant, *Austrian Catholics*, 105 and 110.
46. Ignaz Seipel, "Das Volk und die künftige Staatsform," *Reichspost*, 23 November 1918, 1.
47. The bishops of German Austria, "Hirtenbrief," *Diözesanblatt*, 23 January 1919, 1–2.
48. The bishops of German Austria, "Hirtenbrief," *Diözesanblatt*, 23 January 1919, 4–5.
49. Ibid.
50. See Boyer, *Political Radicalism*, 15–17, on the creation of a system of electoral colleges, known as curia.
51. Leisching, "Die römisch-katholische Kirche," 131.
52. The bishops of German Austria, "Hirtenbrief," *Diözesanblatt*, 23 January 1919, 5–6.
53. Ibid., 6–7.
54. Ibid., 9.
55. The bishops of German Austria, "Hirtenbrief," *Diözesanblatt*, 23 January 1919, 9.
56. For differing perspectives on the election outcomes, see any of the (often uncredited) articles in *Reichspost*, 18 February 1919, 1–4; *Arbeiterzeitung*, 18 February 1919, 1–4.
57. For a general description of political events between 1918 and 1920, see Edmondson, *Heimwehr*, 9–16.
58. The Archbishops and Bishops of Austria, "I. Hirtenbrief," *Diözesanblatt*, 24 November 1919, 66.
59. For Christian Social reactions to the results, see "Bedeutende Wahlerfolge der Christlichsozialen in ganz Österreich," *Reichspost*, 18 October 1920, 1.
60. Hanisch, *Ideologie des politischen*, 9.
61. Benedict XV, "St. Josefs Jubiläum," *Diözesanblatt*, 19 March 1921, 9.
62. See Alfred Kostelecky, "Kirche und Staat," in *Kirche in Österreich 1918–1965*, ed. Ferdinand Klosterman, Hans Kriegl, Otto Mauer, and Erika Weinzierl (Vienna: Herold, 1967), 201–17, 202.
63. Boyer, *Culture and Political Crisis*, 445.
64. J. Robert Wegs, *Growing Up Working Class: Continuity and Change Among Viennese Youth, 1880–1938* (University Park: Pennsylvania State University, 1989), 43–44, describes the limited nature of some Social Democratic building programs.
65. Cardinal Friedrich Gustav Piffl, "Oberhirtlicher Dank," *Diözesanblatt*, 31 December 1921, 67–69; P. Frazer, "A Recent Chapter in the Modernist Controversy," *The American Journal of Theology* 13, no. 2 (1909): 238–59.
66. DAW, parish chronicle of Weinhaus, 1922.
67. DAW, parish chronicle of Weinhaus, 1923.
68. Hanisch, *Ideologie des politischen*, 3. The *Chronik* of the parish of Neulerchenfeld records alarm at the large number of people leaving the Church that year: DAW, parish chronicle of Neulerchenfeld, 1922.
69. For an explanation of the law, see "Religionswechsel und Konfessionslosigkeitserklärung," *Reichspost*, 1 January 1908, 6.
70. See, for example, DAW, St. Anton von Padua parish chronicle, 1920.
71. DAW, Weinhaus parish chronicle, 1923.

72. See Alfred D. Low, *The Anschluss Movement 1931–1938* (New York: East European Monographs, 1984), 39, 42–45. See also Anita Ziegerhofer, "Austria and Aristide Briand's 1930 Memorandum," *Austrian History Yearbook* 29 (1998): 139–60.
73. See John T. Lauridsen, *Nazism and the Radical Right in Austria, 1918–1934* (Copenhagen: Royal Library, 2007), 131–33.
74. DAW, Weinhaus parish chronicle, 1927.
75. See Edmondson, *Heimwehr*, 49–50; and Hanisch, *Ideologie des politischen*, 11–13.
76. Diamant, *Austrian Catholics*, 104–105.
77. Edmondson, *Heimwehr*, 43.
78. Ibid., 51.
79. Hanisch, *Ideologie des politischen*, 13.
80. Lauridsen, *Nazism and the Radical Right*, 133.
81. Edmondson, *Heimwehr*, 76–77.
82. DAW, Weinhaus parish chronicle, 1930.
83. Ibid.
84. Edmondson, *Heimwehr*, 77.
85. On Seipel and authoritarianism, see Edmondson, *Heimwehr*, 90–94.
86. Diamant, *Austrian Catholics*, 86, 266.
87. *St. Laurenz-Getrudsblatt: Mitteilungen der Pfarrgemeinde Währing*, March 1934, 1.
88. DAW, Weinhaus parish chronicle, 1933.
89. "Die Grundsteinlegung zur Gedächtniskirche des befreiten Wien," *Neuigkeits-Welt-Blatt*, 19 April 1934, 3.
90. Ibid.
91. DAW, Schottenfeld parish chronicle, 1934.
92. From Articles 1 and 2 of the constitution, quoted in *Diözesanblatt*, 4 September 1934, 79. See also Diamant, *Austrian Catholics*, 265.
93. A debate on whether Austria was a fascist or fascist-leaning state can be found in Julie Thorpe, *Pan-Germanism and the Austro-Fascist State, 1933–38* (Manchester: Manchester University Press, 2011).
94. DAW, Weinhaus parish chronicle, 1934.
95. "Das Konkordat," *Diözesanblatt*, 7 May 1934, 27–36.
96. Ibid., 27–28.
97. "Die Konsekration der Dr. Dollfuß-Gedächtniskirche in Währing," *Neuigkeits-Welt Blatt*, 10 November 1934, 5; *St. Laurenz-Getrudsblatt*, September–October 1934, 1.
98. Lucile Dreidemy, *Der Dollfuß Mythos: Eine Biographie des Posthumen* (Vienna: Böhlau, 2014).
99. *Neulerchenfelder Pfarrblatt*, Year VI, no. 5 (March 1935): 1.
100. DAW, Neulerchenfeld parish chronicle, 1934. Ernst Hanisch puts the figure for net conversions to Catholicism at over 30,510 for the year (Hanisch, *Ideologie des politischen*, 4).
101. "I. Verfassung 1934," *Diözesanblatt*. 4 September 1934, 79, 79–102.
102. Discussions of the closeness of churches, including the Catholic Church, with various fascist and authoritarian regimes can be found in Matthew Feldman and Marius Turda, eds., *Clerical Fascism in Interwar Europe* (London: Routledge, 2008).
103. Frances Lannon, "The Church's Crusade against the Republic," in *Revolution and War in Spain, 1931–1939*, ed. Paul Preston (London: Routledge, 1984), 35–58.

104. Paul Preston, *The Coming of the Spanish Civil War*, 2nd ed. (London: Routledge, 1994), 39–42.
105. Ibid., 41.
106. Ibid., 40.
107. Paul Preston, *The Spanish Civil War: Reaction, Revolution and Revenge* (London: Routledge, 2006), 41–44.
108. Preston, *Coming of the Spanish Civil War*, 71.
109. Preston, *Spanish Civil War*, 201–2 and 220–22.
110. Cardinal Theodor Innitzer, "II. 30 August: Gebetssonntag für Spanien," *Diözesanblatt*, 29 August 1936, 106.
111. Preston, *Spanish Civil War*, 33–34 and 43–44.
112. Preston, *Coming of the Spanish Civil War*, 40.
113. Peter Pulzer, *The Rise of Political Antisemitism in Germany and Austria* (Cambridge, MA: Harvard University Press, 1988), 122.

Select Bibliography

Boyer, John W. *Culture and Political Crisis in Vienna: Christian Socialism in Power, 1897–1918*. Chicago: University of Chicago Press, 1995.

———. *Political Radicalism in Late Imperial Vienna: Origins of the Christian Social Movement, 1848–1897*. Chicago: University of Chicago Press, 1981.

———. "Silent War and Bitter Peace: The Revolution of 1918 in Austria." *Austrian History Yearbook* 34 (2003): 1–56.

Diamant, Alfred. *Austrian Catholics and the First Republic*. Princeton: Princeton University Press, 1959.

Dreidemy, Lucile. *Der Dollfuß Mythos: Eine Biographie des Posthumen*. Vienna: Böhlau, 2014.

Edmondson, C. Earl. *The Heimwehr and Austrian Politics 1918–1936*. Athens, GA: University of Georgia Press, 1978.

Feldman, Matthew, and Marius Turda, eds. *Clerical Fascism in Interwar Europe*. London: Routledge, 2008.

Frazer, P. "A Recent Chapter in the Modernist Controversy." *The American Journal of Theology* 13, no. 2 (1909): 238–59.

Hanisch, Ernst. *Die Ideologie des politischen Katholizismus in Österreich, 1918–1938*. Salzburg: Geyer, 1977.

Healy, Maureen. *Vienna and the Fall of the Habsburg Empire: Total War and Everyday Life in World War I*. Cambridge, UK: Cambridge University Press, 2004.

Judson, Pieter M. *Guardians of the Nation: Activists on the Language Frontiers of Imperial Austria*. Cambridge, MA: Harvard University Press, 2007.

Kostelecky, Alfred. "Kirche und Staat." In *Kirche in Österreich 1918–1965*, edited by Ferdinand Klosterman, Hans Kriegl, Otto Mauer, and Erika Weinzierl, 201–17. Vienna: Herold, 1967.

Lauridsen, John T. *Nazism and the Radical Right in Austria, 1918–1934*. Copenhagen: Royal Library, 2007.

Leisching, Peter. "Die römisch-katholische Kirche in Cisleithanien." In *Die Habsburgermonarchie 1848–1918*, vol. 4, edited by Adam Wandruszka and Peter Urbanitsch, 1–247. Vienna: Österreichische Akademie der Wissenschaften, 1985.

Low, Alfred D. *The Anschluss Movement 1931–1938*. New York: East European Monographs, 1984.
Pickus, Keith H. "Native Born Strangers: Jews, Catholics and the German Nation." In *Religion und Nation, Nation und Religion: Beiträge zu einer unbewältigten Geschichte*, edited by Michael Geyer and Hartmut Lehmann, 141–56. Göttingen: Wallstein Verlag, 2004.
Preston, Paul. *The Coming of the Spanish Civil War*, 2nd edition. London: Routledge, 1994.
———. *The Spanish Civil War: Reaction, Revolution and Revenge*. London: Routledge, 2006.
Pulzer, Peter. *The Rise of Political Antisemitism in Germany and Austria*. Cambridge, MA: Harvard University Press, 1988.
Sauer, Walter. *Katholisches Vereinswesen in Wien: zur Geschichte des christlichsozial-konservativen Lagers vor 1914*. Salzburg: Neugebauer, 1980.
Seipel, Ignaz. *Nation und Staat*. Vienna: Braumüller, 1916.
Thorpe, Julie. *Pan-Germanism and the Austro-Fascist State, 1933–38*. Manchester: Manchester University Press, 2011.
Wegs, J. Robert. *Growing Up Working Class: Continuity and Change Among Viennese Youth, 1880–1938*. University Park: Pennsylvania State University, 1989.
Ziegerhofer, Anita. "Austria and Aristide Briand's 1930 Memorandum." *Austrian History Yearbook* 29 (1998): 139–60.

Chapter 9

Wealthy Landowners or Weak Remnants of the Imperial Past?
Central European Nobles during and after the First World War

Konstantinos Raptis

A common theme of the literature on the dissolution of the Austro-Hungarian Empire at the end of World War I is the national revolutions that precipitated and pursued it.[1] Yet the venerable regime's collapse in 1918 was not only a matter of border redrawing and state-building—it was a decisive event for the economic, social, and even cultural character of the entire territory. In this respect, the group most affected by the transition from empire to nation-state was the nobility, which had directly identified itself with the three imperial pillars of bureaucracy, military, and dynasty.[2] Overrepresented in the diplomatic corps and dominant in the senior ranks of the army and administration, the Habsburg nobility faced a crisis of legitimacy in the interwar period.[3]

Could the Austro-Hungarian aristocracy remain relevant in the aftermath of World War I and with the advent of nation-state building in Central Europe? In addition to their decline in status and wartime material losses, Habsburg nobles often encountered popular hostility. This was directed mainly at the need for land reform, as the nobility was generally seen as an obsolete and parasitic social group incompatible with democracy and mass political parties like the Social Democrats, Agrarians, Christian Socials, and Communists. The situation was yet worse for nobles who were ethnonationally alien to the new local elites and the majority of the population, above all German and Hungarian aristocrats in Czechoslovakia and Yugoslavia.[4] In the former, the nobility came to represent the most prominent living emblem of the old order, "a symbol of everything the new state's leaders sought to displace: Habsburg imperial institutions, social inequality, and German dominance."[5]

In examining the shifting political, economic, and sociocultural conditions of the Habsburg nobility from 1910 through the postwar era, this chapter illustrates how many noble families not only survived, but thrived—retaining a considerable part of their wealth, social status, and cultural/symbolic capital in the new national states of Austria and Czechoslovakia.[6] They did so, moreover, despite such debilitating circumstances as the abolition of noble titles in the Monarchy's successor states (with the exception of Hungary), land reform in Czechoslovakia, and the leftist revolutionary spirit that followed the Russian Revolution. At the end of World War I and well into the postwar period, the Habsburg aristocracy would prove itself to be fluid, multifaceted, and, indeed, relevant.

Central European nobles (i.e., the nobility of Austria-Hungary) constituted a heterogeneous group in terms of wealth, political power, and social status. Fragmented by rank, origins, profession, and estate size, one of the few consistencies among the Habsburg gentry were their male-dominated heads of household. These men were the landowners and administrators of the family fortune, the family's face in the public sphere, and the chief purveyors of the aristocratic way of life.[7] Yet the divergent circumstances among the Habsburg nobility meant that the Great War affected them differently as well. For example, members of the *Dienstadel* (service gentry) who lived from salaries (typically fixed allowances from family revenues, pensions, or rents) suffered severely from the high inflation between 1917 and 1922.[8] These impoverished "ex-nobles" of aristocratic or bourgeois origin comprised the *Adelsproletariat* (noble proletariat) or the German *Kleinadel* (petty gentry) whose postwar survival depended largely upon the charity of their peers.[9]

For the purposes of this chapter, however, I focus on the upper nobility of large estate owners—that is, those counts and princes in the former crown lands (mainly Bohemia and Lower Austria, but also Galicia and Bukovina) who were the richest and most powerful aristocrats in the Austrian half of the empire.[10] Together with the Magyar nobility, they constituted one of Austria-Hungary's "centripetal forces" due to their steadfast loyalty to imperial unity under the Habsburg dynasty.[11] And while the Hungarian and Polish nobility of Austrian Galicia are also important in this respect, it is already well documented that these landed oligarchies survived largely intact under the *Sanacja* regime in Poland (1926–39) and Hungary's counter-revolutionary Horthy government (1920–44).[12]

More specifically, this chapter focuses on the Counts Harrach, who had possessions in Bohemia and Moravia, Lower and Upper Austria, and Hungary.[13] As members of the core court nobility—the Habsburg Monarchy's so-called *erste Gesellschaft* (first society), which numbered some four hundred families of high landed nobility and has been called "continental Europe's most exclusive elite"[14]—the Harrachs enjoyed hereditary seats in both the *Herrenhaus* (the upper house of the Austrian parliament) and the Bohemian *Landtag* (diet). They also attended the empire's most prestigious annual events—the *Hofball* (court ball), which opened Vienna's carnival season, and the *Ball bei Hof* (ball-at-court), which ended it. Until the Monarchy and court were abolished in 1918, the head of the house, Count Otto Harrach (1863–1935), was chamberlain (*Kämmerer*) to the emperor. His wife, Princess Karoline Oettingen, was a member of the Order of the Star Cross (*Sternkreuzorden*).[15]

Politics: Defeat and Compromise

Clearly, the nobles in the Austrian half of the empire suffered political defeat with the dissolution of the Monarchy and abolition of their privileges. But even in the decades before 1918, the conservative Austrian nobility had been challenged by a gradual democratization that began with the extension of male suffrage to the lower classes (peasants, craftsmen, and skilled workers in 1882; and in 1896 to the entire adult male population, including servants, unskilled workers, and peasant laborers), and peaked in 1907 when the socially unequal distribution of votes in favor of the landowners and the middle classes ended with the abolition of voter classes (*Kurien*).[16] Thus, long before the world war, Austrian nobles were losing political ground to peasants, workers, and the middle classes represented by the Liberals, German Nationals, Christian Socialists, and the Social Democrats.[17] Moreover, the nobility itself was divided between centralists (*Verfassungstreue*, literally meaning loyal to the constitution), who had supported the 1867 Compromise between Austria and Hungary, and the federalists (*Feudale*), who defended Bohemian state rights. In this situation, they were obliged to ally themselves with like-minded middle class parties, such as the German Liberals (*Verfassungspartei*) or the clerical-Slavic-conservative right in the so-called Hohenwart-Klub.[18]

Nevertheless, the Habsburg aristocrats' position was safe as long as they had access to power and the means to advance their goals. This changed radically after the war, when revolution, social upheaval, and the collective condemnation of estate-based society heightened the insecurity of these traditional elites.[19] Even Hungarian nobles who retained their titles and enjoyed the best position in postwar Central Europe risked political elimination under Béla Kun's Soviet Republic (March to August 1919) and the nationalization of estates larger than one hundred hectares. Yet they made a quick comeback thanks to the counter-revolutionary Horthy regime, which revived much of the country's oligarchic past by revoking the large-scale land reform, limiting the suffrage to some 27 to

29 percent of potential voters, and restoring open-ballot voting in the countryside as well as the upper house of the Hungarian parliament.[20]

By contrast, the nobility in democratic Czechoslovakia, who had been stripped of their titles and orders by the Revolutionary National Assembly on 10 December 1918, were politically marginalized as "emblems of Habsburg feudalism and authoritarianism."[21] Titles, ranks, and orders of nobility were also outlawed in rump Austria by the Law on the Abolition of the Nobility (*Adelsaufhebungsgesetz*) of 3 April 1919.[22] "In terms of their longings and frustrations," argues the Austrian historian Lothar Höbelt, Austrian aristocrats were "probably more estranged from their political environment than any other noble society in Europe, except for Bohemia."[23] The three great parties—Social Democrats, Christian Socials, and German Nationals—now constituted the basic poles of political integration, replacing the emperor, bureaucracy, army, and, of course, nobility of the prewar era.[24]

Moreover, apart from allying themselves with the Catholic but socially radical Christian Socials, the possibilities for the aristocracy to resist these developments were minimal.[25] The Catholic faith was the *sine qua non* that bound together the Austrian nobility. The adoption of authoritarian, patriarchal, and antidemocratic ideas by the Christian Socials in the interwar period facilitated a convergence between the party and the conservative nobility. In this way, the nobility found political refuge in a large bloc that gave it access to power during the Dollfuß (1932–34) and, especially, Schuschnigg (1934–38) eras.

Count Rudolf Hoyos-Sprinzenstein, chairman of the Federal State Council (*Staatsrat*) until the *Anschluß*, was the most prominent individual case of a short and limited aristocratic comeback in the Federal State of Austria.[26] He was also an exception—for the most part, nobles did not manage to undertake political initiatives and actions on their own. Even the Union of Catholic Noblemen (*Vereinigung der katholischen Edelleute in Österreich*), the most important organization of the Austrian nobility in the interwar period, focused on social and cultural matters rather than political ones. Indeed, its chief goal was to project aristocratic values such as faith, tradition, honor, and social engagement for the common good of the Austrian people and fatherland. The various monarchist leagues and unions, unified in the so-called Iron Ring (*Eiserne Ring*) on 18 August 1932 (the birthday of Emperor Franz Joseph), were also oriented toward cultural issues and the preservation of tradition. They were unable to attain political power and parliamentary representation for Habsburg legitimism and its noble supporters.[27]

Otto Harrach, who like his father Johann and grandfather Franz belonged to the Feudal Conservatives (Federalists) in the imperial era, offers an interesting case study of how some nobles sought to survive politically.[28] In 1917, he provided 40 percent of the original share capital to found the Phönix publishing house, which took over the weekly *Wiener Neueste Nachrichten*.[29] This respected conservative journal was regarded as the successor of the daily *Das Vaterland*, which from 1861 until its suspension in 1911 (due to a lack of private contributions) constituted the central organ of the Conservatives and was promoted by some of the Empire's most influential and wealthy aristocratic families (including the Schwarzenbergs, Liechtensteins, Czernins, and Lobkowitzes).[30] Additionally, in 1918, Harrach founded the weekly *Die Monarchie* in cooperation with Tyrolia publishers.[31] With the support of other high nobles, he planned to use these publications to promote conservatism, Catholicism, and Habsburg (that is, supranationalist) patriotism, as well as landowning interests generally.[32]

Yet these proved to be maximal goals in those turbulent years. The compromise with the Christian Socials was short-lived. Harrach's demand in September 1918 that *Die Monarchie* be strictly conservative-Catholic and avoid a Christian Social course was rejected by Tyrolia's Christian Social director, the priest Aemilian Schöpfer.[33] Furthermore, financial difficulties and a dearth of subscribers forced Harrach to sell Phönix to the People's Confederation of Austrian Catholics (*Volksbund der Katholiken Österreichs*) in January 1919.[34] After the Monarchy's collapse, *Die Monarchie* continued publication as *Das neue Reich*. In April 1920, Harrach and other nobles, including the counts Thun und Hohenstein, Stollberg, Chotek, and Prince Schwarzenberg, bought back the shares of *Das neue Reich*, which had 2,100 subscribers and a circulation of 4,000.[35] The counts Alfons Mensdorff-Pouilly, Rudolf Czernin-Morzin, Heinrich Clam-Martinic, Karl Auersperg, and Ottokar Czernin wrote regularly for the magazine until it folded in 1932.[36]

The Austrian nobility's immediate losses were mainly political, since land reform, while widely discussed, was sidelined in favor of heavier taxes on large holdings. The aristocracy thus developed "a revisionism without any obvious and clear-cut goals."[37] By contrast, Bohemian nobles sought to reduce the impact of the land reform "through behind-the-scenes lobbying and bribery."[38] In a letter that Otto Harrach wrote to his cousin Franz in June 1920, we see both the networks of nobles in Bohemia, and the local political influence they still wielded thanks in part to the unfavorable circumstances of the 1920s.[39]

> My Dear Cousin!
> I am writing to you in French in order to avoid, if possible, any breach in the confidentiality of my letter. In Vienna, I recently spoke to Vella, who told me that you are practically the prisoner of your employees. This sounds like a case for intervention by the famous *Bodenamt* (pozemkový úřad [Land Office]) in Prague. They no longer organize the so-called *Zwangsverwaltungen* [forced administrations], but rather dispatch employees to conduct inspections at the large landowners' estates for several weeks. Such an inspection (*dočasný dohled*) would not be detrimental to your estate if the delegate was an honest man, like the one who has been at my home and is leaving in a few days since his job here is finished now that the *Zwangsverwaltung* has finally been revoked. He is a former director of Waldstein in Münchengrätz, a pensioner

from there, and I can assure you that I owe him a lot, because he always conducted himself very honestly, always taking my side against the employees' associations as well as those of the workers. If you want, I could tell him to announce to the *Bodenamt* that it would be necessary to send you a mediator in order to conduct an inspection, and that he offer his services for such an assignment. If you agree, telegraph me a "yes" or "no" right away. His name is Mr. Nový. I am certain that he will soon put your estate in order, even though he's a seventy-year-old man.[40]

Mr. Nový, the long-time Czech administrator of the Waldstein estate in the northern Bohemian town of Münchengrätz (now Mnichovo Hradiště), proved useful to Otto Harrach by supporting him as an official mediator in disputes with his employees during the confiscation reviews for the land reform. Otto thus urged his cousin to do the same for his Moravian estates.

Concern about their properties and political survival in interwar Czechoslovakia also led the nobles to become increasingly nationalistic.[41] Whether they were influenced by Karl Rohan's vision of a greater Germany, or by Karel Schwarzenberg's commitment to Bohemian historic rights and Czech national politics, the Bohemian nobles shared ideas of aristocratic elitism, corporatism, antisocialism, antiliberalism, and the traditional values of patriarchal family and paternalistic labor relations. In the late 1930s, this drew many of them to the radical right and, even, to fascism, be it the Czech or German varieties.[42] Among those nobles who identified themselves with the Czech nation were six members from the houses of Kinsky and Lobkowicz; four from the houses of Czernin, Dobrženský, and Schlik; and three from the Colloredo-Mannsfeld, Belcredi, Mensdorff-Pouilly, and Schwarzenberg houses.[43] Ulrich Kinsky, the Khuens, the Clarys, one of the Westphalen brothers, and Hohenlohe were, according to Ashton-Gwatkin's Foreign Office report of 15 August 1938, strong supporters of the pro-German/Hitler Sudeten German Party. Likewise, the counts Karl Buquoy and Karl Waldstein, as well as Franz Anton (Prince) Thun-Hohenstein, were among the many Bohemian German nobles who greeted the dismantling of Czechoslovakia at Munich and Hitler's subsequent annexation of the Sudetenland with considerable public enthusiasm.[44]

However, as the cases of the Kinskys, Czernins, and Harrachs demonstrate, the aristocratic political landscape was quite fluid, and not all members of a noble house solidly supported either the Czechs or the Germans. Otto Harrach was thus quite irritated in August 1927 when he received an invitation to participate in a celebration by the Czech Anglers' Club in Wittingau (now Třeboň) on the expropriated land of his relative Schwarzenberg. To make matters worse, his cousin Franz had signed the invitation as the club's vice-president. Otto accepted that Franz had acted as a Czech patriot, but he had no desire to play a leading role in the Czechoslovak state despite the fact that the Harrachs were regarded as a Czech-friendly family.[45] Moreover, Otto's aversion to National Socialism until the day he died in 1935 did not prevent his son and successor Hans from becoming a Nazi sympathizer, as his library and donations reveal.[46]

In sum, the Bohemian nobility displayed two principal continuities with regard to their prewar political behavior. First, they remained divided along the lines of the imperial era—that is, Czech and German nobles drew on different Bohemian traditions concerning historic rights federalism and Viennese centralism. Secondly, they were and felt loyal to the state, whether it was the Czechoslovak Republic or the Third Reich.[47] Despite their affinities for the authoritarian regimes imposed in 1934 in Austria and in 1939 in Czechoslovakia, the political power and presence of the nobility in these countries, especially the latter, was quite limited. In any case, it certainly did not reflect their strong economic position as great landowners in the interwar period.

Landed Estates and the Economic Situation: Losses, Continuities, Adaptations

Although the nobility's wealth and financial standing were degraded during the war and in its aftermath through a combination of coal and personnel shortages, wartime requisitions, inflation, taxation, land reforms, and the general revolutionary atmosphere, many landlords managed to retain a considerable part of their family's wealth and, furthermore, a good deal of its economic and social influence.[48] One such aristocrat was Otto Harrach, who possessed land holdings in Bohemia and Lower Austria totaling some 26,707 hectares in 1910 (he served as head of the Harrach house from 1909 to 1935). While this was not in the league of such magnates as the Schwarzenbergs, Esterhazys, Liechtensteins, Windisch-Graetzes, Hoyos, Czernins, Fürstenbergs, and Colloredo-Mansfelds, Harrach's properties put him closely behind the Lobkowitzes, Kinskys, Waldsteins, and Thun und Hohensteins as one of the ten largest landowners in Lower Austria (4,970 hectares) and Bohemia (21,737 hectares).[49] Moreover, Otto Harrach owned five manor houses on the family estates—at Prugg and Rohrau in Lower Austria, Hradek, Starkenbach (now Jilemnice), and Strkow (Strkov) in Bohemia, as well as city mansions in Vienna and Prague.[50]

Most Harrach possessions, like many estates of the Austrian aristocracy, were secured through a *fideicommissum* granted by the emperor. This institution of the entailed estate, which was in force in most German-speaking regions, was a de facto privilege of the upper nobility that contributed decisively to maintaining the social position of aristocratic families over generations.[51] It was so important, in fact, that some aristocratic families remained loyal to their traditional principles to bequeath the property intact to the firstborn son, despite the abolition of such entailments in 1924 in Czechoslovakia and 1938 in Austria.[52] During the last decade of his life, Otto Harrach repeatedly asked his son Hans to entail the

Figure 9.1. Prugg Palace (Bruck an der Leitha), rear side, 12 September 2008. Author's photo.

whole property to his own son, and to ensure that this process would continue in the future.[53]

The greatest threat to aristocratic property after the world war was land reform, which the people demanded and their political leaders largely implemented in their efforts to build a cohesive nation-state and socially just democracy. The most extensive and ambitious land reform project took place in Czechoslovakia, which inherited many landed estates from the Austrian (Czech lands) as well as the Hungarian (Slovakia) half of the Dual Monarchy. In Bohemia and Moravia alone, 33.5 percent of the land belonged to the nobility at the end of the war.[54]

The Land Control Act of April 1919 in Czechoslovakia limited arable holdings to 150 hectares and mixed holdings to 250 hectares. The excess land was compulsorily purchased and redistributed to dwarf-holders and landless agricultural laborers (veterans of the Czechoslovak Legion received priority). Through what President Tomáš Masaryk called "the greatest act of the new republic," no single landowner would retain estates larger than 500 hectares (including forests and meadows).[55] A similar act in Yugoslavia limited arable holdings to 75 hectares and mixed estates to 200.[56]

And yet, despite the nobility's understandable fears of this new democratic order, the land reform was not properly implemented in Czechoslovakia and

Yugoslavia. Redistribution became a long and deliberate process by which the nobility managed to retain almost half its land (mainly forest) in Bohemia and Moravia through 1938. In Slovenia (Carniola), nobles succeeded in exempting forests, which comprised three-quarters of the large land holdings.[57] Moreover, the timing and extent of the land reforms in Czechoslovakia and Yugoslavia varied from case-to-case depending upon shifting political constellations, the intensity of national agitation for reform, and the prestige and paternalism of the individual proprietors, not to mention the skills of their lawyers.[58]

The Schwarzenbergs thus managed to retain almost one-third of their estates in southern Bohemia, or some 55,600 hectares in the demesnes of Böhmisch Krumau (now Český Krumlov), Frauenberg (Hluboká nad Vltavou), Winterberg (Vimperk), and Chejnow (Chýnov), as well as 27,747 hectares in Austria and 2,786 in Germany. The Chudenitz-Neuhaus demesne of the Czernin family amounted in the 1930s to 13,000 hectares, more than a third of the 32,000 hectares they held at war's end.[59] The Harrach family did better, maintaining nearly half their landed property in Bohemia (ca. 9,500 hectares) and their entire Lower Austrian estates, which were leased out to an agricultural enterprise.[60] Furthermore, the land lost by the nobles was expropriated rather than confiscated, though the compensation tended to be quite low (some 8 percent of 1920s real estate prices, which were determined on the basis of the 1913–15 prices before the wartime hyperinflation).[61]

The abolition of the entailments in the context of land reform gave these landowners the additional opportunity of rationalizing their estates by restoring their allodial property, disposing of indebted enterprises, and taking out new loans from the banks. In a letter to his cousin Franz in autumn 1922, Otto Harrach expressed his fear of bankruptcy due to the great debts burdening his allodial estate:

> So long as the entailments exist, I am in a very difficult position, because my allodial property is very small, but the substance of the entailed property must stay intact, thus the immense burdens on my estate rest exclusively on my allodial assets, which are however insufficient; the banks will eventually deprive me of any credit, if I do not carry out an aggressive cut, by disposing of all the loss-making properties from my allodial wealth, such as breweries, inns and, probably, the sugar factory.[62]

The anticipated bankruptcy never happened, and by 1925, Harrach had divested himself of the indebted enterprises (which were all sold, except for the sugar factory which was shut down).[63]

Thus, by retaining a considerable part of their property, Bohemian nobles were able to continue those agricultural and forestry enterprises that were so crucial to the national economy of the new state. In this way, too, they perpetuated the choices of their fathers and grandfathers, who, especially after 1848 in

Bohemia and Lower Austria, functioned largely as agrarian capitalists by investing in industry, banking, the stock exchange, and railway companies.[64]

Since the nobles were deprived of most of their arable land, many of their agricultural factories closed or were sold. However, they continued to operate their most important and profitable enterprises. Through the late 1930s, the Harrach estates in Bohemia included two mechanized breweries, a brickworks, two petrol-powered sawmills, a grinding mill, a box factory, a wood-pulp and cardboard factory, and the famous glass works in Neuwelt (Giant Mountains, now Nový Svět). The latter, the pride of the family, produced high quality glassware that was sold in family-owned factory shops in Vienna, Karlsbad (Karlovy Vary), and, until 1917, Moscow and St Petersburg.[65] Glass and beer production were also leading sectors of Czechoslovak industry.[66]

The Harrachs' main source of income came from forestry and related industries, since 76 percent of their total estates consisted of woodland. The timber industry had been built up over many decades. By the end of the nineteenth century, wood, including paper and other products, was already the most important export commodity of the Habsburg Monarchy.[67] In 1933, the Harrachs had a lumber output (*Holzabtrieb*) of 33,256 cubic meters (21,043 m^3 in Starkenbach, which was 94 percent woodland).[68] The subsidies that the Lower Austrian demesnes of Prugg and Rohrau received from Starkenbach amounted to 2,430,581 Austrian schillings in 1936, which gives some indication of the lucrative nature of the forestry sector.[69] During World War II, timber production was so important for the German economy that Hans was exempted from military service until the last months of the conflict.[70]

The Fürstenbergs, who like the Harrachs had estates in Lower Austria and Bohemia, were known in the 1930s for their forestry and brewery operations in Krušovice and Křivoklát, though the latter plant was sold to the Czechoslovak state in 1929 on the condition that Max Egon Fürstenberg could lease it until 1935.[71] The Lobkowitz (or, as they were known after 1918, Lobkowicz) family had a mechanized brewery, two brickworks, an electric plant, and a factory for processing the famous Křimice cabbage.[72] The Schlick and Mitrowitz families also ran breweries and brickworks, as well as saw and grinding mills.[73]

The maintenance of numerous clerks and servants over the decades attests to the size and wealth of the Harrach estates, as well as to their role in the local communities. During World War I, forty-one servants were employed in the Vienna mansion, as well as in the Prugg and Rohrau castles and their surroundings in Lower Austria. Additionally, twelve to fifteen servants (house, kitchen, and stable staff, as well as drivers) accompanied the family to its various residences.[74] Even in 1933 in Bohemia, where the Harrachs lost almost half their estates in the land reform, they employed 114 clerks and others in agriculture and forestry, as well as in their factories (forty-seven fewer than in 1910).[75] Other noble landowners also employed numerous clerks, as indicated in the census for large landed estates and their personnel in the early 1930s.[76]

This does not mean that the nobility lacked financial burdens or loan debt. "I have a personal debt of four million in Zivnobank in Prague, the glass factory owes 3,800,000 to the same bank, and beyond this . . . I have 14,000,000 in unpaid pension contributions for my clerks," Otto confided to his cousin, Franz Harrach, in October 1922.[77] However, the aristocrats did not run out of cash, even in the most difficult times. According to a report from his estate's accounts office dated 28 February 1919, Otto Harrach had current savings of 3,568,617 crowns.[78]

The economic situation of the nobility can also be estimated on the basis of their overall wealth and income during the period in question. The Harrachs' net wealth (that is, the wealth administered by the head of the family), which remained intact during the war, amounted to 148,417,450 German-Austrian crowns in June 1920. Of this, 86.5 percent was held in Czechoslovakia and the rest in Austria.[79] Despite the wealth losses of the 1920s due to the land reform, which led to the expropriation of 12,181 hectares with minimal compensation, Hans inherited from his father a net wealth of 28,567,145 Czechoslovak crowns in September 1935.[80]

Figure 9.2. Harrach Palace in Vienna's First District (Freyung 3), June 2006. Photo courtesy of Gryffindor, Wikimedia Commons.

The regular and extra taxes the nobles paid on their wealth and income also point to the magnitude of their economic position. According to the payment orders as well as the official confirmations of the tax administration in Vienna (dated April and May 1918), Otto paid 1,197,015 crowns in property and income tax. In February 1922, he paid an additional 3,193,512 crowns in a one-off wealth levy in Austria (*einmalige grosse Vermögensabgabe*).[81]

Harrach, as every other aristocratic head of house, was the universal heir and main beneficiary of the family wealth. That also made him the richest person in the family. His declarable income for 1920 was calculated at 6,299,809 Austrian crowns, for which he paid two million in tax three years later.[82] Even his stepbrother Ernst, who depended on an appanage for his living expenses, drew an annual benefit of 70,000 crowns from 1910 to 1917, which was quite a large sum considering that in 1915, Otto offered a yearly salary of 4,800 crowns to his eleven-year-old son's tutor.[83]

Lifestyle and Social Distinction

Although taxation in the interwar period was heavy and the debts and social security contributions for the nobles' staff and employees increased, the lifestyle, consumption habits, and expenses of the nobility, above all noble landowners and heads of the aristocratic houses and their families, showed significant continuities with the imperial past. In his study of the interwar Bohemian aristocracy, Eagle Glassheim writes that the "nobles retained much of their social exclusivity and class solidarity. As before the war, they hunted, rode horses, and frequented noble-only clubs in Prague and Vienna."[84] Harrach's correspondence with his wife, relatives, and compeers during and after the war also reveals a lifestyle in accordance with their rank.[85]

Certainly the frequency of dinner parties, balls, tea parties, and other occasions declined during the war, while court festivities such as the *Hofball* and *Ball bei Hof* in Vienna ended after the death of Emperor Franz Joseph in 1916.[86] Moreover, many aristocrats had served in the war as officers and recruits, and their casualties, especially of young noblemen, cast a shadow over the Empire's former first society. The scarcity of representative social events and festivities organized by the Harrachs or other peers is evident from their absence in the family's correspondence from 1914 to 1918. For instance, in March 1917, Harrach's eldest sister, Anna Hennenberg, wrote: "The social life in Vienna is very small. Nobody has a reason or wish for great pleasure and cheerfulness."[87]

Nevertheless, the Harrachs offer historians a good example of what a rich and stable aristocratic family could afford, even during and after the war's worst episodes of hunger, poverty, and general degradation. These luxuries included vacations, travel to famous spas in Bohemia and Germany for medical reasons,

Figure 9.3. Hradek Palace (bei Nechanic), front view, 30 April 2008. Author's photo.

summer and winter holidays in the countryside, horse-riding, maintaining two cars with drivers, traveling first-class in trains, incessant hunting, and, of course, being attended to by servants in all their mansions.[88] The evidence indicates that the Harrachs maintained this aristocratic lifestyle well into the 1930s.[89]

The regular rotation of the Harrach household between their Vienna mansion and numerous manor houses—in Prugg and Rohrau (in Bruck an der Leitha in Lower Austria), Hradek in Sadowa (Nechanice), Starkenbach (now Jilemnice) in northeastern Bohemia, and Strkow (now Strkov near Tábor) in central Bohemia—also attests to the maintenance of cherished social rituals. In this case, the Harrachs followed an annual pattern of residence: from December/January to the end of April in Vienna; May and June in the Rohrau or Prugg castles or, alternatively, in Strkow; July to mid August in Hradek castle; the second half of August to mid-late September in Starkenbach; and October to the end of December/January again in Rohrau and Prugg.

The Harrachs' move from one mansion to another was crucial to the family's annual travel ritual right up to World War II. It was also, importantly, a Habsburg noble custom going back to the late eighteenth century. Nor was it limited to the Harrachs. The practice of regularly changing residence was followed by the Lobkowitz, Schwarzenberg, Waldburg-Salm, Attems-Gilleis,

Czernin, Colloredo-Mannsfeld, Hoyos, Mensdorff-Pouilly, Thurn and Taxis, Thun und Hohenstein, and Waldstein families, among others.

Concerning male aristocratic culture, Harrach and his high-ranking relatives and friends also continued their avid hunting. As huntmaster (*Jagdherr*), he organized excursions in the family hunting grounds in Lower Austria and Bohemia four to five times a year during and after the war, for which he garnered much appreciation.[90] "Honored uncle," wrote Harrach's nephew, Eduard Lobkowitz, in 1917: "My deepest thanks for the wonderful Hradek hunting. At all times, you were in every respect the most generous house-lord one can ever imagine!"[91] Central European nobles strived for exclusivity in all forms of sociability in the interwar period, just as they always had done. Members of some forty aristocratic families took part in social events in which Harrach and his wife were either guests or hosts in the first quarter of the twentieth century.[92] The guests at a hunting and tennis event hosted by the Habsburg Count Karl Buquoy at his southern Bohemian estate in August 1923 were mostly relatives from the high nobility.[93]

The exclusive sports of tennis, polo, hunting, and riding remained popular among the nobility throughout the interwar era. Otto's younger sister, Maria Theresia, was particularly fond of tennis and played it regularly even during World War I in the Galician capital of Lemberg (now L'viv, in western Ukraine), where she lived after her marriage to the Polish Count Stanislaus Wiśniewski.[94] Upon her marriage to Hans Harrach in 1940, Stephanie, Countess of Eltz, also had a tennis court built for her at the family's castle at Hradek, in Bohemia.[95]

According to the memoirs of Count Leopold of Sternberg's wife Cecilia (born in 1908 to Adolf Cecil, Count of Reventlow-Criminil from Schleswig-Holstein and Alice Lillian, Countess Hoyos), hundreds of nobles attended the *Jubelwoche* (Celebration week) in Vienna, "which consisted of a month of tennis tournaments, polo games, and the Vienna Derby."[96] During the winter social season in Prague, nobles frequented balls sponsored by their wealthiest members, such as the Schwarzenbergs and Clam-Martinics. In spring, "noble sociability moved on to country estates, where nobles gathered for hunting, tennis, polo and preliminaries to the famous Pardubice Steeplechase."[97] As a main attraction for international high society until the late 1930s, the Steeplechase gave Zdeněk Kinský, a member of one of Austria-Hungary's most prominent aristocratic families, the opportunity "to show off his hospitality to a wider audience." In 1937, this highborn assemblage included nobles from Paris, the sister of the Duke of Norfolk (Lady Rachel Howard), and members of the families Schwarzenberg, Auersperg, Harrach, Czernin, and Aehrenthal, among others.[98]

Another indication of continuity with the prewar period can be seen in the consumption patterns of the nobles, including their lavish travels. Regarding the latter, these included trips to Italy that Franz Harrach made with his two daughters and niece (Otto's daughter) in 1925 and 1928 (also with his nephew),

Egypt in 1926, and Otto's weeklong visits to the Italian and French Riviera in the spring of 1926 and 1927.[99] Hans Harrach's receipts from 1936 to 1943 reveal the extent of their wealth and consumerism, including 1,420 Austrian schillings for a black jacket suit, a single-breasted dinner jacket, a pair of black dinner trousers, and a pair of grey flannel trousers; 300 schillings for membership in the Austrian Jockey Club and 120 schillings for membership in the Vienna Riding and Polo Club (from 1936); 1,455 Czechoslovak crowns for a car service (July 1942); 14,480 Czechoslovak crowns in July 1941 and 4,690 in June 1943 for furs, overcoats, dresses, outfits, and blouses for his wife.[100]

Despite income or revenue differences between family members, conviviality within high noble circles in the form of tea societies and social calls, spa tourism, summer holidays, country excursions, and, of course, hunting helped to maintain close family ties. And thanks to the *fideicommissum*, family members received compensation and allowances from the estate's heir and life-tenant, thus assuring them a decent standard of living.[101] Additionally, most difficulties could be managed through family networks. When Harrach's four married sisters faced financial hardship during and after the war, family solidarity came in the form of exceptional allocations, hospitality offers, and food provisions. From 1905 to 1919, Otto regularly allocated funds to the indebted family of his youngest sister, Margarethe Windisch-Graetz, who had five children.[102] He even covered her extended stay at a spa resort in Upper Austrian Gallspach, as well as her accommodation in a local hotel in autumn 1934, shortly before her death.[103] For several weeks during and after the war, Otto Harrach hosted various members of his sisters' families and in-laws in Rohrau castle.[104]

When food was scarce in the last two years of the war,[105] Harrach managed to send precious foodstuffs such as cereals, potatoes, pork, cheese, duck, flour, and sugar from Lower Austria to his sisters in Bohemia, Salzburg, and Budapest, as well as to other nobles in Vienna.[106] A brother-in-law, Gabriel Marenzi, who served as a lieutenant general in the cavalry, sent at least five thank-you letters to Harrach for the cheese, butter, and pheasant he received while in the Galician battlefield or Budapest.[107] Likewise, a neighbor of the Harrachs in Starkenbach, Count Rudolf Czernin-Morzin, wrote in March 1918 about an "unbelievable donation of flour, corn, and groat from Prugg," noting, "nobody is in possession of such great quantities nowadays."[108] Such supplies were absolutely vital during the acute food shortages that brought much of the Empire's population to the brink of starvation from 1917 to 1919.

Moreover, and most crucially for this chapter, such instinctive charity on the part of the nobles was essential to their self-image, as well as to how others perceived them.[109] Harrach received numerous petitions for financial support during and after the war, most of which he answered positively. The countless thank-you letters provide evidence of his considerable donations to charities, relief funds, and other programs between 1914 and 1919. Seventeen of these donations topped one thousand crowns, while eighteen ranged from one hundred to one thousand crowns. The highest sums went to the treatment of soldiers and war victims. Harrach frequently and generously supported the Widows' and Orphans' Fund of the Armed Forces, the War Auxiliary Bureau of the Interior Ministry, the Austrian Red Cross Society, the War Blind Homes Association, the War Welfare Office of the War Ministry, the funds of Catholic organizations, as well as the respective Czech charities. Nobles often played leading roles in these charities and foundations as well: Count Rudolf Abensperg und Traun was president of the Austrian Red Cross and Prince Franz Liechtenstein was director of the Austrian relief operation for the Bulgarian Red Cross.[110] Harrach himself established a convalescent home for wounded officers in his Prugg castle under the direction of the Sovereign Military Order of Malta.[111] And despite the nobles' financial difficulties after the war, Otto Harrach continued his father's philanthropic tradition and old Bohemian patriotism by donating over four hundred thousand crowns to various Czech charities between 1918 and 1925.[112]

Conclusion

The forces for continuity across the World War I divide were quite strong for the East-Central European aristocracy generally. Despite the political and economic losses suffered by the Counts Harrach and much of the old Austrian nobility after 1918, these nobles carried on their lifestyles at a sociocultural level distinguished by wealth, exclusivity, and self-image. Of course, we should not idealize or over-generalize this survival, as some nobles were far more successful than others. In particular, subgroups among the former imperial officers and bureaucrats, as well as unemployed second-born sons, were harshly affected by the processes of decline. In this sense, postwar aristocratic circles were comprised of either wealthy landowners or weak remnants of the imperial past, and individual noble houses often contained both.

Yet neither should the Austrian nobility's losses in the Great War be overestimated, particularly in comparison to those of the middle classes. German-speaking civil servants, officers, pensioners, and rentiers saw their savings and incomes evaporate as a result of wartime and postwar hyperinflation. According to the Austrian Social Democratic leader Otto Bauer, thousands of well-situated prewar *Bürger* only managed to survive by selling jewelry and old glass- or silverware, letting rooms in their homes, dismissing their domestic servants, and even canceling their theatre subscriptions. In terms of fortune, status, and power, they were the real losers of the world war.[113] World War I was by no means as destructive for the Central European nobility as the next world war would be, above all in the countries in which communism was established.

Konstantinos Raptis is Associate Professor in Modern European History at the National and Kapodistrian University of Athens, from which he graduated. He did his PhD at the Institute of Economic and Social History of the University of Vienna. His research interests lie in the history of the middle classes, the nobility, and nationalism in Central Europe, which are the focus of his main publications in German, English, French, and Greek. He recently published *Die Grafen Harrach und ihre Welt 1884–1945* (Vienna: Böhlau, 2017). He has taught and given lectures at universities in Austria, Germany, Slovenia, and the United States.

Notes

1. Ernst Hannisch, *Der lange Schatten des Staates: Österreichische Gesellschaftsgeschichte im 20. Jahrhundert* (Vienna: Ueberreuter, 1994), 263: "How else can the dissolution of the Habsburg Monarchy be characterized if not as a revolution? Whatever was built throughout the centuries collapsed within weeks, days, hours."
2. Ernst Bruckmüller, *Sozialgeschichte Österreichs*, 2nd ed. (Vienna: Verlag für Geschichte und Politik, 2001), 365; Robert Bideleux and Ian Jeffries, *A History of Eastern Europe: Crisis and Change*, 2nd ed. (London: Routledge, 2007), 315–16.
3. Hannes Stekl, "Zwischen Machtverlust und Selbstbehauptung: Österreichs Hocharistokratie vom 18. bis ins 20. Jahrhundert," in *Adel und Bürgertum in der Habsburgermonarchie 18. bis 20. Jahrhundert: Hannes Stekl zum 60. Geburtstag*, ed. Hannes Stekl and Ernst Bruckmüller (Vienna: Verlag für Geschichte und Politik/ Oldenbourg Wissenschaftsverlag, 2004), 30–31; Solomon Wank, "Aristocrats and Politics in Austria, 1867–1914: A Case of Historiographical Neglect," *East European Quarterly* 26, no. 2 (1992): 137–39.
4. These were mainly the cases of the German-speaking nobility in Bohemia and Moravia and the Yugoslav lands of Croatia and Slovenia, as well as the Hungarian nobles in Slovakia (and Transylvania, which was annexed to Romania). See Iván T. Berend, *Decades of Crisis: Central and Eastern Europe before World War II* (Berkeley: University of California Press, 2001), 290.
5. Eagle Glassheim, *Noble Nationalists: The Transformation of the Bohemian Aristocracy* (Cambridge, MA: Harvard University Press, 2005), 5, 53.
6. Bylaws passed on 10 December 1918 in Czechoslovakia and on 10 April 1919 in Austria.
7. Hannes Stekl, "Österreichs Adel im 20. Jahrhundert," in *Deutscher Adel im 19. und 20. Jahrhundert*, ed. Günther Schulz and Markus A. Denzel (St. Katharinen: Scripta Mercaturae, 2004), 35–36.
8. Bruckmüller, *Sozialgeschichte Österreichs*, 364 and 369–70; and Hannisch, *Der lange Schatten des Staates*, 74.
9. See the pioneering work of Stephan Malinowski, *Vom König zum Führer: Sozialer Niedergang und politische Radikalisierung im deutschen Adel zwischen Kaiserreich und NS-Staat* (Berlin: Akademieverlag, 2003), 260–66.
10. Stekl, "Zwischen Machtverlust und Selbstbehauptung," 27 and 32.

11. Oszkár Jászi, *The Dissolution of the Habsburg Monarchy* (Chicago: University of Chicago Press, 1929), 134.
12. Bideleux and Jeffries, *A History of Eastern Europe*, 315 and 359.
13. The Harrachs are regarded as being of Bohemian origin, with a pedigree going back to fourteenth-century Upper Austria. Originally they were knights and barons, elevated by the emperor to imperial counts in 1627. The estate of Stauff zu Aschach in Upper Austria as well as the estates of Janowitz (now Janovice in Rýmařov) and Groß Meseritsch (now Velké Meziříčí) in Moravia belonged to Alfred Harrach, the brother of Johann Nepomuk, head of the house from 1884 to 1909. The possessions in Hungary, situated on the Austro-Hungarian border and after World War I in Austrian Burgenland, constituted a unified complex with the Lower Austrian estate and were administrated from Bruck an der Leitha. See *Gothaischer Genealogischer Hofkalender nebst diplomatisch-statistischem Jahrbuche* (Gotha: Justus Perthes, 1910), 131–32. For an overview of the Harrachs, see Konstantinos Raptis, *Die Grafen Harrach und ihre Welt 1884–1945* (Vienna: Böhlau, 2017).
14. William D. Godsey Jr., "Quarterings and Kinship: The Social Composition of the Habsburg Aristocracy in the Dualist Era," *The Journal of Modern History* 71, no. 1 (1999): 61–62.
15. Franz Planer, ed., *Das Jahrbuch der Wiener Gesellschaft* (Vienna, 1929), 229–30. For the importance of imperial titles and honorary services for members of the court nobility, as well as for the social status of the aristocratic "first society" of the Habsburg Monarchy, see Godsey, "Quarterings and Kinship," 65–75.
16. Cf. Helmut Rumpler and Peter Urbanitsch, eds., *Die Habsburgermonarchie, 1848–1918*, vol. 7, bk. 1, *Verfassung und Parlamentarismus* (Vienna: Verlag der Österreichische Akademie der Wissenschaften, 2000), 1233–40; see also Alois Scheucher, Anton Wald, Hermann Lein, and Eduard Staudinger, *Zeitbilder: Geschichte und Sozialkunde*, vol. 7, *Vom Beginn des Industriezeitalters bis zum Zweiten Weltkrieg* (Vienna: ÖBV Pädagogischer Verlag, 1998), 59–60.
17. Gernot Stimmer, *Eliten in Österreich, 1848–1970* (Vienna: Böhlau, 1997), 1:278–93.
18. Lothar Höbelt, "Adel und Politik seit 1848," in *Die Fürstenberger: 800 Jahre Herrschaft und Kultur in Mitteleuropa*, ed. Erwein H. Eltz and Arno Strohmeyer (Korneuburg: Ueberreuter, 1994), 367.
19. For the radicalization of Austrian society, see, among others, Bruckmüller, *Sozialgeschichte Österreichs*, 360–62.
20. Piotr Stefan Wandycz, *The Price of Freedom: A History of East-Central Europe from the Middle Ages to the Present*, 2nd ed. (London: Routledge, 2001), 216; Berend, *Decades of Crisis*, 128 and 140–42.
21. Eagle Glassheim, "Genteel Nationalists: Nobles and Fascism in Czechoslovakia," in *European Aristocracies and the Radical Right, 1918–1939*, ed. Karina Urbach (Oxford: Oxford University Press, 2007), 149; Stekl, "Österreichs Adel," 38.
22. Berthold Waldstein-Wartenberg, "Das Adelsaufhebungsgesetz von 1919," *Mitteilungen des Österreichischen Staatsarchivs* 25 (1972): 306–14, quoted in Stekl, "Österreichs Adel," 38.
23. Lothar Höbelt, "Nostalgic Agnostics: Austrian Aristocrats and Politics, 1918–1938" in *European Aristocracies and the Radical Right, 1918–1939*, ed. Karina Urbach (Oxford: Oxford University Press, 2007), 161–62.

24. Bruckmüller, *Sozialgeschichte Österreichs*, 369.
25. Höbelt, "Nostalgic Agnostics," 167. Besides, the Christian Socials "represented the only bulwark against socialism."
26. Stekl, "Österreichs Adel," 52–56.
27. Ibid., 41–42 and 50–51.
28. Lothar Höbelt, "Die Konservativen Alt-Österreichs 1848 bis 1918," in *Konservativismus in Österreich: Strömungen, Ideen, Personen und Vereinigungen von den Anfängen bis heute*, ed. Robert Rill and Ulrich E. Zellenberg (Graz: Leopold Stocker, 1999), 119–120; Jiří Georgiev, *Až do těch hrdel a statků? Konzervativní myšlení a otázka samosprávy v politických strategiích české státoprávní šlechty po roce 1848* (Prague: Nakladatelství Lidové Noviny, 2011), 303–4.
29. The *Wiener Neueste Nachrichten* remained in publication until 1945.
30. Höbelt, "Die Konservativen Alt-Österreichs," 113; Stimmer, *Eliten in Österreich*, 304–5; Stekl, "Zwischen Machtverlust und Selbstbehauptung," 29.
31. Österreichisches Staatsarchiv (Austrian State Archives, ÖStA), Allgemeines Verwaltungsarchiv (AVA), Familienarchiv (Fa) Harrach, Karton (Kt.) 877, Phönix Verlagsgesellschaft, Gesellschaftsvertrag laut dem Notariatsakt, 5 September 1917, and Programm für die redaktionelle Führung der Zeitschrift, *Die Monarchie*, 22 April 1918. See also Konstantinos Raptis, "Auf dem Weg zum Niedergang? Österreichischer Hochadel im Ersten Weltkrieg am Beispiel der Familie Harrach," in *Deutscher Adel im 19. und 20. Jahrhundert*, ed. Günther Schulz and Markus A. Denzel (St. Katharinen: Scripta Mercaturae, 2004), 388–94.
32. The other aristocrats who were associated with this project and shareholders in Phönix were Ferdinand Zdenko, Fürst Lobkowitz, Dr. Jaroslav Graf Thun-Hohenstein, and Alfons Graf Mensdorff-Pouilly. ÖStA, AVA, Fa Harrach, Kt. 877, Phönix Verlagsgesellschaft, Gesellschafts-Vertrag laut dem am 5.9.1917 angezeigten Notariatsakt (Geschäftszahl 26964).
33. ÖStA, AVA, Fa Harrach, Korrespondenz Otto, Kt. 866, letter from Dr. Aemilian Schöpfer, 29 September 1918.
34. ÖStA, AVA, Fa Harrach, Korrespondenz Otto, Kt. 861, letters from Dr. Viktor and Ludwig Fuchs, 11 and 16 January 1919; Kt. 877, Phönix, Verlagsgesellschaft, letter from Dr. Aemilian Schöpfer to the People's Confederation of Austrian Catholics, 22 March 1919.
35. ÖStA, AVA, Fa Harrach, Korrespondenz Otto, Kt. 861, letter from Dr. Joseph Eberle, managing editor of *Das neue Reich*, 12 August 1920; Kt. 866, letter from Dr. Schöpfer, 16 November 1918; Kt. 877, Phönix, Verlagsgesellschaft, letter from Dr. Victor Fuchs, 16 April 1920.
36. Stefan Hanzer, "Die Zeitschrift *Das neue Reich*" (PhD diss., University of Vienna, 1973), 31.
37. Höbelt, "Nostalgic Agnostics," 161–62.
38. Glassheim, "Genteel Nationalists," 150.
39. Count Franz Harrach is perhaps most famous for owning the car in which the Archduke Franz Ferdinand and his wife were riding during their procession through Sarajevo on 28 June 1914. At the moment of their assassination, Franz Harrach himself was standing on the car's running board to protect his future sovereign. See Manfried Rauchensteiner, *Der Erste Weltkrieg und das Ende der Habsburgermonarchie* (Vienna: Böhlau, 2013), 108.

40. Moravský zemský archiv v Brně (Moravian Regional Archives in Brno, MZA), G 393, Rodinný Archiv Harrachů (Harrach Family Archive, RAH), Kt. 76, Fol. 1024, letter from Otto Harrach to his cousin Franz Harrach, Hradek, 23 June 1920.
41. Glassheim, "Genteel Nationalists," 152.
42. Ibid., 156–59; Glassheim, *Noble Nationalists*, 149–50 and 157.
43. Glassheim, *Noble Nationalists*, 238–41.
44. Ibid., 178–88.
45. MZA, G 393, RAH, Kt. 76, Fol. 1024, letters from Otto Harrach to Franz Harrach, Strkov, 20 and 31 August 1927.
46. ÖStA, AVA, Fa Harrach, Korrespondenz Otto, Kt. 971, letter to his cousin Hans Albrecht, Hradek, 28 July 1935; Kt. 917, Johann Graf Harrach (Hans), Rechnungen 1936.
47. Glassheim, "Genteel Nationalists," 159.
48. Bruckmüller, *Sozialgeschichte Österreichs*, 359. For the dramatic circumstances in Bohemia, see Otto Urban, *Die tschechische Gesellschaft: 1848 bis 1918* (Vienna: Böhlau, 1994), 1:840–54; Glassheim, "Genteel Nationalists," 149.
49. For data on the Harrach family's possessions, see Ignaz Tittel, *Schematismus und Statistik des Grossgrundbesitzes und grösserer Rustikalgüter im Königreiche Böhmen* (Prague: Josef Springer, 1906), 182–89; Ignaz Tittel, *Schematismus landtäflicher Güter, grösserer Rustikalwirtschaften, Beamten und Pächter* (Prague: Josef Springer, 1910), 126; Sigrid Hanna Knaf, "Die Entwicklung des landtäflichen Großgrundbesitzes in Niederösterreich von 1848 bis 1908" (PhD diss., University of Vienna, 1981), 99–100; *Schematismus des landtäflichen und Großgrund-Besitzes von Nieder-Österreich* (Vienna: Leopold Weiss, 1903), 20 and 168. For a comparative picture of the possessions of the aristocracy in Bohemia and Lower Austria before 1918, see the maps and graphics in Höbelt, "Adel und Politik seit 1848," 367–70.
50. ÖStA, AVA, Fa Harrach, Finanzielles Otto, Kt. 881, Übersichtliche Darstellung des Allod-, Nachlassvermögens nach Johann Grafen Harrach.
51. Godsey, "Quarterings and Kinship," 81–82; Eckart Conze, *Von deutschem Adel: Die Grafen von Bernstorff im zwanzigsten Jahrhundert* (Stuttgart: Deutsche Verlags-Anstalt, 2000), 16.
52. Stekl, "Österreichs Adel," 69.
53. ÖStA, AVA, Fa Harrach, Kt. 971, Otto Harrach to his son Hans, Vienna, 7 March 1925, and Hradek, 5 September 1931.
54. Berend, *Decades of Crisis*, 25.
55. Richard J. Crampton, *Eastern Europe in the Twentieth Century and After* (London: Routledge, 1997), 63.
56. Stekl, "Österreichs Adel," 64. This law came into force on 21 July 1919.
57. Glassheim, "Genteel Nationalists," 150; Berend, *Decades of Crisis*, 290. Stekl, "Österreichs Adel," 64.
58. Stekl, "Österreichs Adel," 64–65.
59. Karl Schwarzenberg, *Geschichte des reichsständischen Hauses Schwarzenberg* (Neustadt an der Aisch: Degener, 1963), 255–58; Vladimír Votýpka, *Böhmischer Adel: Familiengeschichten* (Vienna: Böhlau, 2007), 169.
60. Rudolf Lustig and František Světnička, *Schematismus velkostatků v Čechách* (Prague: Nakladatelství Mars, 1933), 332–35; *Jahr- und Adressbuch der Land- und Forstwirtschaft,*

Ergänzungsband 1930/31, ed. Österreichische Agrarische Zentralstelle in Wien (Vienna: Agrarverlag, 1930), 95.
61. Stekl, "Österreichs Adel," 63.
62. MZA, G 393, RAH, Kt. 76, Fol. 1024, letter from Otto Harrach to Franz Harrach, Hradek, 21 October 1922.
63. Lustig and Světnička, *Schematismus velkostatků*, 332–35; Oldřich Turčín and V. Bečvářová, "Velkostatek [Herrschaft] Sadová 1599–1948," unpublished catalogue compiled by the Státní archiv Zámrsk (State Archives in Zámrsk), 1963, IV.
64. Wank, "Aristocrats and Politics," 136.
65. ÖStA, AVA, Fa Harrach, Kt. 857, Finanzielles Otto, Kt. 881, Übersichtliche Darstellung des Allod-Nachlass-Vermögens nach Johann Grafen Harrach. Tittel, *Schematismus und Statistik*, 182–89, Lustig and Světnička, *Schematismus velkostatků*, 332–35.
66. Karl Bachinger and Vlastislav Lacina, "Wirtschaftliche Ausgangsbedingungen," in *Österreich und die Tschechoslowakei 1919–1938: Die wirtschaftliche Neuordnung in Zentraleuropa in der Zwischenkriegszeit*, ed. Alice Teichova and Herbert Matis (Vienna: Böhlau, 1996), 61.
67. Adam Wandruszka and Peter Urbanitsch, eds., *Die Habsburgermonarchie 1848–1918*, vol. 1, *Die wirtschaftliche Entwicklung* (Vienna: Verlag der Österreichische Akademie der Wissenschaften, 1973), 442.
68. Lustig and Světnička, *Schematismus velkostatků*, 332–35.
69. ÖStA, AVA, Fa Harrach, Kt. 971, Summarische Aufstellung der Aktiven und Passiven, Vienna, 1 September 1936, Nachlass Otto Graf Harrach.
70. Interview with Ernst Leonhard Graf von Harrach, Bruck an der Leitha, 12 September 2008.
71. Josef Fencl, "Die Fürstenbergischen Brauereien in Böhmen," in *Die Fürstenberger*, ed. Eltz and Strohmeyer, 342–50; Jiří Šouša, "Das Fürstenbergische Forstwesen auf der Herrschaft Křivoklát, 1735–1929," in *Die Fürstenberger*, ed. Eltz and Strohmeyer, 351–56. Fürstenberg paid 10,000 Czechoslovak crowns per year to lease the plant.
72. Votýpka, *Böhmischer Adel*, 44.
73. Ibid., 112 and 153–54.
74. ÖStA, AVA, Fa Harrach, Finanzielles Otto, Kt. 881, Rekapitulation mit der Summe der monatlichen Gehälter der Bediensteten 1916; Kt. 882, Verzeichnis von 53 versicherungspflichtigen Beamten in Prugg-Rohrau in Niederösterreich, 23 July 1920.
75. Tittel, *Schematismus landtäflicher Güter*, 121–26; Lustig and Světnička, *Schematismus velkostatků*, 332–35.
76. Lustig and Světnička, *Schematismus velkostatků*.
77. MZA, G 393, RAH, Kt. 76, Fol. 1024, letter from Otto Harrach to his cousin Franz Harrach, Hradek, 21 October 1922.
78. ÖStA, AVA, Fa Harrach, Kt. 885, Wirtschaftskorr. Finanzielles, 1898–1919, Konto-Bilanzen, 1918–1919, Stand der Hauptkassa, 28 February 1919.
79. ÖStA, AVA, Fa Harrach, Kt. 882, Bekenntnis zur einmaligen großen Vermögensabgabe in Österreich (1921), 54. Beilageblatt 8. Ausweis über das an das Ausland gebundene Vermögen des Abgaben-pflichtigen Otto Harrach.
80. ÖStA, AVA, Fa Harrach, Kt. 971, Verlassenschafts-gebühren 1937, Zahlungsauftrag von Berního úřadu v Nechanice (Nechanic tax office), Okresního finančního ředitelství v Hradci Králové (Königgrätz district financial directorate), Hradec Králové, 15 March 1940. In 1920, one Czechoslovak crown was worth 3.75 German-Austrian crowns.

81. ÖStA, AVA, Fa Harrach, Kt. 885, Wirtschaftskorrespondenz-Finanzielles, 1898–1919, Otto Harrach an seine Hauptkassa in Wien, Hrádek, 30 April 1918 (Erlass No 173); Zahlungsbestätigungen der k. k. Steueradministration für den I. Bezirk, Wien, 3–4 May 1918; Kt. 882, Bekenntnis zur einmaligen großen Vermögensabgabe, Empfangsbestätigung der Taxamtskasse Wien, 8 February 1922.
82. ÖStA, AVA, Fa Harrach, Kt. 883, Steuerakten. Steueradministration für den I. Bezirk in Wien an Otto Harrach, 14 May, 23 June and 13 September 1923.
83. ÖStA, AVA, Fa Harrach, Kt. 913, Testament Johann Graf Harrach, 22 August 1904, para. 1, 4; Kt. 654, Johann Nepomuk Familiensachen-Verlassenschaft; Kt. 856, Otto an Franz Josef Emmler, August 1915.
84. Glassheim, *Noble Nationalists*, 122.
85. ÖStA, AVA, Fa Harrach, Korrespondenz Otto, Kt. 856, letters from his wife, Karoline, 17 August 1907, 20 and 30 April 1909, 31 March and 13 June 1909, 28 February 1911, 23 and 25 August 1915, 7 October and 4 December 1916.
86. Entry for *Hofball* in Felix Czeike, *Historisches Lexikon Wien* (Vienna: Kremayr & Scheriau, 1994), 2:219; and entry for *Ball bei Hof* in Czeike, *Historisches Lexikon Wien* (Vienna: Kremayr & Scheriau, 1992), 1:237.
87. ÖStA, AVA, Fa Harrach, Korrespondenz Otto, Kt. 857, letter from his sister baroness Anna Henn von Henneberg-Spiegel, 8 February 1917.
88. ÖStA, AVA, Fa Harrach, Kt. 856, letter from his wife, Karoline, Strkow, 15 September 1916; Kt. 857, letter from his sister Gabriele Marenzi, Neupernstein (Kirchdorf an der Krems, Upper Austria), 14 July 1918; letter from Franz Czernin, Schönhof (now Krásný Dvůr), 6 April 1918. Otto's wife, Karoline, spent September 1916 and April 1918 in Karlsbad and the two last weeks of June 1918 in Bad Liebenstein.
89. ÖStA, AVA, Fa Harrach, Korrespondenz Otto, Kt. 856, letters from his wife, Karoline, 23 and 25 August 1915, 7 October and 4 December 1916; Kt. 857, letters from his sister Anna Henn von Henneberg-Spiegel, 9 August 1914, 16 August 1917 and 5 October 1918, letters from his sister Gabriele Marenzi, April 1915 and 20 June 1919; Kt. 858, letter from his sister Margarethe Windisch-Graetz, 17 September 1916; interview with Stephanie Harrach, 28 September 2004.
90. ÖStA, AVA, Fa Harrach, Korrespondenz Otto, Kt. 856, letters from his wife, Karoline, 5 April 1902, 15 April 1904, 20 November 1904, 25 April 1907, 1 May 1908, 17 April 1909, 25 May 1910, 28 March 1913, 23 September 1916, 26 July 1917; see also Kt. 864, letters from Prince August Lobkowitz, 21 October 1909, 19 October 1911, 23 October 1913, 15 August 1916, and 4 December 1918; Kt. 862, letters from Count Ferdinand Hildprandt, 4 May 1908, 5 May 1914, 29 April 1916, and 9 May 1918, as well as almost the entire correspondence Otto received from his stepbrother Ernst Harrach from 1905 to 1919 (Kt. 859).
91. ÖStA, AVA, Fa Harrach, Korrespondenz Otto, Kt. 864, letter from Eduard Lobkowitz, Wiener Neustadt, 27 November 1917.
92. Among them were members of the Abensperg-Traun, Auersperg, Belcredi, Bellegard, Buquoy, Chorinsky, Clam, Clary, Colloredo, Czernin, Esterhazy, Gudenus, Hardegg, Hohenlohe, Hoyos, Kinský, Kuefstein, Lazansky, Ledebur, Lanckoronski, Lobkowitz, Lubomirski, Ludwigstorff, Mensdorff, Palffy, Pallavicini, Potocki, Salm, Schönborn, Schönburg, Schwarzenberg, Sternberg, Thun, Thurn-Taxis, Trauttmansdorf, Waldburg, Walterskirchen, Wamboldt, Windisch-Graetz, and Zichy families.

93. See Appendix in Godsey, "Quarterings and Kinship," 96; Zdenko Radslav Kinský, *Zu Pferd und zu Fuss: 70 Jahre aus den Erinnerungen* (Vienna, 1974), 122–23, quoted in Glassheim, *Noble Nationalists*, 125.
94. ÖStA, AVA, Fa Harrach, Korrespondenz Otto, Kt. 858, letters from his sister Maria Theresia Wisniewski, Lemberg, 12 and 16 June 1916.
95. Interview with Stephanie Harrach und Arco-Zinneberg, 28 September 2004.
96. Cecilia Sternberg, *The Journey* (London: Collins, 1977), 71 and 18, quoted in Glassheim, *Noble Nationalists*, 122–23.
97. Glassheim, *Noble Nationalists*, 124.
98. Kinský, *Zu Pferd und zu Fuss*, 137 (cited in Glassheim, *Noble Nationalists*, 124–25).
99. MZA, G 393, RAH, Kt. 76, Fol. 1024, letters from Otto Harrach to his cousin Franz, dated 24 November 1924, 23 April 1925, 4 April 1926, 1 February 1927, 15 March 1928 (all sent from Prugg), and 17 April 1928 from Vienna.
100. ÖStA, AVA, Fa Harrach, Kt. 917, Johann Graf Harrach, Rechnungen 1936, 1942, and Stephanie Gräfin Harrach, Rechnungen 1941–43.
101. ÖStA, AVA, Fa Harrach, Familiensachen, Otto, Kt. 856, Testamentskonzept von 1925; interview with Stephanie Harrach, 28 September 2004.
102. ÖStA, AVA, Fa Harrach, Korrespondenz Otto, Kt. 858, letters from his sister Margarethe Windisch-Graetz, 24 June 1906, 1 July 1908, 9 December 1910, 29 September 1915, 11 January 1916, 5 March 1918.
103. ÖStA, AVA, Fa Harrach, Korrespondenz Otto, Kt. 859, letter from his sister Margarethe Windisch-Graetz, Grand Hotel, Gallspach, 10 November 1934.
104. ÖStA, AVA, Fa Harrach, Korrespondenz Otto, Kt. 857, letters from his brother-in-law Count Gabriel Marenzi, 27 May 1918, 12 March 1919; interview with Stephanie Harrach, 28 September 2004.
105. Zdeněk Jindra, "Der wirtschaftliche Zerfall Österreich-Ungarns," in *Österreich und die Tschechoslowakei 1919–1938: Die wirtschaftliche Neuordnung in Zentraleuropa in der Zwischenkriegszeit*, ed. Alice Teichova and Herbert Matis (Vienna, 1996), 20 and 38–44; Roman Sandgruber, *Ökonomie und Politik: Österreichische Wirtschaftsgeschichte vom Mittelalter bis zur Gegenwart* (Vienna, 1995), 323–26.
106. ÖStA, AVA, Fa Harrach, Korrespondenz Otto, Kt. 857, letters from his sister Anna Henn von Henneberg-Spiegel, 21 November 1916, 30 June 1917, 17 November 1917, 28 August 1918; his sister Gabriele Marenzi, 29 April 1915, 25 December 1918; and his brother-in-law Gabriel Marenzi, 20 February and 29 September 1916, 21 November 1917, 6 March 1918; Kt. 858, his sister Margarethe Windisch-Graetz, 19 October and 14 December 1917, 21 January and 22 September 1918; Kt. 857, his sister Gabriele Marenzi, 22 October 1917; Kt. 867, letter from Count Vincenz Thurn und Valsassina, 10 November 1917; Kt. 861, letter from Prince Max Croy, 6 September 1918; Kt. 860, letter from Countess Giulietta Berchtold, February 1919.
107. ÖStA, AVA, Fa Harrach, Korrespondenz Otto, Kt. 857, letters from his sister Gabriele Marenzi, 29 April 1915, 25 December 1918; his brother-in-law Gabriel Marenzi, 20 February and 29 September 1916, 21 November 1917, 6 March 1918.
108. ÖStA, AVA, Fa Harrach, Korrespondenz Otto, Kt. 859, letters from his aunt Anna Harrach, 7 and 15 November 1916; Kt. 861, letter from Rudolf, Count of Czernin-Morzin, 13 March 1918.
109. "Das wohltätige war immer dabei" (the charity was always part of it), according to Stephanie Harrach, interview with Stephanie Harrach, 28 September 2004.

110. ÖStA, AVA, Fa Harrach, Korrespondenz Otto, Kt. 872, 873, Verbände und Vereine 1900–1919, letters from Franz Liechtenstein, Vienna, 21 and 27 October 1915; Rudolf Abensperg und Traun, Vienna, 10 January 1916.
111. ÖStA, AVA, Fa Harrach, Korrespondenz Otto, Kt. 872, 873, Verbände und Vereine 1900–1919; Planer, *Das Jahrbuch*, 229–30; *Gothaischer Genealogischer Hofkalender nebst diplomatisch-statistischem Jahrbuche* (Gotha: Julius Perthes, 1915), 134–35.
112. Glassheim, *Noble Nationalists*, 96. Glassheim's source is a letter dated 16 June 1926 from the director of the Harrach estate in Starkenbach to the Czechoslovak president.
113. Otto Bauer, *Die österreichische Revolution* (Vienna: Wiener Volksbuchhandlung, 1923), 75; Sandgruber, *Ökonomie und Politik*, 357–59; Ernst Bruckmüller, "Das österreichische Bürgertum zwischen Monarchie und Republik," *Zeitgeschichte* 20, no. 3–4 (1993): 67–70.

Bibliography

Bauer, Otto. *Die österreichische Revolution*. Vienna: Wiener Volksbuchhandlung, 1923.
Berend, Iván T. *Decades of Crisis: Central and Eastern Europe before World War II*. Berkeley: University of California Press, 2001.
Bideleux, Robert and Ian Jeffries. *A History of Eastern Europe: Crisis and Change*. 2nd ed. London: Routledge, 2007.
Bruckmüller, Ernst. "Das österreichische Bürgertum zwischen Monarchie und Republik." *Zeitgeschichte* 20, no. 3–4 (1993): 60–84.
———. *Sozialgeschichte Österreichs*. 2nd ed. Vienna: Verlag für Geschichte und Politik, 2001.
Conze, Eckart. *Von deutschem Adel: Die Grafen von Bernstorff im zwanzigsten Jahrhundert*. Stuttgart: Deutsche Verlags-Anstalt, 2000.
Crampton Richard J. *Eastern Europe in the Twentieth Century and After*. London: Routledge, 1997.
Czeike, Felix. *Historisches Lexikon Wien*. 2 volumes. Vienna: Kremayr & Scheriau, 1992–94.
Eltz, Erwein H. and Arno Strohmeyer, eds. *Die Fürstenberger: 800 Jahre Herrschaft und Kultur in Mitteleuropa*. Korneuburg: Ueberreuter, 1994.
Georgiev, Jiří. *Až do těch hrdel a statků? Konzervativní myšlení a otázka samosprávy v politických strategiích české státoprávní šlechty po roce 1848*. Prague: Nakladatelství Lidové Noviny, 2011.
Glassheim, Eagle. *Noble Nationalists: The Transformation of the Bohemian Aristocracy*. Cambridge, MA: Harvard University Press, 2005.
Godsey, William D., Jr. "Quarterings and Kinship: The Social Composition of the Habsburg Aristocracy in the Dualist Era." *The Journal of Modern History* 71, no. 1 (1999): 56–104.
Gothaischer Genealogischer Hofkalender nebst diplomatisch-statistischem Jahrbuche. Gotha: Justus Perthes, 1910 and 1915.
Hanisch, Ernst. *Der lange Schatten des Staates: Österreichische Gesellschaftsgeschichte im 20. Jahrhundert*. Vienna: Ueberreuter, 1994.
Hanzer, Stefan. "Die Zeitschrift *Das neue Reich*." PhD diss., University of Vienna, 1973.
Höbelt, Lothar. "Die Konservativen Alt-Österreichs 1848 bis 1918." In *Konservativismus in Österreich: Strömungen, Ideen, Personen und Vereinigungen von den Anfängen bis heute*, edited by Robert Rill and Ulrich E. Zellenberg, 109–52. Graz: Leopold Stocker, 1999.

Jászi, Oszkár. *The Dissolution of the Habsburg Monarchy*. Chicago: University of Chicago Press, 1929.
Knaf, Sigrid Hanna. "Die Entwicklung des landtäflichen Großgrundbesitzes in Niederösterreich von 1848 bis 1908." PhD diss., University of Vienna, 1981.
Lustig, Rudolf and František Světnička. *Schematismus velkostatků v Čechách*. Prague: Nakladatelství Mars, 1933.
Malinowski, Stephan. *Vom König zum Führer: Sozialer Niedergang und politische Radikalisierung im deutschen Adel zwischen Kaiserreich und NS-Staat*. Berlin: Akademieverlag, 2003.
Österreichische Agrarische Zentralstelle in Wien, ed. *Jahr- und Adressbuch der Land- und Forstwirtschaft, Ergänzungsband 1930/31*. Vienna: Agrarverlag, 1930.
Planer, Franz, ed. *Das Jahrbuch der Wiener Gesellschaft*. Vienna: Franz Planer, 1929.
Raptis, Konstantinos. "Auf dem Weg zum Niedergang? Österreichischer Hochadel im Ersten Weltkrieg am Beispiel der Familie Harrach." In *Deutscher Adel im 19. und 20. Jahrhundert*, edited by Günther Schulz and Markus A. Denzel, 377–96. St. Katharinen: Scripta Mercaturae, 2004.
———. *Die Grafen Harrach und ihre Welt 1884–1945*. Vienna: Böhlau, 2017.
Rauchensteiner, Manfried. *Der Erste Weltkrieg und das Ende der Habsburgermonarchie*. Vienna: Böhlau, 2013.
Rumpler, Helmut and Peter Urbanitsch, eds. *Die Habsburgermonarchie, 1848–1918*. Vol. 7, *Verfassung und Parlamentarismus*. Vienna: Verlag der Österreichische Akademie der Wissenschaften, 2000.
Sandgruber, Roman. *Ökonomie und Politik: Österreichische Wirtschaftsgeschichte vom Mittelalter bis zur Gegenwart*. Vienna: Ueberreuter, 1995.
Schematismus des landtäflichen und Großgrund-Besitzes von Nieder-Österreich. Vienna: Leopold Weiss, 1903.
Scheucher, Alois, Anton Wald, Hermann Lein, and Eduard Staudinger. *Zeitbilder: Geschichte und Sozialkunde*, vol. 7, *Vom Beginn des Industriezeitalters bis zum Zweiten Weltkrieg*. Vienna: ÖBV Pädagogischer Verlag, 1998.
Schwarzenberg, Karl. *Geschichte des reichsständischen Hauses Schwarzenberg*. Neustadt an der Aisch: Degener, 1963.
Stekl, Hannes. "Österreichs Adel im 20. Jahrhundert." In *Deutscher Adel im 19. und 20. Jahrhundert*, edited by Günther Schulz and Markus A. Denzel, 35–80. St. Katharinen: Scripta Mercaturae, 2004.
———. "Zwischen Machtverlust und Selbstbehauptung: Österreichs Hocharistokratie vom 18. bis ins 20. Jahrhundert." In *Adel und Bürgertum in der Habsburgermonarchie 18. bis 20. Jahrhundert: Hannes Stekl zum 60. Geburtstag*, edited by Hannes Stekl and Ernst Bruckmüller, 14–34. Vienna: Verlag für Geschichte und Politik/Oldenbourg Wissenschaftsverlag, 2004.
Stimmer, Gernot. *Eliten in Österreich, 1848–1970*. 2 vols. Vienna: Böhlau, 1997.
Teichova, Alice and Herbert Matis, eds. *Österreich und die Tschechoslowakei 1919–1938: Die wirtschaftliche Neuordnung in Zentraleuropa in der Zwischenkriegszeit*. Vienna: Böhlau, 1996.
Tittel, Ignaz. *Schematismus und Statistik des Grossgrundbesitzes und grösserer Rustikalgüter im Königreiche Böhmen*. Prague: Josef Springer, 1906.
———. *Schematismus landtäflicher Güter, grösserer Rustikalwirtschaften, Beamten und Pächter*. Prague: Josef Springer, 1910.

Turčín, Oldřich and V. Bečvářová. "Velkostatek [Herrschaft] Sadová 1599–1948," unpublished catalogue compiled by the Státni archiv Zámrsk. State Archives in Zámrsk, 1963, IV.

Urbach, Karina, ed. *European Aristocracies and the Radical Right 1918–1939*. Oxford: Oxford University Press, 2007.

Urban, Otto. *Die tschechische Gesellschaft: 1848 bis 1918*. Vol. 1. Vienna: Böhlau, 1994.

Votýpka, Vladimír. *Böhmischer Adel: Familiengeschichten*. Vienna: Böhlau, 2007.

Wandruszka, Adam and Peter Urbanitsch, eds. *Die Habsburgermonarchie 1848–1918*. Vol. 1, *Die wirtschaftliche Entwicklung*. Vienna: Verlag der Österreichische Akademie der Wissenschaften, 1973.

Wandycz, Piotr Stefan. *The Price of Freedom: A History of East-Central Europe from the Middle Ages to the Present*. 2nd ed. London: Routledge, 2001.

Wank, Solomon. "Aristocrats and Politics in Austria, 1867–1914: A Case of Historiographical Neglect." *East European Quarterly* 26, no. 2 (1992): 133–48.

Chapter 10

SINNER, SAINT—OR CIPHER?
The Austrian Republic and the Death of Emperor Karl I

Christopher Brennan

In November 1919, when the "Emperor Karl" section of Vienna's *Ringstrasse* reverted to its original name (*Opernring*), the city's most tangible reminder of the last Habsburg ruler disappeared.[1] After World War I, sixty-one streets and twelve bridges had their monarchist name changed, with rare exceptions such as Emperors Franz Joseph I and Franz I, Archduke Karl, and the *Habsburgergasse*.[2] The former Karl I, however, was still alive, banished not only from Vienna's streetscape, but also from his Austrian homeland. Since he had never formally abdicated any of his thrones, his brief internal exile in Eckartsau Castle after the collapse of the Habsburg Monarchy rapidly became untenable to the new republican government in Vienna and to the empire's successor states, not to mention a danger to Karl himself and his family.[3] Thus, in March 1919, Colonel Edward Lisle Strutt, who had been sent by King George V to provide Karl with protection as well as "moral and material support," besought the Swiss for asylum.[4] Karl had no choice but to leave.[5] A few days later, the so-called "Law of 3 April 1919" banned the House of Habsburg-Lorraine from Austria, removing in perpetuity its right to rule and nationalizing its property. Only family members who renounced their membership of the dynasty and any associated claims, and who swore fidelity to the republic, were allowed to stay.[6] Such a surrender was inconceivable to Karl. Yet he kept a low profile in his Swiss exile. During 1919 and 1920, the often-ill ex-ruler did not return to the lands of his former empire.[7]

Only in March 1921 did Karl first decide to reclaim his throne. The obvious place to do so was Hungary, a monarchy without a king under the regency of the still oath-bound Miklós Horthy.[8] Karl's attempt, however, ended in humiliation.[9] Although he had boasted of French support, Paris denied it. International pressure and Horthy's refusal to relinquish the crown forced Karl to retreat to Switzerland via Austria, where a hostile reception awaited him at the train station in Bruck an der Leitha.[10] The restless crowd exalted the republic, booed the Habsburgs, and hurled such insults at the former emperor as "syphilitic pimp, mass murderer, child kidnapper; throw him in the sewer, hang him." The incident was particularly revealing of working-class hatred toward Karl, much to his astonishment. The local mayor told him that the crowd was outraged by his "betrayal of the German people [during the war]" and "illegal appropriation of the crown jewels."[11]

While Karl played no role whatsoever in starting the world war, and genuinely sought to make peace and minimize bloodshed throughout his short reign, his reputation was not unsullied. Foremost, it suffered from his alleged treachery toward Germany in the Sixtus Affair, Karl's secret attempt to negotiate peace through his brother-in-law Sixtus of Bourbon-Parma, by which he committed to supporting France's "just claims to Alsace-Lorraine."[12] This was, in the words of the former German Plenipotentiary to Austro-Hungarian Headquarters, "the height of [his] scheming."[13] Even the Social Democrat Karl Renner, a German nationalist at heart, decried Karl in parliament in October 1921 as "the man who in the moment of defeat wanted to disown and betray his people, his state and its whole history!"[14] This alone condemned him as a traitor in the eyes of Germans both inside and outside Austria.

For others, Karl's amnesty for political prisoners in July 1917—unfairly remembered as "the Czech Amnesty"—constituted the greatest blot on his copybook. According to the pan-German Infantry General Alfred Krauß, "Back then, all loyal supporters of Austria turned away from the emperor, he lost their confidence; back then, the death throes of Austria began."[15] Other detractors focused on Karl's alleged failure to stand up to the Hungarians, his sacking of Chief of Staff Franz Conrad von Hötzendorf, his dismissal of the old guard at court, his purported cronyism, his risible last-gasp October Manifesto in 1918, and even his religious zeal and supposed susceptibility to female influences. In particular, the groundless, though widespread, portrayal of Karl's wife, the Empress Zita, as a Franco-Italian anti-German Lady Macbeth created a type of Austrian *Dolchstoßlegende*.[16] Despite the general enthusiasm inspired by Karl's youth and modesty, his easy charm, picturesque family, and his own bravery in the war, not to mention his blamelessness for its outbreak and sensible—if belatedly expressed—desire for a general peace in October/November 1918, the ex-emperor's immediate postwar legacy was a mixed bag.[17]

Undeterred, Karl unexpectedly mounted a second coup attempt later that year.[18] In October 1921, accompanied by Zita, he flew into western Hungary, swore in troops from the local garrison, and named a cabinet before heading toward Budapest by train in order to demand that Horthy surrender power to him unconditionally. The admiral, however, again stood his ground, emboldened this time by the anti-Habsburg consensus abroad, the manageable number of putschists (approximately four thousand men), the successful mobilization of his own soldiers, and by the relative calm in Budapest, which was under martial law.[19] A few shots were fired but Karl quickly gave up. On 26 October, he and Zita were whisked away to Tihany Abbey on Lake Balaton for temporary internment.[20] Yet despite surrendering unconditionally, Karl still refused to abdicate, or even to leave Hungarian territory.[21] Under foreign pressure, the Hungarian Prime Minister István Bethlen presented the hurriedly convened parliament with a bill for "The Removal of the Ruling Rights of His Majesty the King Karl IV and the Succession of the House of Habsburg," which was unanimously adopted on 6 November 1921 and became effective the following day.[22]

On the night of 31 October, the former imperial couple was taken to southern Hungary to board the British gunboat HMS *Glowworm* on the Danube.[23] The journey continued until Galați in Romania, where Karl and Zita embarked on the light cruiser HMS *Cardiff* to Constantinople. There, they would await their fate at the hands of the Great Powers.[24] They did not have to wait long. The *Bundesrat* in Bern swiftly decided to expel all members of Karl's household, including those Habsburgs not essential to his children's care.[25] Meanwhile, in Austria, business resumed as usual and Karl—whose foolhardy ventures had created a storm of controversy in the Lower House of Parliament[26] and the press[27]—gradually disappeared from newspaper columns and parliamentary minutes.[28] No notable figures came to his defense.

Eventually, the British suggestion of Madeira was accepted for Karl's banishment—an improvement on the Czechoslovaks' alleged proposal of Saint Helena, though a remoter venue than Malta, originally mooted by the Great Powers.[29] Karl's stay on the Portuguese island was to be short. When he disembarked on 18 November 1921, he only had 135 days left to live. It did not come entirely as a surprise.[30] As Josef Redlich, the last Austrian Finance Minister and a mourner of the monarchy (and, incidentally, a distinguished jurist and historian), wrote to his friend, the writer Hermann Bahr, in mid-October: "I fear that the young man will ultimately end up tragically. What fate for one who—despite the best of wills—does not have the talent to prove himself as an imperial and royal ruler."[31]

Karl's death at age thirty-four was indeed tragic: expelled from his homeland, forced to live in pitiable circumstances, physically and mentally defeated, and the focus of hatred and derision, he left a widow with seven children and an eighth in her womb on a faraway island whose damp and cool inland climate likely precipitated his death.[32] How was Karl's passing received by Austrians? What can the conflicting responses to his death tell us about changing attitudes toward the Habsburg regime as a whole? Surprisingly, there was little continued dynastic support in postwar Austria. Subjects who had suffered through the war and its deprivations generally considered Karl's reign to have been such a disaster that they opposed the very idea of a restoration. This is particularly paradoxical in light of the fact that most Austrians also considered their new country risible and unviable. Many pined for annexation with Germany. In a country almost entirely shaped by the Habsburgs, whose citizens were among the most dynastically minded of the bygone empire and whose institutions remained unchanged from imperial times, monarchism was neither a political force nor, even, a popular ideology.

As we will see below, the variety and virulence of the reactions to Karl's inglorious end were representative of the confusion, bitterness, fear, and uncertainty that had gripped Austria by 1922. Thus, a detailed examination of attitudes toward his death can help clarify the extraordinary shift in dynastic support that occurred between 1914 and 1922 (or even 1918 and 1922). This shift appears to indicate a violent rupture with the past. But closer examination will reveal less obvious elements of continuity as well.

Legally for republican Austria, Karl was merely a private person whose death required no official statement, though this silence was eased by the fact that the most prominent Christian Social monarchist, party chairman, prelate, and future

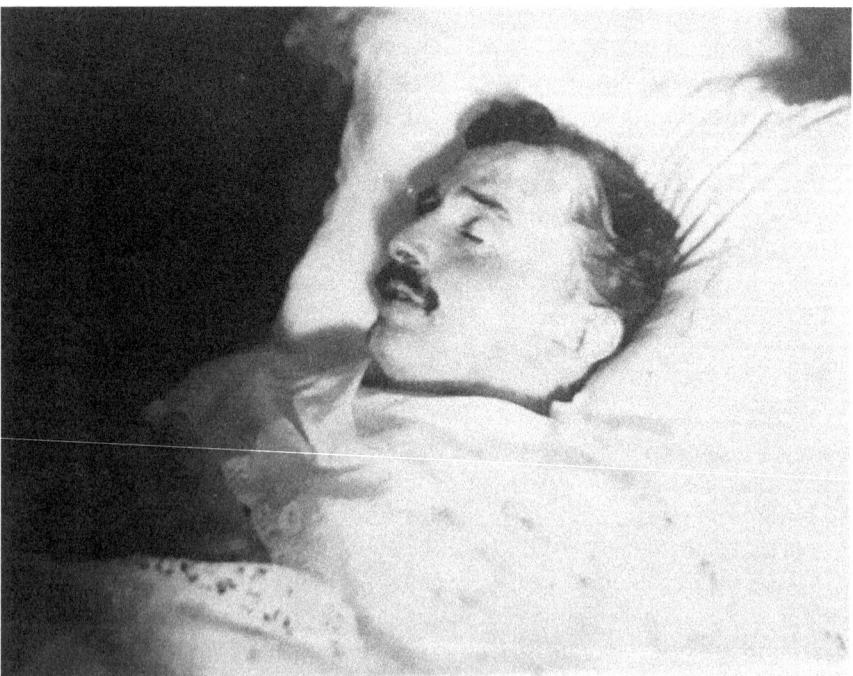

Figure 10.1. Karl on his deathbed in Madeira, 1922. Author's collection.

chancellor Ignaz Seipel was out of power.³³ In Hungary, Horthy and Prime Minister István Bethlen sent condolences to "Her Majesty the Empress and Queen Zita" in Funchal. Additionally, the Party of the Austrian Monarchists sent a telegraphic message to Zita expressing its "deepest patriotic pain upon the passing of Emperor Karl and its unshakeable loyalty to the heir [Karl's nine-year-old son Otto]."³⁴ The monarchist Party of all Black-and-Yellow Legitimists also sent a condolence telegram and planned a mourning rally and elegy in the Capuchin Church, the traditional resting place of Habsburg monarchs.³⁵ The Catholic Imperial Women's Organization wrote its commiserations to the former empress on behalf of three hundred thousand women.³⁶ Zita thanked all loyal royalists in the name of King Otto, but responded neither to the regent nor his government.³⁷ Consequently, the fiercest rhetorical debates over Karl's legacy played out in the Austrian press.

The liberal and historically pro-Habsburg *Neue Freie Presse* manifested understanding for Karl: "Far from the homeland, a solitary man has died. . . . Profound tragedy suffused the life which has now found its end, and human sympathy cannot be repressed upon seeing the bier. . . . The ex-Emperor Karl seemed born for happiness, but misfortune was in fact the lot which marked him out." Nevertheless, the paper did not shy from sharp criticism of Karl's political ability, including his lack of strength, inconsistency, poor training, and his tendency to make "rash decisions . . . [despite] proofs of goodness and goodwill."³⁸ It also criticized Karl's failure to win over the Czechs with the amnesty, the Hungarians with Tisza's removal, and the Entente with the letters to Sixtus.³⁹ These mistakes still rankled.

Similarly, the *Neues Wiener Journal*, a nonpartisan daily that described in detail Karl's agonizing last days, expressed its sincere grief: "A human tragedy has ended. . . . Ex-Emperor Karl has died in exile, young in years, a broken man, the victim of colossal events of volcanic violence, before which even a stronger man would have been too weak." The paper underlined both the abysmal situation Karl inherited as emperor, and his efforts toward peace. Repeating a well-worn refrain, it lamented Karl's choice of advisers and ministers, as well as his youthful fickleness, "which did not repel the catastrophe but accelerated it." The paper pithily concluded, "Emperor Karl wanted what was right and did what was wrong," even as it took pity on him as "one of the unluckiest [Habsburgs], above all because none of them faced so great a conflict between mission and power, between will and actions."⁴⁰

By contrast, the *Reichspost*, which always took care to address the ex-monarch as "Emperor Karl," "King Karl IV," or "the crowned Hungarian King," would only concede that he had "perhaps [been] too gentle and soft," not to mention too young.⁴¹ Despite Karl's clear insights and good intentions, editor Friedrich Funder argued, the situation by late 1916 was almost insoluble: it was "the perennial human motif of the ultimately vain struggles of a will directed only at pure and noble aims against forces beyond his reach."[42] The *Reichspost* went on ruefully:

> Today, in all the lands which were once the inheritance of the deceased, no bells are ringing, no black flags are announcing the death of this dethroned, banished man, who once counted among the most powerful in the world. But a hundred thousand heads and hearts bow—regardless of their political thoughts and feelings—before the painful majesty of this death.

Funder squarely blamed the Entente for killing Karl in a manner "less bloody, but no less cruel" than the Bolsheviks murdered the Tsar: "The shame of it will ring out for centuries to come." Nevertheless, Funder was careful to end on a conciliatory, if opaque, note of support for the republic.[43]

The Christian Social press was predictably unanimous in its praise for Karl, extolling his personality, noble character, and sincerity.[44] The *Linzer Volksblatt* noted that "Emperor Karl was a deeply religious man ... who felt no anger towards his enemies" and had never lost his faith. "God will glorify him," the paper insisted, "and make him triumph over all his enemies." The *Salzburger Chronik* concentrated on Karl's quest for peace, noting that it did "not belittle Karl's merit that he sought to save both his empire and his throne by undertaking peace initiatives." The front page of the *Allgemeiner Tiroler Anzeiger* bore a large portrait of Karl as emperor-king, surrounded by a black border. Its opening lines were unequivocal: "The life of the martyr emperor is extinct. Seized by deep pain, all those who listened to the public expressions of mourning, who remained true to him despite the scorn and mockery of almost overpowering violence, proved thereby that even in these sad times there are men who do not bow before the slogans of new intellectual fashions."[45] The *Kärntner Tagblatt* defended Karl's controversial restoration attempts as efforts to save Hungary from the horrors of Bolshevism and to restore her serenity and security. Grandiosely comparing his dilettantish putsches to Napoleon's Hundred Days, the paper regretted that "Karl negotiated when he should have acted."[46] Similarly, the veteran Christian Social politician Leopold Kunschak had nothing but praise for "the man who carried the proudest crown of Europe," and he found it particularly galling that so many viewed Karl's attempts at extracting Austria from the world war, a conflict for which he bore no responsibility, as undermining the military effort. Kunschak expressed his conviction that future generations of objective historians would rehabilitate Karl.[47]

Naturally, the little-read, if fervently legitimist, newspaper *Staatswehr*, whose motto was "Black and Yellow to the Bone," mourned Karl's death "from a broken heart." On the front page of its 14 April edition, the weekly called upon "honest working people" to denounce "the red terror," "the most egregious tyranny," "the worst kind of ochlocracy" of the Social Democrats. It then bemoaned the passing of "bright sunny days, when all of old Vienna showed its loyalty, love and devotion to its late emperor." Ever conspiratorial, another article expounded on the "international band of assassins," allegedly supported by the *Arbeiter-Zeitung*, who had on their conscience the death of Franz Ferdinand, his wife, the Romanovs, Empress Elisabeth, Austrian Prime Minister Karl von Stürgkh, and now Karl.[48] The newspaper also blamed the "Prussian, pan- and Greater Germans" who had prevented the conclusion of peace in good time, and the Social Democrats (and Freemasons) who had taken advantage of the lost war to achieve total collapse and "world domination." It singled out Otto Bauer, Victor Adler, and Friedrich Austerlitz (three Jewish Social Democrats) for criticism. Thus of all the protagonists, Karl was least to blame. The issue's largest headline was devoted to the new monarch, technically Otto the First, "by the grace of God, Emperor of Austria, King of Bohemia etc., and Apostolic King of Hungary second in name." It did not matter that there had been no official or clerical proclamation, for "whoever in Austria is a true patriot knows that for him Otto II is the guarantor of a better future, that it is incumbent upon him to fight and to succeed for the salvation of the Austrian people."[49]

Elsewhere on the cultural spectrum, the *Jüdische Presse* (the "Organ for the Interests of Orthodox Jewry") paid brief homage to Karl on page six: "Thus this regal drama faded into the nimbus of martyrdom. Beyond the political pros and cons, the memory of the last unfortunate ruler of the Danube Monarchy will remain in the heart of the people. His attitude towards Jewry corresponded to the tradition of his House." The article added that toward the end of the war, and after the revolution, Karl had resisted the antisemitic velleities of his environment and built new ties with Jewish legitimists.[50] He thus enjoyed the sympathy of both scarcely veiled antisemites and Orthodox Jews.

Neutral or sympathetic newspapers often published personal recollections by those who had known Karl, such as Franz Schießl, the long-serving director of Franz Joseph's Private Office who retired shortly after Karl's accession to power. In the *Neues Wiener Journal*, he admitted that Karl's passing had touched him deeply, and that his exilic death at such a young age, during which he experienced the bitterness of both a lost war and throne, made him a tragic figure.[51] In the same paper, the eccentric Count Adalbert Sternberg described Karl as "the best young man, most ideally invested with a modesty and a will for good, such as I have never seen in any other ruler in the world." Yet Sternberg also argued that Karl's sensitivity, apparently acquired from his mother's Saxon side, had ruined him: "The Habsburgs and Lorraines have had many good qualities, but heart was never one of them. They were diplomatic and they could also be benevolent, but they always lacked the empathy and emotion which Emperor Karl showed." Like many eulogists, Sternberg pointed out that Karl had played no role in the outbreak of war and had striven to bring back peace at any price, though he conceded that Karl's "misfortune" lay in "his lack of knowledge of human nature. . . . He was not born to be a ruler, he was not brought up to be a ruler. But even if he had been, he could not have withstood the collapse, because he was also the inheritor of a monarchic system which was no longer viable, like Louis XVI." He finished with a prescient flourish: "And however the future might and will think upon the present, it will think better of Emperor Karl than of those who betrayed him, maltreated him and broke his heart."[52]

Some of Karl's acquaintances felt duty-bound to defend the former emperor from calumny. Emmerich Zeno von Schonta, an aide-de-camp who followed Karl into exile and compiled a panegyric to his former master,[53] wrote a letter to

Figure 10.2. Memorial Bust of Emperor Karl I of Austria (Blessed Karl) in Vienna's Imperial (Capuchin) Crypt. Dedicated in a memorial mass on Karl's name day, 4 November 1931. Author's photo.

the *Reichspost* in an effort to quash the long-standing and false rumors of Karl's alcoholism.[54] "I had the honor of being around him almost uninterruptedly since January 1917," wrote Schonta, and "to see him at every hour of the day and night. Never in these five years did I see him even tiddly."[55] Karl consumed a glass of beer during midday and evening meals, as well as a glass of light Hungarian wine. As far as Schonta knew, nobody had ever dared put their name to these slanderous claims: "Anybody who spreads this rumor further [is] a disgraceful liar and [I] will treat him accordingly if I catch him."[56] Friedrich Austerlitz, the editor of the Social Democratic mouthpiece the *Arbeiter-Zeitung*, wasted no time in doing so, writing of Karl's last days: "a flu which his body, weakened by a fondness for alcohol, was not able to withstand, took him away."[57] Baron Albert von Margutti, who had known and liked Karl (despite some rather ambiguous writings about him),[58] wrote in his recollections of the period: "On 1 April 1922, in an almost naked room, in a faraway and inhospitable land, having eaten, six months long, the bread of a bitter exile, soaked, one can say, in his tears, the Emperor Karl of Habsburg, last in name, gave up the ghost."[59]

Finally, tabloid coverage of Karl's death—for instance, in the *Wiener Bilder, Illustrierte Kronen Zeitung, Wiener Illustrierte Zeitung, Das Interessante Blatt*, or the *Neuigkeits-Welt-Blatt*—showed that there was plenty of public interest left for royal drama, photographs, and anecdotes.

The Reaction of the Left

The Social Democrats' loathing of all things monarchic (and clerical) was nothing if not thorough. On 4 April 1922, three days after Karl's death, the Vienna city senate voted (admittedly with the help of the Christian Socials) to rename numerous institutions with imperial connections. Franz Joseph, Elisabeth, and Rudolf, among others, disappeared from many public buildings; and Karl, whose name was now attached only to a war veterans' home, was also consigned to history when the *Kaiser Karl-Kriegerheimstätten in Aspern* became, simply, *the Kriegerheimstätten in Aspern*.[60]

The unmoved *Arbeiter-Zeitung*, which always referred to the former emperor as "Karl Habsburg" (his legal name under the republic) or even "Karl the Last," came out with guns blazing, having informed readers two days earlier that reports of Karl's illness were exaggerated: "A man dying before his time is naturally sad," began the article.[61] However, it continued, the death of one individual paled in comparison to the millions who perished in the war and its aftermath—a war criminally begun by the Habsburgs. Furthermore, since Karl had refused to abdicate and retire into private life like a "stubborn child," his death was "certainly not a sentimental matter but a purely political one." Had he disappeared from the public eye, he could have lived peacefully in Eckartsau—a clear lie—or spent the rest of his days in Switzerland: "Whoever finds it so distressing that Karl had to live and die on the beautiful island of Madeira should bear in mind that nobody but the last Habsburg himself brought about his fate." Crushing the widespread notion that Karl would have been a successful peacetime emperor, the paper claimed his reign would have been "a true agony" for the people: "He was a completely ordinary man, who lacked everything that constitutes greatness: everything about him was vapid and insignificant." In sum, the world had lost nothing, and the Habsburgs were not to be pitied: "Their destiny is only the retribution of Nemesis for their conduct."[62] Even Social Democrats who had known Karl and cooperated with him (such as Karl Renner, the first chancellor of both the First and Second Republics) had no good word to spare for the deceased.

Yet crueller voices came from the far left. As he lay on his deathbed, the communist press, exemplified by *Die Rote Fahne*, poured scorn on the already condemned man:

> The Madeira cretin Karl Habsburg is allegedly seriously ill. The reports are so contradictory that one cannot tell whether it is a con, mere mawkishness, or a small case of alcohol poisoning. In any case, one would do well to wait for the official news of his death. At least then one will know that, for the first time in his life, Karl has not lied.[63]

The only disease the newspaper would concede to this "crummy scoundrel" was brain damage from birth: "His death would be the one and only judicious event in his life." After confirmation of Karl's dying, the journal commented: "Somebody has passed away, upon whose orders hundreds of thousands died and withered in agony. If anything is noteworthy about the death of Karl Habsburg, it is the fact that he was allowed to die peacefully in bed and that he was not hanged by the masses."[64] It concluded by warning workers to "observe precisely all the messages of sympathy, because they give clear evidence of the sharpness of the monarchic claw which hides in the republican-democratic cat's paw."[65]

Political Bickering

The ex-emperor was the subject of passionate debate between the Social Democrat and Christian Social parties, though minimal decorum was observed. The chairman of the *Bundesrat* (the Federal Parliament, or Upper House), the Christian Social Josef Zwetzbacher, announced in advance of the day's session that he would open with an obituary for Karl. However, he insisted that he would stress his own commitment to democracy and the republic, and that Karl was only being commemorated as the former head of state and a man whose fate could but evoke sympathy. The Social Democrats initially appeared to accept this purely personal statement, though soon changed course, arguing that the declaration was superfluous since Karl had been stripped of his Austrian citizenship, was banished from the country, and had not died as its ruler. Moreover, it was unjustifiable "childish sentimentality" to honor Karl, since the "overwhelming majority of the population" held a "highly derogatory opinion" of him.[66] After much wrangling, the Christian Socials dropped their eulogy but took revenge during the subsequent proceedings by refusing to fast-track important social legislation.[67] The Social Democrats responded tit for tat and, in the end, not a single item on the agenda was settled.[68]

Similarly, Richard Weiskirchner, the President of the *Nationalrat* (a Christian Social politician and former wartime Mayor of Vienna) had planned to mention Karl's death at the beginning of the parliamentary sitting on 5 April. Yet he failed to gain the approval of the other parties. Both the pan-Germans and Social Democrats refused to accept any form of obituary. Again, the Christian Socials backed down to avoid unseemly scenes.[69] The *Arbeiter-Zeitung* reported with satisfaction that the National Assembly was able to fulfill its agenda "without being importuned by provocative sentimentalities."[70]

Despite the bickering over Karl's legacy in the Austrian parliament and press, the monarchist British historian Herbert Vivian, who would write a highly sympathetic biography of Karl ten years later, reported almost universal mourning in Austria, especially among the poorest classes, and that he witnessed "flags ... flying at half-mast, shops closed, and dour Tyrolese peasants in tears." Vivian added that "only the worst ruffians among the new masters remained callous, and their sneers roused indignation even in the fly-blown parliament of a Socialist Republic."[71] Similarly, the *Reichspost* reported that a number of houses "whose owners had the courage to express the mood of the population" were adorned with black flags. One such building belonged to the Hungarian embassy on *Bankgasse*.[72] Additionally, numerous Viennese signed the condolence books left in the *Habsburgergasse* and Augarten Palace by Albin Schager-Eckartsau, the imperial family's representative in the capital.[73]

Princess Maria Josepha, Karl's mother, who had long cared for Vienna's poor and ill, received numerous letters of sympathy.[74] A certain Captain Emmerich Lippert, himself a war invalid, wrote indignantly to the *Reichspost* about the spoliation of the Habsburgs to subsidize invalids' pensions. Even the imperial couple's private properties, like Wartholz and Feistritz, had been sequestered to pay for the fund. In light of Zita and her children's precarious situation, Lippert suggested that every Austrian invalid forego some of his pension in order to compensate Karl's widow and orphans so as to return the properties or pay the equal amount in annuities.[75] In Linz, the Upper Austrian faction of the *Reichsbund der Österreicher*[76] raised one hundred thousand crowns from its members to set up an Emperor Karl Memorial Foundation, which made a donation to a needy local widow every year on the anniversary of Karl's death.[77] Such gestures testified to Karl's enduring respect and popularity among considerable segments of the population.

Conversely, the German center-right *Kölnische Zeitung* marvelled that Vienna seemed to remain "completely mute and cold-blooded" at the news of Karl's death. While red Berlin and republican Munich had treated their last royals with pomp, ceremony, and commiseration, Vienna had responded "without any visible emotion": "nowhere a black flag, no memento in a shop window, no government announcement, no declaration in parliament." In fact, "scarcely a word of sympathy" could be heard, and there was "hardly an expression of resentment" in response to this disrespectful treatment. The newspaper explained the anger against Karl and the Habsburg dynasty as a result of the appalling misfortune brought about by the war. Rather less plausibly, it also claimed that the deepest resentment was reserved for Karl's treason against Germany, committed merely to save himself, and that unlike Wilhelm II, Karl had not accepted his fate and retired.[78] It concluded: "The emperor dies and Vienna does not cry a single tear." This was not quite true; in fact, it was a barefaced lie.

In this confused atmosphere, it was no surprise that tongues loosened in the political world, despite the obligatory genuflections to democracy and republicanism. Ignaz Seipel—who had served in Karl's last cabinet—declared in a meeting at the Old Town Hall: "I am sure there are people who will mightily resent me and my party if we publicly express our mourning for the deceased."[79] He then pointed out that, as long as the old state existed, the Christian Socials had been loyal to empire and emperor, adding that they were not ashamed of this now. Seipel further recalled his first and last audience with Karl, the emperor's strivings for peace, his courage and refusal to flee. He admitted that the party and emperor had to go their separate ways in the autumn of 1918, because the Christian Socials had to choose between doomed legitimism, which would have paved the way for parties with no tradition, and *Realpolitik*, which allowed them to continue focusing on the welfare of the people. He concluded that the party "today steps up to the bier of the dead emperor, blameless in his personal and political misfortune, and deposes, without damaging in any way its position in the new state, a funeral wreath of compassionate remembrance."[80]

On 4 April, the Christian Social Union met in Vienna before all its national and federal deputies. Seipel again gave a warm eulogy for Karl, recalling the humanity that so many who had worked with him had witnessed. He also praised Karl's peace initiatives, and added that no ruler could have avoided defeat and the destruction of the empire. Throughout his speech, the audience stayed standing.[81]

Naturally, such scenes also occurred in the provinces, usually at the instigation of the somewhat torn Christian Socials. Before the plenary session of the Lower Austrian Diet, the deputy governor of the region Zwetzbacher sought to justify this ambiguity, although during the session itself, Karl was not mentioned.[82] In Klosterneuburg, just north of Vienna, members of the club of Christian Social municipal councillors made a declaration of mourning.[83] And in Innsbruck, the regional deputy governor held a eulogy for Karl during the sitting of the Diet and with the consent of the House majority.[84]

Austria in (Partial) Mourning

Unsurprisingly, masses and other church ceremonies took place throughout Austria.[85] In Vienna, between 5 and 10 April, such well-attended events occurred in almost twenty churches. In Salzburg, thousands were present at a service in the cathedral, including city officials, entire municipalities, local Christian Social politicians, and members of various organizations. In Linz, a requiem was attended by large numbers of people in mourning attire. Inside the church, a symbolic tomb was decorated with an imperial crown, the double-headed eagle, and laurel. Many officers, civilian dignitaries, and politicians were present (with the Christian Socials particularly well represented). The Tyrol displayed particular fervor. On 10 April, mourning services were held in every church in the region, including Bozen (by then Bolzano in Italy), and the local government allowed its civil servants to take time off work to attend the requiem in Innsbruck's *Propsteipfarrkirche*.[86]

The most impressive requiem occurred in Vienna's Saint Stephen's Cathedral on 6 April. In the middle of the church, a catafalque surrounded by burning girandoles represented the absent body. Gustav Piffl, the Archbishop of Vienna, conducted the service before a massive audience (although no official invitations had been issued)—in fact, the building was full well before the requiem was scheduled to start, forcing police to close the cathedral entrance.[87] The square around the *Stephansdom* likewise thronged with people. To the dismay of the Social Democrats, the chancellor, vice-chancellor, and several ministers attended.[88] Others who paid their respects included deputies of the Christian Social Union under the leadership of President Weiskirchner and Chairman Seipel, as well as former archdukes and archduchesses, members of aristocratic families such as the Liechtensteins, various ecclesiasts, and numerous state and court dignitaries who had served under Karl, including Count István Burián, Count Heinrich Clam-Martinic, Ernst Seidler von Feuchtenegg, and Baron Max Hussarek von Heinlein.[89] Former ministers of Karl who attended included Banhans, Georgi, Gayer, Homann, and Spitzmüller.[90] The once Chief of the General Staff, Arz, had published an appeal in the *Neue Freie Presse* for all former members of the Austro-Hungarian army to attend the requiem.[91] Among the notable soldiers present were the last Commander-in-Chief of Austria-Hungary General Field Marshal Hermann Kövess von Kövessháza, the one-time Minister of War General Auffenberg von Komarów, and Colonel Generals Viktor Dankl and Josef Roth von Limanowa-Łapanów.[92] (Noticeably absent was the embittered Field Marshal Conrad von Hötzendorf, who led Austria-Hungary to war as Chief of the General Staff in 1914, and was removed by Karl in early 1917). Among the grandees of the former empire, dynastic loyalty lived on.

After the requiem, as the crowd streamed into the square, screams of "*Hoch*" were suddenly heard from a young band of monarchists, who started singing the imperial anthem. Heads were instantly uncovered. Scarves were waved in approval from neighboring houses.[93] Friedrich Funder witnessed the scene: "I watched as the traffic of the city center suddenly stopped. Many people were crying. People from the windows of the high houses joined in the singing. People were waving and saluting as for a loving goodbye."[94] As the monarchist demonstrators (estimated at between two thousand and ten thousand) and active army officers moved along the *Graben*, cries against the republic (or even "the Jew republic") were heard along with "Up with Emperor Otto! Up with the monarchy! Up with the Habsburgs!"[95] The troublemakers eventually made their way to parliament, still bellowing the old anthem. By midday, the demonstrators had been dispersed and several arrests made,[96] though no serious incident had occurred and their proposal to honor the emperor with an announcement in the National Assembly and the flying of flags at half-mast was, obviously, not honored by a House that was against even a formal obituary.[97]

Karl's death certainly provided an outlet for the heretofore discreet and disparaged monarchists. But it did not help to organize the movement. On 2 April, the *Arbeiter-Zeitung* reported contentedly that the monarchists had split and a new Monarchist State Party had emerged from the public house gatherings of the Wolff group (named for *Staatswehr* editor Colonel Wolff).[98] One of its members, a certain Kuno Hoynigg (a "known monarchist agitator"), was sentenced to fourteen days prison for having instigated the troubles.[99]

The Social Democrats were unforgiving of even the slightest sign of monarchist sympathies. A day after the demonstrations, they raised the question in parliament.[100] Twenty-six signatories asked whether members of the federal government had taken part in a monarchist demonstration under the guise of a mourning service for Karl Habsburg, and how they intended to justify their involvement.[101] Social Democrat deputy Karl Leuthner went on the offensive, quipping that the chancellor and ministers in the church "must really be the only citizens of Vienna not to read any newspapers, otherwise they would have known what spirit and aim this mourning service in Saint Stephen's had, with what intention it was organized, what would necessarily accompany [it] and indeed did." To the nominally nonpolitical Chancellor Johannes Schober's protestation that he had merely attended as a private person, Leuthner retorted that, outside his dining room and bedroom, he was not a private person, and wherever he appeared, he embodied the honor and reputation of the republic. Leuthner further noted that out of nine cabinet members, six were present, as well as the *Nationalrat* President Weiskirchner, all Christian Social deputies of both Houses (who had apparently turned up as a group and sung the imperial anthem enthusiastically), and a host of former government ministers. Leuthner then expounded on the disastrous impression this display would make abroad, on Schober's failings as Interior Minister (a portfolio he held with the chancellorship), and on the irony of the antirepublicanism of duty- and oath-bound people paid wages and pensions by the system. As he spoke, he was interrupted by heckles and catcalls from the opposite benches.[102]

Karl Renner added his voice to Leuthner's, arguing that a prime minister could not appear in a public procession as a private person. He further reminded the audience that every Habsburg was technically allowed to stay and live in Austria as an ordinary citizen, and that demonstrating in favor of someone who had opposed the laws of the republic was setting a poor example. Finally, Renner inveighed against the political involvement of the Catholic Church and the dichotomy of the Christian Social Party, warning the chancellor that behind the monarchist movement lurked the threat of civil war.[103]

The attack on Schober continued in the *Arbeiter-Zeitung*, which questioned whether the Christian Socials were republicans simply because there was no alternative.[104] The newspaper bemoaned Schober's "astounding and distressing" lack of insight into the danger of the situation, and denounced the silence on the part of the pan-Germans.[105] Later in the edition, the paper poked fun at monarchist gatherings in Innsbruck, sarcastically suggesting that the local clerics, worn-out aristocrats, and stupid bourgeoisie also had reason to mourn: "because along with the last Habsburg their time ha[d] irrevocably sunk into the grave of the past."[106]

Schober himself, in the name of the government and to rapturous Christian Social approval, expressly distinguished the religious memorial service from the street demonstrations.[107] He also emphasized that the cabinet had neither been invited to the requiem nor attended as a group. "Concerning my person in particular," Schober said, "I belong to those who drop their sword even before the bier of a fallen opponent out of reverence for the majesty of death." He insisted that his commitment to the republic was beyond doubt and that he had every right to attend the funeral of a man he had known, and who had made him Police Superintendent of Vienna in imperial times.[108]

The *Reichspost* offered its support, denouncing the Social Democrats as a party whose "actions always sneer at good morals" and defending Karl as "the man who did his very best for the welfare of this country, [yet] was kicked out like a thief and murderer ... with even his private property confiscated through an outrageous breach of the law." The proud, thousand-year tradition that he embodied had been dumped on the rubbish heap and turned into a joke. However, the *Reichspost* insisted, Vienna and the country as a whole were on Karl's side. The Socialist Democrats were just too obsessed with power to listen to the voices of the people. The memorial service, the paper insisted, was neither a political demonstration nor a monarchist provocation, but rather an expression of genuine support for tradition and the Austrian idea of gratitude for the past, and the "commemoration of a noble-hearted man."[109]

Nevertheless, scarcely a day passed without the *Arbeiter-Zeitung* attacking or mocking the fallen dynasty. On 9 April, it feigned to understand what monarchists meant when they boasted of Karl's sacrifice for his people. It recounted that, exhausted after the rehearsal for his coronation in Budapest in December 1916, he had been spotted entering a small pub and ordering a couple of sausages and a glass of beer; and that, on another occasion, he had been seen riding the tram from Baden (thus from the Front!) to Vienna. Sausages, beer, and tram travel had been Karl's sacrifice for his people: he had deigned to lower himself to their level.[110] On the next page, the newspaper reported that the Ambassadors' Conference estimated that the Habsburgs had property in Hungary worth some thirty million gold crowns—enough for all Karl's children to learn a manual trade so that they could earn their bread honestly, like millions of other workers.[111]

Two days after the 6 April memorial, a clash between monarchists and republicans occurred in Vienna's Inner City.[112] After a requiem for Karl in the Capuchin Church organized by the Black-Yellow Legitimists (one of nine such events that day in the Austrian capital), a deputation led by Colonel Wolff made its way to Vice-Chancellor Walter Breisky's office.[113] On their way, they were confronted by a number of republicans, leading to a collision of words and bodies on the street.[114] Security guards stepped in and dispersed the crowd. The delegation eventually reached its destination and asked Breisky to ensure that Karl was buried in Austria, to guarantee that his widow and children received support from their rightful property, and to rescind the law banning the Habsburgs from living in Austria. Breisky politely promised to present these demands to the government.[115] The delegation—that is, the "nutcases," according to the *Arbeiter-Zeitung*—then proceeded to the Hungarian consul to express their condolences. The previous evening, they had taken an oath of fidelity toward "Emperor Otto" on the party flag.[116] In an article entitled "From the Monarchist Madhouse," the *Arbeiter-Zeitung* commented: "A few straitjackets and asylum guards seem necessary."[117]

Three days later, in the large hall of Vienna's *Konzerthaus*, thousands of people—including former court members, officers, state dignitaries, senior civil servants, university professors, writers, artists, ecclesiasts, Catholic students, aristocrats, and society ladies—attended an invitation-only commemorative service presided over by Prince Johann von und zu Liechtenstein.[118] To a standing, silent audience, he gave a biography of Karl, praising his character and strivings to save Austria-Hungary—a task beyond even "the strength of a Titan." He then read out a telegram from Zita in Funchal, assuring Karl's followers that: "His last words were a goodbye to all the children in his beloved Austria."[119]

Myriad requiems and eulogies, public signs of mourning, a suicide, a shop on the *Graben* forced to remove Karl's portrait from its window, much singing, two days of (relatively harmless) unrest in Vienna's streets, virulent opinion pieces in the press, and indignant exchanges in parliament: Karl's death had certainly not gone unnoticed; nor had it caused a storm or opened up debate on an Austrian restoration.[120] After the hectic sitting of 6 April, the *Nationalrat* calmly returned to business the following day.[121] As Redlich wrote in his diary: "Karl's death did trouble me for a few days. Had he been a little more potent as a man, it would have been a tragedy. But he was too little, too insignificant a man."[122] Count Albert von Mensdorff-Pouilly-Dietrichstein—the last Austro-Hungarian Ambassador to London—wrote rather more emotionally in his diary: "What a tragic destiny! . . . Since the Atreides, no family has been so persecuted by tragedies as our dynasty."[123] Arz noted in his memoirs that Karl had passed away in his prime, "filled with glowing love for the fatherland and warm longing for home, dying while still thinking of his people."[124]

Within ten days of his death, Karl had virtually disappeared from the newspapers, replaced by the Genoa Conference (to rebuild Europe's economy), the organization of the newly acquired Burgenland, and elections to the Salzburg Diet. When the Habsburgs did appear in the press, it was typically in the form of speculation regarding the location of Karl's permanent grave,[125] the allowance and residence to be provided for Zita and her children,[126] the family's actual wealth,[127] and the location of the crown jewels (which the left-wing press claimed for the Austrian people).[128] The aftermath of Karl's death confirmed that legitimism in Austria was dead—indeed, it had never existed in any meaningful form since the empire's collapse, despite the fact that most Austro-Germans had remained loyal until the end of the war.[129] Although monarchist sentiment remained strong among many former aristocrats, officers and civil servants, clerics and students, it posed no threat as a political movement. The Communist *Rote Fahne* had commented that Karl's passing would give monarchists a "heritage" they could exploit politically.[130] But this never happened—not even after the collapse of the republic. In fact, the Catholic rather than monarchist cause ultimately benefited most from Karl's death.

Beatification and Canonization

Karl's religious significance was almost as old as the man himself. In 1895, when the eight-year-old had no realistic prospect of coming to power, a prayer league—The *Kaiser-Karl-Gebetsliga für den Völkerfrieden*, or Emperor Karl Prayer League for Peace among Nations—was established after an Ursuline mystic prophesied an unhappy emperorship for him.[131] Even as events brought the young archduke closer to fulfilling this premonition, his circle of faithful expanded its activities. Karl's fall, exile, and death prompted the group to seek his beatification.[132]

Ironically, the Austrian Catholic Church had not been especially supportive of Karl after the collapse of the empire. In a joint pastoral letter signed on 23 January 1919, the Archbishops and Bishops of German Austria stated that the religion of Christ allowed its flock to choose its form of state: "Whether men will be free or not, whether they will be ruled by monarchs or republicans: the Church remains in calm possession of the truth, which it took from Jesus Christ via the apostles."[133] Karl had already written to Vienna's Archbishop, Cardinal Piffl, insisting that he remained the legal ruler of German Austria and would never abdicate.[134] The letter was published and read out in churches across the country in late January and early February, before the coming elections.[135] But it was to no avail.

On 1 April 1923, the first anniversary of Karl's passing, the future Austrian President Wilhelm Miklas, a Christian Social who, like many in his party, had (with difficulty) come to terms with the republic and did not toy with the idea of a restoration,[136] petitioned Cardinal Piffl to initiate the beatification process.[137] The Prayer League obtained ecclesiastical sanction for beatification in 1925.[138] Henceforth, it pursued three aims: atonement for the repeated injustice done to God and Karl, glorification of the former emperor's name, and protection for his family. By 1929, the League counted over one thousand members throughout Austria, but also in the monarchy's former lands, as well as in Switzerland and Germany.[139] That year, it began publishing a yearbook, which continues to this day. The 1929 edition was purchased by ten thousand to twelve thousand people.[140] The journal compiled such personal memories of Karl as childhood descriptions, sayings, testimonies by former comrades, and hagiographies.[141]

With the encouragement of the clerical and Habsburg-friendly *Ständestaat* from 1934, Prayer League membership swelled. Although the membership lists were burnt in 1938 to avoid falling into the hands of the Gestapo, the League estimates that it had twenty-five thousand adherents worldwide by that time.[142] The beatification process was to be initiated at the end of 1938, but the National Socialists disbanded the League, deporting and killing one of its leading members (and editor of the yearbook), Hans Karl Zeßner-Spitzenberg. Undeterred, the organization reformed and reinitiated its endeavors after World War II, gaining official approval from the Vatican in 1949.[143] In 2004, their work was finally crowned with success, and the Habsburg Empire's last Kaiser became the Blessed Karl of Austria.

Conclusion

The death of the last Emperor-King of Austria-Hungary elicited a polarized and emotional reaction in the new, vulnerable, and insecure Austria—the "republic without republicans," as the popular expression went.[144] Similar tensions had arisen during his lamentable restoration attempts.[145] Yet the events of Karl's life between his renunciation of power and untimely death neither helped to consolidate the republican state nor to revive monarchism. While the political establishment repudiated Karl's actions, it did not make them into a rallying point for the republic. The major parties merely displayed a veneer of unity in their commitment to republican Austria. The budding war between Christian Socials and Social Democrats was already detectable in their respective responses to Karl's death, whether in the press, parliament, or in the streets. These tensions would escalate into the July 1927 Revolt, the end of parliamentary life in 1933, the 1934 Austrian Civil War, and, ultimately, precipitate the downfall of democracy in Austria.

What Karl represented—the Old World, the Habsburgs, Catholicism, divine right, privilege, even World War I—turned out to be more important than who he was. Beyond the calumnies and gratuitous personal invectives, Karl was a decent and courageous man of conviction who cared deeply for his peoples, his faith, and his mission as monarch. Yet his fleeting and blundering wartime reign, not to mention his tragicomic attempts to reclaim the throne, made him an easier target than the hallowed Franz Joseph, who was already an entrenched, untouchable figure when he died in late 1916, after nearly seventy years on the throne. Karl was also more vulnerable than the warmongering generals, belligerent diplomats, gung-ho politicians, pan-Germans, intransigent Magyars, and national chauvinists who bore responsibility for the war and its stubborn pursuit to the catastrophic end. In the confused, embittered, and violent years after the collapse of the Austro-Hungarian Empire, Karl concentrated a range of popular sentiment on his person alone. He was everything to everyone: a sinner to anti-Habsburg pan-Germans and the republican left (which had nevertheless been loyal to him during the war); a saint for unshakeable imperial loyalists and Catholics; and a cipher for those who saw him as a feeble and unimpressive figure of no consequence, barely worthy of a footnote in history.[146]

Undeniably, the imperial past still inspired strong, positive feelings among much of the Austrian population, unlike in the other successor states of the Dual Monarchy with the exception of Hungary. Indeed, they had largely become little empires in and of themselves, with their own strongmen and wartime mythologies.[147] In Austria, none of the three main political parties—the Social Democrats, the Christian Socials, and the German Nationalists—wished to claim the legacy of the empire or to defend the dynasty.[148] The wartime imperial governments and, by extension, the Habsburgs had failed to feed, heat, clothe, and protect their people and their territory, and thus had lost all legitimacy and respect.[149] Furthermore, Karl had made mistakes that nobody had forgotten and few were willing to condone or forgive.

But it was not simply these concrete failures that averted people from the empire. As the historian Adam Kożuchowski points out, the "enormous changes in everyday life during the Great War and its aftermath" had the effect of making it appear as if time itself had accelerated: "Hence, the last years of Austria-Hungary seemed to represent a past much more remote a decade after the monarchy's breakdown than, say, the turn of the century had represented in the spring of 1914." Karl was arguably irrelevant months before November 1918. By 1922, he was anachronistic. As far as the future was concerned, Austrians of virtually all backgrounds opted for what appeared to be the only face-saving option for a defeated, traumatized, poor, embittered, mutilated, and diplomatically isolated Austria: unification with Germany. Monarchism and legitimism thus never carried any serious political weight in the interwar period. Nor, even, did plans for a supranational federation in Central Europe. Simply put, the prevailing opinion was that the Habsburgs belonged to the past. Or as Kożuchowski put it, "the Habsburg Monarchy already seemed an antiquated idea a few years, if not months, after it had broken down."[150] There can therefore have been no genuine fear of a Habsburg restoration—at least not one involving Karl or including several countries.

For many Austrians, Karl was a popular and amicable figure whose tragic destiny echoed that of Austria herself. As *Der Morgen* commented shortly after he expired: "Death has made a man who had to carry the hatred caused by others who are now long gone, into an object of general human sympathy."[151] Nobody blamed Karl personally for the collapse of Austria-Hungary. Indeed, historian Gergely Romsics's systematic review of thirty-two "Old Austrian" memoirists of the monarchy's political elite revealed that the most cited cause of Austria-Hungary's dissolution was not Karl, but the "chauvinistic, selfish and inconsistent behavior of its Hungarian part."[152] All this, however, was not enough to save Karl's reputation. As his supporters in the Prayer League lamented in their 1929 yearbook: "The current generation will barely succeed in recognizing Karl's greatness. Only historical hindsight will allow that." For many, he remained "'the weak', or 'the unfortunate' in the best of cases."[153] To his champions, on the contrary, he was "a martyr of his belief, of his duty, of his oath, his conscience."[154]

Unexpectedly, considering the political climate surrounding Karl's death in 1922, the Habsburgs made a return of sorts under Chancellors Dollfuß and Schuschnigg's corporate state (the *Ständestaat*). This entailed Schuschnigg's rather feeble and desperate attempts to oppose German nationalism with a Habsburg version by, for example, repealing most of the 1919 anti-Habsburg laws in July 1935.[155] Schuschnigg also occasionally toyed with the idea of a Habsburg restoration, though he was well aware that it would be suicidal for his government and country.[156] In the dying days of independent Austria, as Hitler prepared to annex the country, Karl's son Otto, "as the legitimate Emperor of Austria," asked Schuschnigg to appoint him chancellor.[157] Schuschnigg would not take the risk, responding on 2 March 1938: "Your Majesty . . . Any attempt at restoration in the immediate future would 100 percent imply the ruin of Austria."[158] Eleven days later, the country ceased to exist.

Thereafter, Karl fell into oblivion. Recent steps toward sainthood have not made him more popular or well-known either (indeed, today most Austrians struggle even to recall the name of the last Habsburg emperor). What they have done, however, is to help fashion the predominant contemporary image of Karl, one in which the memory of his tragic death, however controversial at the time, overshadows that of anything he achieved during his life. In all likelihood, Karl's martyrdom and impending canonization are his only remaining chances to leave a mark on history, however minor it may be.

Christopher Brennan completed his doctoral thesis on the role of the last Habsburg Emperor/King, Karl I/IV, at the London School of Economics, where he also taught. He has published "The Memory of the First World War in the former lands of Austria-Hungary," in *Memorias contemporáneas de la Gran Guerra: Narrativas nacionales 1914–1918*, *Comillas Journal of International Relations*, vol. 2 (Madrid: Universidad Pontificia Comillas, 2015). He wrote the entry "Balkan Wars, 1912–13" for *The Encyclopedia of Diplomacy* (Hoboken: Wiley-Blackwell, 2018), and "Hesitant Heir and Reluctant Ruler: Karl I/IV of Austria-Hungary during the Great War," in *Monarchies and the Great War*, edited by J. Rowbotham and M. Glencross (Basingstoke: Palgrave Macmillan, 2018).

Notes

1. There seemingly remained only the *Kaiser Karl-Kriegerheimstätten in Aspern*, a nursing and retirement home for war veterans. The Museum of Austrian Ethnology in Vienna had been renamed *k.k. Kaiser Karl-Museum für österreichische Volkskunde* in March 1917, but removed its imperial connotations ten days after the end of the war, on 21 November 1918. See Michael Haberlandt, ed., *Zeitschrift für österreichische Volkskunde: Organ des Vereines für österreichische Volkskunde in Wien*, XXIII (Vienna: Verein für Volkskunde in Wien, 1917), V; Ibid., XXIV (1918), 141–42.
2. Report on the city council meeting of 6 November 1919, *Amtsblatt der Stadt Wien* 94, 22 November 1919, 2880; *Arbeiter-Zeitung, Morgenblatt (AZM)*, 15 May 1919, 4; 9 November 1919, 2.
3. Julius Deutsch, *Ein weiter Weg: Lebenserinnerungen* (Vienna: Amalthea, 1960); *AZM*, 21 March 1919, 2–3; 24 March 1919, 1.
4. Emmerich Zeno von Schonta, *Erinnerungen eines Flügeladjutanten an Weiland Seine Majestät den Kaiser und König Karl* (Vienna: Reichsbund der Oesterreicher, 1928), 60–61.
5. Deutsch, *Ein weiter Weg*, 85–86; Karl Freiherr von Werkmann, *Der Tote auf Madeira* (Munich: Verlag für Kulturpolitik, 1923), 34–35.

6. *Staatsgesetzblatt für den Staat Deutschösterreich* 71, 10 April 1919, 209: "Law of 3 April concerning the territorial ban and the transfer of the assets of the House of Habsburg-Lorraine," 513–14.
7. *Reichspost, Morgenblatt* (*RPM*) (15 January 1919), 5; Werkmann, *Der Tote auf Madeira*, 53; Anton Lehár, *Erinnerungen: Gegenrevolution und Restaurationsversuche in Ungarn*, ed. Peter Broucek, 1918–21 (Vienna: Geschichte und Politik, 1973).
8. Karl Freiherr von Werkmann, ed., *Aus Kaiser Karls Nachlass* (Berlin: Verlag für Kulturpolitik, 1925), 163–66; *RPM* (15 November 1918), 4; handwritten letter by Karl from his internal exile (13 November). For Karl's Easter Putsch, see Paul Szemere and Erich Czech, eds., *Die Memoiren des Grafen Tamás von Erdödy: Habsburgs Weg von Wilhelm zu Briand. Vom Kurier des Sixtus-Briefe zum Königsputschisten* (Zurich: Amalthea, 1931), 209–56; Admiral Nicholas Horthy, *A Life for Hungary: Memoirs of Admiral Nicholas Horthy Regent of Hungary* (New York: Ishi Press, 2011), 116–21; Aladár von Boroviczény, *Der König und sein Reichsverweser* (Munich: Verlag für Kulturpolitik, 1924), 95–143; Lehár, *Erinnerungen*, 171–214.
9. Elisabeth Kovács, ed., *Untergang oder Rettung der Donaumonarchie? Politische Dokumente zu Kaiser und König Karl I. (IV.) aus Internationalen Archiven*, vol. II (Vienna: Böhlau, 2004), document 237, 13 May 1921, 737; Horthy, *A Life for Hungary*, 118–19.
10. Lehár, *Erinnerungen*, 183; Carvel de Bussy, ed., *Memoirs of Alexander Spitzmüller Freiherr von Harmersbach* (New York: Columbia University Press, 1987), 215; Horthy, *A Life for Hungary*, 118–21. For a study of the incident, which was widely reported in the papers at the time, see Georg Fingerlos, "Als die Leute von Bruck a. d. Mur ihren ehemaligen Kaiser, den seligen Karl, töten wollten," *Wiener Zeitschrift zur Geschichte der Neuzeit* 6, no. 1 (2006), 117–32; a detailed report sent to the Interior Minister on 18 April 1921 exists: Österreichisches Staatsarchiv (Austrian State Archives, henceforth ÖStA), Archiv der Republik (AdR), Bundeskanzleramt (BKA), Abteilung 5, 22 in genere, 130729 (1921); there is a witness account in Albert Sever, *Ein Mann aus dem Volk. Selbstbiographie* (Vienna: Landesorganisation Wien der SPÖ, 1956), 34–44; Karl's own version of the Easter restoration attempt is in Kovács, *Untergang oder Rettung*, 237, 732–55.
11. ÖStA, AdR, BKA, Abt. 5, 130729 (1921); Sever, *Ein Mann aus dem Volk*, 42.
12. For a detailed description and explanation of the Sixtus scandal, see Robert A. Kann, *Die Sixtus Affäre und die geheimen Friedensverhandlung Österreich-Ungarns im Ersten Weltkrieg* (Vienna: Verlag für Geschichte und Politik, 1966).
13. August von Cramon, *Unser österreich-ungarischer Bundesgenosse im Weltkriege: Erinnerungen aus meiner vierjährigen Tätigkeit als bevollmächtigter deutscher General beim k.u.k. Armeeoberkommando* (Berlin: Mittler & Sohn, 1920), 115.
14. *Stenographisches Protokoll*, 61. Sitzung des Nationalrates der Republik Österreich (*SPN*) 61, 25 October 1921, 2220.
15. Alfred Krauß, *Die Ursachen unserer Niederlage. Erinnerungen und Urteile aus dem Weltkrieg* (Munich: J. F. Lehmanns, 1921), 279–80.
16. Général Baron Albert de Margutti, *La Tragédie des Habsbourg: Mémoires d'un aide de camp* (Vienna: Les Éd. G. Crès, 1923), 159–60.
17. Marga Lammasch and Hans Sperl, eds., *Heinrich Lammasch, Seine Aufzeichnungen, sein Wirken und seine Politik* (Vienna: F. Deuticke, 1922), 184; Deutsch, *Ein weiter Weg*, 8–9.

18. For the second coup attempt, see von Boroviczény, *Der König und sein Reichsverweser*, 269–340; Szemere and Czech, *Die Memoiren des Grafen Tamás von Erdödy*, 273–93; Horthy, *A Life for Hungary*, 122–26; Lehár, *Erinnerungen*, 220–25.
19. *Neue Freie Presse, Morgenblatt* (*NFPM*), 23 October 1921, 2–3; 24 October 1921, 1, 3–4; *AZM*, 23 October 1921, 3; 25 October 1921, 1, 3; *RPM*, 25 October 1921, 2–3; 30 October 1921, 1; 31 October 1921, 3.
20. *NFPM*, 28 October 1921; *RPM*, 26 October 1921, 1; 27 October 1921, 2.
21. *RPM*, 26 October 1921, 1; 1 November 1921, 3.
22. Ibid., 4 November 1921, 1; 6 November 1921, 3; 7 November 1921, 1; *AZM*, 1 November 1921, 1; *RPM*, 8 November 1921, 3.
23. *NFPM*, 1 November 1921, 3; 2 November 1921, 1–3.
24. *RPM*, 29 October 1921, 2; 6 November 1921, 3; 7 November 1921, 1.
25. *RPM*, 24 October 1921, 1; 26 October 1921, 2; 27 October 1921, 2; *NFPM*, 23 October 1921, 1; 24 October 1921, 4; 26 October 1921, 1; 27 October 1921, 4.
26. *SPN*, 31, 1 April 1921, 1248–54; Ibid., 61, 25 October 1921, 2213–22, 2224–28, 2230, 2232–35; *RPM*, 26 October 1921, 4; *AZM*, 26 October 1921, 3; *NFPM*, 26 October 1921, 1, 4.
27. The vitriol from the *Arbeiter-Zeitung* appeared on most days during the Easter Putsch (*AZM*, 30 March 1921, 1–2; 31 March 1921, 1–2; 1 April 1921, 1; 5 April 1921, 1–2; 7 April 1921, 1–2; 9 April 1921, 1) and October Putsch (*AZM*, 23 October 1921, 1; 25 October 1921, 1–2, 4; 26 October 1921, 5; 27 October 1921, 5; 29 October 1921, 5; 30 October 1921, 4–6; *AZMG*, 24 October 1921, 1). On the other hand, the *Neue Freie Presse* showed plenty of sympathy, while expressing mild disapproval and bafflement at his adventures (*NFPM*, 30 March 1921, 1; *Neue Freie Presse, Abendblatt* [*NFPA*], 30 March 1921, 1; *NFPM*, 1 April 1921, 2; *NFPA*, 1 April 1921, 1; *NFPM*, 2 April 1921, 1; 25 October 1921, 1; 2 November 1921, 1); meanwhile, over Easter, the *Reichspost* appeared to support him tacitly in what it considered a purely Hungarian matter (*RPM*, 30 March 1921, 1; 31 March 1921, 1; 1 April 1921, 1; 2 April 1921, 1; 5 April 1921, 1; 7 April 1921, 1). In October, however, it refrained from any judgement.
28. From 11 to 15 November, for example, there was virtually nothing about Karl in the *Reichspost*.
29. *Erdödy*, 291; *AZM*, 27 October 1921, 1, 5; *RPM*, 26 October 1921, 1, 3; 27 October 1921, 2; 29 October 1921, 2.
30. See, for example, *Staatswehr*, 14 April 1922, 3.
31. Fritz Fellner, ed., *Dichter und Gelehrter: Hermann Bahr und Josef Redlich in ihren Briefen 1898–1934* (Salzburg: Verlag Wolfgang Neugebauer, 1980), Redlich to Bahr, 24 October 1921, 463.
32. *NFPA*, 28 October 1921, 2 and 4 April 1922, 2. The official cause of death was pneumonia as a result of complications from flu.
33. *Neues Wiener Journal* (*NWJ*), 3 April 1922, 1.
34. *RPM*, 4 April 1922, 2.
35. *NFPN*, 3 April 1922, 2.
36. *RPM*, 9 April 1922, 5.
37. *AZM*, 9 April 1922, 3.
38. For an overview of Karl's training, see Christopher Brennan, "Reforming Austria-Hungary: Beyond His Control or Beyond His Capacity? The Domestic Policies of

Emperor Karl I: November 1916–May 1917" (PhD thesis, London School of Economics, 2012), chapter 1.
39. *NFPM*, 2 April 1922, 1.
40. *NWJ*, 2 April 1922, 1–3. No publication shied away from describing Karl's pitiful last weeks on Madeira (*RPM*, 4 April 1922, 3), his final hours (*AZM*, 1 April 1922, 4) or his last words (*NFPN*, 3 April 1922, 2; *RPM*, 4 April 1922, 1).
41. *RPM*, 15 January 1919, 5; 31 March 1921, 1; 2 April 1922, 1.
42. Friedrich Funder, *Vom Gestern ins Heute, Aus dem Kaiserreich in die Republik* (Vienna: Herold, 1953), 672.
43. *RPM*, 2 April 1922, 1.
44. Ibid., 5 April 1922, 2.
45. *Tiroler Anzeiger*, 3 April 1922, 1.
46. *RPM*, 5 April 1922, 2.
47. *RPM*, 4 April 1922, 2.
48. *Staatswehr*, 14 April 1922, 1–3.
49. Ibid., 2.
50. *Jüdische Presse*, 7 April 1922, 6.
51. *NWJ*, 2 April 1922, 3.
52. Ibid., 4.
53. von Schonta, *Erinnerungen eines Flügeladjutanten*.
54. Count Arthur Polzer-Hoditz, *The Emperor Karl* (London: Putnam, 1930), 48–49; *AZM*, 27 October 1921, 5.
55. *RPM*, 5 April 1922, 2.
56. von Schonta, *Erinnerungen eines Flügeladjutanten*, 18–22.
57. *RPM*, 8 April 1922, 3.
58. Albert Freiherr von Margutti, *Von alten Kaiser: Persönliche Erinnerungen an Franz Joseph I. Kaiser von Österreich und apostolischen König von Ungarn* (Leipzig: Leonhardt, 1921); Albert Freiherr von Margutti, *La Tragédie des Habsbourg: Mémoires d'un aide de camp* (1923); Albert Freiherr von Margutti, *Kaiser Franz Joseph: Persönliche Erinnerungen* (Vienna: Manz'sche Verlags- und Universitätsbuchhandlung, 1924). His second opus, in French, was at times mordant and vitriolic, but his final work, published in German the following year, was rather contrite and, at times, glowing about Karl and Zita.
59. von Margutti, *La Tragédie des Habsbourg*, 205–6.
60. *NFPM*, 6 April 1922, 8.
61. *RPM*, 3 April 1922, 1–2.
62. *AZM*, 2 April 1922, 1.
63. *Die Rote Fahne*, 1 April 1922, 5.
64. Ibid., 2 April 1922, 1.
65. Ibid.
66. *RPM*, 5 April 1922, 2; *NFPA*, 5 April 1922, 4; *AZM*, 5 April 1922, 3.
67. Stenographisches Protokoll, 22. Sitzung des Bundesrates der Republik Österreich (*SPB*) 22, 4 April 1922, 477; *NFPA*, 5 April 1922, 4–5; *AZM*, 5 April 1922, 3.
68. *SPB* 22, 4 April 1922, 477; *NFPA*, 5 April 1922, 4–5; *AZM*, 5 April 1922, 3.
69. Ibid., 6 April 1922, 2; *NFPA*, 5 April 1922, 3; *SPN* 102, 5 April 1922, 3365–92.
70. *AZM*, 6 April 1922, 2.
71. Herbert Vivian, *The Life of the Emperor Charles of Austria* (London: Grayson & Grayson, 1932), 281–82.

72. *RPM*, 3 April 1922, 2.
73. Ibid., 4 April 1922, 2; 6 April 1922, 2; *NFPN*, 3 April 1922, 2.
74. *RPM*, 3 April 1922, 2.
75. Ibid., 6 April 1922, 2.
76. "The Imperial League of Austrians," see "The Appeal for the Creation of the Imperial League of Austrians," *Das Neue Reich*, 1 May 1921, 1.
77. Ibid., 12 April 1922, 5.
78. *AZM*, 14 April 1922, 6.
79. *RPM*, 3 April 1922, 1.
80. Ibid.
81. Ibid., 5 April 1922, 1.
82. *NFPA*, 5 April 1922, 3.
83. *RPM*, 11 April 1922, 4.
84. *NFPM*, 9 April 1922, 10.
85. *RPM*, 10 April 1922, 3; 4 April 1922, 2; 5 April 1922, 2; 6 April 1922, 2; 7 April 1922, 4; 8 April 1922, 3; 9 April 1922, 5; 11 April 1922, 4; 12 April 1922, 5; 15 April 1922, 3; *NFPM*, 4 April 1922, 4; 6 April 1922, 5.
86. *RPM*, 10 April 1922, 3; 11 April 1922, 4; 12 April 1922, 5.
87. *RPM*, 4 April 1922, 2.
88. *NFPA*, 6 April 1922, 3; *AZM*, 7 April 1922, 1; *SPN* 103, 6 April 1922, 3408.
89. *NFPA*, 5 April 1922, 3; 6 April 1922, 3; *AZM*, 7 April 1922, 7; *SPN* 103, 6 April 1922, 3408; *RPM*, 7 April 1922, 3–4.
90. *RPM*, 7 April 1922, 3–4.
91. *NFPM*, 4 April 1922, 4.
92. Ibid.; *NFPA*, 6 April 1922, 3.
93. *NFPA*, 6 April 1922, 3; *AZM*, 7 April 1922, 7.
94. Funder, *Vom Gestern ins Heute*, 673.
95. *NFPM*, 7 April 1922, 8; *RPM*, 7 April 1922, 4; *AZM*, 7 April 1922, 7.
96. *RPM*, 7 April 1922, 4; *NFPA*, 6 April 1922, 3.
97. *NFPM*, 6 April 1922, 5; 7 April 1922, 8; *SPN* 103, 6 April 1922, 3410; *AZM*, 7 April 1922, 7.
98. *AZM*, 2 April 1922, 7.
99. *NFPM*, 8 April 1922, 5.
100. *SPN* 103, 6 April 1922, 3394.
101. Ibid., 3397–98.
102. Ibid., 3408–12.
103. Ibid., 3414.
104. *AZM*, 7 April 1922, 1.
105. Ibid., 2; 8 April 1922, 4.
106. Ibid., 7 April 1922, 6.
107. *NFPM*, 7 April 1922, 5.
108. *SPN* 103, 6 April 1922, 3412.
109. *RPM*, 7 April 1922, 1–2.
110. Ibid., 9 April 1922, 6.
111. Ibid., 7. Schager, their representative, countered that the property was worth at most eight million Swiss Francs—in Austrian currency 11,760 million crowns, "still a stately sum today."

112. *NFPA*, 8 April 1922, 3.
113. The legitimists' version of the meeting is in *Staatswehr*, 14 April 1922, 2–3.
114. *NFPA*, 8 April 1922, 3–4; *AZM*, 9 April 1922, 6.
115. Ibid.; *Staatswehr*, 14 April 1922, 2–3.
116. *NFPA*, 8 April 1922, 4.
117. *AZM*, 9 April 1922, 6.
118. *NFPM*, 12 April 1922, 7; *RPM*, 12 April 1922, 5.
119. Ibid.
120. *Staatswehr*, 14 April 1922, 3.
121. *RPM*, 8 April 1922, 2.
122. Fritz Fellner and Doris A. Corradini, eds., *Schicksalsjahre Österreichs 1869–1936: Die Erinnerungen und Tagebücher Josef Redlichs*, vol. 2 (Vienna: Böhlau, 2011), 6 April 1922, 597.
123. ÖStA, Haus-, Hof- und Staatsarchiv, Nachlass Mensdorff, K4, Diary, 2 April 1922.
124. Arthur A. Arz, *Zur Geschichte des Grossen Krieges: 1914–1918* (Vienna: Rikola-Verlag, 1924), 387.
125. *NWJ*, 2 April 1922, 1; 3 April 1922, 1; *RPM*, 3 April 1922, 1; 4 April 1922, 2; *NFPN*, 3 April 1922, 2; *NFPM*, 4 April 1922, 4; 6 April 1922, 5; 7 April 1922, 7; *NFPA*, 6 April 1922, 3. Much speculation surrounded Karl's burial. During their demonstration on 6 April, the monarchists demanded his body be buried in Austria. Yet that very day, he was laid to rest in Funchal.
126. *NFPA*, 6 April 1922, 3; 15 April 1922, 1; 4 April 1922, 2; *NFPM*, 7 April 1922, 7; *NWJ*, 4 April 1922, 1.
127. *AZM*, 9 April 1922, 7; *NFPM*, 9 April 1922, 10.
128. *NFPM*, 11 April 1922, 4; *NFPA*, 8 April 1922, 3.
129. Max Schiavon, *L'Autriche-Hongrie dans la Première Guerre mondiale: La Fin d'un Empire* (Saint-Cloud: Publisher, 2011), 236.
130. *Die Rote Fahne*, 1 April 1922, 1.
131. Hans Zeßner, ed., *Zu Kaiser Karls Gedächtnis: Ein österreichisches Jahrbuch; 1929* (Vienna: Verlag der Arbeitsgemeinschaft österreichische Vereine, 1928), 58; Emmy Gehrig, "Der Weg unserer Liga," *Die stille Schar: Jahrbuch der Gebetsliga* 1 (1953): 8. According to the legend, she had said: "Yes—one must pray for him a lot because one day he will be emperor and he will have to suffer greatly."
132. Ibid, 9–10.
133. The letter is reproduced in *RPM*, 24 January 1919, 8–10.
134. Kovács, *Untergang oder Rettung*, 130, Karl to Cardinal Piffl, 15 January 1919, 432–35.
135. *RPM*, 24 January 1919, 10.
136. Anneliese Harasek, "Bundespräsident Wilhelm Miklas" (PhD diss., University of Vienna, 1967), 44.
137. Maria Habacher, "Die Geschichte des Seligsprechungsprozesses und der religiösen Verehrungsformen des Dieners Gottes Karl von Habsburg," in *Kaiser Karl I (IV.) als Christ, Staatsmann, Ehemann und Familienvater*, ed. Jan Mikrut (Vienna: Dom Verlag, 2004), 261. This is one of the rare documents that survived the *Anschluss*. It can be found in the Archive of the Prayer League (Archiv der Gebetsliga) in Sankt-Pölten, Ordner I.
138. Hans Zeßner, ed., *Gedächtnis-Jahrbuch. Dem Andenken an Karl von Österreich gewidmet. 1930* (Vienna: Verlag und Vertrieb der Arbeitsgemeinschaft österreichische Vereine, 1929), 54.

139. *Gedächtnis-Jahrbuch* (1929), 47.
140. *Gedächtnis-Jahrbuch* (1930), 41. The league had originally counted on selling three thousand.
141. *Gedächtnis-Jahrbuch* (1929), 54–62.
142. Maria Habacher, *Geschichte der Gebetsliga 1895–1995* (Vienna: Selbstverlag der Gebetsliga, 1995), 27, 32; Habacher, "Die Geschichte des Seligsprechungsprozesses," 261; Gehrig, "Der Weg unserer Liga," 14. This is according to Gehrig's recollection. By 1964, the re-formed league had over thirty-two thousand members, which makes the prewar figures plausible.
143. Eva Demmerle, *Kaiser Karl I: "Selig, die Frieden stiften"* (Vienna: Amalthea, 2004), 260.
144. von Werkmann, *Der Tote auf Madeira*, 25.
145. Kovács, *Untergang oder Rettung*, 816, footnote 1.
146. For example, Alexander von Spitzmüller, Karl's first candidate for prime minister and later finance minister, wrote in his diary that the emperor was "an agreeable, lovable person beyond all measure, but in no way an historical type of leader": de Bussy, *Memoirs of Alexander Spitzmüller*, 214.
147. Pieter M. Judson, *The Habsburg Empire: A New History* (Cambridge, MA: Harvard University Press, 2016), 448; Robert Gerwarth, *The Vanquished: Why the First World War Failed to End, 1917–1923* (London: Farrar, Straus and Giroux, 2016), 14.
148. Adam Kożuchowski, *The Afterlife of Austria-Hungary: The Image of the Habsburg Monarchy in Interwar Europe* (Pittsburgh: University of Pittsburgh Press, 2013), 11–12.
149. Maureen Healy, *Vienna and the Fall of the Habsburg Empire: Total War and Everyday Life in World War I* (Cambridge: Cambridge University Press, 2004), 309.
150. Kożuchowski, *The Afterlife of Austria-Hungary*, 11, 174.
151. *RPM*, 3 April 1922, 2.
152. Gergely Romsics, *Myth and Remembrance: The Dissolution of the Habsburg Empire in the Memoir Literature of the Austro-Hungarian Political Elite* (Boulder, CO: Social Science Monographs, 2006), 39.
153. *Gedächtnis-Jahrbuch* (1930), 43.
154. *Gedächtnis-Jahrbuch* (1929), 48.
155. Kożuchowski, *The Afterlife of Austria-Hungary*, 12. *Bundesgesetzblatt für den Bundesstaat Österreich*, Nr. 80, 13 July 1935, Law 299, "Federal law concerning the revocation of the expulsion and the return of the assets of the House of Habsburg-Lorraine," 1355.
156. Kożuchowski, *The Afterlife of Austria-Hungary*, 93.
157. Kurt von Schuschnigg, *The Brutal Takeover: The Austrian ex-Chancellor's Account of the Anschluss of Austria by Hitler* (London: Weidenfeld and Nicolson, 1971), Otto to von Schuschnigg, 17 February 1938, 9.
158. Ibid., von Schuschnigg to Otto, 2 March 1938, 13–15.

Select Bibliography

Arz von Straußenburg, Arthur. *Zur Geschichte des Grossen Krieges: 1914–1918*. Vienna: Rikola-Verlag, 1924.

Brennan, Christopher. "Reforming Austria-Hungary: Beyond His Control or Beyond His Capacity? The Domestic Policies of Emperor Karl I: November 1916–May 1917." PhD thesis, London School of Economics, 2012.

de Bussy, Carvel, ed. *Memoirs of Alexander Spitzmüller Freiherr von Harmersbach*. New York: Columbia University Press, 1987.

Demmerle, Eva. *Kaiser Karl I: "Selig, die Frieden stiften."* Vienna: Amalthea, 2004.

Deutsch, Julius. *Ein weiter Weg: Lebenserinnerungen*. Vienna: Amalthea, 1960.

Fellner, Fritz, ed., *Dichter und Gelehrter: Hermann Bahr und Josef Redlich in ihren Briefen 1898–1934*. Salzburg: Verlag Wolfgang Neugebauer, 1980.

———, and Doris A. Corradini, eds. *Schicksalsjahre Österreichs 1869–1936: Die Erinnerungen und Tagebücher Josef Redlichs*. 3 Vols. Vienna: Böhlau, 2011.

Fingerlos, Georg. "Als die Leute von Bruck a. d. Mur ihren ehemaligen Kaiser, den seligen Karl, töten wollten." *Wiener Zeitschrift zur Geschichte der Neuzeit* 6, no. 1 (2006): 117–32.

Funder, Friedrich. *Vom Gestern ins Heute, Aus dem Kaiserreich in die Republik*. Vienna: Herold, 1953.

Habacher, Maria. *Geschichte der Gebetsliga 1895–1995*. Vienna: Selbstverlag der Gebetsliga, 1995.

Harasek, Anneliese. "Bundespräsident Wilhelm Miklas." PhD diss., University of Vienna, 1967.

Horthy, Admiral Nicholas. *A Life for Hungary: Memoirs of Admiral Nicholas Horthy Regent of Hungary*. New York: Ishi Press, 2011.

Judson, Pieter M. *The Habsburg Empire: A New History*. Cambridge, MA: Harvard University Press, 2016.

Kożuchowski, Adam. *The Afterlife of Austria-Hungary: The Image of the Habsburg Monarchy in Interwar Europe*. Pittsburgh: University of Pittsburgh Press, 2013.

Krauß, Alfred. *Die Ursachen unserer Niederlage. Erinnerungen und Urteile aus dem Weltkrieg*. Munich: J. F. Lehmanns, 1921.

Polzer-Hoditz, Count Arthur. *The Emperor Karl*. London: Putnam, 1930.

Romsics, Gergely. *Myth and Remembrance: The Dissolution of the Habsburg Empire in the Memoir Literature of the Austro-Hungarian Political Elite*. Boulder, CO: Social Science Monographs, 2006.

Szemere, Paul and Erich Czech, eds. *Die Memoiren des Grafen Tamás von Erdödy: Habsburgs Weg von Wilhelm zu Briand. Vom Kurier des Sixtus-Briefe zum Königsputschisten*. Zurich: Amalthea, 1931.

Vivian, Herbert. *The Life of the Emperor Charles of Austria*. London: Grayson & Grayson, 1932.

von Boroviczény, Aladár. *Der König und sein Reichsverweser*. Munich: Verlag für Kulturpolitik, 1924.

von Cramon, August. *Unser österreich-ungarischer Bundesgenosse im Weltkriege: Erinnerungen aus meiner vierjährigen Tätigkeit als bevollmächtigter deutscher General beim k.u.k. Armeeoberkommando*. Berlin: Mittler & Sohn, 1920.

von Margutti, Albert Freiherr. *Von alten Kaiser: Persönliche Erinnerungen an Franz Joseph I. Kaiser von Österreich und apostolischen König von Ungarn*. Leipzig: Leonhardt, 1921.

———. *Kaiser Franz Joseph: Persönliche Erinnerungen*. Vienna: Manz'sche Verlags- und Universitätsbuchhandlung, 1924.

———. *La Tragédie des Habsbourg: Mémoires d'un aide de camp*. Paris: Éditions Crès, 1923.

von Schonta, Emmerich Zeno. *Erinnerungen eines Flügeladjutanten an Weiland Seine Majestät den Kaiser und König Karl*. Vienna: Reichsbund der Oesterreicher, 1928.

von Schuschnigg, Kurt. *The Brutal Takeover: The Austrian ex-Chancellor's account of the Anschluss of Austria by Hitler*. London: Weidenfeld and Nicolson, 1971.

von Werkmann, Karl Freiherr. *Der Tote auf Madeira*. Munich: Verlag für Kulturpolitik, 1923.
——. ed. *Aus Kaiser Karls Nachlass*. Berlin: Verlag für Kulturpolitik, 1925.

Newspapers/Yearbooks
Arbeiter-Zeitung
Die Rote Fahne
Gedächtnis-Jahrbuch. Dem Andenken an Karl von Österreich gewidmet
Jüdische Presse
Neue Freie Presse
Neues Wiener Journal
Reichspost
Staatswehr
Tiroler Anzeiger

Protocols and Documents
Amtsblatt der Stadt Wien
Kovács, Elisabeth, ed. *Untergang oder Rettung der Donaumonarchie? Politische Dokumente zu Kaiser und König Karl I. (IV.) aus Internationalen Archiven*. Vol. II. Vienna: Böhlau, 2004.
Staatsgesetzblatt für den Staat Deutschösterreich
Stenographisches Protokoll des Bundesrates der Republik Österreich
Stenographisches Protokoll des Nationalrates der Republik Österreich

Part IV

HISTORY, MEMORY, MENTALITÉ: PROCESSING THE EMPIRE'S PASSING

Chapter 11

"What Did They Die For?"
War Remembrance in Austria in the Transition from Empire to Nation State

Christoph Mick

Public war remembrance has multiple functions: to honor the dead, comfort the bereaved, conciliate the veterans, and legitimize the political order. In order to fulfill these tasks, war has to be invested with meaning. This is easier for states that win, or at least survive, a war. After the German army attacked France and Belgium in 1914, their soldiers did not need convincing that they had to fight. The British government, meanwhile, told its soldiers that they were fighting Germany to uphold liberal values and the rule of law as ensconced in the Treaty of London (1839), which guaranteed Belgian neutrality and to which Germany (then Prussia) was a signatory. But, of course, the main reason Britain entered the war was to maintain the balance of power in Europe and prevent the Belgian seaports from falling into German hands. Britain, France, Belgium, and the other victorious powers could thus draw meaning from the world war in a way that was not possible for Bulgarian or German soldiers. And yet, despite defeat, their countries had at least survived the epic conflict. The same could not be said for the Austro-Hungarian Empire, which collapsed in 1918. What did its soldiers die for?

It proved difficult for the eponymous successor states of Austria-Hungary to give meaning to the Great War and integrate it into their national narratives. While Czechs, Slovaks, Poles, Croats, Slovenians, and Bosnians could all draw sustenance from their own successful state-building, Austrian Germans and

Hungarians had been the dominant nations in an empire that no longer existed. The new postwar borders, moreover, meant that 3.3 million Hungarians and more than three million Austrian Germans now found themselves as minorities in states dominated by other nations. And Austria herself was a small republic consisting of just a few German-speaking provinces with a total population of some six million. Only Vienna, the former imperial capital, still bore witness to Austria's vanished status as a great power.

This chapter analyzes Austrian attempts to give meaning to World War I. It will not examine how the bereaved sought to come to terms with their loss, but rather discuss the meaning offered them by their government, political parties, and elites. Public war remembrance plays an important role in political conflicts. The design of memorials and the form and content of national rituals are negotiated between government and society. They thus stand a better chance of finding wide acceptance if they result from compromise and are open to multiple interpretations, rather than when governments and interest groups try to impose their views onto the memorials and memorialization process. Such partisanship risks alienating those parts of the population that do not accept the "official" version of the war. In so doing, they can undermine one of the main purposes of war remembrance: furthering national unity. Governments and interest groups count on their control of the public space and narrative to shift, eventually, opinion in their favor. Yet this does not always work out and national unity can, in fact, actually be weakened. Such was the case in interwar Austria.[1]

I have set out to make this argument by analyzing Austrian attempts to create a national memorial that would give meaning to the world war. My focus is on the *Heldendenkmal* (Heroes' Memorial) on *Heldenplatz* (Heroes' Square) in Vienna. Although the initial ideas for such a memorial were floated in the 1920s, when Austria was still a democratic republic, the memorial was only completed a decade later under Austro-fascism. As we will see, this had a profound impact on the memorial's design and meaning. First, however, I will examine an earlier memorial project that promoted democratic and pacifist values and was closely connected with Vienna's then socialist city government: the war memorial on the *Zentralfriedhof* (Central Cemetery).

The War Memorial on the *Zentralfriedhof* in Vienna

After the world war, successive Austrian governments faced a monumental task: almost every Austrian had lost a son, friend, husband, or close relative. How could the bereaved be comforted in the wake of the empire's collapse? They went to war—like so many other soldiers in 1914–18—believing they had to fight to defend their families and homes. Retrospectively, they had rather defended a now deposed dynasty and dismantled empire. Had the soldiers therefore not died in vain? Was their death not futile? Religion offered some comfort, but it was difficult to find national meaning for their "ultimate sacrifice." Liberals could at least welcome one consequence of the defeat: Austria had become a democratic republic. Yet the soldiers had not fought for republican/democratic values, or even for an Austrian or German nation-state. For most Austrians, the solution to their dilemma was thus to become part of Germany. Yet the victorious powers expressly forbade *Anschluß* (in this context: union) and denied Austrians the right of self-determination. Instead, Austria became an independent state largely against the will of her people.[2]

For Austrian socialists, the war provided a different message: it had been a capitalist crime chiefly committed by the old elites. Socialists thus invoked the dead as a warning against militarism and on behalf of revolutionary action. Accordingly, only a socialist revolution would prevent a new imperialist war. Nevertheless, these were still not the ideals for which the k. (u.) k. soldiers had fought.

In the 1920s and early 1930s, most Austrian war memorials arose from local initiatives and were made by and for local communities and military units. For example, every day at noon since 3 May 1931, an organist plays the *Heldenorgel* (heroes' organ) in the Kufstein fortress (Tyrol) for ten minutes.[3] Yet despite being the biggest open-air organ in the world, the concert only commemorates the Austrian and German war dead, which originally had a pan-German meaning. Such local memorials and monuments to specific peoples or military units could not compensate for the lack of a national war memorial in the capital.

On the other hand, the memorials created during the war had imperial rather than national meanings. Thus, the postwar Austrian government was forced either to redefine these monuments or to build new ones that would privilege republican values. This was easier said than done. Austria, after all, was still trying to find her raison d'être, and the government was undecided as to how to use the war to integrate the population and reconcile social and political divisions. Moreover, political parties and varying veterans' organizations dominated war remembrance and used it to promote their particular interests. Most agreed that a national war memorial was needed, but it proved exceedingly difficult to settle on a representation of the war that would be acceptable to the majority of conflicting interest groups.

It is in this atmosphere that the Vienna city council and the organization of Viennese war invalids commissioned the monument for the city's *Zentralfriedhof* in 1924. Never intended to be a national war memorial, the socialist magistrate tasked the sculptor, Anton Hanak, to design a structure that would combine mourning for the fallen with a clear antiwar message. The outcome was a monument depicting a mother sinking to her knees and raising her arms in pain and desperation. Above her juts a stone overhang—symbol of war's heavy burden and threat. The monument was erected at the entrance to the cemetery's war graves

Figure 11.1. War memorial in Vienna's Central Cemetery (*Zentralfriedhof*). Photo courtesy of Dr. Christopher Brennan.

section containing the remains of some seventeen thousand soldiers who died in Vienna's military hospitals. On the rear of the monument was the inscription "NIE WIEDER KRIEG" (Never Again War) (Figure 11.1).[4]

The socialist newspapers praised the monument. The *Arbeiter-Zeitung* welcomed the fact that it conveyed a universal rather than more narrowly national message—"a monument of nameless humanity [*Menschheit*] mourning her lost sons."[5] Proponents even saw the chalkstone material used for the sculpture as a deliberate statement against traditional heroic monuments typically made from more expensive granite or "noble" marble or bronze. Hanak had originally planned to group male bronze figures representing sacrifice, superhuman struggle, truth, and loyalty (*Treue*) around the "mother of sorrows" (*Schmerzensmutter*).[6] This did not come to fruition and the mother figure stood alone. Without the bronze figures, the monument's antiwar message was even stronger than the artist originally intended.

Although the *Zentralfriedhof* monument could not satisfy all national groups, socialist newspapers and republican organizations went to great lengths to popularize its pacifist appeal. The war, the *Arbeiter-Zeitung* reminded readers, had made widows and invalids out of far too many women and men. The newspaper also blamed the military conflict for the high unemployment and general impoverishment of the Austrian populace. In this way, socialists hoped to unite the nation through suffering rather than triumph, and thus to mobilize Austria against war: "A shout resounds from the depths of this miserable hell suffered by the masses, a call to all subsequent generations: Never again war!" The *Arbeiter-Zeitung* argued that only democracy could prevent war, and that proletarian pacifism had to incorporate a patriotism that was capable of defending itself ("*wehrhafter Patriotismus*"). But it was up to the whole nation to resist the return of the Habsburg dynasty and to prevent capitalists and the ruling classes from again sending Austrians to war.[7]

On 31 October 1925, socialist Vienna and various republican organizations honored what the *Arbeiter-Zeitung* referred to as the "murdered soldiers" whose death had been "meaningless and useless." The demonstrations brought together memorialization and pacifist discourse. Members of the *Republikanischer Schutzbund* (the Social Democratic Party's paramilitary) marched to the cemetery in disciplined formations. The socialists agitated against capitalist society and any restoration of the Habsburg dynasty, using war remembrance to reinforce democracy, socialism, and pacifism.[8] Speeches by city officials during the monument's unveiling delivered a clear antiwar message. Moreover, the social-democratic mayor Karl Seitz reemphasized the non-national significance of the memorial, which was dedicated to *all* soldiers and war victims (*Opfer des Krieges*). He thus compared the monument to the "tombs of the unknown soldier" in other countries:

> When we celebrate [the nameless soldier], we are certainly not doing so in order to pay homage to the arts of war and violence; we are not honoring him as the tool but rather as the victim of war, as one who had to die. The monument's inscription—"Never again war!"—is the cry of all cultured humanity, a cry of culture and civilization against the barbarity of war.[9]

The government newspaper *Wiener Zeitung* likewise extolled the fact that, unlike other war memorials, this one neither glorified war nor called for revenge. Rather, it was an expression of "unspeakable pain" (*eines unsäglichen Schmerzes*) and "harrowing calamity" (*eines grauenvollen Unglückes*), the main purpose of which was to comfort the bereaved. The monument would thus serve as a warning to future generations and promote reconciliation.

Nevertheless, the *Wiener Zeitung* was none too happy about the antiwar inscription. Indeed, it expressed concern that some citizens might be offended by the message, "which shouts out at us—all too loudly!—from this monument." Moreover, if political infighting should stop when remembering the dead, then the monument's "fierce and fervent pagan spirit" (*heidnischer Geist heftig und brennend*) was unhelpful.[10] The conservative Christian Social journal *Reichspost* also expressed displeasure with the inscription, as well as with the monument's lack of religious symbols. In one of the many letters-to-the-editor published by the newspaper, a reader not only took umbrage at the inscription's political connotation, but also with the sculpture itself: rather than seeing a mother mourning her heroic sons, he imagined "a hyena, a Fury." The reader also found the monument to be deeply materialistic and devoid of any sign of Christian hope.[11]

Despite its pacifist message, the war memorial was not the sole prerogative of socialists and democrats—in 1925–26, it also became a rallying point for the political right. One day after the socialists gathered in front of it on All Saints' Day (1 November 1925), conservative veterans organizations and student corporations gathered around what they called the "heroes' monument" (*Heldendenkmal*) rather than the "mother of sorrows." The chairman of the right-wing *Frontkämpfervereinigung* (Frontline Fighters' Organization) of German-Austria, Colonel von Zeiß, abstained from openly criticizing the memorial's antiwar message. Yet he loudly declared that while veterans did not "frivolously" wish for war, they would always be ready to do their duty should the people (*Volkstum*) be threatened (though not necessarily with the same enthusiasm as in 1914). He further promised that those present were inspired by the fallen to work together for a better future, even if the fatherland had not shown adequate gratitude to its soldiers.[12]

Similar dueling ceremonies took place the following year. After the right-wing Frontline Fighters' Organization met near the memorial on 1 November to honor the world war dead, the leftist *Schutzbund* held its own gathering on *Totensonntag* ("Dead Sunday," 21 November 1926).[13] This time, *Frontkämpfer* chairman Colonel Zeiß did not spare the monument his criticism. He stirred his audience by declaring that the memorial failed to live up to the Austrian people's expectations—the *Frontkämpfer* would thus not rest until a new one had been built on the same site.[14] From this 1 November forward, the *Frontkämpferverband*, as it was also called, appears to have held its annual memorial ceremony beside the graves of former leaders, rather than at the monument itself. The army, meanwhile, commemorated the fallen in Vienna's St. Charles's Church (*Karlskirche*). Only the *Republikanische Schutzbund* continued to meet at the Viennese war memorial, though these gatherings received less press coverage than in previous years.

The political right maintained that the inscription "Never Again War" was an unacceptable politicization of war remembrance. However, they were not above evoking the fallen soldiers to promote their own political aims. The *Heldendenkmal* in central Vienna would be the very epitome of this politicization.

The *Heldendenkmal*

By 1930, Austrian cities including Vienna, Eisenstadt, Klagenfurt, Salzburg, and Innsbruck all had impressive World War I memorials. Yet these were no substitute for a national memorial. Ideas for what was already being called a *Heldendenkmal* went back to the first Austrian postwar democratic governments, and in 1925, several front fighter associations put forward concrete proposals. Yet, as with similar attempts in Germany, these early Austrian commemorative efforts came to naught.[15] Even in 1930, it was unclear where the memorial would be located and what it would look like. One idea was to erect a twenty-five meter iron cross on the Kahlenberg, at the edge of Vienna's nineteenth district. The remains of an unknown soldier would then be buried there. Other proposed sites included the classical Theseus temple in the Volksgarten; Austria's tallest mountain, the Grossglockner (the tomb would be blasted into the rock immediately beneath the peak); and the island of Wörth in the Danube.[16]

In 1932, the government finally settled on a site that was already a war memorial in its own right—the outer castle gate (*Äußeres Burgtor*) on Vienna's *Heldenplatz* (Figure 11.2). Designed by the Neoclassicist architect Peter (Pietro) Nobile and built by soldiers of the Imperial Austrian Army, the *Äußeres Burgtor* was unveiled in 1823 to commemorate the tenth anniversary of the victory over Napoleon's army at the Battle of Nations in Leipzig (1813). Later, equestrian statues of Prince Eugène de Savoy (1663–1736) and the Archduke Karl, Duke of Teschen (1771–1847)—arguably Austria's greatest military leaders—were erected on *Heldenplatz*. In 1916, laurel leaves were attached to the gate to honor the fallen soldiers of the Austro-Hungarian Army. The gate was thus already intimately connected with war remembrance.[17]

The Association for the Erection of an Austrian Heroes' Memorial (*Vereinigung zur Errichtung eines Österreichischen Heldendenkmals,* or simply *Heldendenkmalskomitee*) was established in 1932. Dominated by high-ranking

Figure 11.2. The outer castle gate (*Äußeres Burgtor*) on Vienna's Heroes' Square (*Heldenplatz*). Photo courtesy of Tofko, Wikimedia Commons.

officers of the imperial army and representatives of right-wing veterans' organizations, the Association was chaired by the veteran Major General Carl Jaschke. Colonel General (Count) Viktor Dankl von Kraśnik—the oldest living member of the imperial army in Austria—served as its patron.[18]

In the midst of the planning for the Heroes' Monument, the political landscape in Austria changed dramatically. On 4 March 1933, Federal Chancellor Engelbert Dollfuß suspended parliament and transformed the democratic republic into an authoritarian Austro-fascist "*Ständestaat*" (corporative state). Dollfuß soon created the Patriotic Front (*Vaterländische Front*) by merging the *Heimwehr* (the paramilitary organization of the political right) with the Christian Social Party and other conservative organizations. The government, which could now rule by decree, gradually suspended civil rights and dissolved the Social Democrats' paramilitary organization, the *Republikanische Schutzbund*. It also closed down the main workers' newspaper, the *Arbeiter-Zeitung*. Yet the repression did not merely target pro-republican organizations—it went after enemies of the new regime on both the far left and right (i.e., the communists and national-socialists) as well. In February 1934, resistance by the *Schutzbund* in Linz led to a brief civil war that ended victoriously for the government, its paramilitary organizations, and the federal army. The civil war cost 356 lives, 88 of whom were members of the *Schutzbund* or its allies. The remaining dead included 111 who fought for the state (police, gendarmerie, army, and volunteers), 112 noncombatants, and 45 who could not be allocated to any group. Nine *Schutzbund* members had been executed and ten to fifteen committed suicide. Following the civil war, scores of *Schutzbund* members were arrested and the government dissolved the Social-Democratic Party and its affiliated trade unions.[19]

The *Heldendenkmal* now became a joint project of right-wing veterans' organizations and the emerging Austro-fascist state. Yet despite this ideological uniformity, the planning process proved challenging due to the need to maintain the historical unity and consistency of the *Heldenplatz* site itself. In this respect, the committee stipulated that the memorial design fulfill the following criteria: (1) a monument to a "nameless soldier" of the Great War and the cornerstone in a network of local war memorials; (2) a monument to the "glorious imperial army" and its history over the past three centuries; and (3) a site for the obsequies of important personalities. In short, the *Ständestaat* and federal army (*Bundesheer*) would link themselves to the Austrian empire through war remembrance and the glorification of the imperial army.

They would ideally do so, moreover, with voluntary funding by the Austrian people rather than as a solely top-down government project. The Association for the Erection of an Austrian Heroes' Memorial held its first fundraising event in the ceremonial hall of the Habsburg Imperial Palace (the *Hofburg*) on 17 January 1934. It was hardly a populist occasion. Former Austrian counts and countesses, princes and princesses, archdukes and archduchesses met with retired generals and high-ranking representatives of the new government, including Federal Chancellor Dollfuß and Ministers Kurt Schuschnigg, Karl Buresch, Robert Kerber, and their wives. A state secretary in the Army Ministry, Prince Alois von Schönburg-Hartenstein, welcomed the guests with a speech emphasizing the objectives of the *Heldendenkmal*: to honor the dead heroes, their living comrades, and the war invalids. Schönburg-Hartenstein went on to praise the dutiful soldiers who had sacrificed their lives for the fatherland;[20] and Cardinal Theodor Innitzer, the provincial governors, and the federal government were named patrons (*Ehrenschützer*) of the *Heldendenkmalskomitee* and of the memorial itself.[21]

While the organizers considered the event a success, fundraising for the memorial proved more difficult. Veterans' organization members were reluctant to top up their membership fees to support the project, and the contributions from fundraising events and general collections did not meet the organizers' expectations. The fact that additional state funding was granted in the midst of the global economic crisis is not only indicative of this dilemma, but also of the government's eagerness to legitimize the new political order. In the end, more than 40 percent (three hundred thousand schillings) of the memorial's total cost of seven hundred thousand was covered by public money. The remainder came mostly from collections and voluntary contributions, with veterans' organizations contributing approximately one hundred thousand schillings.[22]

The design competition itself fared better in terms of public support: 173 artists and groups submitted some one thousand different project proposals. These projects had to comply with such conditions as confining the memorial to the internal halls of the *Burgtor* (which would thus have to be transformed) and maintaining the general external appearance of Heroes' Square and the castle gate. In light of these restrictions on artistic imagination, the *Reichspost* complained that it might have been better to create something new altogether.[23] But the organizers favored traditional designs over abstract or "unaesthetic" forms that were less likely to appeal to most Austrians. Thus the *Neue Freie Presse* judged a design by the prominent architects Max Fellerer and Eugen Wörle as inappropriate, since it included sculptures by the Austrian modernist Fritz Wotruba. The journal described Fellerer and Wörle as talented men who were incapable of satisfying the "sense of beauty" (*Schönheitssinn*) the memorial demanded: "The future heroes' monument must have in its decor figures which will really be liked by the 'ordinary man' and 'ordinary woman,' graceful but full of power so that they will become popular."[24] In the end, a jury of artists, committee members, and state representatives narrowed the field to nine projects, three of which won awards.

In opening an exhibition of the contest designs, retired Colonel General Dankl emphasized that the Austrian capital was the appropriate place for the national war memorial. Federal Chancellor Dollfuß, for his part, stressed that the monument should be a "symbol of the unity of all war comrades . . . [and] preserve the spirit of the past and love for our free, independent homeland in our youth." The monument would also symbolize "our freedom . . . [and] unity, irrespective of world view, language and of profession."[25]

The St. Pölten architect Rudolf Wondracek won the competition. Rather than placing the Hall of Honor (*Ehrenhalle*) for the imperial army in one of the *Burgtor*'s wings as in the Fellerer/Wörle design (which would then have decorated it with ceiling reliefs depicting the Empire's military history) or in a large crypt under the castle gate as in another proposal (an idea the *Reichspost* deemed too expensive),[26] Wondracek put it on top of the gate itself. The Hall thus had no roof—or in Wondracek's words, it "had the most wonderful roof in the world: the sky." Dedicated to the army, the Hall was filled with sculptures of imperial symbols such as the imperial eagle and relief portraits of Austrian generals from Wallenstein to Franz Conrad von Hötzendorf (the Chief of the General Staff from December 1912 through March 1917), as well as of representatives of Austria-Hungary's eight main nations and of soldiers from the previous three centuries.

The Austrian national character of the project was expressed through the deliberate use of native materials. The sculptures and reliefs were carved from local stone, and the unknown soldier was shaped from red Austrian marble. The latter was located in a wing of the *Burgtor*, which served the monument's second purpose: war remembrance. Designed by the sculptor and former frontline soldier Wilhelm Frass, the 2.70-meter sculpture of the dead warrior lies upon a sarcophagus inside the wing's crypt and chapel. Indeed, he can still be seen there today, in the uniform of an Austrian infantry soldier right down to the steel helmet. His left hand rests upon his heart, symbolizing the blood he spilled for his fatherland. In his right, he's holding a gun. An eternal flame burns behind the altar, and the walls on either side of it bear inscriptions commemorating Archduke Franz Ferdinand, "murdered in Sarajevo"; and Emperor Karl, who "died in exile" (*Verbannung*).[27]

Since the sculpture had not been completed when the *Heldendenkmal* (Figure 11.3) was unveiled on 9 September 1934, a cast copy was substituted (indeed, the entire building, including the sculpture, was not finalized until 26 October 1935).[28] In the meantime, on 25 July 1934, less than seven weeks before the unveiling, Austrian National Socialists murdered Dollfuß. The dead chancellor quickly became the patron saint of the *Ständestaat*, with a devoted following linked at once to the cult of the fallen soldiers and the glorification of the imperial army.[29] On 8 August 1934, his memorial service on the *Heldenplatz* drew some two hundred thousand faithful and prompted a state-wide industry of Dollfuß chapels, altar pictures, and renamed streets during the *Ständestaat*'s few remaining years before Nazi Germany occupied Austria in March 1938.[30]

Despite the heavy mood following Dollfuß's murder, there was broad acclaim in the press for the *Ehrenhalle* and its closeness to nature (i.e., with the sky as its

Figure 11.3. Heroes' Memorial (*Heldendenkmal*) inside the castle gate. Photo courtesy of Paul Miller.

ceiling). Virtually every newspaper dutifully cited Wondracek's sentiment that, with the exception of the St. Stephen's Cathedral (*Stephansdom*), nowhere in Vienna did one come closer to God.[31] When I began researching the Austrian Unknown Soldier, I was unsure whether the actual physical remains of an anonymous soldier had been buried in the crypt. It was discussed whether to bring the body of an unidentified soldier from the Italian front to the memorial. The Austrian Black Cross (war graves commission) supported the initiative. But the generals of the former army, the memorial committee, and finally the government opposed it on the nationalist grounds that burying an unknown soldier would be an imitation of the Entente countries.[32] To this day, there are no physical remains in the crypt.

On 8–9 September, the government staged two mass meetings on the *Heldenplatz*. Since the unveiling had been purposely timed with the national meeting of war veterans (*Kameradschaftstreffen*), some fifty thousand gathered in Vienna on the eighth. The city was abuzz with delegations from across the country, and the old imperial uniforms appeared everywhere. The "coordinated" (*gleichgeschaltet*) Austrian press published in full or extensively quoted from the many official speeches that sought to give meaning to the mass death of Austrian soldiers, in part by popularizing the Austro-fascist and clerical-conservative interpretation of the Great War. On the first day, the main speakers were the chairman of the *Heldendenkmalskomitee*, Carl Jaschke; the president of the Patriotic front and former leader of the *Heimwehr*, Vice Chancellor Ernst Rüdiger Starhemberg;

Austrian president Wilhelm Miklas; and Chancellor Kurt Schuschnigg. At the end of his speech, Schuschnigg raised his right hand and, according to the press, was "enthusiastically" cheered by the crowd. The federal anthem played and Starhemberg and Schuschnigg marched together to the *Äußeres Burgtor* to lay a wreath at a plaque commemorating the recently deceased Chancellor Dollfuß.

The first-day celebrations culminated at 5 p.m. with a rally by the Patriotic Front and its military arm (*Wehrfront*). Imperial army generals, former archdukes, barons, and their wives all took up their places of honor in the rally. Above the scene floated an image of the assassinated chancellor Dollfuß, while a black flag emblazoned with his white death mask hung from a building on the square.[33] The evening ended with fireworks meant to illustrate the last three hundred years of Austrian history.[34] Throughout the ceremony, oppositional voices were silenced.

The next day's unveiling ceremony was also staged such that it was almost impossible to disrupt the regime's display of self-adulation. The arrangement of the audience left little space for ordinary civilian participation, and the army, the *Wehrbund* (formerly *Heimwehr*), and various uniformed veterans' formations occupied the area in front of the gate. The main speakers, moreover, were a virtual who's who of the authoritarian *Ständestaat*: the Archbishop of Vienna, Cardinal Theodor Innitzer; the former defense minister, retired Colonel General Alois Schönburg-Hartenstein; retired Colonel General Viktor Dankl; Vienna's last Christian Social Mayor, Richard Schmitz; Chancellor Schuschnigg; and Austrian President Miklas. Cardinal Innitzer gave the state ceremony a religious component by celebrating a *Feldmesse* (field Mass) on a platform above the gate.

On both days, the speeches focused on seven themes, the first four of which were universal to modern war commemoration: (1) the duty to remember and honor the sacrifice of the fallen soldiers; (2) the importance of educating the younger generation; (3) the need to comfort the bereaved; and (4) a call for national unity invoking the unity that supposedly existed during the war, as well as that of the front-line soldiers themselves. The final themes were tailored to Austria: (5) the legitimization of the current political system (the *Ständestaat*) by placing it on a continuum of Austrian history; (6) the meaning of the sacrifice specifically for Austria; (7) and what might be termed the ceremony's *leitmotiv* —the propagation of the "Austrian idea" (*österreichische Idee*), which stood for the healing of national conflicts and overcoming class divisions.

Many of the speeches and newspaper articles criticized the treatment of veterans and the general lack of respect accorded the fallen soldiers in the immediate aftermath of the war. According to this argument, the returning soldiers were mocked and humiliated in the democratic republic—forced to watch powerlessly as Austria's dignity and honor were trampled in the mud. And now the *Ständestaat* was giving the fallen the kind of dignified memorial they deserved.[35] Cardinal Innitzer heard the dead soldiers say, "Do not forget us!"[36] And Austria answered, "They, the unknown soldiers," will never be forgotten.[37] The "deep and noble debt of gratitude owed the victims and warriors of the world war" was at last being discharged, exclaimed Captain Reichel, the *Wehrfront*'s Chief of Staff. In short, with the erection of the *Heldendenkmal*, Austria—that is, the *Ständestaat*—had finally fulfilled her duty toward "her heroic sons" (*Heldensöhne*). In the crypt, books were laid out bearing the names of every fallen Austrian. Each day, a page was turned to reveal new names and a mass was read for the dead soldiers.[38]

The two-day celebrations aimed to unite the war generation with Austria's youth.[39] The soldiers had done their duty, risking and often sacrificing their lives for the nation. Now it was up to the new generation to emulate them. The dead were thus an exhortation to the living to create Austria anew and to validate the soldiers' sacrifices.[40] In their readiness to defend Austria, moreover, the youth should learn not only from the military virtues of their forebears in World War I, but from Dollfuß himself, who supposedly also had sacrificed his life for Austria.[41] In his speech, Vice-Chancellor Starhemberg referred to "the heroic death of our Federal Chancellor and leader Dr. Dollfuß, who has joined the martyrs and heroes of our past."[42] He then absolved the front-line soldiers from guilt in the defeat, drawing on the Austrian version of the popular German "stab-in-the-back legend" (*Dolchstoßlegende*) in which "treason in the Hinterland" rather than military defeat made Austria's demise inevitable.[43] Cardinal Innitzer, for his part, agreed with the politicians though did not specify Dollfuß: the soldiers had died so that the next generation could live, and the next generation was obliged to work for a "strong Austria and a new nation [*Volk*]."[44]

Besides Cardinal Innitzer, the former Social-Democratic paper *Das kleine Blatt* alone also emphasized the importance of the monument for the bereaved. The newspaper, which had been brought into line by the new regime, reminded readers of how the soldiers had gone off to war, leaving their families and friends with "a terrible anxiety" (*eine furchtbare Ungewißheit*). Now the thoughts of the bereaved were in the distant countries where their sons lay buried. The journal continued:

> And yet, the pain suffered has been lightened by our gratitude. Of course, war as such is senseless—a crime, a wicked attack on flesh and blood. But the fate of the individual in war is not meaningless. Every person who lies out there gave his life in the fulfillment of the duty demanded of him. And in so doing he transcended himself to become a shining example for all those for whom service to an ideal constitutes the final fulfillment of life.[45]

The unity at the front, moreover, was to be reproduced through shared remembrance, which for the government represented a means to overcoming political and class divisions. As Schönburg-Hartenstein had said at an earlier event in 1934, the memorial should constitute a reminder "of the great unity [*Geschlossenheit*] of all nations [*Völker*] of our great erstwhile fatherland," and of the "enthusiasm with which we went to war [together] twenty years ago." In this way, continued Schönburg-Hartenstein, the memorial should also teach contemporary youth of the importance of such unity [*Einigkeit*] in the new, smaller fatherland.[46] According to most of the 9 September press, the monument admirably fulfilled this task, as the fallen soldier became "a symbol of the unity and communion of all good Austrians."[47] One speaker patriotically exclaimed: "The Austrian has a fatherland."[48]

Austrian workers, however, had not yet been reconciled to the new system. This task was taken up by the *Christliche Arbeiterzeitung*, the Christian Social newspaper for the working classes. On 15 September 1934, the paper stated that the present generation had to prove itself worthy of the heroes of Austria's great past. It was imperative to guide workers back toward the history of Austria and of the Austrian people—after all, this was their heritage as well. In short, the journal advocated using history to reconcile the working classes with the state: "Austria herself needs a workforce that is conscious of Austrian history and connected with this history, as out of this flows [*erfließt*] the bond between state and labor."[49]

The fallen soldiers would thus set examples for subsequent generations of Austrians—by demonstrating the power of unity, standing in the glorious traditions of the old imperial army, and providing the link between the former empire and the authoritarian *Ständestaat*. The democratic republic, meanwhile, was deemed an aberration. "The old love of country [*Vaterland*] has once again come alive," exclaimed Federal Minister Fey.[50] The president of the *Wehrfront*, Vice-Chancellor Starhemberg, placed his organization in the tradition of the "glorious old Austro-Hungarian Army," just as the *Ständestaat* put itself in the tradition of the Empire as a whole.[51] The speakers thus not only linked Dollfuß, the *Ständestaat*'s founder, to the Great War fallen ("a front-line soldier from our midst"), but to the imperial family itself: "Three great men died a martyr's death for Austria: Archduke Franz Ferdinand, Emperor Karl, and Chancellor Dr. Dollfuß. They died because they wished to make Austria free and happy. Their legacy lives on and is holy."[52]

It was not unusual for the cult of the fallen after World War I to be construed religiously. The soldiers' deaths were equated with that of Christ. And just as Christ's martyrdom had redeemed mankind, the fallen soldiers had redeemed the nation. The lead article in the *Reichspost* on 9 September expressed it this way: "New life arises out of [the soldiers'] death. For sacrifice is stronger than success, more sublime than victory, more imperishable than glory. It is holy. . . . Their sacrifice has the power to inspire the present, no matter how difficult life may be, with the willingness to win the future for Austria."[53]

Of course, Austria had no realistic possibility of regaining her old empire. Indeed, the small state was more likely to be swallowed up by its powerful

German neighbor than to reincorporate the imperial crownlands. Thus, a less revisionist-sounding mission statement for the new nation was needed. But what mission could convincingly integrate Austria's powerful imperial past with the diminished and vulnerable nation-state of the present? The solution was to glorify neither the old nor the new Austria, but rather the "eternal Austria, the idea of Austria, which stands for the idea of the reconciliation between nations, of peace between classes." This became the sacred calling for which the soldiers of the multinational army had fought and died. Crucial too was the fact that this idea was not invented by the *Ständestaat*, but took shape during the war itself.[54]

In this sense, then, the "mission" of the new Austrian state was consistent with that of the old Austrian Empire, without being dependent upon its recreation. Just as the Habsburg dynasty had brought Christianity, culture, and peace to its peoples and protected them against "the storm of barbarism," Austrians would go on defending "European culture." Indeed, they had done just that during the world war.[55] The new Austria was thus held up as the gateway to Europe, a task that had been "entrusted to our ancestors—honest [*schlichten*], quiet and reliable gatekeepers." Austria's "mission," in sum, was that which it had always been: to serve as Europe's "spiritual and moral bulwark" (*Bollwerk des Geistes und der Gesittung*).[56] Starhemberg went so far as to argue that Austria was destined to write European history, even world history. The world would only be "healed" from the Great War when Austria's historical importance was restored and recognized.[57]

Cardinal Innitzer set a slightly more pacific tone in affirming his support for the *Ständestaat* and expressing his sense of an Austrian mission. Austrian soldiers had gone to war in 1914, he argued, to fight for peace: "our heroes set forth for the sake of peace, so as to protect family, homeland, nation [*Volk*] and fatherland." The legacy of the fallen soldiers was the call for peace, and the living must build a "holy, new Austria." As the "guarantor of Europe's peace," Austria would enable "a strong, Christian West [*Abendland*]" to rise again.[58]

Thus did the *Heldendenkmal* go further than providing a national monument for Austria's world war dead: it honored the "victors of an eternal idea." This theme was embellished through the notion that Austria was "not dead, but resurrected." And since only "the Christian ethos [could] save European civilization," Austria would "once again be the model for a Europe torn asunder."[59]

In constructing Austria as the flag bearer for western/Christian civilization, *Ständestaat* leaders were also making a sly dig at Germany. There, they argued, the Nazi Party had come to power "in times of national confusion," whereas Austria had faithfully protected "the most precious treasures [*edelste Schätze*] of the German spirit [*deutsches Wesen*]."[60] Austria, proclaimed President Miklas, was the "redeeming idea for all Europe, for the happiness and peace of the world, and not least for the honor of the German name."[61] In other words, Austrian soldiers had died so that German and European civilization could live and, ultimately, world peace could be restored. Similarly, Schuschnigg ended his speech on 9 September by reciting the slogan of the Dollfuß government, which itself came from the title of an 1848 book by the Austrian politician Franz Schuselk: "Austria above all else, if only she wants it." The Chancellor then followed this with his own slogan: "Austria above all else. Comrades, we want it!" (*Österreich über alles! Kameraden, wir wollen!*). His speech reminded the audience of Austria's "thousand-year-old historical mission," before ending with the refrain: "Austria will remain forever."[62]

The *Ständestaat* did face the question of how much it should emphasize its "Austrian-ness," versus the German essence of Austria. Dollfuß had founded the Patriotic Front in 1933 to unite all right-wing and Christian organizations. He professed its adherence to Austria, though did not speak of Austria as a nation. Dollfuß's successor, Schuschnigg, also spoke of Austria's "German nature" and avoided the term "Austrian nation." Austro-fascism thus promoted an independent Austrian state of the German nation. After Hitler came to power in Germany in 1933, Austro-fascists presented their country as the better Germany and the Austrian people as a second, *better* German nation.[63] War remembrance was one of the main vehicles to propagate these ideas, which formed the very basis of the *Ständestaat*'s ideology.

Following the speeches on 9 September, dignitaries led by the Federal President and other government leaders laid wreaths in the *Ehrenhalle*. Archduke Eugen contributed an enormous laurel wreath on behalf of the former Empress Zita, the wife of the last Austrian Emperor Karl. The German Army minister, a Hungarian delegation, and a Chinese military delegation also laid wreaths. The guests then moved to the crypt with the Tomb of the Dying Soldier (*Grab des Sterbenden Soldaten*) to pay their final respects on behalf of a reborn Austria.

Epilogue

The war memorial in the *Zentralfriedhof* divided the Austrian public. Initially, right-wing veterans' organizations tried to claim the space and monument, though they later preferred to hold their meetings and memorial rituals at sites with less pacifist associations. Social-democratic and republican organizations, however, continued to remember the war dead at this monument. After the Austro-fascists came to power, the controversial inscription at the center of these political divisions—"Never Again War"—was replaced with the more anodyne words "God, grant us peace! To the Fallen of the World War [from] the City of Vienna" (*Herr, gib uns den Frieden! Den Gefallenen des Weltkrieges die Stadt Wien*). The new government additionally placed a cross atop the monument, thus giving it a Christian meaning not present in the original design. Today, the *Zentralfriedhof* memorial still resonates powerfully, even if it is often overlooked by tourists more interested in the graves of Austrian authors, artists, composers, actors, and politicians. Bereft of its original, provocative conceptualization, it has become a marginal monument.

Ironically, the *Heldendenkmal* in the center of the capital has come to share the fate of Vienna's official war memorial in the *Zentralfriedhof*. Its marginalization, however, is due to its origins and function during Austro-fascism. The unveiling of the memorial was an opportunity the *Ständestaat* simply could not resist. It thus stamped the ideology of Austro-fascism onto the discourse surrounding the war memorial. And this was certainly not a message shared by all Austrians: on 9 September 1934, both the socialist workers and the national-socialists were absent from the dedication ceremonies on the *Heldenplatz*.

Dollfuß's state funeral in July 1934 and the unveiling of the *Heldendenkmal* that September have since been overshadowed by another mass meeting that took place on the *Heldenplatz* just four years later: on 15 March 1938, Adolf Hitler proclaimed the return of his homeland (*meine Heimat*) to Germany to a cheering crowd of some three hundred thousand. Today, the *Heldenplatz* evokes the memory of the *Anschluß*, Nazi Germany's annexation of Austria (belittlingly renamed the *Ostmark*). Ironically, considering the *Ständestaat*'s opposition to National Socialism, the Nazis found much to recycle in Austro-fascist ideology, including the oft-invoked German nature of Austria and Austria's role as a bulwark against invading eastern hordes.[64] Yet while the Nazis also destroyed many *Ständestaat* monuments and all those that honored Dollfuß, they did not alter the *Heldendenkmal*. Even its hall of honor and the crypt with the dead warrior—where Hitler and other Nazi leaders laid wreaths—were left untouched. The SA (*Sturmabteilung*, or NS paramilitary) was given its own monument just below the central passage of the castle gate, which in former times had been reserved for the emperor.

The SA monument was removed in 1945, but one symbol of the national-socialist years remained until quite recently. In 1934, Wilhelm Frass, who created the sculpture of the dead warrior, belonged to the then illegal National Socialist Party. After the *Anschluß*, he proudly recounted how he had deliberately subverted the intentions of the *Ständestaat* by slipping a metal capsule with a national-socialist message underneath the marble sculpture when it finally replaced the temporary statue in 1935. In 2012, Austrian defense minister Norbert Darabos decided to investigate whether there was any truth to Frass's story, and ordered the sculpture searched. Sure enough, the following message was discovered:

> After all the terrible events, after all the humiliation, may God put an end to the unspeakably distressing feud between brothers and lead our united glorious people under the banner of the sun wheel [i.e., swastika] to the Most High. Then, my comrades, you will not have fallen in vain.[65]

Thus, since 1945, Austrian chancellors, presidents, foreign ambassadors, and state guests have bowed their heads before a monument bearing a concealed pro-Nazi message.

This was not, however, the complete story. To everyone's surprise, a second capsule was found bearing a message from Frass' coworker, the sculptor Alfons Riedel. His missive was also addressed to the German nation, though it had a decidedly more pacifist tone: "I hope that future generations of our immortal nation will not again be faced with the need to erect monuments for those who fell in violent conflicts between nations."[66] There are many layers of meaning to the *Heldendenkmal*, though it never became a popular site of memory in Austria. According to the historian Peter Stachel, most Austrians have never heard of it. Fewer still, it follows, have ever paid their respects at the crypt with the unknown warrior.[67]

Christoph Mick is Professor of History at the University of Warwick. He received his PhD and habilitated at the University of Tübingen, Germany. He is a specialist in twentieth-century Russian, Polish, and Ukrainian history and is currently writing a transnational history of the cult of unknown soldier in interwar Europe. His last monograph examined the experience of war in the city of L'viv, Ukraine: *Lemberg—Lwów—L'viv, 1914–1947: Violence and Ethnicity in a Contested City* (West Lafayette: Purdue University Press, 2016).

Notes

1. T. G. Ashplant, Graham Dawson, and Michael Roper, "The Politics of War Memory and Commemoration: Contexts, Structures and Dynamics," in *Commemorating War: The Politics of Memory*, ed. T. G. Ashplant, Graham Dawson, and Michael Roper (London: Routledge, 2000), 3–85; Jay Winter and Emmanuel Sivan, "Setting the Framework," in *War and Remembrance in the Twentieth Century*, ed. Jay Winter and Emmanuel Sivan (Cambridge, UK: Cambridge University Press, 1999), 6–39; J. M. Mayo, "War Memorials as Political Memory," *Geographical Review* 78 (1988): 62–75.
2. According to the provisions of the Treaty of Saint-Germain (10 September 1919), German-Austria had to change its name to Austria, and the new state had to accept that "the independence of Austria is inalienable." This could only be changed with the consent of the League of Nations.
3. Author, "Die Heldenorgel in Kufstein," *Wiener Zeitung* 103, 5 May 1931, 3.
4. Josef Seiter, "Politische Denkmäler im Wien der Ersten Republik (1918–1934)," in *Steinernes Bewußtsein: die öffentliche Repräsentation staatlicher und nationaler Identität Österreichs in seinen Denkmälern*, ed. Stefan Riesenfellner (Wien: Böhlau, 1998), 427–29.
5. "Wehrhafter Friedenswille," *Arbeiter-Zeitung* 300, 1 November 1925, 1.
6. "Das Kriegerdenkmal der Gemeinde Wien im Zentralfriedhof," *Arbeiter-Zeitung* 297, 29 October 1925, 8.

7. "Wehrhafter Friedenswille," *Arbeiter-Zeitung*, 1. In German: "Aus dieser Hölle der Massennot tönt es allen nachkommenden Geschlechtern entgegen: Nie wieder Krieg!"
8. "Die Totenfeier des Republikanischen Schutzbundes," *Arbeiter-Zeitung* 300, 1 November 1925, 7.
9. "Das Kriegerdenkmal der Gemeinde Wien," *Arbeiter-Zeitung* 300, 1 November 1925, 7. In German: "Wenn wir diesen [den namenlosen Soldaten] feiern, dann gewiß nicht im Sinne einer Huldigung für das Handwerk des Krieges und für die Gewalt, wir huldigen ihm nicht als dem Werkzeug, sondern als dem Opfer des Krieges, das sterben mußte. Das Wort am Denkmal, das sagt: 'Nie wieder Krieg!', das ist der Schrei der gesamten Kulturmenschheit, ein Schrei der Kultur und Zivilisation über die Barbarei des Krieges . . ." See also "Enthüllung des Kriegerdenkmals auf dem Zentralfriedhofe," *Wiener Zeitung* 250, 1 November 1925, 4.
10. "Das Kriegerdenkmal auf dem Zentralfriedhofe," *Wiener Zeitung* 248, 30 October 1925, 2.
11. "Das neue Kriegerdenkmal," *Reichspost* 302, 3 November 1925, 5.
12. "Die Totengedenkfeier des Bundesheeres," *Reichspost* 301, 2 November 1925, 4.
13. "Der Republikanische Schutzbund ehrt die Kriegsgefallenen," *Arbeiter-Zeitung* 302, 2 November 1926, 12. *Totensonntag* is the Sunday before Advent on which the dead are commemorated (thus it always falls between 20 and 26 November).
14. "Die Tage der Toten," *Reichspost* 302, 2 November 1926, 6.
15. On Germany, see Benjamin Ziemann, *Contested Commemorations: Republican War Veterans and Weimar Political Culture* (Cambridge, UK: Cambridge University Press, 2013).
16. C. Jaschke, "Die Grundlagen zum Werden des österreichischen Heldenkmales," in *Österreichisches Heldendenkmal: Gedenkschrift anläßlich der Weihe des österreichischen Heldendenkmales am 9. September 1934*, ed. the Vereinigung zur Errichtung eines österreichischen Heldendenkmals (Wien: Steyrermühl, 1934). On the Großglockner project, see "Ein Grab für den unbekannten Soldaten Österreichs," *Vorarlberger Tagblatt* 254, 5 November 1924, 1; "Das Denkmal des unbekannten Soldaten," *Vorarlberger Tagblatt* 53, 5 March 1926, 1.
17. *Lorbeer für unsere Helden 1914–1916: Denkschrift zur Enthüllung der Kränze am äußeren Burgtor in Wien* (Wien: Militär-Witwen u. Waisenfond, 1916).
18. "Oesterreich gedenkt seiner Helden," *Reichspost* 46, 17 February 1934, 9.
19. Kurt Bauer, "Die Opfer des Februar 1934: Auszug aus dem Projektbericht 'Die Opfer des Februar 1934. Sozialstrukturelle und kollektivbiografische Untersuchungen,'" accessed 13 November 2015, http://www.kurt-bauer-geschichte.at/PDF_Forschung_Unterseiten/Kurt-Bauer_Opfer-Februar-34.pdf. The project was based in the Ludwig-Boltzmann-Institut für Historische Sozialwissenschaft. On the Austrian civil war, see also Emmerich Tálos, *Das austrofaschistische Herrschaftssystem: Österreich 1933–1938* (Berlin: Lit, 2013); Manfred Scheuch, *Der Weg zum Heldenplatz: Eine Geschichte der österreichischen Diktatur 1933–1938* (Wien: Kremayr & Scheriau, 2005); Roland Jezussek, *Der "Austrofaschismus"—ein Modell autoritärer Staatsform: Ideologie, Entstehung und Scheitern des österreichischen Ständestaates* (Saarbrücken: VDM, 2009).
20. "Dem unbekannten Soldaten Österreichs!" *Reichspost* 15, 17 January 1934, 7.
21. Ibid.
22. Österreichisches Staatsarchiv—Archiv der Republik (Austrian State Archives, Archives of the Republic), Landesverteidigung (Defense), Bundesministerium für Landesverteidigung 1. Republik (Federal Ministry of Defense of the First Republic), Vereinigung zur

Errichtung eines Heldendenkmales in Wien l (previously 07R118/1, 302–06.) Urkunde zur Schlussteinlegung im Österreichischen Heldendenkmal in Wien, 26. Oktober 1933.
23. "Das äußere Burgtor als Heldendenkmal," *Reichspost* 49, 20 February 1934, 10.
24. "Das österreichische Heldendenkmal," *Neue Freie Presse* 24940, 18 February 1934, 14.
25. "Das Heldendenkmal ein Sinnbild unserer Freiheit," *Reichspost* 48, 19 February 1934, 5.
26. "Das äußere Burgtor als Heldendenkmal," *Reichspost* 49, 20 February 1934, 10.
27. "Erster Blick auf das Heldendenkmal," *Reichspost* 251, 9 September 1934, 2.
28. "Das österreichische Heldendenkmal," *Neue Freie Presse* 25140, 8 September 1934, 11.
29. Tálos, *Das austrofaschistische Herrschaftssystem*, 116.
30. David Clay Large, *Between Two Fires: Europe's Path in the 1930s* (New York: Norton, 1990), 96. For more on the Dollfuß cult, see Lucile Dreidemy, *Der Dollfuß-Mythos: Eine Biographie des Posthumen* (Wien: Böhlau, 2014), 61–154.
31. "Das äußere Burgtor als Heldendenkmal," *Reichspost* 49, 20 February 1934, 10.
32. Wilhelm Wenk, "Heldendenkmäler und Heldenehrung," *Reichspost* 251, 9 September 1934, 8.
33. "Heldenfeier im Heeresmuseum," *Reichspost* 245, 3 September 1934, 7.
34. "Oesterreich über alles: Wir wollen!" *Reichspost* 245, 3 September 1934, 4; "Das Soldatentreffen auf dem Heldenplatz," *Neue Freie Presse* 25141, 9 September 1934, 6–7; "Wien im Zeichen der Heldenfeier," *Das kleine Blatt* 233, 9 September 1934, 2.
35. From Starhemberg's speech. "Wir sind kampfesfroher denn je!" *Reichspost* 251, 9 September 1934, 4; "Das Soldatentreffen auf dem Heldenplatz," *Neue Freie Presse* 25141, 9 September 1934, 6.
36. "Den für Österreich Gefallenen," *Wiener Zeitung* 252, 10 September 1934, 1–3.
37. "Dem unbekannten Soldaten," *Das kleine Blatt* 233, 9 September 1934, 2.
38. "Das Soldatentreffen auf dem Heldenplatz," *Neue Freie Presse* 25141, 9 September 1934, 6; "Die vaterländische Kundgebung auf dem Heldenplatz," *Wiener Zeitung* 251, 9 September 1934, 2f; "Die vaterländische Kundgebung auf dem Heldenplatz," *Wiener Zeitung* 251, 9 September 1934, 2f.
39. "Heldenfeier im Heeresmuseum," *Reichspost* 251, 9 September 1934, 7.
40. Jaschke, "Die Grundlagen zum Werden," in *Österreichisches Heldendenkmal*, 43–48.
41. "Dem Unbekannten Soldaten Österreichs," *Reichspost* 15, 17 January 1934, 7.
42. "'Wir sind kampfesfroher denn je,'" *Reichspost* 251, 9 September 1934, 4.
43. "Der unglückliche Ausgang des Krieges 1918, den nicht der Frontsoldat verschuldet hat, sondern den der Verrat im Hinterland herbeigeführt hat, kann für uns nicht eine endgültige Lösung für Österreich bedeuten." Starhemberg, "Das Soldatentreffen auf dem Heldenplatz," *Neue Freie Presse* 25141, 9 September 1934, 6.
44. "Unsere Helden zogen um des Friedens willen aus, um Familie, Heimat, Volk und Vaterland zu schützen." Cardinal Innitzer, "Den für Österreich Gefallenen," *Wiener Zeitung* 252, 10 September 1934, 1–3.
45. "Dem unbekannten Soldaten," *Das kleine Blatt* 233, 9 September 1934, 2.
46. "Dem Unbekannten Soldaten Österreichs," *Reichspost* 15, 17 January 1934, 7.
47. "Das Soldatentreffen auf dem Heldenplatz," *Neue Freie Presse* 25141, 9 September 1934, 6. The newspaper is quoting the speech of the chairman of the *Heldendenkmalskomitee*, Major General (Army Reserve) Jaschke.
48. "Das Soldatentreffen auf dem Heldenplatz," *Neue Freie Presse* 25141, 9 September 1934, 6; "Die vaterländische Kundgebung auf dem Heldenplatz," *Wiener Zeitung* 251, 9 September 1934, 2.

49. "Österreich selbst braucht eine Arbeiterschaft, die sich der österreichischen Geschichte bewußt ist und die dieser Geschichte verbunden ist, weil daraus die Verbundenheit zwischen Staat und Arbeiterschaft erfließt." "Das österreichische Heldendenkmal," *Österreichische Arbeiter-Zeitung* 37, 15 September 1934, 5.
50. "Das Soldatentreffen auf dem Heldenplatz," *Neue Freie Presse* 25141, 9 September 1934, 6.
51. "'Wir sind kampfesfroher denn je,'" *Reichspost* 251, 9 September 1934, 4.
52. "Das Soldatentreffen auf dem Heldenplatz," *Neue Freie Presse* 25141, 9 September 1934, 6; "Die vaterländische Kundgebung auf dem Heldenplatz," *Wiener Zeitung* 251, 9 September 1934, 2f.
53. "Aus dem Tode das neue Leben," *Reichspost* 251, 9 September 1934, 1.
54. Markus Erwin Haider, *Im Streit um die österreichische Nation: Nationale Leitwörter in Österreich 1866–1938* (Wien: Böhlau, 1998), 172–80.
55. "Das Soldatentreffen auf dem Heldenplatz," *Neue Freie Presse* 25141, 9 September 1934, 6; "Die vaterländische Kundgebung auf dem Heldenplatz," *Wiener Zeitung* 251, 9 September 1934, 2.
56. "Und setzet ihr nicht das Leben ein . . . ," *Wiener Zeitung* 251, 9 September 1934, 1.
57. "'Wir sind kampfesfroher denn je,'" *Reichspost* 251, 9 September 1934, 4; "Das Soldatentreffen auf dem Heldenplatz," *Neue Freie Presse* 25141, 9 September 1934, 6.
58. "Den für Österreich Gefallenen," *Wiener Zeitung* 252, 10 September 1934, 1–2.
59. "Aus dem Tode das neue Leben," *Reichspost* 251, 9 September 1934, 1.
60. Ibid.
61. "Den für Österreich Gefallenen," *Wiener Zeitung* 252, 10 September 1934, 1–3.
62. Franz Schuselka, *Oesterreich über alles, wenn es nur will!* (Hamburg: Hoffmann und Campe, 1848); "Den für Österreich Gefallenen," *Wiener Zeitung*, 10 September 1934, 1–3.
63. Friedrich Grassegger, "Nationalsozialistische Denkmäler in Österreich," in *Steinernes Bewußtsein*, ed. Stefan Riesenfellner, 547–73.
64. Peter Diem, *Die Symbole Österreichs: Zeit und Geschichte in Zeichen* (Wien: Kremayr & Scheriau, 1995), 203–6.
65. "'Gefallener Krieger': Nazi-Metallkapsel in Burgtor-Krypta gefunden," *Der Standard*, 19 Juli 2012, http://derstandard.at/1342139530529/Gefallener-Krieger-Nazi-Metallkapsel-in-Burgtor-Krypta-gefunden.
66. Ibid.
67. Peter Stachel, "Der Heldenplatz: Zur Semiotik eines österreichischen Gedächtnis-Ortes," in *Steinernes Bewußtsein*, ed. Stefan Riesenfellner, 619–56. Abridged version: "Der Heldenplatz als österreichischer Gedächtnisort," *Österreichische Akademie der Wissenschaften*, accessed 17 September 2015, http://www.oeaw.ac.at/ikt/mitarbeiterinnen/publikationen-der-mitarbeiter/peter-stachel-werkverzeichnis-seit-1999/peter-stachel-werkverzeichnis-vor-1999/der-heldenplatz-als-oesterreichischer-gedaechtnisort/.

Bibliography

Ashplant, T. G., Graham Dawson, and Michael Roper, eds. *Commemorating War: The Politics of Memory*. London: Routledge, 2000.

Bauer, Kurt. "Die Opfer des Februar 1934: Auszug aus dem Projektbericht 'Die Opfer des Februar 1934. Sozialstrukturelle und kollektivbiografische Untersuchungen.'" Accessed 13 November 2015. http://www.kurt-bauer-geschichte.at/PDF_Forschung_Unterseiten/Kurt-Bauer_Opfer-Februar-34.pdf.

Botz, Gerhard. *Gewalt in der Politik: Attentate, Zusammenstöße, Putschversuche, Unruhen in Österreich 1918 bis 1938*. 2nd ed. München: Wilhelm Fink, 1983.

Brook-Shephard, Gordon. *Dollfuss*. London: Macmillan, 1961.

Bußhoff, Heinrich. *Das Dollfuß-Regime in Österreich*. Berlin: Duncker & Humblot, 1968.

Cornwall, Mark and John-Paul Newman, eds. *Sacrifice and Rebirth: The Legacy of the Last Habsburg War*. New York: Berghahn Books, 2016.

Diem, Peter. *Die Symbole Österreichs: Zeit und Geschichte in Zeichen*. Wien: Kremayr & Scheriau, 1995.

Dreidemy, Lucile. *Der Dollfuß-Mythos: Eine Biographie des Posthumen*. Wien: Böhlau, 2014.

Goebel, Stefan. *The Great War and Medieval History: War, Remembrance and Medievalism in Britain and Germany, 1914–1940*. Cambridge, UK: Cambridge University Press, 2007.

Haider, Markus Erwin. *Im Streit um die österreichische Nation: Nationale Leitwörter in Österreich 1866–1938*. Wien: Böhlau, 1998.

Hettling, Manfred and Jörg Echternkamp, eds. *Gefallenengedenken im globalen Vergleich: Nationale Tradition, politische Legitimation und Individualisierung der Erinnerung*. München: Oldenbourg, 2013.

Jezussek, Roland. *Der "Austrofaschismus"—ein Modell autoritärer Staatsform: Ideologie, Entstehung und Scheitern des österreichischen Ständestaates*. Saarbrücken: VDM, 2009.

Kluge, Ulrich. *Der österreichische Ständestaat 1934–1938: Entstehung und Scheitern*. Wien: Verlag für Geschichte und Politik, 1984.

Koselleck, Reinhard and Michael Jeismann, eds. *Der politische Totenkult: Kriegerdenkmäler in der Moderne*. München: Wilhelm Fink, 1993.

Large, David Clay. *Between Two Fires: Europe's Path in the 1930s*. New York: Norton, 1990.

Lorbeer für unsere Helden 1914–1916: Denkschrift zur Enthüllung der Kränze am äußeren Burgtor in Wien. Wien: Militär-Witwen u. Waisenfond, 1916.

Mayo, J. M. "War Memorials as Political Memory." *Geographical Review* 78 (1988): 62–75.

Meysels, Lucian O. *Der Austrofaschismus—Das Ende der ersten Republik und ihr letzter Kanzler*. Wien: Amalthea, 1992.

Mosse, George L. *Fallen Soldiers: Reshaping the Memory of the World Wars*. Oxford: Oxford University Press, 1994.

Naderer, Otto. *Der bewaffnete Aufstand: Der Republikanische Schutzbund der österreichischen Sozialdemokratie und die militärische Vorbereitung auf den Bürgerkrieg (1923–1934)*. Graz: Ares, 2005.

Neuhäuser, Stephan, ed. *"Wir werden ganze Arbeit leisten." Der austrofaschistische Staatsstreich 1934*. Norderstedt: Books on demand, 2004.

Österreichisches Heldendenkmal: Gedenkschrift anläßlich der Weihe des österreichischen Heldendenkmales am 9. September 1934. Edited by the Vereinigung zur Errichtung eines österreichischen Heldendenkmals. Wien: Steyrermühl, 1934.

Riesenfellner, Stefan, ed. *Steinernes Bewußtsein: die öffentliche Repräsentation staatlicher und nationaler Identität Österreichs in seinen Denkmälern*. Wien: Böhlau, 1998.

Schafranek, Hans. *"Sommerfest mit Preisschießen." Die unbekannte Geschichte des NS-Putsches im Juli 1934*. Wien: Czernin, 2006.

Schausberger, Franz. *Letzte Chance für die Demokratie*. Wien: Böhlau, 1993.

Scheuch, Manfred. *Der Weg zum Heldenplatz: Eine Geschichte der österreichischen Diktatur 1933–1938*. Wien: Kremayr & Scheriau, 2005.
Schuselka, Franz. *Oesterreich über alles, wenn es nur will!* Hamburg: Hoffmann und Campe, 1848.
Tálos, Emmerich. *Das austrofaschistische Herrschaftssystem: Österreich 1933–1938*. Berlin: Lit, 2013.
Tálos, Emmerich and Wolfgang Neugebauer, eds. *Austrofaschismus—Politik, Ökonomie, Kultur 1933–1938*. 5th ed. Münster: Lit, 2005.
Walterkirchen, Gundula. *Engelbert Dollfuß—Arbeitermörder oder Heldenkanzler*. Wien: Molden, 2004.
Weinzierl, Erika and Kurt Skalnik. *Österreich 1918–38*. 2 vols. Graz: Styria, 1983.
Winter, Jay. *Sites of Memory—Sites of Mourning: The Great War in European Cultural History*. Cambridge, UK: Cambridge University Press, 1998.
Winter, Jay and Emmanuel Sivan, eds. *War and Remembrance in the Twentieth Century*. Cambridge, UK: Cambridge University Press, 1999.
Ziemann, Benjamin. *Contested Commemorations: Republican War Veterans and Weimar Political Culture*. Cambridge, UK: Cambridge University Press, 2013.

Newspapers
Reichspost
Neue Freie Presse
Das kleine Blatt
Wiener Zeitung
Österreichische Arbeiter Zeitung
Arbeiter-Zeitung
Vorarlberger Tagblatt

Chapter 12

"THE FIRST VICTIM OF THE FIRST WORLD WAR"
Franz Ferdinand in Austrian Memory

Paul Miller

In 1909, at age forty-six, Franz Ferdinand made a decision about his death that would shape the memory of his life: he would be buried beside his morganatic wife, Sophie Chotek, at his palace in Artstetten (Lower Austria). That may not seem like much from the perspective of our own era. But in the context of the tradition-bound Habsburg dynasty, and in view of the Archduke's exalted place in it as next-in-line for the imperial throne, it was pure rebellion. For what the Successor had also determined was where he would *not* be interred—with his esteemed ancestors in Vienna's Kaiser Crypt, which was strictly off-limits to lesser nobility like the Duchess of Hohenberg.

Franz Ferdinand's decision came from love for his wife rather than any lack of regal airs. In fact, his corpse would have found good company amongst forbears like Joseph II (r. 1780–90), whose reforms in everything from taxation to religious toleration had aimed to unite his realm under a more uniform and centralized rule. For his own epoch, the Archduke was also planning reforms—this time to combat the secular nationalism that threatened to pull apart the imperial crownlands and, the heir feared, push Europe's Great Powers into a war that Austria-Hungary could never survive.[1]

The Archduke's model, however, was Franz I (r. 1804–35), who reconsolidated the regime following Napoleon's dismemberment of the Habsburg-ruled Holy Roman Empire. In his "Program for the Change of Rule," the

Figure 12.1. Artstetten crypt with tombs of Franz Ferdinand and Sophie von Hohenberg. Author's photo.

Successor stipulated that he would ascend the throne as Franz II rather than Franz Ferdinand I, thus constructing a "self-narrative."[2] The tragedy, of course, is that the Archduke would be dead before the narrative by which he longed to be remembered could actually be embarked upon. The irony is still harsher: his death would always be associated with the war that, as he had warned, the Monarchy did not survive.

Franz Ferdinand's entire life was shot through with such paradox. The Successor who placed private feeling before family custom and called Habsburg rulership a "crown of thorns" also staked his legacy upon assuring the continuity of the imperial patrimony.[3] Was Franz Ferdinand truly the man to steady the Monarchy? Did he possess the personal and political acumen needed to advance the "serious organizational change" essential to satisfying the national aspirations of the Empire's diverse population?[4] Or rather was the multinational state "increasingly becoming an anachronism" in the age of nationalism and democratization?[5] Was the conservative Archduke so distant from his own era that he "would have succumbed beneath [the Empire's] ruins"?[6]

This question, though counterfactual, dominates the historiography of Franz Ferdinand. After all, everything his life had been leading to ended with his death on 28 June 1914. It's no wonder so many works carry such titles as *The Obstructed Sovereign*, "Stymied Savior?", *The Hindered Dynasty*, and *Europe's Lost Hope*.[7] When a scholar of Robert Kann's stature refers to Franz Ferdinand as "this potentially great and genuinely tragic personality," it's hard to think about him without also considering the Empire's future.[8]

This chapter takes a different tack to exploring the Archduke's legacy. Since we know how Franz Ferdinand had hoped to be remembered, the question here is: How has he been? Unlike the qualitative historical inquiry that entails scrutinizing the heir's political plans, probing his difficult personality, and then analyzing it all in the context of late imperial problems, memory concerns itself with how a particular group contemplates a specific past. In Franz Ferdinand's case, it enables us to interrogate the extent to which his presumed role as the Empire's reformer figures into how the final years of the Monarchy itself, including the Sarajevo assassination, are remembered and interpreted.[9]

To whose memory do we refer? While all former Habsburg subjects constructed their identities in part through the prism of their imperial past, the dynasty's collapse was particularly disorienting for Austrians. As a crucial component of a vast empire, the new Austrian state of some 6.2 million people had to redefine its place in Europe. What this meant for ordinary Austrians was no less than a collective identity crisis: Were they actually ethnic Germans whose best prospects lie in union (*Anschluß*) with their powerful neighbor to the north? Or did "Austria" embody a distinct ethnonational identity to be conserved in an independent entity? And if so, what was the Habsburgs' role in this new identity?

During the First Republic, when the victorious Entente powers forbade *Anschluß*, most Austrians saw it as the optimal solution to their political predicament.[10] With the emergence of the "*Ständestaat*" (the Austro-Fascist "corporate state") from 1933 to 1938, however, the newly ascendant conservative right adopted a pro-Austrian position in order to combat threats from the communist left and the "Germanist" Austro-Nazis on the right.[11] And how better to emphasize national distinctiveness than by invoking the Habsburg legacy? The Nazis unraveled this synthesis when they annexed the state in 1938 and assailed "the very concept of Austria itself," including what Hitler reviled as the anti-German Habsburg empire.[12] The horrors of World War II and the "first victim" status conferred upon Austria by the Allies (and embraced by complicit Austrians) ended all serious political impetus toward *Anschluß*. Thus, the Second Republic that gained full independence in 1955 could finally fix Habsburg memory in the Austrian psyche and give Franz Ferdinand his full due for trying to protect it from the very collapse that had created the Austrian identity crisis in the first place.

If it were only so simple. Memory is never static. Through time, place, and political context, it takes on different forms and formulations. And Franz Ferdinand's memory is no exception. Which seems all the more reason for starting with his startling death—both as a locus for looking at how the Archduke was regarded in his own time, and for understanding how the link between his end and that of the Empire has been understood since.

The Sarajevo Assassination: "Death Knell" of the Empire

If memory begins with mourning, then the night the coffins carrying the Successor and his wife fled their shameful "third-class funeral" in Vienna for burial in Artstetten was fraught with meaning.[13] Just as the train pulled into the station and the caskets were unloaded, a storm broke. Writing during World War II, General Edmund Glaise von Horstenau described everyone running for cover while the royal couple's coffins were left behind, "alone and abandoned, in the wind and the rain."[14] The scene thus suggests the symbolic desertion of the Archduke's heritage as the Empire's potential reformer.

Many others have interpreted the murder and mourning of Franz Ferdinand as omens of the Empire's end. "The bullet in Sarajevo struck the Monarchy in its very heart," wrote the Archduke's doctor, Victor Eisenmenger.[15] In his novel *Apis und Este* (1931), Bruno Brehm glimpsed the dynasty's dying days in the crowd watching the nobility process with the caskets to Vienna's West Rail Station.[16] Another powerful (and literal) metaphor for the sinking Monarchy occurred as the coffins were being ferried across the Danube toward Artstetten, and a clap of thunder spooked the horses and nearly plunged the hearse into the river. In the 1960s, an Austrian journalist described "the eerie circumstances that accompanied the funeral, which also symbolically announced the end of the Monarchy."[17] And who could forget the foreboding thunderstorm that greeted news of the Archduke's death in Joseph Roth's novel *Radetzkymarsch*?[18]

Even the immediate aftermath of the assassination could be construed cataclysmically. In his reflections on the first memorial to the slain couple—the tolling of church bells in Sarajevo—Count Ottokar Czernin hears "the death knell of the Monarchy." It's a melancholic sensation, even if Czernin was not actually there, the Monarchy was very much alive, and the war that would end it far from foreordained, let alone lost. More than six decades later, the biographer Friedrich Weissensteiner evoked the chiming bells as "the dirge of the Monarchy."[19]

The point is not to mock these retrospective representations of the Archduke's political murder. The problem is that in conflating his tragic death with that of the Monarchy, they distract readers from the war's origins and uncertain outcome. It's a soothing distraction, which is why it is as widespread today as it was in 1915, when an article in the *Neue Freie Presse* began: "An entire year has passed since the first shots were fired in this world war," and ended with Artstetten: "in this crypt lie the first victims of this war."[20] After the war, the Sarajevo murder was blamed for robbing "the people of Austria-Hungary of the chance to build a more secure future."[21] On the tenth anniversary, the *Oesterreichische Wehrzeitung* pronounced the assassination "a death sentence against the Monarchy" and Franz Ferdinand the "first victim" of the Great War.[22] A decade later, the *Reichspost* proclaimed that Princip's pistol shots "struck down ... the peace and future of Europe."[23] Even in the Second Republic, Sarajevo is often constructed as the *coup de grâce* of a once great empire. In his biography of Franz Ferdinand, Gerd Holler wrote of Princip's shots piercing "not only the representatives of a tottering Empire, but the very heart of the Monarchy."[24]

Certainly there are non-Austrian sources that hold the assassination responsible for everything from ending Europe's golden age to deferring dialogue on women's rights.[25] Yet the case of Austria is exceptional both because of Vienna's role in the looming clash, and the reference frame for reflecting on Sarajevo is the Archduke's determination to reform the Empire. Thus, the assassination has slid easily into the trope of the Habsburgs' "tragic fate," signified in titles like *Austria's Fateful Years*, *Austria's Fateful Days*, and *Austria's Fateful Places*, and focused on such subjects as Mayerling and Empress Elisabeth's murder.[26] "Nevertheless," wrote von Horstenau, "it was fate's tragedy that Franz Ferdinand had to be the first to fall on the battlefield of the world war."[27] To this day, 28 June is regularly invoked as "a fateful date/day" for the Habsburg Empire.[28]

In ruling out "fate" in Vienna's decision to invade Serbia, scholars cite such reasons as fear of encirclement, the chance to end a long-standing regional conflict, and worries over domestic dissolution.[29] Regardless of which factor may have been foremost in 1914, historians largely concur that the Monarchy's determination to take "decisive action" was uncoerced.[30] Yet the language typically incorporated into collective memory has tended toward the deterministic. During the "*Ständestaat*," schoolbooks made Austrian intervention a matter of honor, thus standing not only against "the restrained and peace-loving" regime's agency, but for the war's inevitability: "Any other solution to the conflict would have been construed as weakness and merely deferred the shooting war."[31]

"Honor" was certainly relevant for Austro-Hungarian leaders in July 1914. However, this argument justifies the war's origins in terms of official Serbia's alleged offense, leaving little room to explore the larger context for the Empire's belligerence. Moreover, it was the murder of the regime's leading voice *against* war that produced the conflict that destroyed the dynasty, just as Franz Ferdinand had warned it would. This irony begs the question: What is actually known about the heir apparent and his political reform plans?

According to Alma Hannig's recent biography, Franz Ferdinand was one of the most politically active and Habsburg-loyal Successors in the dynasty's history. Yet he was also, according to virtually all scholars, one of the least popular and appreciated, a distinction that is as much due to his difficult personality as to his ill-defined plans to reform the Monarchy. On the one hand, the Archduke was an intensely private family man with such a headstrong, haughty, and impetuous personality that many judged him unfit for rulership. On the other, he kept intimately abreast of state affairs through his Military Chancellery in Vienna, was powerful enough to influence ministerial appointments, and was deeply committed to addressing the Monarchy's most pressing problem: nationalism.[32]

Thus, the paradox that plagued Franz Ferdinand in life and has hounded him in the hereafter: for friends, followers, and many scholars, the fact that he survived the disease that killed his mother (tuberculosis) and surmounted the court's conventions by marrying beneath his rank signified a strength of character superbly suited to political power. "Notwithstanding the glaring weaknesses of his persona, he was the only one in the era of the *Götterdämmerung* of the monarchical idea who represented the incarnation of the ruler in his sense of mission, determination and, despite his false inferences, also in his faculties," wrote the respected specialist, Robert Kann.[33] Yet for untold others, it was precisely Franz Ferdinand's trying and mistrustful personality that rendered him unfit for rulership.

"Wherever there is strong light, there is sharp shadow."[34] Goethe's quote is cited by Dr. Victor Eisenmenger, who saw the Archduke through his battle with tuberculosis and later sought to staunch the "spiteful rumors" propagated by his enemies. The doctor was among the faithful who believed that Franz Ferdinand would have saved the Empire. But what he also wished to commit to remembrance was something less subjective: "Basically, [the Archduke] was right. His Cassandra-calls fell on deaf ears and unfortunately we lived to see the fulfillment of his prophetic fear that our policy was driving us into war and ruin."[35]

Remembering Franz Ferdinand

On 28 June 1917, in the midst of the war and not a year-and-a-half from the ruin, the first memorial to Franz Ferdinand was unveiled in Sarajevo, directly opposite the assassination site. Dedicated in a Catholic ceremony, the "Atonement Monument" consisted of two pillars supporting a massive medallion emblazoned with the likenesses of the royal couple. It soared some twelve meters (thirty-nine feet), partially blocking the mountain views on the postcards peddled in its wake.

Those cards quickly became collector's items once Bosnians destroyed the structure in March 1919. How had it collapsed so quickly? What sort of memorial had Austria-Hungary actually erected? Initiated by one Major Piffl, the monument was designed by a Hungarian, financed by the German-language Bosnian press, and dedicated by Foreign Minister István Burián, the retired commander-in-chief Archduke Friedrich, and the province's Commanding General, Stefan Sarkotić.[36] Yet despite this diverse and distinguished roster, only one report on the monument circulated in the Austrian papers. And it appeared on page twelve of the *Neue Freie Presse* and ten in the conservative *Reichspost*.[37]

Franz Ferdinand's first memorial had not been made for Austrians, as such. Rather, the regime's faithful had sought to put the heir's memory to use among restless Bosnians. During the war, the main champion for Franz Ferdinand and the Atonement Monument was the Jesuit priest Anton Puntigam, who had lived more than twenty years in Bosnia. The pastor also came to possess the murder weapon, which vanished into the Jesuits' vaults in Vienna.[38] It would be "discovered" there in 2004. A year later, the pistol was featured in the exhibition "The New Austria" in Belvedere Palace, where the signing of the State Treaty had restored Austrian sovereignty a half-century earlier.[39] No indication was given of what went on in that palace in the latter years of the "old Austria," when the man murdered by that gun had lived and labored there for a *renewed* "Austria-Hungary."[40]

From 1914 to 1918, on the cusp of the birth of the first "new Austria" after World War I, and decades before the *new* "new Austria" commemorated in the 2005 exhibition, Father Puntigam had tremendous faith in the fixity of the old one. And he was not alone, for otherwise he never would have successfully raised funds for a "Franz Ferdinand Memorial Atonement Church" and "Sophie Chotek Youth Home," or been awarded the Military Cross for Civil Service by Kaiser Karl, who supported Puntigam's memorial plans. Private citizens, the Bosnian state government, and the Finance and War Ministries did too. The State Printing Office contributed three stamps commemorating the couple and depicting the Church design. After selecting a construction site, the land purchase began in August 1917. By June 1918, "preparations were in full gear" for a prominent and practical memorial to the victims, even if not in Austria proper.[41]

Puntigam had expressed concern that the building site might be prone to mud slides, even hiring a commission to test it. Whatever the outcome, "by this time the entire Monarchy was 'slip terrain.'" What kept the memorial going was the energy of its originator, who was as devoted to the slain couple's memory as he was to his country's continuity. That's why this memorial was so meaningful—like the multinational Empire itself, it was to be built by and for Sarajevo's diverse citizenry. The largest donor, in fact, was a Bosnian Muslim. In the end, the only force that could destroy the project was the world war, which did so by destroying the Monarchy.[42]

That today virtually nothing is known in Austria of this memorial project is a somber précis of the Archduke's legacy. For once the war and regime were lost, his memory was bound more to the afterlife of the assassination than to the actual life of the Successor. Surely the economic deprivations and political instability in interwar Austria ensured that ordinary citizens had other imperatives than funding a memorial church to a Habsburg prince who never reached power. Yet that does not explain why, despite dozens of articles on the Archduke in the interwar era, I have not found one on Puntigam's project or, even, any memorial for Franz Ferdinand.[43] And there was virtually nothing in the Austrian press about the destruction of the Atonement Monument. The "new Austrians," though not yet validated by the Saint-Germain Treaty, were, evidently, already eager to get on.

This distancing entailed implicit avoidance of Franz Ferdinand's memory. Whereas the wartime Kaisers had decreed memorial masses and military obsequies for the Archduke and Duchess on 28 June, such events now became private affairs. According to one secondary source, "thousands of pilgrims" braved the poor postwar roads and railways to Artstetten each year.[44] In 1924, the Hohenberg children welcomed hundreds of aristocratic acquaintances at Artstetten. Nearly three years after the lately deceased Emperor Karl's last attempt to retake the throne, they swore an oath of Habsburg allegiance upon the sarcophagi.[45]

These annual excursions may well have attracted some Austrians. Yet all I found with regard to anything one could call a "pilgrimage" to Artstetten was a short piece in the *Neue Freie Presse* for the tenth anniversary obsequies.[46] And if ever there was a "Society of Franz Ferdinand" or some such group, then no reference has emerged in my research. The late Archduke undoubtedly had a following, yet nothing like the "hero-cult" Yugoslavists built around his assassin.[47] Moreover, the Habsburg-inhospitable politics of the First Republic did more for forgetfulness and ambivalence than remembrance and reverence. If Emperor Karl decreed Artstetten a memorial site and saved its church bells from being melted into ammunition, in interwar Austria, the funds to construct more permanent coffins came from private coffers.[48]

Further, the Austrian government did not try to resurrect the Sarajevo monument inside its own borders, or even to establish any memorial to the Successor. To this day, there has never been a public monument to the Archduke outside of Artstetten, not to mention a street or square named for him. In 1935, a Franz Ferdinand Girls' School was established in his birth house, the Khuenburg Palace in Graz. But the Nazis removed the name and it was never restored to the building. Likewise, the "Franz Ferdinand caserne" in Vienna was renamed for the Starhemberg family in 1967. A marble plaque from the k. (u.) k. Uhlan regiment in Vienna's *Karlskirche* and a stained glass window above the altar in the basilica Maria Taferl (near Artstetten) indicate that the Church and armed forces had not forgotten the Archduke. Once tracked down, however, these memorials tell us little more about the Successor than the two eateries that today carry his name (in Perchtoldsdorf and St. Florian in Steyr).

Just like the Monarchy he had lived to rehabilitate, Franz Ferdinand would fade quickly from public memory, as the new Austrian state sought to establish its own national identity by disestablishing its imperial one. By no means did this denote the dismissal of all that was Habsburg.[49] On the contrary, the suddenness of the Empire's disappearance triggered the kind of confusion that often takes refuge in nostalgia, as "Old Austrians" looked back on "the loss of greatness, harmony, and stability, the end of an idyllic world."[50] For many, 28 June 1914, rather than the war's actual end, came to be reviled as the day when this dependable world was "smashed into a thousand pieces like a hollow clay vessel."[51] Stefan Zweig's fellow Austrian writer Joseph Roth also aimed his anguish at the assassination: "The world is wrecked. And Sarajevo stands. It should not be a city. It should be a monument, to make everyone remember with horror."[52]

In the wrecked, interwar world in which Austrians found themselves, only Franz Ferdinand's most steadfast followers—Eisenmenger, *Reichspost* editor Friedrich Funder, journalist Leopold von Chlumecky, and others in his "Belvedere Circle"—kept his memory alive with writings that elevated the heir and corrected the myths and malignings. "Franz Ferdinand, as He Really Was," was the title of an article in the *Neues Wiener Journal*, in which a director at the State Archives strove to staunch such "misinformation" as that the Archduke had been plotting to establish Slavic kingdoms for his sons.[53] Others stressed the Successor's irrepressible energies and unconditional affection for family and fatherland.[54] The first two biographies of Franz Ferdinand situated him as a confident and serious statesman.[55]

If time did not favor the would-be reformer of what Austrian elites were increasingly constructing as a doomed empire, timing all but annihilated him. Newspaper articles regularly appeared on the anniversary of the Archduke's death rather than his birth on 18 December. For what would have been his sixtieth birthday and the start of his seventh year as sovereign, there was nothing on the heir in any major Austrian paper.[56] It was the exceptions, many of them literary, that helped shape the long-term and largely negative image of Franz Ferdinand.

One of the earliest and most important was Bruno Brehm's novel *Apis und Este*. Before becoming a committed Nazi, this k. (u.) k. officer's son penned an international bestseller endorsed by Robert Kann, prefaced by Harvard historian Sidney Fay, and printed in multiple languages.[57] The first of a trilogy on the Empire's collapse, Brehm's work is also an outright character assassination of the assassinated Archduke.

From Franz Ferdinand's first appearance at a pageant for the Emperor in 1903, his reputation is ruined: "Everyone is afraid of him; it is as though he personified the dangerous clouds which are now threatening the Empire." Like many antagonists, Brehm dwells on his protagonist's compulsive hunting. In one scene, the Successor forces a peasant to drive into a ditch so that his hunting party can pass. Brehm's Franz Ferdinand may believe in his capacity to save his country, but gratuitous scenes such as when he publicly insults a Dragoon (i.e., a professional defender of that country) do little to persuade readers of his prospects.[58]

Yet herein lies the novel's revealing tension, which is the tension inside its author as well. While some of Franz Ferdinand's followers tried to align the heir's nonracial thinking with their Nazi leanings, Brehm's depiction is truer to the Archduke's multinational ideals.[59] What the writer got right (just not for the right reasons) was that the Successor would have hated the Nazis as much as he did the Pan Germanists of his own day. Yet in pointing up the real Franz Ferdinand—Habsburg imperialist and, as the assassination's Serbian abettor

Apis puts it: "the only man over there who still believes in his rotten crumbling country"—Brehm held little back in his belittlement of the insufficiently *völkisch* Archduke, a man so vain he flatters himself before a mirror.[60] In short, Franz Ferdinand's mission to rescue the Monarchy is easily mocked, though not necessarily minimized. After all, before Brehm himself tasted the *völkisch* Kool-Aid, he too had been emotionally devastated by the Empire's downfall.

That may explain why the novel evinces some sympathy toward the fallen, future emperor in its critique of the disrespectful funeral arrangements. Brehm also has several officers defend the Archduke for supporting the army.[61] If the author's Franz Ferdinand were merely some unfeeling slayer of animals driven along by his grasping wife,[62] then how is it that he also gets this obituary:

> There lies the silent man in whom [the officers] had centered all their hopes . . . who was to lead them out of the dark confusion. . . . His death marks not only the end of a dynasty . . . it is the end of the Holy German Empire's last uncrowned emperor . . . for the sovereigns of all great countries are really carried to their graves with this man.[63]

Brehm by no means makes Franz Ferdinand into the lost savior of the Habsburg state. But neither does his novel make the Monarchy and the Archduke's attachment to it look foolish, or fanciful.[64]

If *Apis und Este* teetered between respecting the imperial past and resenting the man of its future, Roth and Zweig came right to the point. In *Radetzkymarsch* (1932), Joseph Roth only evokes the heir toward the end of his novel, when the assassination is announced to a drunken group of officers. Yet the effect on this multinational microcosm of the Monarchy is immediate, as the Hungarians cannot curb their ethnic pride. "The son of a bitch is dead!" shouts Count Benkyö in his native language rather than the army's official German.[65] In his memoir *Die Welt von Gestern* (1942), Stefan Zweig likewise has so little sympathy for the deceased Archduke "with the bulldog neck and stone cold eyes" that he insists most Austrians were little stirred by the news of the assassination, and that many "secretly sighed with relief" at the prospect of "the much more beloved young Archduke Karl" becoming Kaiser. After all, Zweig writes, the humorless Successor and his insufferable wife "lacked everything that counts for real popularity in Austria: amiability, personal charm and easygoingness." It's hard to imagine two more devastating, formative influences for Franz Ferdinand's memory.[66]

Unless, that is, Ludwig Winder's Jewishness had not prevented the Prague writer from publishing his acclaimed novel *Der Thronfolger* (1937) in Germany or Austria. First printed in Zürich and later (1984, 1989) in the DDR, the work only recently became known to the Austrian public thanks to a 2014 edition reviewed widely and glowingly.[67] Nevertheless, and like his contemporary literati, Winder offered an unsparing psychological portrait of the Crown Prince.

Winder first returns us to the protagonist's childhood rivalry with his brother Otto, imagining how this awakened feelings of rage and self-reproach: "I know it well," the youthful Archduke thinks to himself. "The world is so mean, so base. In order to be happy, one has to be as brash, bold, and barefaced as [Otto] is." Over the course of the novel, Franz Ferdinand relearns this lesson and reaffirms his aloofness. In the army, he wonders: "Why do people find me so repulsive? . . . Why is there this dreadful wall between me and the world?" And later, when his political confidant Max Wladimir von Beck agrees to become the Kaiser's prime minister, the Successor is beside himself with a sense of betrayal: "Because if Beck were a traitor, where was there a man who was not a traitor?"[68]

Thus, shaped by this all-consuming mistrust and Frankenstein-like longing for love, the Archduke's alienation morphs into megalomania; he begins to begrudge his powerlessness, bewail his wasted potential. During the struggle over marrying Sophie, Franz Ferdinand imagines: "Now it must be my turn. Now I could show what's inside of me." And elsewhere in the work he assures himself, if not the readers, of his capacity "to renew the old Reich . . . [and] redress all that his uncle has debased and depraved." Self-pitying, wildly restless, and with an abiding sense that everyone was out to get him, Winder's Successor is by no means a man who could hold together a Monarchy. The fact that the renunciation oath also occurred on 28 June (1900) thus becomes, for the author, a portent of historical providence rather than a mere coincidence.[69]

As a literary contemplation of the Archduke's inner turmoil, Winder's novel may work on some level. Even Robert Kann commended its "truly artistic value."[70] Yet the historian overlooked a key factor for any fair reflection on Franz Ferdinand: his strong caution when it came to military conflict.[71] During the 1908–09 Bosnian Crisis, the Archduke had not only opposed war with Serbia, he had initially stood against annexing Bosnia-Herzegovina. Yet Winder's impatient protagonist comes off almost as belligerent as his Chief of Staff and the Empire's outspoken proponent of preventive war, General Conrad von Hötzendorf: "It was the voice of having to hold oneself back year in and year out . . . of rebellion against constraint and the powerlessness to do anything but wait idly by. . . . Was not war the only way to end this deadly dormancy?"[72]

The Archduke-as-warmonger myth did not originate with Winder—it was widespread before the war and boosted after by books like journalist Heinrich Kanner's popular *Kaiserliche Katastrophenpolitik* (1922).[73] But it gained credence from Winder's depiction of an heir who views violence as a cathartic escape from a life squandered in the seemingly endless expectation of power. Franz Ferdinand desperately wants to restore the Empire's preeminence and Winder reviews his fluctuating plans to do so. Yet the novel presents this ambition as private and pathological—less a higher cause or calling than a symptom of the Archduke's insurmountable insecurities.

If neither of these novels lifted the image of Franz Ferdinand, the authoritarian *"Ständestaat"* did try to clamp down on the calumnies. Winder's work was banned and censors buried all but the most positive portrayals of the Archduke and Habsburg regime generally.[74] At a time when sympathy for the Monarchy and cultivation of Austrian identity went so far as to repeal the Habsburg return law and dress the army in imperial uniforms, it's not surprising to find loud praise for Franz Ferdinand on the twentieth anniversary of his assassination. A front-page piece in the *Neue Freie Presse* described the purposeful and "most charming" Archduke who understood what was best for the people: "Economic cooperation with political independence!"[75] Similarly, a cover story in the *Reichspost* asserted, "Had Franz Ferdinand ascended the throne, a powerful personality for maintaining peace in Europe would have strode to the fore of international politics."[76] For the Austro-fascist state straddling the line between the Third Reich and its founding commitment to forging an independent Austrian identity, warding off war was also a priority.

In this respect, a perfect occasion came soon after the May 1934 Constitution installed one-party rule in Austria. September 9 marked the start of three days of dedication festivities for a national memorial to k. (u.) k. soldiers who fell in the world war. The site of the ceremonies was the *Burgtor* (Castle Gate), at the southwest entrance to the *Heldenplatz* (Heroes' Square). Completed in 1824 to commemorate the victory over Napoleon, this neo-classical structure was transformed into a war memorial under the First Republic.[77] Yet by the time of its inauguration, the *"Ständestaat"* had appropriated the memorial as the "Austrian Heroes' Monument." The opening thus became a consciously orchestrated act of national representation.[78] In a pageant that pointed up the nation's longstanding ties to the Habsburg family, political leaders consecrated a tomb to the unknown soldier meant to represent "the eternal Austria, the idea of Austria, which is the idea of the conciliation of peoples."[79]

That was the language of *Das Kleine Blatt* and much of the rest of the unfree press. Officially and insistently, this "was a memorial for old Austria's heroic sons from 1618 to 1918!"[80] Historical continuity mattered for *Ständestaat* leaders, as it often does with authoritarian regimes. That attitude assured Franz Ferdinand a prominent place in the memorial, even if he neither fought nor fell in the war. To the left of the concave wall facing the anonymous tomb, in large block letters, one reads: "Archduke Franz Ferdinand; Assassinated in Sarajevo; 28 June 1914." This was not the first time the heir's peacetime political murder was equated with the Great War fallen. As of 1934, however, this mode of remembrance was woven into official discourse.

The 1938 *Anschluß* that promptly ended the Austrian identity crisis did not so much burnish the negative image of Franz Ferdinand as render it irrelevant, since the Third Reich was anti-Austria-Hungary to begin with. The Archduke's death was thus deemed a liberating *Stunde der Bewährung* (moment of truth) rather than the fateful tragedy of Austrian interpretation.[81] Articles marking the thirtieth anniversary of the Sarajevo assassination conceived it less as the trigger for a tragic war than for the decisive "Thirty-Years War" to regenerate all *Germans*. From this "undivided war,"[82] the Archduke's missed opportunity to reform the multinational Monarchy—"the most guilt-ridden dynasty the German people ever had to endure"[83]—was never an effort worth undertaking. As Hitler himself put it:

> In the north and south, the poison of foreign races was eating into our people's body ... it was the hand of the goddess of eternal justice ... that caused the most deadly enemy of Germanism in Austria, the Archduke Franz Ferdinand, to fall by the very bullets he had helped to cast ... he was the chief patron of the movement to make Austria a Slav State.[84]

For the Nazis, any polity that interfered with unifying and amplifying the *Volk*—be it the Empire *or* interwar Austria—was anathema to a worldview based on "race" and bent upon weakening or wiping out the non-German ones. Thus, Thomas Grischany's point that Hitler's relationship to Austria "cannot be reduced to a sweeping hatred" is well taken; for, as long as the Austro-German "master race" reigned supreme, then even the Monarchy had some merit. The question for Third Reich historians was: What sort of ruler might Franz Ferdinand have been when one weighs his unwavering German-Austrian identity against his hopes to stabilize the multinational state?[85]

Ironically, academics in the Third Reich presented a relatively nuanced portrait of the Crown Prince. With the Successor's murder, wrote one, "A final great hope was snatched from the Danube Monarchy." He then flattered the *Führer* for bringing the *Volk* (that is, the ethnic Germans of Austria-Hungary) back to its true, Germanic fold.[86] No love lost here, though no disrespect for the heir either. Konrad Klaser, a bigoted "specialist" in Balkan conspiracies, also admitted, "Hardly any other member of the privileged classes comprehended the Monarchy's weaknesses ... [and] appreciated the strengths of the German administrative apparatus" so well as Franz Ferdinand.[87]

A nice illustration of this ambiguity appears in a biography by Georg Franz-Willing. Drawing on such reliable witnesses as Czernin and Chlumecky, Franz-Willing ventures no major new interpretation. Yet he is so thorough in his summary of the literature on Franz Ferdinand that he validates those authors who set out to combat the stereotypes and convey the Crown Prince in a constructive, nonideological light. The Nazi-era author acknowledges that the Archduke was a "fervent Catholic," but also insists that he never would have let his religious passions conflict with his political plans. And he praises the Successor's "intelligence and willpower, quick learning ... [and] clear judgment" before affirming the better known "blemishes."[88]

As a devout Catholic and multinationalist hated by Hitler, Franz Ferdinand should not have fared this well during the Third Reich.[89] But like Brehm, whose novel was awarded Nazi Germany's National Book and Film Prize in 1939, Franz-Willing recognized that if Austria-Hungary were not worth saving for "Aryan civilization," neither were Franz Ferdinand's imperial pretensions not worth respecting.[90] After all, the Third Reich was also an empire, and some of its staunchest Austrian adherents had belonged to the Archduke's inner circle.[91] Further, if Franz Ferdinand failed as a *völkisch* hero, his murderers fared far worse. Klaser's work is so anti-Serb that even the Serbian prime minister teaches Bosnians to throw bombs![92] And in numerous textbooks and the Nazis' official mouthpiece *Völkischer Beobachter*, Gavrilo Princip is portrayed as a Jew and a Freemason.[93] That Franz Ferdinand often came off better than Nazi purists presented him, while his rabidly nationalist, anti-Habsburg assassins appeared worse, is an ironic tribute from a racial state.

The Third Reich, like all ideological systems, was conveniently inconsistent. The Second Austrian Republic that emerged from its ruins thus did so forcefully, aided by the "first victim" status bestowed by the Allies and aiming to carve out a path in which "every historical continuity was a nuisance . . . now history was not merely Austrified (*austrifiziert*), but even more: It was virtually 'little Austrified' [*verkleinösterreichert*]."[94] In short, all imperial aspirations were off, including *Anschluß*. The new "new Austria" was determined to go it alone as a small Republic.

The historian Laurence Cole identifies three "phases" in the postwar "Habsburg Myth." After 1945, the conservative Austrian People's Party (ÖVP) instrumentalized Habsburg history in its nation-building practices. This era brought the sappy yet successful *Sisi* films (1955–57) romanticizing the life of Empress Elisabeth and creating a lasting icon for Austrian identity. It also gave rise to published works, memorial ceremonies, and cultural events exhibiting a "good old days" image of the Empire.[95]

This phase of purposeful Habsburg revival petered out around 1970 with the ascent of the Austrian Socialist Party (SPÖ). For the next dozen years, the nation-building project promoted contemporary cultural figures over traditional Habsburg ones. Certainly the public's nostalgic impulse for imperial kitsch never completely cooled, and the myth's "recovery," which Cole dates to around 1983, was a seamless one. Starting with a historical reconstruction of Maria Theresia for the two-hundredth anniversary of her death, this period saw two exhibitions on Kaiser Franz Joseph (1984, 1987); the celebrated return and subsequent burial (in the Kaiser Crypt) of ex-Empress Zita (1982, 1989); and a booming "museumification" that included the 1982 opening of the Franz Ferdinand Museum in Artstetten.[96]

By the late 1980s, the Habsburg myth was on its way to staking a permanent place in Austrian self-perception. Cole knows that not all Austrians appreciated the "Habsburgiana" spectacle, especially when it constrained confronting less savory parts of their recent past. During the Waldheim affair in 1986, it was all too easy to take refuge in an idealized imperial identity while repressing the reality of Austrian complicity in Nazi crimes. But all myths have their comeuppances, and how Franz Ferdinand would fit into this one is, if not the last chapter on his memory, certainly the one that appears most lasting.[97]

In a piece published in *Neues Österreich* for the fiftieth anniversary of the Sarajevo assassination, the historian Gerald Stourzh concluded: "Hence the heir apparent has become the symbol for a renewal of the multinational state."[98] Yet Stourzh focused far more on the Archduke's murder than his ideas for reform. Indeed, it's highly debatable as to how well his statement holds up, even under the democratic Second Republic and in the midst of the Habsburg revival.

After all, no memorials for the "would-be renewer" had materialized. And the assassination's fortieth anniversary largely failed to examine the Archduke's political aspirations. As in interwar Austria, the press produced plentiful articles on "the fateful day in Sarajevo" that destroyed the Empire and "wrecked an entire world order."[99] In short, what Franz Ferdinand had hoped to do was still being displaced by what his assassin singlehandedly did, thus forcing the "peace Kaiser" to "take up the sword." This article, also in the prestigious journal *Neues Österreich*, ends by rehashing the "fateful paradox" that linked "the Reich's presumptive reformer" to the regime's regrettable departure.[100]

Equally paradoxical is this author's failure to incorporate a study of Franz Ferdinand published a year earlier by former k. (u.) k. officer Rudolf Kiszling, who had gained access to the Archduke's papers as director of the war archives. The work praised the heir's political skills so highly that some accused Kiszling of hagiography. Yet the biographer was no Eisenmenger, and what he wrote about the Successor deserved more attention in 1954 than the normative nostalgia that foretold the Empire's implosion and forgave Franz Joseph for going to war.[101]

A year later, when the Second Republic came into existence, the moment seemed auspicious for a dramatization of the incident that, allegedly, led to the First Austrian Republic. That's what the director Fritz Kortner calculated with *Sarajevo—Um Thron und Liebe* (1955).[102] The problem for Austrian filmgoers, however, is that Kortner was more attuned to the assassins and their anti-imperial motives than to Franz Ferdinand's plans to improve the Empire through political reform. In one implausible scene, Sophie Chotek argues over the legitimacy of political murder as a means of protest with three arrested conspirators.

As for her husband, he comes off as a headstrong and heedless soldier with a major chip on his shoulder. We see this plainly each time he envyingly eyes his uncle's bust in the hotel room. The Archduke's willful character is also evident in his habitual smoking, which Sophie repeatedly tries to stop until his temper flares as they are leaving City Hall, and she lovingly hands him a (final) cigarette.

The resigned gesture foreshadows the murder, since Franz Ferdinand seems too obstinate ever to amount to anything.

Um Thron und Liebe does venture a "viewpoint," though it is unoriginal in the extreme. "Fate is fate," says one inebriated chauffeur to the other as they await the couple outside of City Hall. This message, as we have seen, has long dominated Austrian discourse on both the Archduke's and the Empire's end. Although a formidable artist, Kortner was no better equipped to transcend the triteness of "destiny" than the interwar interlocutors. Even in the film's final scene, as black flags unfurl from the town hall's tall windows, it's as if they had always been there, just waiting to mourn the Monarchy.

If Austrian memory of the Archduke received any reprieve prior to Professor Stourzh's improbable pronouncement on his symbolic stature as political reformer, then it came only in a few minor historical novels. Eduard Danszky's *Krone und Herz* (1952) sets up a sublime analogy between the Successor's desire for marriage and family, and the larger "family of nations" he envisions for a federalized Empire. In E. J. Görlich's *Der Thronfolger* (1961), a colorful cast of ordinary Austrians gradually grasp just how much the Archduke means to them as the Monarchy's reformer-in-chief. Görlich never idealizes Franz Ferdinand, who is stiff, irritable, and self-righteous. Yet his Successor is also capable and clever, and the novel traces a growing public perception of him as the last and best hope for transforming the Empire into a truly equal "union of peoples."[103]

Neither of these novels has been translated or reprinted, nor achieved nearly the impact of Winder's *Der Thronfolger* (republished in 2014) and *Apis und Este* (reissued four times during the Habsburg revival). Certainly the back-to-back one-hundredth birthday of the Archduke in December 1963 and the fiftieth anniversary of his assassination six months later kept Franz Ferdinand in the public eye. Yet the focus stayed on the assassins rather than the plans and passions of their victim. Indeed, the only "Portrait of the Murdered" piece I came across was by the Successor's grandson, Georg Hohenberg.[104]

Part of the problem with confronting Franz Ferdinand in 1964 was that most Austrians had not meaningfully confronted the Empire's role in the outbreak of war in 1914. Since Fritz Fischer's groundbreaking 1961 work on German responsibility, Austria had been off the hook and out of the public eye.[105] In 1975, Austrian Friedrich Würthle's study of the links between the assassination and Serbian administration further relieved pressure to readdress the war's origins, let alone the heir's politics.[106] Moreover, Austrians had bigger historical fish to fry in terms of facing their less equivocal culpability as part of another empire—the Nazi one.

It's doubtful there was any relationship between Austria's late encounter with its Nazi past and the fact that Franz Ferdinand's arrival in the "Habsburg revival" came so late as well. Yet it was at about the same time, in the early 1980s, that we see a surge in attention to the Archduke in more positive ways than previously.

One need only compare the scant interest in him during the sixtieth anniversary of the assassination to the articles and events on the seventieth, including an exhibition on this "historically significant personality" in the Graz City Museum, housed since 1972 in the Khuenburg Palace. A decade later, the museum put on a repeat performance. And although the Palace was never renamed for the heir, a plaque on its facade now memorializes his birth there.[107]

With an academic assist from Robert Kann's groundbreaking *Franz Ferdinand Studien* (1976), the Successor's presence in Austria has progressively risen. In addition to the wealth of press in 1984, four popular biographies appeared that decade.[108] One, *Europas verlorene Hoffnung* (*Europe's Lost Hope*, 1989), cautiously argued that the Archduke's death kept him from having to suffer full-on defeat in his reform effort. Yet, as in the other studies, the author was sympathetic to his subject.

In subsequent decades, popular works probed the heir's softer and more secluded side. *Habsburgs grösste Liebesgeschichte* (*Habsburgs' Greatest Love Story*, 2001) and *Verbotene Liebe am Kaiserhof* (*Forbidden Love in the Imperial Court*, 2004) suffered from the kind of kitschiness one would expect from books centered on someone's personal life.[109] But that does not make their stories less truthful, especially considering Franz Ferdinand's professional unfulfillment. In recognition of the reliable appeal of royal intimacy, Artstetten mounted the exhibit "Throne or Love" for the couple's ninetieth anniversary in 1990.[110] Franz Ferdinand may mostly be remembered for the murder that made him miss out on the former, but today, the museum's permanent exhibit is entitled "For Heart and Crown".[111]

Certainly there have been more ways to access the Archduke since the 1980s. In 1999, the Austrian Mint mounted "Franz Ferdinand: 'The End of an Era,'" an exhibition that examined the fullness of its subject's life even as it gave the usual, inordinate attention to his death.[112] And in addition to the aforementioned books, the archivist Wladimir Aichelburg published numerous articles to complement the Artstetten exhibits; three volumes of annotated *Notes on an Unusual Journal of an Exceptional Life* (2014); and booklets on such themes as "The Successor and the Sea" and "Franz Ferdinand as Building Contractor."[113] As for the latter, rising interest in the heir's work in nature, monument, and urban preservation has spawned several new studies.[114] His unusual (for an Archduke) world voyage also came into public focus thanks to a 2010 exhibit on his time in India at Vienna's *Weltmuseum*. Four years later, the museum advertised, "Franz is here!" for a exhibition on the entire trip. It may have been timed with the centenary of his death, but it was the first time Franz Ferdinand's life became part of the Habsburg myth right on the Ringstraße.[115]

There are more examples of the Archduke's recent emergence in the Austrian public sphere. The problem with alighting upon them, however, is that it's unclear to what extent they reshaped Austrian collective memory, or merely the

"The First Victim of the First World War" | 301

Figure 12.2. Vienna *Weltmuseum* exhibition: "Franz is here!" 2014. Photo courtesy of Dr. David Schriffl.

individual memory of those who read the works and saw the exhibits. Moreover, there have always been impactful counternarratives. The 1984 Graz exhibit, for instance, coincided with one in Pottenbrunn Palace (St. Pölten) entitled *Austria in the Fateful Year 1914*. And for anyone interested in further exploring the Successor's world voyage after visiting the *Weltmuseum*, there was a newly edited and, in 2013–14, widely reviewed edition of his travel journals which paints a decidedly unpretty picture of Franz Ferdinand.[116]

The more positive and nuanced portrayals of the Archduke did not, in other words, preclude the preponderance of the usual stereotypes of a "stiff, cold, impersonable" man—"one of the most problematic personalities of the House of Habsburg." In another news article from the 2000s entitled "Franz Ferdinand: Swindler, Stupid Fool—and an Archduke," the author insists the heir "would probably have become a nasty dictator."[117] Franz Ferdinand's nastiness and narrow-mindedness are displayed in popular works from the 1980s renaissance up to the present, including those by Hilde Spiel and Frederic Morton. And while the latter does reference the Successor's political skills, it's his "martial mustache" and "imperial gestures" that stand out in Morton's depiction of the "fearsome" Franz Ferdinand.[118] More recently, Florian Illies's highly successful work, *1913: Der Sommer des Jahrhunderts*, paints Franz Ferdinand as an "irascible, uncontrollable power-politician" nearly gone mad from waiting for his uncle's passing.[119]

Film has been consistently unkind to the Crown Prince. From the stiff, stolid, and chain-smoking cameos in *Maresi* (1948) and *Um Thron und Liebe*, to István Szabó's *Colonel Redl* (1985), in which he deceitfully (and nonfactually) frames the famed Austrian spy Alfred Redl in order to coax the army into war in the Balkans, Franz Ferdinand invariably looks belligerent and unbecoming on the big screen.[120] In Austrian director Peter Patzak's character study of the assassins, *Gavre Princip—Himmel unter Steinen* (1990), the Archduke is degraded to little more than the over-decorated representative of a ruthless colonial power. And in a new, 2014 Austrian Broadcasting (ORF) film insipidly entitled *Das Attentat—Sarajevo 1914*, the director's conspiracy-driven rendition of world history focuses on the examining magistrate Leo Pfeffer rather than the crime's real victim.[121]

Austrian popular memory has not exactly refired a fatal shot through the "ill-fated" Franz Ferdinand, though he has slipped through a Habsburg memory hole of sorts. His name, best associated with the "Okidoki Mascot" on Austrian KidsTV (where he appears as a purple cow with an earring), never became popular in the Second Republic.[122] Artstetten, of course, remains the main arbiter of the Archduke's memory in Austria. Yet the Franz Ferdinand Museum, which receives no regular state-level support, welcomes just twenty- to thirty thousand mostly non-Austrians a year.[123] Like all collective efforts to commemorate the Archduke, the museum has an intrinsic problem—the man it honors, honorable as he was, never ascended to his life's purpose. One thus learns about the heir's personal history and Military Chancellery with a sense that all the letters, furniture, photographs, and so forth belong more to a family heirloom than a public museum. This is not an argument against Artstetten, which is a notable achievement by any measure. But despite its efforts, Austrian memory remains fixated on Franz Ferdinand's death at the expense of the life the museum so ardently promotes, and few Austrians will ever visit. As one scholar put it: "From the viewpoint of both historical research, as from general public interest, [the heir's life] was and is interpreted and appreciated primarily as a sub-species of his death."[124]

Indeed, even efforts to correct this often draw in their audiences with allusions to the assassination. The catalogue cover for the aforementioned exhibition in Graz featured the iconic illustration of the Sarajevo murders in the *Kronen Zeitung* (30 June 1914), even as the Introduction decried the kneejerk linkage between the Archduke and his demise. Thirty years later for the centenary, the museum presented *Konigsmörde*, a "psychopolitical installation" in which "the epochal Sarajevo assassination [illustrates] the fateful culmination of a sequence of (attempted) murder, execution and suicide in the Austrian ruling House."[125] In order to visualize what Austrians mostly imagine of the Archduke, just look at the commemorative coin the National Mint manufactured for its 1999 exhibition. On one side is a flattering image of Franz Ferdinand and his Frau. On the other, they're leaving Sarajevo's City Hall moments before their momentous murder.

Where else in Austria could one confront the Archduke? I asked everyone this question when I arrived for my research, though apart from specialists, no one I met had visited Artstetten; nor noticed the tablet for Franz Ferdinand in *Karlskirche*; nor seen the stained glass window in Maria Taferl; nor set foot inside the *Burgtor*. According to one scholar, "even Vienna cognoscente" have no inkling that this huge structure on *Heldenplatz* houses Austria's official memorial for the two world wars, let alone that Franz Ferdinand is commemorated there as a fallen soldier of the first one.[126]

The centenary did little to uplift the heir's image. For those interested, there were endless print articles and public broadcasts, two new biographies (in addition to Aichelburg's aforementioned volumes), interviews with family members fawning over the "*Friedensfürst,*" and even trips "on the trail" of the Successor from Vienna to Sarajevo. Yet the best subscribed books, plays, and films focused on the assassination to such an extent that Vienna's *Schauspielhaus* hosted the world premiere of its commissioned work *Princip (Dieses Grab ist mir zu klein)* by the Serbian playwright Biljana Srbljanović. Meanwhile, there was not even a documentary about the Archduke on the centennial of his death, let alone a major conference or other public event. As usual, the former imperial capital never paused for an official memorial. Instead, those honors were outsourced to Artstetten, where Church leaders led mass and politicians kept their distance.[127]

Is this a problem? Are we asking too much of Austrian collective remembrance in the case of the uncrowned Crown Prince, whose however remarkable life is unlikely ever to escape the specter of his over determined death? And even if it occasionally does, what can this then tell us?

Conclusion

"His prejudices and feudal bearing notwithstanding," wrote Robert Kann, Franz Ferdinand "was a man of stature." Count Czernin fashioned him "a known quantity." And soon after Sarajevo, the British scholar and energetic antagonist of the Habsburg Empire R. W. Seton-Watson conceded: "I had pinned all my hopes for the future upon [Franz Ferdinand] . . . all Europe is the loser by his death."[128] Whatever one may say about the Successor, scholars and close contemporaries mostly concur: Franz Ferdinand was neither a foolish nor frivolous man.[129] He was obstinate, insolent, arrogant, and abrupt. But if the Archduke knew one thing, it was that the Empire he would someday rule was in dire need of reform, and war would only endanger, if not undo, that eventuality. This was no small thing.

Indeed, when seen from the perspective of the past century, it's hard not to feel nostalgic for the central European empire Franz Ferdinand so ardently wished to preserve. Some contemporaries, of course, had already written the regime off, as since have scholars with the assistance of hindsight. Yet as the historian Timothy Snyder argued with regard to another Habsburg prince who kept faith with the "fading" Monarchy: "It lasted long, and might have lasted longer."[130] Few contemporaries would so instinctively have agreed as Franz Ferdinand. Perhaps that's why so many who have judged him so severely based on his trying personality and authoritarian tendencies have also praised his political talents and principled ideals. In this sense, there's sad irony in the fact that this was especially true during the undemocratic *Ständestaat* and Nazi periods.

As for the Second Republic, outside the privately created Artstetten museum, it has proven little inspired in presenting Franz Ferdinand in all his paradoxical ways. Certainly by the 1980s, new works and exhibitions were probing the Successor's life such that, for those interested, his political activity and individuality—foremost as family man and world traveler—could better be appreciated. Schoolbooks and media, moreover, increasingly indicate that his reform plans may well have been what antagonized south Slavic nationalists in the first place. Yet public remembrance still privileges the Archduke's tragically exploited death over his independently minded life. Thus, while Vienna officials have yet to honor Franz Ferdinand with so much as a street name, some Church leaders felt it was finally time for him and his wife to be brought together in the hallowed Habsburg Crypt. In a small ceremony held on 25 June 1986, a marble

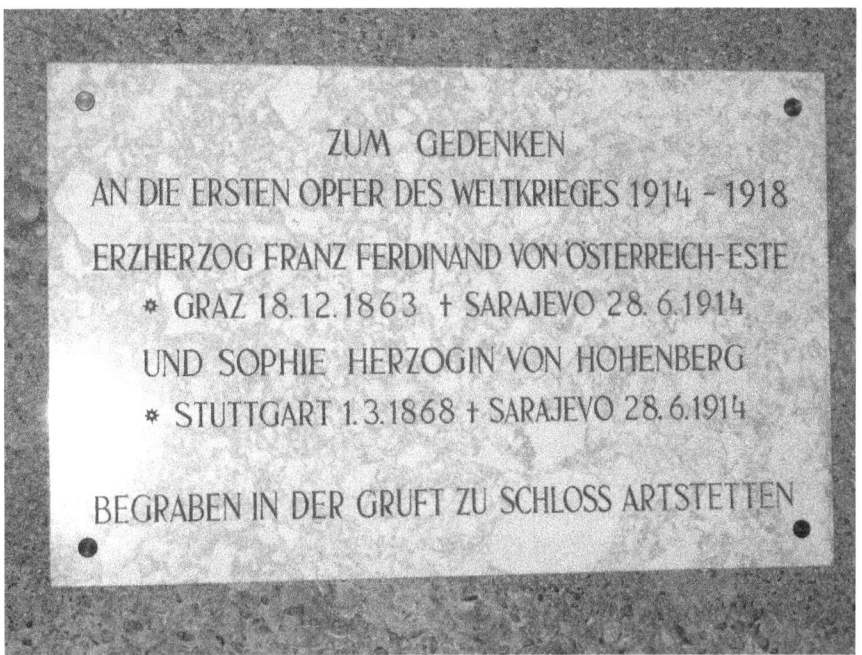

Figure 12.3. 1986 Memorial Plaque in Vienna's Imperial Crypt. Author's photo.

plaque was unveiled at the entrance to the chamber containing Franz Joseph's formidable tomb. Scant articles on the memorial appeared in the Austrian press. Its language was also unsurprising: "In memory of the first victims of the First World War, 1914–1918."[131]

One could argue that this is the most consistent construction of Franz Ferdinand's memory in Austria. Besides its appearance in countless media outlets and the memoirs of many who mourned him, like von Horstenau and Kiszling, the Austrian writers Friedrich Würthle, Erika Bestenreiner, and Gerhard Tötschinger all put it at the beginning of their histories.[132] Thus in 1986, the same year that Austrian President and former UN Secretary-General Kurt Waldheim was bringing his small and otherwise quiescent state to the forefront of world affairs through accusations of Nazi war crimes, this modest marker to imperial victimization eased a few more consciences concerning the century everyone was anxious to put behind them, if not consign to collective forgetfulness altogether. After all, if Austrians could hardly avoid the fact that one of their own started World War II, they were far less ready to accept responsibility for the mythicized Monarchy's role in the first.

The problem for the historian, however, is that World War I did not begin until several weeks after the Archduke's assassination. And while Franz Ferdinand was the victim of a lot of things—the abysmal security in Sarajevo, the blinkered pride of Bosnian Governor-General Oskar Potiorek, his own bloated ego—he was *not* a victim of the war any more than Austria was the "first victim" of Nazi Germany, as collective national memory only started rejecting in the 1980s. The pleasing phraseology that adorns the memorial plaque in the Kaiser Crypt, is implicit in the *Burgtor*, and has cropped up in public, private, and even scholarly discourse ever since the onset of hostilities is no more than an efficient, if instinctive, way to distort the memory of the one man who would have done everything in his power to prevent the war his death propelled and to promote the peace his Empire required.

Was such reform actually feasible for Austria-Hungary? Was Franz Ferdinand the man to mandate it? Such counterfactual inquiry can never be known, even if it will always be tied to the Successor's legacy. Memory, however, does not have to adhere to facts in order to shape our understanding of the past. Its purpose is more emotional, easing our consciences by allowing us to privilege those aspects of history we find most comforting. Because as all Austrians and all of us surely know, the first victim of World War I was a much younger man than Franz Ferdinand, who also had his life's ambitions before him. If that were to become central to collective Austrian remembrance, then it would be hard to forget that not only was there nothing "fateful" about 28 June 1914, but there was still an Empire to be stabilized and secured for the modern era.

Paul Miller is Associate Professor of history at McDaniel College in Westminster, Maryland (USA). His scholarship has covered topics including antimilitarism in nineteenth-century France, the bombing of Auschwitz controversy, and genocide in Bosnia. His recent work on the history/memory of the Sarajevo assassination has been generously supported by the Fulbright Program, the National Endowment for the Humanities, the EU's Marie Curie Actions, the Woodrow Wilson International Center for Scholars, and the American Philosophical Society.

Notes

1. Alma Hannig, *Franz Ferdinand: Die Biographie* (Wien: Amalthea, 2013), 275; Ottokar Czernin, *Im Weltkriege* (Wien: Ullstein, 1919), 56: "I am nevertheless convinced that [Franz Ferdinand] instinctively felt that the Monarchy could never withstand war's frightful trial of strength." On his insistence that the Empire's internal consolidation be "the precondition for a vigorous foreign policy," see Alma Hannig, "'Wir schauen in der Loge zu': Thronfolger Franz Ferdinand und die Außenpolitik Oesterreich-Ungarns vor dem Ersten Weltkrieg," *Etudes Danubiennes* 27, no. 1–2 (2011): 56–57; Friedrich

Funder, *Vom Gestern ins Heute: aus dem Kaiserreich in die Republik* (Wien: Herold, 1952), 515; Carl Freiherr von Bardolff, *Soldat im alten Österreich: Erinnerungen aus meinem Leben* (Jena: Diederichs, 1938), 177; Robert Kann, "Kaiser Franz Joseph und der Ausbruch des Weltkrieges: Eine Betrachtung über den Quellenwert der Aufzeichnungen von Dr. Heinrich Kanner," in series, *Österreichische Akademie der Wissenschaften, Sitzungsberichte*, 274, Bd. 3 (Wien: Böhlau, 1971), 13f., 21f; Feldmarschall Conrad, *Aus meiner Dienstzeit, 1906–1918*, vol. 3 (Wien: Rikola, 1921), 434–42.

2. For Franz Ferdinand's "Programm für den Thronwechsel," see Georg Franz-Willing, *Erzherzog Franz Ferdinand und die Pläne zur Reform der Habsburger Monarchie* (Brünn: R. M. Rohrer, 1943), 123–49; Ulric Neisser, "Self-narratives: True and False," in *The Remembering Self: Construction and Accuracy in the Self-Narrative*, eds. Ulric Neisser and Robyn Fivush (Cambridge, Cambridge UP, 1994), 1–18.
3. Funder, *Vom Gestern ins Heute*, 383.
4. John W. Boyer, *Culture and Political Crisis in Vienna: Christian Socialism in Power, 1897–1918* (Chicago: University of Chicago Press, 1995), 366–67.
5. Hannig, *Franz Ferdinand*, 278–79.
6. Czernin, *Im Weltkriege*, 62. Literature supporting this paragraph includes Adam Wandruszka and Peter Urbanitsch, eds., *Die Habsburgermonarchie 1848–1918*, vol. 6. *Die Habsburgermonarchie im System der internationalen Beziehungen* (Wien: Österreichische Akademie der Wissenschaften, 1993); Helmut Rumpler and Herwig Wolfram, eds., *Österreichische Geschichte 1804–1914. Eine Chance für Mitteleuropa: Bürgerliche Emanzipation und Staatsverfall in der Habsburgermonarchie* (Wien: Ueberreuter, 1997). For recent examples of this counterfactual deliberation, compare the conclusions of Hannig, *Franz Ferdinand*, and Jean-Paul Bled, *François-Ferdinand d'Autriche* (Paris: Tallandier, 2012). The conference "The Long Shadow of Austria-Hungary: A Counterfactual Exploration" was held at the Diplomatische Akademie Wien (November 2014).
7. Friedrich Weissensteiner, *Franz Ferdinand: Der verhinderte Herrscher* (Wien: Österr. Bundesverlag, 1983); Günther Kronenbitter, "Verhinderter Retter? Erzherzog Franz Ferdinand und die Erhaltung der Habsburgermonarchie," in *Konservative Profile: Ideen & Praxis in der Politik zwischen FM Radetzky, Karl Kraus und Alois Mock*, ed. Ulrich E. Zellenberg (Graz: Stocker, 2003), 267–83; Lucian O. Meysels, *Die verhinderte Dynastie: Erzherzog Franz Ferdinand und das Haus Hohenberg* (Wien: Molden, 2000); Max Polatschek, *Franz Ferdinand: Europas Verlorene Hoffnung* (Wien: Amalthea, 1989).
8. Robert Kann, "Franz Ferdinand and the Bohemian Question," in *Dynasty, Politics, and Culture: Selected Essays*, ed. Stanley B. Winters (Boulder, CO: Social Science Monographs, 1991), 189.
9. Rudolf de Cillia, Martin Reisigl, and Ruth Wodak, "The Discursive Construction of National Identities," *Discourse & Society* 10, no. 2 (1999): 149–73.
10. Laurence Cole argues that being for or against the Monarchy was "increasingly irrelevant" in the *Anschluß* debate, which centered on the Republic's economic future: "Der Habsburger-Mythos," in *Memoria Austriae I: Menschen Mythen Zeiten*, ed. Emil Brix, Ernst Bruckmüller, and Hannes Stekl (Wien: Verlag für Geschichte und Politik, 2004), 476.
11. Béla Rásky, "Erinnern und Vergessen der Habsburger in Österreich und Ungarn nach 1918," in *Österreich 1918 und die Folgen: Geschichte, Literatur, Theater und Film*, ed. Karl Müller and Hans Wagener (Wien: Böhlau, 2009), 33.

12. Douglas Patrick Campbell, "The Shadow of the Habsburgs: Memory and National Identity in Austrian Politics and Education, 1919–1955" (PhD diss., Univ. of Maryland, 2006), 17.
13. The phrase "Begräbnis dritter Klasse" was likely coined by Karl Kraus in his play *Die letzten Tage der Menschheit* (Wien: *Die Fackel*, 1922): Ch. 2, Vorspiel, Scene 3; Ch. 3, Act I, Scene 22; and Ch. 6, Act IV, Scene 31. Gordon Brook-Shepherd notes that it appears in the final pages of Baron Alfred Morsey's unpublished reminiscences (Morsey was one of the Archduke's secretaries): *Archduke of Sarajevo: The Romance and Tragedy of Franz Ferdinand of Austria* (Boston: Little, Brown, 1984), 261 (n. 292).
14. Peter Broucek, ed., *Ein General im Zwielicht: Die Erinnerungen Edmund Glaise von Horstenau*, vol. 1 (Wien: Böhlau, 1980), 278, 10–11.
15. Victor Eisenmenger, *Erzherzog Franz Ferdinand* (Wien: Amalthea, 1930), 180.
16. Bruno Brehm, *Apis und Este: Ein Franz Ferdinand-Roman* (München: R. Piper & co., 1931), 478.
17. Peter Wolf, "Hol' über—beim "Weltuntergang," *Die Presse*, 18 Feb. 1962, 9.
18. Josef Roth, *Radetzkymarsch* (Berlin: Aufbau-Verl, 1979), 299.
19. Czernin, *Im Weltkriege*, 41; Weissensteiner, *Franz Ferdinand*, 29.
20. "Der Jahrestag der Ermordung des Erzherzogs Franz Ferdinand," *Neue Freie Presse*, 29 June 1915, 15.
21. Dr. Rudolf Fürer, "Persönliche Erinnerungen an Franz Ferdinand," *Neue Freie Presse*, 6 July 1919, 5.
22. "Erzherzog Franz Ferdinand. Zum 10. Jahrestag der Tragödie von Sarajevo," *Oesterreichische Wehrzeitung* 26, 27 June 1924, 1–2.
23. "Nach zwanzig Jahren," *Reichspost*, 28 June 1934, 1–2.
24. Gerd Holler, *Franz Ferdinand von Österreich-Este* (Wien: Ueberreuter, 1982), 349, 18.
25. Olaf Storbeck, "Die Logik der Globalisierung," *Handelsblatt: Wirtschafts- und Finanzzeitung*, 016 (23 Jan. 2007): 102; Alex Capus, *Eine Frage der Zeit* (München, 2007), 102. Among countless other examples, see: Der Spiegel, 18 Jan. 1999, 3; H.A.L. Fisher, *A History of Europe*, Vol. II (London, 1935), 1213.
26. Josef Redlich, *Schicksalsjahre Österreichs, 1908–1919: Das politische Tagebuch Josef Redlichs* (Graz: H. Böhlaus, 1953–54); Friedrich Weissensteiner, *Schicksalstage Österreichs: Wendepunkte, Krisen, Entwicklungen* (Wien: Ueberreuter, 1989); Johannes Sachslehner, *365 Schicksalstage: Der Gedächtnis-Kalender Österreichs* (Graz: Pichler, 2012); Rudolf Kiszling, *Erzherzog Franz Ferdinand von Österreich-Este: Leben, Pläne und Wirken am Schicksalsweg der Donaumonarchie* (Graz: Böhlau, 1953).
27. Edmund Glaise-Horstenau, "Erzherzog Franz Ferdinand, 1863 bis 1914," in *Oesterreichische Biographie*, vol. 3, ed. Anton Bettelheim (Wien: Amalthea, 1926): 9–33.
28. "Der 28. Juni: Ein Datum als Schicksal," [Linzer] *Tages-Post* 147, 28 June 1934, 1; Friedrich Oppenheimer, *Sarajevo—Das Schicksal Europas* (Wien: Phaidon, 1931); Anita von Hohenberg and Christiane Scholler, *Er war mein Urgroßvater: Anita Hohenberg über Thronfolger Erzherzog Franz Ferdinand* (Graz: Verl.-Gruppe Styria, 2011), 11, 49, back cover; *28. Juni 1914 als Schicksalstag für Generationen*, accessed 6 January 2018, https://www.wien.gv.at/kultur/chronik/gedenken2008/archiv/sarajewo.html.
29. Paul W. Schroeder, "World War I as Galloping Gertie: A Reply to Joachim Remak," *Journal of Modern History* 44, no. 3 (Sept. 1972): 319–44; Joachim Remak, "The Third Balkan War: World War I Origins Reconsidered," *Journal of Modern History* 43, no. 3

(Sept. 1971): 353–66; David G. Herrmann, *The Arming of Europe and the Making of the First World War* (Princeton: Princeton UP, 1996), 225; Jürgen Angelow, *Kalkül und Prestige: Der Zweibund am Vorabend des Ersten Weltkrieges* (Cologne: Böhlau, 2000); Samuel R. Williamson Jr., *Austria-Hungary and the Origins of the First World War* (New York: St. Martin's, 1991), 214–16; Jonathan E. Gumz, *The Resurrection and Collapse of Empire in Habsburg Serbia, 1914–1918* (Cambridge: Cambridge UP, 2009), 3.
30. Günther Kronenbitter, *"Krieg im Frieden": Die Führung der k.u.k. Armee und die Großmachtpolitik Österreich-Ungarns 1906–1914* (München: Oldenbourg, 2003), 429.
31. Werner Suppanz, *Österreichische Geschichtsbilder: Historische Legitimationen in Ständestaat und Zweiter Republik* (Wien: Böhlau, 1998), 227–28; Joseph August Lux, *Das goldene Buch der Vaterländischen Geschichte für Volk und Jugend Österreichs* (Wien: Gerlach & Wiedling, 1935), 319–20; Fritz Herndl, *Österreich: Seine Geschichte für Jugend und Volk* (Innsbruck: Tyrolia, 1934), 212.
32. Hannig, *Franz Ferdinand*, 99–103, 276; Robert Kann, *Erzherzog Franz Ferdinand Studien* (Wien: Verlag für Geschichte und Politik, 1976), 39.
33. Kann, *Erzherzog*, 23; Hannig, *Franz Ferdinand*, 11–12.
34. See *Götz von Berlichingen mit der eisernen Hand*, Chapter 2, First Act, accessed 6 January 2018, http://gutenberg.spiegel.de/buch/3672/2.
35. Eisenmenger, *Erzherzog Franz Ferdinand*, 167, 162, 119; Ludwig Jedlicka, "Erzherzog Franz Ferdinand," in *Gestalter der Geschicke Österreichs*, ed. Hugo Hantsch (Innsbruck: Tyrolia, 1962), 537.
36. "Ein Sühne Denkmal," *Reichspost* 304, 2 July 1914, 3.
37. "Enthüllung des Sühnedenkmals für Erzherzog Franz Ferdinand und Gemahlin, *Neue Freie Presse* 18984, 29 June 1917, 12; "Das Sühne Denkmal in Sarajevo," *Reichspost* 296, 29 June 1917, 10.
38. Leo Ashley Nicoll Jr., *Anton Puntigam S. J.: Leben und Wirken eines Jesuiten in Bosnien* (Phil. diss., Universität Wien, 1970), 179–81.
39. Sarah Chalmers, "Gun That Started WWI: Amazing Tale of the Priest and a Pistol That Vanished for 90 Years," *The Daily Mail*, 22 June 2004, 22.
40. Günter Düriegl and Gerbert Frodl, *Das Neue Österreich: Die Ausstellung zum Staatsvertragsjubiläum 1955/2005* (Wien: Österreichische Galerie Belvedere, 2005), 31–32, 43.
41. Nicoll, *Anton Puntigam*, 194–95, 202–26, 229, and Appendix, 87–90. The stamps were issued on 28 June 1917, as part of the fundraising effort.
42. Nicoll, *Anton Puntigam*, 205, 221–22, 230–32, and Appendix, 25–29.
43. A few articles referenced the project: "Der 28. Juni. Ein Datum als Schicksal," *Wiener Zeitung*, 28 June 1935, 5.
44. "Die Ermordung des Erzherzogs Franz Ferdinand und seiner Gemahlin. Die militärische Trauerfeier," *Neue Freie Presse*, 28 June 1915, 8; Wladimir Aichelburg, *Erzherzog Franz Ferdinand von Österreich-Este und Artstetten* (Wien: Verlagsbüro Lehner, 2000), 7, 64; "Der Jahrestag der Ermordung des Erzherzogs Franz Ferdinand," *Neue Freie Presse*, 29 June 1915, 15–16; Nicoll, *Anton Puntigam*, 189–90.
45. "Inland: Eine Trauerfeier in Artstetten," *Neue Freie Presse*, 1 July 1924, 8; C. M., "Bei Franz Ferdinand in Artstetten," *Neues Wiener Journal*, 27 June 1924, 5.
46. *Neue Freie Presse*, 1 July 1924, 8.
47. Luigi Albertini, *The Origins of the War of 1914*, vol. 2 (New York: Enigma Books, 2005), 47n.

48. Aichelburg, *Erzherzog Franz Ferdinand von Österreich-Este*, 64–66.
49. Gergely Romsics, *The Memory of the Habsburg Empire in German, Austrian and Hungarian Right-Wing Historiography and Political Thinking 1918–1941* (Boulder, CO: Social Science Monographs, 2010), 195.
50. Cole, "Der Habsburger-Mythos," 480. Gergely Romsics uses the term "Old Austrian" for memoirs written mainly by German-speaking Austro-Hungarians, "who after 1918 looked back on the Monarchy as the anchor of their primary identity," in *Myth and Remembrance: The Dissolution of the Habsburg Empire in the Memoir Literature of the Austro-Hungarian Political Elite* (Boulder, CO: Social Science Monographs, 2006), 3. Also: Claudio Magris, *Der habsburgische Mythos in der modernen österreichischen Literatur* (Wien: Zsolnay, 2000).
51. Stefan Zweig, *Die Welt von Gestern: Erinnerungen eines Europäers* (Stockholm: Bermann-Fischer, 1942), 247.
52. Klaus Westermann, ed., *Joseph Roth Werke 2: Das journalistische Werk, 1924–1928* (Köln: Kiepenhauer & Witsch, 1990), 731–33 (*Frankfurter Zeitung*, 3 July 1927).
53. Hans Ritter von Schlitter, "Franz Ferdinand, wie er wirklich war," *Neues Wiener Journal*, 9 March 1932, 4–5.
54. József Kristóffy, "Die Persönlichkeit Franz Ferdinand," *Neues Wiener Journal*, 14 Nov. 1926; Fritz Stritzl-Artstatt, "Erzherzog Franz Ferdinand und Herzogin von Hohenberg. Im neuesten Lichte der Tagespresse," *Reichspost*, 20 Nov. 1927, 7; Silvester Blume, "Der Mann neben dem Thron," *Neues Wiener Tagblatt (Wochen-Ausgabe)*, 1 May 1926, 1–3; Moritz von Auffenberg-Komarow, "In memoriam. Am zehnten Jahrestage des 28. Juni 1914," *Neue Freie Presse*, 28 June 1924, 2.
55. Theodor von Sosnosky, *Franz Ferdinand* (München: Oldenbourg, 1929); Leopold von Chlumecky, *Erzherzog Franz Ferdinands Wirken und Wollen* (Berlin: Verlag für Kulturpolitik, 1929).
56. In addition to *Neue Freie Presse* and *Reichspost*, I consulted *Neues 8 Uhr Blatt, Die Neue Zeitung, Wiener Zeitung, Bregenzer/Vorarlberger Tagblatt, Tagblatt* (Linz), *Tages-Post* (Linz), *Linzer Volksblatt*, and *Vorarlberger Volksblatt*.
57. Kann, *Erzherzog*, 33n. Fay wrote the foreword to the American edition, *They Call It Patriotism* (Boston: Little, Brown, 1932). Eva Reichmann, "Franz Ferdinand als literarische Figur," *Studia austriaca VIII* (2000): 140, 135–47.
58. Brehm, *Apis und Este*, 91, 133–58, 270–72, 200–06 (*They Call It Patriotism*, 60, 92–94, 186, 138–40).
59. Romsics, *The Memory of the Habsburg Empire*, 292–93.
60. Brehm, *Apis und Este*, 180, 156–57 (*They Call It Patriotism*, 122, 106).
61. Ibid., 483, 356 (*They Call It Patriotism*, 319–24, 326, 242).
62. In *Apis und Este*, Sophie tries to convince her husband that the renunciation oath does not apply to the unborn, and thus has no bearing on their children (386–87).
63. Ibid., 435, 443 (*They Call It Patriotism*, 295, 300).
64. Bruno Brehm, "Wie ich Apis und Este schrieb," in *Der Piperbote für Kunst und Literatur* 5 (1931): 1–4; Eva Freiin von Plotho, *Berliner Monatshefte* 1 (Jan. 1932): 90–93.
65. Roth, *Radetzkymarsch*, 302–7.
66. Zweig, *Die Welt von Gestern*, 248–50.
67. The original edition of *Der Thronfolger* was published in Zürich by Humanitas in 1937. On the novel's history and reception, see Ulrich Weinzierl, "Ein Gerechter unter den

Schreibern: Ludwig Winder und sein *Thronfolger*," in Ludwig Winder, *Der Thronfolger: ein Franz-Ferdinand-Roman* (Wien: Zsolnay, 2014), 553–69.
68. Winder, *Der Thronfolger* (Berlin: Rütten & Loenig, 1984), 104, 124–25, 429–30.
69. Ibid., 278, 161, 138, 563ff.
70. Kann, *Erzherzog*, 33.
71. See note no. 1 above. The biographies of Hannig and Bled support this position, though Hannig stresses that this by no means made Franz Ferdinand a pacifist. Indeed, she shows that he strongly, if exceptionally, supported intervention during the First Balkan War. Historians Lothar Höbelt and Christopher Clark have described the Archduke as a "dove": Anne-Catherine Simon, "Erster Weltkrieg: 'Franz Ferdinand war die führende Taube,'" *Die Presse*, 21 March 2014; Clark, *Sleepwalkers: How Europe Went to War in 1914* (London: Allen Lane, 2013), 109–10; Höbelt, *Franz Joseph I: Der Kaiser und sein Reich. Eine politische Geschichte* (Wien: Böhlau, 2009), 133–34, 145.
72. Winder, *Der Thronfolger*, 459.
73. Heinrich Kanner, *Kaiserliche Katastrophenpolitik: Ein Stück zeitgenössischer Geschichte* (Leipzig: E.P. Tal, 1922), 80, 114, 192.
74. Christiane Ida Spirek, *Von Habsburg bis Heydrich: Die mitteleuropäische Krise im Spät- und Exilwerk Ludwig Winders* (Wuppertal: Arco, 2005), 71–72.
75. Baron Johann Andreas Eichhoff, "Franz Ferdinand. Gedenkworte zum zwanzigsten Jahrestage seines Todes," *Neue Freie Presse*, 29 June 1934, 1–2.
76. "Nach zwanzig Jahren," *Reichspost*, 28 June 1934, 1–2.
77. Barbara Feller, "Ein Ort patriotischen Gedenkens: Das österreichische Heldendenkmal im Burgtor in Wien," in *Kunst und Diktatur: Architektur, Bildhauerei und Malerei in Österreich, Deutschland, Italien und der Sowjetunion 1922–1956*, ed. Jan Tabor, vol. 1 (Baden bei Wien: Grasl, 1994), 142–47; Christoph Mick, "'What Did They Die For?': War Remembrance in Austria in the Transition from Empire to Nation State," in the present collection.
78. Peter Stachel, "Der Heldenplatz: Zur Semiotik eines österreichischen Gedächtnis-Ortes," in *Steinernes Bewußtsein I. Die öffentliche Repräsentation staatlicher und nationaler Identität Österreichs in seinen Denkmälern*, ed. Stefan Riesenfellner (Wien: Böhlau, 1998), 619–56; Peter Stachel, *Mythos Heldenplatz* (Wien: Pichler, 2002); Rásky, "Erinnern und Vergessen," 33; Irene Nierhaus, "Orte der nationalen Narration in Österreich," in *Symbole und Rituale des Politischen: Ost- und Westeuropa im Vergleich*, ed. Andreas Pribersky and Berthold Unfried (Frankfurt am Main: P. Lang, 1999), 281–94.
79. "Dem unbekannten Soldaten," *Das Kleine Blatt*, 9 Sept. 1934, 2.
80. Generalmajor a. D. Dr. Egon von Lauppert, "Das künstlerische Problem des Heldendenkmales," in *Gedenkschrift anläßlich der Weihe des österreichischen Heldendenkmales am 9. September 1934* (Wien: Steyrermühl, 1934), 49. Also see Friedrich Grassegger, "Denkmäler des autoritären Ständestaates: Repräsentation staatlicher und nationaler Identität Österreichs 1934–1938," in *Steinernes Bewußtsein*, ed. Riesenfellner, 495–546.
81. Karl Hederich, *Adolf Hitler* (Leipzig: Bibliog. Inst., 1942), 23–24.
82. Wilhelm Koppen, "Dreißig Jahre Krieg . . . Die Schüsse von Sarajewo," *Völkischer Beobachter*, 27 June 1944, 1–2; Emil Landkarte, "Der ungeteilte Krieg," *Neues Wiener Tagblatt (Wochen-Ausgabe)* 26, 30 June 1944; "30 Jahre seit dem Sarajewo-Attentat: Die Tat von Chauvinisten entzündete den ersten Weltkrieg," *Tagespost* (Graz), 27 June 1944, 2.

83. Gerhard L. Weinberg, ed., *Hitlers Zweites Buch: ein Dokument aus dem Jahr 1928* (Stuttgart: Deutsche Verlags-Anstalt, 1961), 185.
84. Adolf Hitler, *Mein Kampf* (München: Zentralverlag der NSDAP, 1941), 13, 173–74. For the Hitlerian version of the "anti-Germanic" Archduke, see Wilhelm Granner, *Franz Ferdinand, seine Entwicklung und seine politischen Ideen* (phil. diss., Universität Wien, 1942).
85. Thomas Grischany, *Der "Österreicher" Adolf Hitler: Der Anteil Österreichischer Elemente An Hitlers Historischer Erscheinung* (Diplomarbeit, Universität Wien, June 1994), 139.
86. Walter Hoffmann, *Donauraum Völkerschicksal* (Leipzig: F. Meiner, 1939), 46–47. See also Romsics, *The Memory of the Habsburg Empire*, 136, 180; Wilhelm Mommsen, *Politische Geschichte von Bismarck bis zur Gegenwart, 1850–1933* (Frankfurt am Main: M. Diesterweg, 1935), 147.
87. Konard Hans Klaser, *Spione, Bomben und Verschwörer in der serbischen Politik* (Zagreb: Europa Verlag, 1941), 77–78.
88. Franz-Willing, *Erzherzog Franz Ferdinand*, 15–16; "Georg Franz-Willing: Die Hitlerbewegung," *Der Spiegel*, 20 June 1962, accessed 6 January 2018, http://www.spiegel.de/spiegel/print/d-45140548.html; Fritz Stern, "Der Zweite Weltkrieg: Ursachen und Anlass," *Foreign Affairs* 58, no. 5 (Summer 1980): 1198.
89. Certainly his sons did not—both were in Dachau. Gudula Walterskirchen, *Blaues Blut für Österreich: Adelige im Widerstand gegen den Nationalsozialismus* (Wien: Amalthea, 2000).
90. Andrew Barker, *Fictions from an Orphan State: Literary Reflections of Austria Between Habsburg and Hitler* (Rochester: Camden House, 2012), 86–87.
91. For a list of those closest to Franz Ferdinand ("the future leading figures in the case of [his] ascension to the throne"), see: Franz-Willing, *Erzherzog Franz Ferdinand*, 69–71.
92. Klaser, *Spione, Bomben und Verschwörer*, 68.
93. *Völkischer Beobachter*, 8 Jan. 1936; Bernhard Kumsteller, Ulrich Haacke, and Benno Schneider, *Geschichtsbuch für die deutsche Jugend* (Wien: Braumüller, 1940); Karl Grunwald and Otto Lukas, *Von der Urzeit zur Gegenwart: Aufgabe und Stoff eines Geschichtsunterrichts auf rassischer Grundlage* (Frankfurt am Main: Diesterweg, 1938), 108; Dietrich Klagge and Walter Franke, *Volk und Führer: Deutsche Geschichte für Schulen* (Frankfurt am Main: Diesterweg, 1939), 85; Eduard Ebner and Josef Habisreutinger, *Geschichte der Neuzeit* (Bamberg: C. C. Buchner, 1936), 186.
94. Rásky, "Erinnern und Vergessen," 41.
95. Cole, "Der Habsburger-Mythos," 485–91.
96. Ibid., 492–96.
97. Ibid., 497–98, 496.
98. Gerald Stourzh, "50 Jahre nach Sarajewo," *Neues Österreich*, 27 June 1964.
99. E. A. J., "Der Schicksalstag von Sarajewo," *Weltpresse: Das österreichische Informationsblatt*, June 26, 1954, 7; L. F. Jedlicka, "Das Attentat auf das Abendland," *Neue Wiener Tageszeitung*, 27 June 1954, 5–6; Otto Habsburg-Lothringen, "Vierzig Jahre ohne Europa," *Die Presse*, 26 June 1954, 1–2.
100. P. D., "Vierzig Jahre nach Sarajewo," *Neues Österreich*, 27 June 1954, 1–2.
101. Kiszling, *Erzherzog Franz Ferdinand*.
102. Robert Dassanowsky, "Finis Austriae, vivat Austria: The Re/Vision of 1918 in Austrian Film," in *Österreich 1918 und die Folgen*, ed. Müller and Wagener, 189.

103. Ernst Joseph Görlich, *Der Thronfolger* (Wien: Wancura, 1961), 310.
104. Georg Hohenberg, "Portrait des Ermordeten," *Forum* (June/July 1964): 293–95; Friedrich Wallisch, "Der Mann an der Weltenwende," *Wiener Zeitung*, 14 December 1963.
105. Fritz Fischer, *Griff nach der Weltmacht: die Kriegszielpolitik des kaiserlichen Deutschland 1914/18* (Düsseldorf: Droste, 1961).
106. Friedrich Würthle, *Die Spur führt nach Belgrad: Sarajevo 1914* (Wien: Molden, 1975).
107. Wilhelm Steinböck, "Erzherzog Franz Ferdinand von Österreich-Este (1863–1914) Zur Ausstellung," in *Ausstellung im Geburtshaus, Kulturreferat der Landeshauptstadt Graz Stadtmuseum, 2. Juli bis 28 Juli 1984*, ed. Wilhelm Steinböck (Graz: Stadtmuseum, 1984); Gerhard M. Dienes, "'Erzherzog Franz Ferdinand von Österreich-Este': Ausstellung im Grazer Stadtmuseum," *Österreichische Ärztezeitung* 12–25 (June 1984): 906.
108. Holler, *Franz Ferdinand* (1982); Weissensteiner, *Verhinderte Herrscher* (1983); Gordon Brook-Shepherd, *Die Opfer von Sarajevo* (Stuttgart: Engelhorn, 1988); Polatschek, *Franz Ferdinand* (1989).
109. Beate Hammond, *Habsburgs größte Liebesgeschichte* (Wien: Ueberreuter, 2001); Erika Bestenreiner, *Franz Ferdinand und Sophie von Hohenberg: Verbotene Liebe am Kaiserhof* (München: Piper, 2005); Sigrid-Maria Größing, *Amor im Hause Habsburg: Eine Chronique scandaleuse* (München: Heyne, 2001), 273–97.
110. Schloß Artstetten, *Thron oder Liebe: 90 Jahre Hochzeit des Thronfolgers* (Marbach: Sandler J & H, 1990); Wladimir Aichelburg, "Habsburger-Leid," *Morgen: Kulturzeitschrift aus Niederösterreich Kulturberichte* (Aug. 2003): 18–19.
111. Robert Müller, "Jung-Österreichs Hoffnungen: Erzherzog Franz Ferdinand," in *Werkausgabe in Einzelbänden: Gesammelte Essays*, ed. Michael Matthias Schardt and Günter Helmes (Paderborn: Igel-Verl., 1995), 48.
112. ÖstA, Br. no. 10.368. Also see *Die Münze* (June/August 1999).
113. Wladimir Aichelburg, *Erzherzog Franz Ferdinand und Artstetten: Der Thronfolger und das Meer* (Wien: Neuer Wissenschaftlicher-Verl, 2001); Wladimir Aichelburg, *Der Thronfolger und die Architektur* (Wien: Neuer Wissenschaftlicher-Verlag, 2003); Wladimir Aichelburg, *Erzherzog Franz Ferdinand von Österreich-Este 1863–1914: Notizen zu einem ungewöhnlichen Tagebuch eines außergewöhnlichen Lebens* (Wien: Horn/Berger, 2014).
114. Theodor Brückler, *Thronfolger Franz Ferdinand als Denkmalpfleger: die "Kunstakten" der Militärkanzlei im Österreichischen Staatsarchiv* (Wien: Böhlau, 2009); Brigitta Mader, *Die Sphinx vom Belvedere: Erzherzog Franz Ferdinand und die Denkmalpflege in Istrien* (Koper-Capodistria: Zgodovinsko Društvo za Južno Primorsko, 2000); Robert Hoffmann, *Erzherzog Franz Ferdinand und der Fortschritt. Altstadterhaltung und bürgerliche Modernisierungswille in Salzburg* (Wien: Böhlau, 1994); Samuel D. Werner Telesko, "Der Gemäldezyklus Erzherzog Franz Ferdinands in der 'Neuen Burg' in Wien," *Österreichische Zeitschrift für Kunst und Denkmalpflege* 65, Heft 1/2 (2011): 121–33.
115. "Imperial Sightseeing: Die Indienreise von Erzherzog Franz Ferdinand von Österreich-Este," accessed 6 January 2018, http://imperial-sightseeing.univie.ac.at/; "Franz is here! Franz Ferdinands Reise um die Erde," accessed 6 January 2018, https://www.weltmuseumwien.at/en/exhibitions/franz-is-here/.

116. Frank Gerbert, ed., *Franz Ferdinand von Österreich-Este: "Die Eingeborenen machten keinen besonders günstigen Eindruck"; Tagebuch meiner Reise um die Erde 1892–1893* (Wien: K & S, 2013).
117. Hans Werner Scheidl, "Starr, kalt, unpersönlich," *Die Presse—Spectrum*, 18 November 2000; "Franz Ferdinand: Schwindler, Heuochsen—und ein Erzherzog," *Die Presse*, 12 December 2009.
118. Hilde Spiel, *Glanz und Untergang: Wien 1866–1938* (Wien: Kremayr & Scheriau, 1987), 186–87; Frederic Morton, *Wetterleuchten: Wien, 1913/1914* (Wien: Ueberreuter, 1990), 13–15, 84–86, 116–19, 156. Also see Reichmann, "Franz Ferdinand als literarische Figur," 138.
119. Florian Illies, *1913: Der Sommer des Jahrhunderts* (Frankfurt am Main: S. Fischer, 2012), 39, 177–78, 244, 286–87, 307.
120. Hans Thimig, *Maresi* (Austria/W. Germany, 1948); István Szabó, *Colonel Redl* (Hungary, 1985); Peter G. Christensen, "Szabó's *Colonel Redl* and the Habsburg Myth," *CLCWeb: Comparative Literature and Culture* 8, no. 1 (March 2006).
121. Andreas Prochaska, *Das Attentat—Sarajevo 1914* (2014), http://oe1.orf.at/artikel/373082; Sebastian Hammelehle, "ZDF-Film über Franz Ferdinand: Weltgeschichte als Kaiserschmarrn," *Spiegel Online*, 28 April 2014, http://www.spiegel.de/kultur/tv/das-attentat-sarajevo-1914-zdf-film-ueber-anschlag-auf-franz-ferdinand-a-966106.html. The same can be said of Austrian writer Franzobel's new drama *Sarajevo 14 oder der Urknall in Europa*, which also relegates the Archduke to the background: World premiere at Tiroler Landestheater, Innsbruck (11 October 2014).
122. Österreichischer Rundfunk (ÖRF), accessed 6 January 2018, http://okidoki.orf.at/videos/video.php?encrypted_id=ODc4M2hqZDcyOTNrbWQxNDA3Mzg4NQ. The name Franz Ferdinand occasionally crops up in popular culture, like the children's books *Das Vehikel* (Sauerländer: Patmos, 2006), by Karla Schneider and Katharina Grossmann-Hensel; and Stefanie Holzer's *Franz Ferdinand: Ein Katzenleben* (Hohenems: Limbus, 2010). For a "Habsburg first-name hit list" from 1984 to 2004, see: Harald Havas, *Habsburger Sammelsurium* (Wien: Pichler, 2006), 122.
123. According to Anita von Hohenberg, Franz Ferdinand's granddaughter who lives at Artstetten and runs the museum, they receive one hundred thousand Euros per year from the city, and the Education Ministry made a one-time contribution of thirty thousand Euros (2009 interview).
124. Mader, *Die Sphinx vom Belvedere*, 9.
125. "Königsmorde: Gewalttaten in der Donaumonarchie," *GrazMuseum*, 30 April to 17 November 2014.
126. Feller, "Ein Ort patriotischen Gedenkens," in *Kunst und Diktatur*, ed. Tabor 147.
127. Schauspielhaus world premiere (16 October 2013).
128. Robert Kann, *A History of the Habsburg Empire, 1526–1918* (Berkeley: University of California Press, 1974), 418; Czernin, *Im Weltkriege*, 49; Seton-Watson to Madame Gruić (21 July 1914), cited in Arthur J. May, *The Passing of the Hapsburg Monarchy 1914–1918*, vol. 1 (Philadelphia: University of Pennsylvania Press, 1966), 27–28. In *Sarajevo: A Study in the Origins of the Great War* (London: Hutchinson, 1926,), Seton-Watson "affirmed that in the second decade of our century Francis Ferdinand was the most singular figure of any of the reigning dynasties of Europe" (80), though he also questioned the Archduke's mental and physical health (90–92).

129. Hannig, *Franz Ferdinand*, chapters 13 and 14.
130. Timothy Snyder, *The Red Prince: The Secret Lives of a Habsburg Archduke* (New York: Basic Books, 2008), 24.
131. Gigi Beutler, *Die Kaisergruft, bei den PP Kapuzinern zu Wien (Kapuzinergruft)* (Wien: Beutler-Heldenstern, 2008), 85; and Magdalena Hawlik-van de Water, *Die Kapuzinergruft: Begräbnisstätte der Habsburger in Wien* (Wien: Herder, 1987), 248–50.
132. Glaise-Horstenau, "Erzherzog Franz Ferdinand, 1863 bis 1914"; Rudolf Kiszling, "Erzherzog Franz Ferdinand: Ein Rückblick auf den Beginn des Erstens Weltkrieges vor 50 Jahren," *Südostdeutsche Vierteljahresblätter*, Sonderdruck aus Heft Nr. 3 (1964): 134–39; Würthle, *Die Spur führt nach Belgrad*, 9; Bestenreiner, *Franz Ferdinand und Sophie*, 11; Gerhard Tötschinger, *Auf den Spuren der Habsburger* (Wien: Amalthea, 1992), 107.

Select Bibliography

Aichelburg, Wladimir. *Erzherzog Franz Ferdinand von Österreich-Este und Artstetten*. Wien: Verlagsbüro Lehner, 2000.

———. *Erzherzog Franz Ferdinand von Österreich-Este 1863–1914: Notizen zu einem ungewöhnlichen Tagebuch eines außergewöhnlichen Lebens*. Wien: Horn/Berger, 2014.

Bestenreiner, Erika. *Franz Ferdinand und Sophie von Hohenberg: Verbotene Liebe am Kaiserhof*. München: Piper, 2005.

Bled, Jean-Paul. *François-Ferdinand d'Autriche*. Paris: Tallandier, 2012.

Brehm, Bruno. *Apis und Este: Ein Franz Ferdinand-Roman*. München: R. Piper & co., 1931.

Brückler, Theodor. *Thronfolger Franz Ferdinand als Denkmalpfleger: die "Kunstakten" der Militärkanzlei im Österreichischen Staatsarchiv*. Wien: Böhlau, 2009.

Campbell, Douglas Patrick. "The Shadow of the Habsburgs: Memory and National Identity in Austrian Politics and Education, 1919–1955." PhD diss., Univ. of Maryland, 2006.

Clark, Christopher. *The Sleepwalkers: How Europe Went to War in 1914*. London: Allen Lane, 2013.

Cole, Laurence. "Der Habsburger-Mythos." In *Memoria Austria I: Menschen Mythen Zeiten*, edited by Emil Brix, Ernst Bruckmüller, and Hannes Stekl, 473–504. Wien: Verlag für Geschichte und Politik, 2004.

Czernin, Ottokar. *Im Weltkriege*. Wien: Ullstein, 1919.

de Cillia, Rudolf, Martin Reisigl, and Ruth Wodak. "The Discursive Construction of National Identities." *Discourse & Society* 10, no. 2 (1999): 149–73.

Eisenmenger, Victor. *Erzherzog Franz Ferdinand*. Wien: Amalthea, 1930.

Franz-Willing, Georg. *Erzherzog Franz Ferdinand und die Pläne zur Reform der Habsburger Monarchie*. Brünn: R. M. Rohrer, 1943.

Gerbert, Frank, ed. *Franz Ferdinand von Österreich-Este: "Die Eingeborenen machten keinen besonders günstigen Eindruck"; Tagebuch meiner Reise um die Erde 1892–1893*. Wien: K & S, 2013.

Glaise-Horstenau, Edmund. "Erzherzog Franz Ferdinand, 1863 bis 1914." In *Oesterreichische Biographie*, Volume 3, edited by Anton Bettelheim, 9–33. Wien: Amalthea, 1926.

Görlich, Ernst Joseph. *Der Thronfolger*. Wien: Wancura, 1961.

Granner, Wilhelm. *Franz Ferdinand, seine Entwicklung und seine politischen Ideen.* Phil. diss., Universität Wien, 1942.
Hammond, Beate. *Habsburgs größte Liebesgeschichte.* Wien: Ueberreuter, 2001.
Hannig, Alma. *Franz Ferdinand: Die Biographie.* Wien: Amalthea, 2013.
———. "'Wir schauen in der Loge zu': Thronfolger Franz Ferdinand und die Außenpolitik Oesterreich-Ungarns vor dem Ersten Weltkrieg." *Etudes Danubiennes* 27, no. 1–2 (2011): 51–66.
Hoffmann, Robert. *Erzherzog Franz Ferdinand und der Fortschritt. Altstadterhaltung und bürgerliche Modernisierungswille in Salzburg.* Wien: Böhlau, 1994.
Holler, Gerd. *Franz Ferdinand von Österreich-Este.* Wien: Ueberreuter, 1982.
Jedlicka, Ludwig. "Erzherzog Franz Ferdinand." In *Gestalter der Geschicke Österreichs*, edited by Hugo Hantsch, 527–38. Innsbruck: Tyrolia, 1962.
Kann, Robert. *Erzherzog Franz Ferdinand Studien.* Wien: Verlag für Geschichte und Politik, 1976.
Kiszling, Rudolf. *Erzherzog Franz Ferdinand von Österreich-Este: Leben, Pläne und Wirken am Schicksalsweg der Donaumonarchie.* Graz: Böhlau, 1953.
Kraus, Karl. *Die letzten Tage der Menschheit.* Wien: *Die Fackel*, 1922.
Kronenbitter, Günther. "Verhinderter Retter? Erzherzog Franz Ferdinand und die Erhaltung der Habsburgermonarchie." In *Konservative Profile: Ideen & Praxis in der Politik zwischen FM Radetzky, Karl Kraus und Alois Mock*, edited by Ulrich E. Zellenberg, 267–83. Graz: Stocker, 2003.
Mader, Brigitta. *Die Sphinx vom Belvedere: Erzherzog Franz Ferdinand und die Denkmalpflege in Istrien.* Koper-Capodistria: Zgodovinsko Društvo za Južno Primorsko, 2000.
Nicoll, Leo Ashley, Jr. *Anton Puntigam S. J.: Leben und Wirken eines Jesuiten in Bosnien.* Phil. diss., Universität Wien: 1970.
Polatschek, Max. *Franz Ferdinand: Europas Verlorene Hoffnung.* Wien: Amalthea, 1989.
Rásky, Béla. "Erinnern und Vergessen der Habsburger in Österreich und Ungarn nach 1918." In *Österreich 1918 und die Folgen: Geschichte, Literatur, Theater und Film*, edited by Karl Müller and Hans Wagener, 25–58. Wien: Böhlau, 2009.
Reichmann, Eva. "Franz Ferdinand als literarische Figur." *Studia austriaca VIII* (2000): 135–47.
Remak, Joachim. "The Third Balkan War: World War I Origins Reconsidered." *Journal of Modern History* 43, no. 3 (Sept. 1971): 353–66.
Romsics, Gergely. *Myth and Remembrance: The Dissolution of the Habsburg Empire in the Memoir Literature of the Austro-Hungarian Political Elite.* Boulder: Social Science Monographs, 2006.
Schloss Artstetten. *Thron oder Liebe: 90 Jahre Hochzeit des Thronfolgers.* Marbach: Sandler, J & H, 1990.
Schroeder, Paul W. "World War I as Galloping Gertie: A Reply to Joachim Remak." *Journal of Modern History* 44, no. 3 (Sept. 1972): 319–44.
Stachel, Peter. *Mythos Heldenplatz.* Wien: Pichler, 2002.
Stourzh, Gerald. "50 Jahre nach Sarajewo." *Neues Österreich.* 27 June 1964.
von Chlumecky, Leopold. *Erzherzog Franz Ferdinands Wirken und Wollen.* Berlin: Verlag für Kulturpolitik, 1929.
von Hohenberg, Anita, and Christiane Scholler. *Er war mein Urgroßvater: Anita Hohenberg über Thronfolger Erzherzog Franz Ferdinand.* Graz: Verl.-Gruppe Styria, 2013.
von Sosnosky, Theodor. *Franz Ferdinand.* München: Oldenbourg, 1929.

Weissensteiner, Friedrich. *Franz Ferdinand: Der verhinderte Herrscher.* Wien: Österr. Bundesverlag, 1983.
Williamson, Samuel R., Jr. *Austria-Hungary and the Origins of the First World War.* New York: St. Martin's, 1991.
Winder, Ludwig. *Der Thronfolger: ein Franz-Ferdinand-Roman.* Berlin: Rütten & Loenig, 1984.
Winder, Ludwig. *Der Thronfolger: ein Franz-Ferdinand-Roman.* Wien: Zsolnay, 2014.
Würthle, Friedrich. *Die Spur führt nach Belgrad: Sarajevo 1914.* Wien: Molden, 1975.

Afterword

Pieter M. Judson

Hermann Pirich's 1939 novel *Südsteierisches Grenzland* (*The South-Styrian Frontier*) is a typical "frontier novel" of the period 1880–1945, a popular genre among nationalist readers of all languages in Habsburg Central Europe.[1] This particular novel recounts how a diverse group of German speakers in the mythical town of Schlossau, in formerly Austrian South Styria, come to terms with life under the new Yugoslav regime after the world war.[2] Toward the end of the novel, one of the characters, a German-speaking veteran of the Austro-Hungarian army, observes a regiment of young Yugoslav pioneers as they march across the Drava/Drau river bridge in the early morning mist.

> Certainly many fine young men could be found among these swashbuckling faces, dashing lads, who could in fact be capable of winning any war. And an old soldier's heart like his should have been happy at the sight of them. But in a city with such an originally German character as Schlossau, whose look hardly differed from that of her little sisters on the Neckar or the Rhine or the Mosel, these soldiers seemed alien in their appearance, and even stranger in their beings. Didn't they instead resemble an eternally hostile occupation force, [despite their] respectable and restrained behavior toward the local population?[3]

There is no reason to believe that the young pioneers described here were not themselves recruited from the local population. After all, both the Slovene and

German languages had long been in use in South Styria, and both languages had enjoyed official status under the old Empire. Yet Pirich's veteran characterizes these youths as somehow alien to the town because they represent an institution fostered by the new Kingdom of the Serbs, Croats, and Slovenes. The fundamental identity of the town, its very look, Pirich asserts here, is unquestionably German. Yet since the end of the war in this region, the town had been occupied first by Slovene military units formerly of the Austro-Hungarian army, and then by what Pirich's veteran refers to as alien occupiers sent by a South Slav state.

Pirich's novelistic assertions are familiar to us because they rest on a nationalist logic that has dominated historical approaches to the Habsburg Monarchy and its successor states at least since the end of World War I. The general narratives about this period still cast local events at the end of the War in terms of national revolutions that produced nationalist winners and losers, national majorities and national minorities. Such narratives recount the history of the region as nationalist teleologies that gain their final fulfillment in the destruction of the Habsburg Monarchy and the founding or enlarging of its successor states. Readers of Pirich's narrative might have debated to which nation this town belonged, given its linguistic or ethnic makeup. They would have imagined, however, that for the inhabitants of a town like Ptui/Pettau on which Schlossau was modeled, the question of national belonging was paramount in 1918. And yet an examination of local and regional histories at the end of the War would find many such towns in Habsburg Central Europe taking into account factors other than purely nationalist ones in their efforts to negotiate their futures.

What is missing both from Pirich's tragic description of Ptui/Pettau and, indeed, from most historical narratives about the region and period after 1918 even today is Empire itself. No longer in existence, its former institutions, administrative practices, networks of clienteles, and cultural values all seem to have vanished overnight and exerted no influence whatsoever on the postwar settlements, the new regimes, or their societies. In the above quotation, as throughout the novel, Pirich completely erases the empire and replaces its history with a misleading claim that the past had in fact been German—that is national—rather than imperial. In the same way, the collapse of Austria-Hungary and the creation of Yugoslavia in the novel are refigured specifically as a defeat of Germans and a victory for Serbs. The town's inhabitants, it is claimed, are forced to give up their nationality to live under an alien one. But as the insightful essays in this volume argue, the facts of the political transformations that followed the collapse of Empire, and how those transformations were understood and negotiated by actors on the ground, often tell a far different story.

The Empire may have vanished overnight from nationalist writings, but the Empire's legacies hardly vanished so easily from the historical record. The essays here remind us critically that, in the first place, the nationalist claims of the new or enlarged states regarding the significance of 1918 would not have been easily recognizable to those who experienced the events of 1918–23 on the ground. In part, this is because most local administrations or civic organizations operated under familiar rules and practices forged under imperial regimes, whether the Austrian or Hungarian. As the imperial and royal bureaucracies collapsed, to say nothing of supply links, local administrators and civic organizations took initiatives whose logic had been formed under imperial institutions. They asserted regional—not exactly national—powers, and they did so in order to ensure people's very survival. In regions occupied by foreign militaries—such as Transylvania, Bukovina, northern Slovenia, or today's Slovakia (to mention a few)—civic organizations and civil servants often understandably treated the new situation as if there had been a switch in imperial metropoles, not necessarily as if they now adhered to an ethnically defined nation state.

These points are also reflected in many popular concerns that did not involve nationhood. Some contemporary accounts, for example, document how in the early postwar years, a broad range of relationships, interests, and local networks left over from imperial times were far more pressing to former Austro-Hungarians than were the simple triumphs of ethnic nationhood. Events that later historians, novelists, and journalists portrayed in purely nationalist terms may have held quite different meanings to contemporaries. Local actors in South Styria, for example, may have largely weighed Ptui/Pettau's significance and future in terms of the location of local markets or the presence of railway links to the outside world and, thus, access to particular trading or supplying partners.[4] Whatever their language, they might have seen the town primarily as a regional center for Catholic religious life. They may also have perceived it as normal that they had used both local languages to some degree, because their daily lives had involved constant interaction rather than national separation. Most importantly, they may have viewed the state (all states) in imperial rather than national terms, offering their loyalty to an imperial metropole that could guarantee their physical and economic well-being. After a devastating war that destroyed imperial bonds—both infrastructural and emotional—local actors sought the best options for the physical survival of their regions when they had the chance. Whoever could deliver food or coal or medical supplies, whoever could guarantee economic continuity, may have been far more important to them than the purist rhetorical claims of the National Councils in 1918. Almost all of the options contemporaries conceived of in 1918 for their futures had been shaped by their experiences as part of a large, multilingual empire in their recent past.[5]

A related point to bear in mind is that while some local people after the War may have indulged in nationalist rhetoric to describe and pursue their interests, they rarely agreed on what exactly that national interest demanded when it came to daily life decisions. Pirich's presumption that a kind of universally applicable Germanness somehow bound those sister towns on the Neckar, Rhine, Mosel, or the Drava/Drau Rivers not only erases an imperial past, it also erases powerful local and regional interests that often challenged nationalist presumptions. What was good for Italian, Czech, or German nationalists in one region of Central Europe, for example, may hardly have been good for their Italian, Czech, or German counterparts in other regions. Moreover, in those first confused months and years after the collapse of the Habsburg state, presumptions and practices inherited from the imperial world often shaped initiatives from below. When civic organizations and local officials undertook to negotiate the terms by which they would accept new rulers, for example, they did so presuming their place in a civic society whose structures and habits had been shaped by imperial institutions.

The perceptive essays in this volume argue that we should look beyond nationalist assertions about the postimperial world in order to recapture both the contemporary and historic legacies of the collapse of the Habsburg Monarchy. In so doing, their authors show us a variety of highly credible strategies for recapturing contemporaries' experiences. The exploration of imperial legacies and continuities is complex, and the essays here not only incorporate different fields of history and diverse methodological approaches, they also examine a variety of geographic regions and, above all, fruitfully relate various scales of analysis (biographical, local, regional, national, imperial) to one another.

In reorienting historians' approaches to the events that spanned the wartime collapse of the Monarchy and the rise of several new or enlarged successor states, these authors invite us to pay close attention to crucial continuities that linked pre- and postwar societies, and that historians have too often ignored. If we make the individual, the local, or the regional into the subject of the analysis, we repeatedly encounter exceptions to the rules of the popular narratives that take nations as their subjects. Neither people nor states, it seems, conformed to the expectations nationalists held for them. The postwar states rarely had access to sufficient resources to enable them to impose fresh administrative structures on newly acquired regions, to train and hire new personnel, and to dispense with the military, technological, and bureaucratic expertise of former imperial professionals. They certainly lacked resources to build up new cultural institutions to spread the national visions of the successor states. Rather, they constantly compromised their nationalization programs, even as they reiterated their importance in increasingly radical ideological terms.[6]

At the same time, the self-confident claims of these states to represent nations in democratic terms (through national self-determination) masked the degree to which each state adopted strategies, behaviors, and practices—not to mention personnel—from the former Empire. Despite their confident assertions of nationhood, these states all resembled the Habsburg Monarchy in its multilingual character. Many also followed prewar Hungary in their efforts to nationalize linguistically and religiously diverse populations through draconian education laws. Many even developed internal colonization schemes to move populations in order to minimize the political effects of so-called national minorities.[7] Some also sought control over neighboring territories within Europe or colonies outside of Europe, citing security, geography, or even "civilization" when there was little or no ethnic/national justification for annexation.[8] The point here is that, despite how successor states positioned themselves ideologically as new, modern, and democratic regimes separate from the anachronistic empire, they actually practiced many forms of rule inherited from Imperial Austria and Royal Hungary.

Without question, both during and immediately after the War, the populations of Habsburg Central Europe were desperate for survival. They thus often framed their needs in terms of specific social reforms that they believed would produce greater fairness in society. Ironically, in 1918–19, many of these reforms resembled schemes that had been hatched under the duress of war in the Empire, especially the new relationships of mutuality and sacrifice that developed between state and people even though the state could never fulfill its ever-expanding wartime commitments.[9] Demands for food, fuel, land reform, and improved work conditions all forced the hands of the post-Habsburg regimes in the early postwar years. Invariably, however, even the regimes representing the victors of 1918 (much less the losers—the Austrian Republic and Royal Hungary) could hardly respond adequately and quickly enough to the immediate material needs. Not only did the seemingly endless continuation of wartime privation cause many to question the value of the recent changes that had allegedly transformed society, it often led them to treat the new regimes with suspicion, as nothing more than prolongations of the former empire. The continuities of personnel that many of the new regimes found themselves forced to tolerate only magnified the general impression that nothing, in fact, had changed.[10]

This argument about continuities does not imply that no ruptures took place in Habsburg Central Europe. But as we also learn from the chapters in this volume, those ruptures cannot simply be understood in terms of nationhood and national revolutions. Indeed, a range of useful narratives helped local societies to restore complex meanings to the immediate postwar events. In analyzing critical issues of long-term constructed cultural memory, for example, several of the book's chapters show why and how some older nationalist narratives have remained so compelling one hundred years after the collapse of the Habsburg Monarchy, despite their utter inability to explain historical events on the ground. Here, we can learn more about the many political uses to which the memory of empire has been harnessed, from its role as alleged "prison of the peoples" to its characterization as a lost golden world subject to nostalgia to a possible example that proves either the benefits or the ills of the multinational European Union to a crass commercialized object used to promote regional tourism.

The Habsburg Empire may indeed serve these and many other purposes today. Given the methodological developments of the past thirty years in the study of history, however, it has not been credible for some time now to narrate the history of this region purely in terms of successful nationalist revolutions and, thereby, to erase the importance of empire to twentieth-century Central Europe. It is clear from these essays that a century after the Empire's collapse, historians can venture effectively outside of those nationalist paradigms that have made nations into historical subjects, and to restore to people their role as the proper subjects of history.

Pieter M. Judson is Professor and Chair of the Department of History and Civilization at the European University Institute in Florence and former editor of the *Austrian History Yearbook* (2006–16). His most recent book, *The Habsburg Empire: A New History*, was published in 2016 (Cambridge, MA: Harvard University Press) and is currently being translated into eight languages. He is also the author of *Guardians of the Nation: Activists on the Language Frontiers of Imperial Austria* (Cambridge, MA: Harvard University Press, 2006), *Wien Brennt. Die Revolution von 1848 und ihr liberales Erbe* (Vienna: Böhlau, 1998), and *Exclusive Revolutionaries: Liberal Politics, Social Experience, and National Identity* (Ann Arbor, MI: University of Michigan Press, 1996).

Notes

1. On the frontier novel as genre in Habsburg Central Europe, see Pieter M. Judson, "Marking National Space on the Habsburg Austrian Borderlands, 1880–1918," in *Shatterzone of Empire: Coexistence and Violence in the German, Habsburg, Russian, and Ottoman Borderlands*, ed. Omer Bartov and Eric D. Weitz (Bloomington: Indiana University Press, 2013), 122–35.
2. "Schlossau" is clearly based on the South Styrian town Ptui/Pettau on the Drava/Drau River.
3. Hermann Pirich, *Südsteierisches Grenzland* (Salzburg: "Das Bergland Buch," 1939).
4. For examples of non-nationalist concerns among Slovene speakers in South Styria and Carinthia, see Rolf Wörsdörfer, "Ethnisch-nationale Differenzierung in den Ostalpen: 'Deutsch-Windisch-Slowenisch' (1920–1991)," in *Die Nationalisierung von Grenzen. Zur Konstruktion nationaler Identität in sprachlich gemischten Grenzregionen*, ed. Michael G. Müller and Rolf Petri (Marburg: Herder Verlag, 2002), 137–60.
5. See, for example, the statement of loyalty expressed by the German civic associations of Chernivtsi to their new Romanian rulers on 17 November 1918, a statement that clearly expressed the traditional logic of empire between metropole and a region, reproduced in Emanuel Turczynski, "Das Vereinswesen der Deutschen in der Bukowina," in *Buchenland Hundertfünfzig Jahre Deutschtum in der Bukowina*, ed. Franz Lang (Munich: Verlag des Südostdeutschen Kulturwerks, 1961), 118–19. See also several telling examples cited by Gábor Egry in his chapter in this volume.
6. For Czechoslovakia, see Tara Zahra, *Kidnapped Souls: National Indifference and the Battle for Children in the Bohemian Lands, 1900–1948* (Ithaca: Cornell University

Press, 2008); for Italy, see Roberta Pergher, *Mussolini's Nation Empire: Sovereignty and Settlement in Italy's Borderlands 1922–1943* (Cambridge, UK: Cambridge University Press, 2017); on Romania, see Irina Livezeanu, *Cultural Politics in Greater Romania: Regionalism, Nation Building, and Ethnic Struggle, 1918–1930* (Ithaca: Cornell University Press, 1995).
7. See, in general, Eric D. Weitz, "From the Vienna to the Paris System: International Politics and the Entangled Histories of Human Rights, Forced Deportations, and Civilizing Missions," *American Historical Review* 113 (2008): 313–43; on efforts to marginalize, nationalize, or minimize linguistic minorities, see Livezeanu, *Cultural Politics*; on Czechoslovakia, see Zahra, *Kidnapped Souls*.
8. Pieter M. Judson, *The Habsburg Empire: A New History* (Cambridge, MA: Harvard University Press, 2016), 444–51.
9. Maureen Healy, *Vienna and the Fall of the Habsburg Empire: Total War and Everyday Life in World War I* (Cambridge, UK: Cambridge University Press, 2004); Tara Zahra, "'Each Nation Cares Only for Its Own': Empire, Nation, and Child Welfare Activism in the Bohemian Lands, 1900–1918," *American Historical Review* 111, no. 5 (December 2006): 1378–1402; Ke-Chin Hsia, "Who Provided Care for Wounded and Disabled Soldiers? Conceptualizing State-Civil Society Relationship in WWI Austria," in *Other Fronts, Other Wars? First World War Studies on the Eve of the Centennial*, ed. Joachim Bürgschwentner, Matthias Egger, and Gunda Barth-Scalmani (Leiden: Brill, 2014), 303–28; Rudolf Kučera, *Rationed Life: Science, Everyday Life, and Working-Class Politics in the Bohemian Lands, 1914–1918* (New York: Berghahn Books, 2016).
10. See the many telling examples of this public disappointment cited in Claire Morelon, "Street Fronts: War, State Legitimacy and Urban Space, Prague 1914–1920" (PhD diss., University of Birmingham and École Doctorale de Sciences Po, 2015).

Bibliography

Healy, Maureen. *Vienna and the Fall of the Habsburg Empire: Total War and Everyday Life in World War I*. Cambridge, UK: Cambridge University Press, 2004.
Hsia, Ke-Chin. "Who Provided Care for Wounded and Disabled Soldiers? Conceptualizing State-Civil Society Relationship in WWI Austria." In *Other Fronts, Other Wars? First World War Studies on the Eve of the Centennial*, edited by Joachim Bürgschwentner, Matthias Egger, and Gunda Barth-Scalmani, 303–28. Leiden: Brill, 2014.
Judson, Pieter M. "Marking National Space on the Habsburg Austrian Borderlands, 1880–1918." In *Shatterzone of Empire: Coexistence and Violence in the German, Habsburg, Russian, and Ottoman Borderlands*, edited by Omer Bartov and Eric D. Weitz, 122–35. Bloomington: Indiana University Press, 2013.
———. *The Habsburg Empire: A New History*. Cambridge, MA: Harvard University Press, 2016.
Kučera, Rudolf. *Rationed Life: Science, Everyday Life, and Working-Class Politics in the Bohemian Lands, 1914–1918*. New York: Berghahn Books, 2016.
Lang, Franz, ed. *Buchenland Hundertfünfzig Jahre Deutschtum in der Bukowina*. Munich: Verlag des Südostdeutschen Kulturwerks, 1961.
Livezeanu, Irina. *Cultural Politics in Greater Romania: Regionalism, Nation Building, and Ethnic Struggle, 1918–1930*. Ithaca: Cornell University Press, 1995.

Morelon, Claire. "Street Fronts: War, State Legitimacy and Urban Space, Prague 1914–1920." PhD diss., University of Birmingham and École Doctorale de Sciences Po, 2015.
Pergher, Roberta. *Mussolini's Nation Empire: Sovereignty and Settlement in Italy's Borderlands 1922–1943*. Cambridge, UK: Cambridge University Press, 2017.
Pirich, Hermann. *Südsteierisches Grenzland*. Salzburg: "Das Bergland Buch," 1939.
Weitz, Eric D. "From the Vienna to the Paris System: International Politics and the Entangled Histories of Human Rights, Forced Deportations, and Civilizing Missions." *American Historical Review* 113 (2008): 313–43.
Wörsdörfer, Rolf. "Ethnisch-nationale Differenzierung in den Ostalpen: 'Deutsch-Windisch-Slowenisch' (1920–1991)." In *Die Nationalisierung von Grenzen. Zur Konstruktion nationaler Identität in sprachlich gemischten Grenzregionen*, edited by Michael G. Müller and Rolf Petri, 137–60. Marburg: Herder Verlag, 2002.
Zahra, Tara. "'Each Nation Cares Only for Its Own': Empire, Nation, and Child Welfare Activism in the Bohemian Lands, 1900–1918." *American Historical Review* 111, no. 5 (December 2006): 1378–1402.
———. *Kidnapped Souls: National Indifference and the Battle for Children in the Bohemian Lands, 1900–1948*. Ithaca: Cornell University Press, 2008.

INDEX

Agrarian parties
　Austrian, 191
　Czechoslovak, 105, 203
　Romanian, 149
　See also rural/Agrarian world
Alba Iulia, National Assembly, 19, 149
Albania, 119, 127
Aleksandar, King of Yugoslavia, 168–70
Anschluss
　army, 123–24, 128–29
　Austrian identity, 295–97
　Catholics, 183
　Saint-Germain, 188, 263, 286, 290
antisemitism
　army, 124, 129–30
　Catholic Church, 179–80, 183
　Polish politics, 67
　in postwar Austria, 235, 242
Antonescu, Ion (regime), 23, 149
Arbeiter-Zeitung
　Karl's death, 235, 237, 243–44
　Ständestaat, 268
　World War I, 118–19
　Zentralfriedhof war monument, 264–65
aristocracy. *See* nobility
army. *See* Military
Artstetten
　burial of Franz Ferdinand, 284, 287, 291
　museum, 297, 300, 302–3
Atonement Monument, 289–90
Äußeres Burgtor on *Heldenplatz*. *See* *Heldendenkmal*
Austrianity, 50–56

Banat
　army officers from the, 140–44, 149

　monuments, 28–29
　transition, 16–17, 25, 31
Bánffy, Miklós, 147, 151
Belgrade, 129, 163–64, 167, 168
Biliński, Leon, 63–82
Bohemia, 43–56, 69
　exhibitions, 92–95, 98–100
　local administration, 45
　nobility, 204–9, 211–12, 215–18
　State rights, 66, 205
　World War I, 118
Bolshevism, 44, 50–51
　Bolshevik army, 63, 76
　fear of, 24, 183, 185, 192, 234
Boroević von Bojna, Svetozar, 120–23
Bosnia, 71, 161, 169, 289–90
　Bosnian crisis of 1908, 294
Brașov/Brassó/Kronstadt, 19, 26, 29
Bratislava/Pozsony/Pressburg, 20, 24, 27–29, 104
Brehm, Bruno (*Apis und Este*), 287, 292–93
Brest-Litovsk, Treaty of, 72
Brno/Brünn, 90, 99–108
Budapest, 20–23, 158–59
　exhibitions, 92–93, 98
　Karl's coronation, 127, 244
　media, 29
　National Council, 20
　restoration attempt, 231
　Romanian troops, 144
　World War I, 118, 217
Bukovina, 70, 147, 320
bureaucracy. *See* civil Servants

Carinthia, 121, 320n4
Carniola. *See* Slovenia

Carpatho-Ukraine, 16, 90
Catholic Church, 177–96, 243
  clergy participating in National Councils, 20
  in exhibitions, 103, 108
Catholicism
  Biliński, 64
  Franz Ferdinand, 296
  Karl, 245–46
  locality, 320
  nobility, 206–7
Christian Social Party
  antisemitism, 183
  elections, 187–89, 191, 207
  imperial legacy, 240–41
  newspapers, 184, 234, 274
  nobility, 206
  Slovak Christian Socialists, 20, 22
  Social Democrats, 238–39, 247
  ties with the Church, 178, 182
  Vaterländische Front, 268
  See also Miklas, Wilhelm; Seipel, Monsignor Ignaz
civil servants
  incomes, 218
  monarchist sentiment, 241, 244–45
  Serbia, 162
  transition, 1, 23–25, 45, 50, 54–56, 320
Civil War, Austrian, 123, 128, 247, 268
Civil War, Spanish, 195
Cluj/Kolozsvár, 26–27
coffeehouses, 29–30, 66, 73
Conrad von Hötzendorf, Franz, 144, 230, 241–42, 270, 294
Croatia, Croatians, 121, 157–70
  Croatian Peasant Party, 167
  Independent State of (NDH), 124, 160
Czechoslovakia
  army, 126, 131
  borders, 18
  exhibitions, 99–106
  finances, 78–79
  historical narrative, 3, 161–62
  nationalization policies, 20
  nobility, 204–13
  transition, 1, 22–30, 43–56
  See also Bohemia; Moravia; Slovakia
Czechs, 43–56, 90–108
  amnesty, 230, 233
  Austro-Hungarian politics, 68–69
  bureaucracy, 24, 45, 54
  nobility, 208, 218
  other national groups in Czechoslovakia, 100, 104–5
  Slovak perception of, 30

Daszyński, Ignacy, 69, 73, 75–77
Davidović, Ljubomir, 164, 167
Diamand, Herman, 69, 74–76
Diamant, Alfred, 177–78, 185, 190–91, 196
Die Monarchie/Das neue Reich, 207
Doda, Trajan, 139–40, 143–44
Dollfuß, Engelbert, 123, 192–93, 268–77 passim

Elisabeth, Empress, 235, 237, 288, 297
exhibitions, 90–108, 290, 297, 300–1

fascism, 158–59, 208
  Austro-fascism, 191, 193n93, 268, 271, 276–77
  Fascist Italy, 128, 169
fideicommissum, 209–10, 217
First World War. *See* World War I
Frankists (Pure Party of Right), 161–70
Franz Ferdinand, Archduke, 284–306
  assassination, 179, 207n39, 235, 287–89
  Heldendenkmal, 270, 274
Franz Joseph, Habsburg Emperor
  actor playing, 130–31
  Albanian king Zog, 127
  antisemitism, 128, 130
  Bruckner, Anton, 123
  death, 148, 214, 247
  exhibitions on, 297
  jubilee of 1908, 142
  Masaryk, 26, 46, 106
  statue, 29, 106
  street names, 45, 229, 237
  tomb, 305
  visit to Galicia, 97
Freemasons, 183, 195, 235, 297
Frontkämpfervereinigung (Frontline Fighters' Organization), 266

Galicia, 1, 64–76, 79–81
  exhibition, 96–97
  nobility, 204, 216
  refugees, 48

Germans (in former Austria-Hungary)
  Austro-Hungarian politics, 68, 76
  in Bohemia, 47–53, 55, 95, 98–101,
    103–4, 108, 126, 209
  exhibitions, 93–108 passim
  German Austria, 182–85, 193, 246, 266,
    286
  language, 53, 55, 65–67, 69, 74–75, 119,
    149
  nationalism, 124, 128, 187–88, 191, 206,
    208, 235, 248, 263, 276, 292
  in Slovakia, 16, 20, 26–28
  in Transylvania, 16, 18, 25, 29, 31
Germany
  exhibitions and architecture, 92, 102
  historiography, 4
  Polish politics, 71–73
  Nazi Germany, 160, 270, 275–77, 297,
    306
  relationship with Austria, 123–24, 183,
    188, 208, 232, 248, 263
  World War I, 230, 240, 261
Głąbiński, Stanisław, 68–71, 75, 80, 82
Glaise-Horstenau, Edmund, 119, 124, 129,
  287
Graz, 129, 291, 300, 302–3
Greek Catholics, 16, 24, 28, 32

Habsburg dynasty, 6, 97, 182, 203–4, 229,
  240, 244–45, 275, 296
  Franz Ferdinand, 284, 288, 293
  loyalty to, 2, 26, 72, 119–22, 125, 147,
    291
  restoration, 163, 265
  World War I, 162, 262, 288
Harrach, Otto, 205–13, 217–18
Heimwehr, 163, 191, 268, 271–72
Heldendenkmal, 266–78, 295
Heldendenkmalskomitee, 267–69,
  271–72
Heldenplatz (Heroes' Square), 262, 267–68,
  270–71, 277, 295, 303
Hitler, Adolf, 124, 128, 159–60, 208, 277,
  286, 296–97
Hodža, Milan, 18, 105
Hofburg, 122, 147–48, 268
Honvéd, 18, 27, 30, 119
Horthy, Miklós, 30, 125–26, 204–5, 230–31,
  233

Hungary
  historiography, 4
  interwar, 30, 108, 125–26, 163, 204
  prewar, 16, 26, 29, 31, 66, 143, 166,
    321
  transition, 17–22, 80, 147, 148, 151,
    231–34
  World War I, 98

Innitzer, Theodor, 192–93, 195, 269,
  272–73, 275
Innsbruck, 240–41, 243, 266
Italy, 241
  Fascist, 159, 169, 194
  Poland, 79
  World War I, 117, 121, 166
  World War II, 128

Jászi, Oszkár, 6, 17, 21n28
Jews, 16, 64
  army, 120, 124, 128–30
  Hermann Diamand, 69, 75
  Orthodox, 235
  Polish politics, 71

Kann, Robert, 285–86, 289, 292, 294, 300,
  304
Karl, Habsburg Emperor, 229–49, 270, 274,
  276, 291
  leaving power, 121–22, 125, 182
  loyalty to, 72, 148
Kingdom of Serbs, Croats, and Slovenes. *See*
  Yugoslavia
Kortner, Fritz, 298–99, 302
Krleža, Miroslav, 158–59
Kun, Béla, 80, 205

land reforms, 17, 203–13, 322
Legions, Czechoslovak, 45–48, 50–55, 126,
  210
legitimacy (political), 19–20, 44–56, 69, 184,
  203, 247
Lemberg/L'viv/Lwów, 64, 66, 68, 72–74,
  216
  exhibition in 1894, 92, 93, 96
liberalism, 67, 179, 205, 208
Linz, 239, 241, 268
Lojka, Father Leopold, 189–93
Lower Austria, 209–12, 215–17, 240

loyalty, 151, 160, 193–94, 233, 264, 320
   to Habsburg dynasty, 2, 29, 69–70, 72–73, 77, 120, 139, 142, 147–48, 204, 234, 242
   to new nation-states, 23–24, 26, 125, 179, 182, 184, 187, 320n5

Madeira exile, 231–32, 238
magyárons, 24, 29
Masaryk, Tomáš G., 30, 45, 48, 50–51, 53, 100, 106–107, 126, 158, 210
   cult of, 26, 46–47
memory, 6, 278, 322
   of the *Anschluss*, 277
   of Franz Ferdinand, 284, 286–93, 298–300, 302–06
   of the last Kaiser Karl, 235, 249
   Polish national, 71–72
Miklas, Wilhelm, 246, 272, 275
Military (Austro-Hungarian), 5, 25, 29, 44, 117–31, 131n54, 137–39, 142–43, 145–47, 158–62, 165–66, 180, 205, 234, 263, 267, 273
Military Border, 136, 139–46, 151
Military Chancellery (Franz Ferdinand's), 288, 302
Montenegro, 118, 163, 167
Moravia, 93–95, 99–105, 208, 210–11

Národní Listy, 56, 63, 93, 99, 113
National Councils, 17, 20–23, 21n28, 320
   Czechoslovak, 45, 52, 54
   Hungarian, 17
   Romanian, 19
   Slovak, 18, 31
National Democrats (Polish Party), 67–68, 71, 75, 80
national heroes, 97, 124
   Austrian, 266–75, 295
   Croatian, 166, 168
   Czech, 54
   Hungarian, 28
   Romanian, 143
   Slovak, 28
   Yugoslav, 291
nationalism, 122, 127, 131, 139, 173
   Croat, 164
   Czech, 93, 108

   German, 248
   prewar, 2, 69, 160–61, 284–85, 288
Nazis, 128–29, 208–09, 275, 277–78, 304–06
   Austrian, 193, 286, 291–92, 296–99
   defeat of Yugoslavia, 160
   and Hungary, 126
   and Slovak Republic, 21
   and Ustasha, 124
Neue Freie Presse, 269, 283
   on Karl, 231n27, 233, 241, 257
   on Franz Ferdinand, 287, 289, 291, 295
nobility, 7–8, 138, 138n13, 203–19 passim, 284, 287
   Artstetten, 291
   exhibitions, 96
   Hungarian, 126
   Karl's death, 241, 244
   monarchist restoration, 51
   Polish, 75

Orthodoxy, 120, 141–42, 145–46, 149, 164
Ottoman Empire, 4, 27, 142, 161–62, 164

Parliament, 66
   Austrian *Bundesrat*, 238–39
   Austrian *Herrenhaus*, 205
   Austrian *Nationalrat*, 177, 179, 185–86, 188–95, 230, 239–42, 245, 247, 268
   Austrian *Reichsrat*, 64, 67–70, 182
   Croatian *Sabor*, 161, 164
   Czechoslovak, 47, 54
   Hungarian, 18, 139, 143, 206, 231
   Polish *Sejm*, 73–75, 73n30, 73n33, 80, 82
   Romanian, 149
   Yugoslav, 167–70
Pavelić, Ante, 124n29, 163, 167–70
Piffl, Cardinal Friedrich Gustav (Archbishop of Vienna), 183–85, 187, 192, 241, 246
Piłsudski, Józef, 65, 71, 73, 81, 125
Pirich, Hermann, 318–20
Poland, 1, 5, 43, 48, 64–82 passim, 99, 125, 161, 204
police, 1, 13, 25, 32, 168, 191, 241, 243, 268
   Czechoslovak, 45, 47, 51–56, 63
Poznań/Posen, 73, 99, 102
Prague, 5, 20, 30, 92, 98, 101, 131, 207, 209, 213–16, 293

destruction of Marian column, 126
exhibitions in, 93–96, 99–103, 105–08
transition after World War I, 43–57
Protestants, 50, 120, 122, 183
Puntigam, Father Anton, 289–90

Radetzky, Field Marshall
  monument in Prague, 45, 54, 126
Radić, Stjepan (Peasant Party), 163–64
  assassination of, 167–68
Rašín, Alois, 1, 54, 77
Redlich, Joseph, 65n4, 74n38, 231, 245
Reichenberg/Liberec, 92, 97–98, 108
Reichspost, 184, 233–34, 237, 239, 243, 257, 265, 269–70, 274, 283
  on Franz Ferdinand's assassination, 287, 289, 292, 295
renaming streets, 24, 26–28
  in Prague, 45
  in Vienna, 229, 270, 291, 304
Renner, Karl, 76, 78, 187–88
  on Kaiser Karl I, 230, 238, 243
Republic, Austrian First, 3, 3n18, 6, 12, 79, 123, 148, 177–97 passim, 201, 229–49 passim, 261–78 passim, 286, 291, 295, 298, 322
Republic, Austrian Second, 130, 286, 288, 297–98, 304
Republikanische Schutzbund, 265–66, 268
restoration attempts, 128, 230–32, 234, 246, 248
  fears of, 51, 79, 163
revolution(s), 1, 2n13, 6–7, 15–22, 27–31, 44–45, 57, 62, 66, 103, 118, 120, 131, 162, 165, 179–85, 188–89, 203–09, 226, 263, 319, 322–23
  Bolshevik, 24, 44, 50, 53, 181
  Croatian Revolutionary Organization, 159
  Macedonian Revolutionary Organization, 169
Romania, 6–8, 16–33 passim, 39, 80, 93, 100, 117–18, 129, 136–51 passim, 161, 165n33, 231, 324
Romanian National Party, 18, 143–44, 149
Roth, Joseph (*Radetzkymarsch*), 131, 131n54, 287, 293
rural/Agrarian world, 17, 20, 30–31, 93, 105, 165, 178, 212

Russia, 22, 41, 50, 52, 63, 70–71, 78, 90, 117–18, 141, 183–84
  and Poland, 66–68, 72–73, 77, 80–81, 97, 125

Saint-Germain, Treaty of, 78, 78n58, 263n2, 290
Salzburg, 217, 234, 241, 245, 266
Sarajevo assassination, 71, 164, 207n39, 270, 286–89, 295–96, 298, 302–06
Schober, Chancellor Johannes, 242–43
Schuschnigg, Kurt von, 206, 248, 269, 272, 276
Seipel, Monsignor Ignaz, 184–85, 189–92, 233, 240–41
Serbia, 71, 78, 117–18, 135, 140–41, 160–68 passim, 288, 294
  and Sarajevo assassination, 297, 299
  Serbian People's Radical Party, 167
Sibiu/Hermannstadt/Nagyszeben, 19, 149–50
Silesia, 15, 95
Slovenia, 123, 128, 211, 320
Slovakia, 5, 16, 20, 22, 28–31, 42–43, 47–48, 56, 95, 100, 104–05, 140, 210, 320
Social Democratic Party, 20, 187, 189, 265
  dissolution of, 268
Sophie Chotek, Duchess of Hohenberg, 284–85, 290, 294, 298
  children of, 291, 299
Ständestaat (Austrian Corporate State), 177, 246, 248, 268, 270, 272–77, 282, 286, 288, 295, 304
Styria, 118, 121, 318–320, 323

Thirty Years' War, 122
Timişoara/Temesvár/Temeschwar, 20, 149
Tito, 124–25
Transylvania, 5, 16, 18–21, 23, 25, 27, 29, 31, 140, 143–44, 147–49, 320
Trianon, Treaty of, 100, 125, 148
Trieste, 79, 127–28, 135
Tyrol, 128, 239, 241, 263

Ukraine, 16, 72, 79–81, 216, 278
Upper Austria, 121, 204, 217
Ustaše, 6, 124, 159–60, 163, 167–70

veterans, 18, 52, 165, 167, 169–70, 173, 190, 210, 234, 237, 261, 263, 266–72 passim, 276, 283, 318–19
Vidovdan Constitution, 164
Vienna, 20, 45, 54, 62, 64–77 passim, 80–82, 98, 101, 106, 118, 123, 126–31, 138, 146–47, 169, 201, 205, 207, 209, 212–17, 229, 234, 237, 244, 262, 284, 287–91, 301, 303–05
   and the Catholich Church, 177–96 passim
   at the end of World War I, 121
   Kaiser Karl I memorial, 236
   mourning Kaiser Karl I, 239–46
   Romanians in, 140–42, 149–50
   war memorialization, 262–67, 271–72, 276–77
   Weltausstellung (1873), 92–96, 103

war memorial, 28, 48, 192–93, 262–78 passim, 295, 303, 305–06
Warsaw, 64, 67, 71, 73–82
   Uprising, 125
Wasylko, Mykola, 70–72, 72n25, 79–81
Weltausstellung, 92–93, 95–96, 101, 103
Wiener Diözesanblatt (Vienna Diocesan Journal), 178, 183, 185, 188–89, 193

Wilhelm II, German Emperor, 55, 240
Winder, Ludwig, 293–95, 293n67, 299
Wondracek, Rudolf, 270–71
World War I, 71–72, 117–21, 144–47, 217
   continuation of war conditions, 47–49
   first victims of, 305–6
   historiography, 2, 5
   memorials, 28, 262–76
   Serbian interpretation of, 162
World War II, 82, 124–25, 128–29, 149, 160, 212, 287, 305

Yugoslavia (Kingdom of Serbs, Croats and Slovenes), 3, 5, 121, 124, 160, 162, 164–70 passim, 173–74, 203, 210–11, 319

Zagreb, 161, 163, 165–68
Zentralfriedhof (Vienna), 123, 262–64, 276–77
Zita, Empress, 237n58, 239, 276
   burial in Capuchin crypt, 130, 297
   in Funchal, 233, 244–45
   negative portrayals of, 230
   restoration attempts, 231
Zweig, Stefan, 131, 291, 293

CPSIA information can be obtained
at www.ICGtesting.com
Printed in the USA
LVHW080852191021
700803LV00001B/4